D1525512

—

Publius Quinctilius Varus

Publius Quinctilius Varus

The Man Who Lost Three Roman Legions in the Teutoburg Disaster

Joanne Ball

Pen & Sword
MILITARY

First published in Great Britain in 2023 by
Pen & Sword Military
An imprint of Pen & Sword Books Limited
Yorkshire – Philadelphia

ISBN 978 1 39908 832 9

A CIP catalogue record for this book is
available from the British Library

Typeset by Mac Style
Printed in the UK by CPI Group (UK) Ltd, Croydon, CR0 4YY.

Pen & Sword Books Limited incorporates the imprints of After
the Battle, Atlas, Archaeology, Aviation, Discovery, Family History,
Fiction, History, Maritime, Military, Military Classics, Politics,
Select, Transport, True Crime, Air World, Frontline Publishing, Leo
Cooper, Remember When, Seaforth Publishing, The Praetorian Press,
Wharncliffe Local History, Wharncliffe Transport, Wharncliffe True
Crime and White Owl.

For a complete list of Pen & Sword titles please contact

PEN & SWORD BOOKS LIMITED
47 Church Street, Barnsley, South Yorkshire, S70 2AS, England
E-mail: enquiries@pen-and-sword.co.uk
Website: www.pen-and-sword.co.uk
or
PEN AND SWORD BOOKS
1950 Lawrence Rd, Havertown, PA 19083, USA
E-mail: Uspen-and-sword@casematepublishers.com
Website: www.penandswordbooks.com

Contents

Acknowledgements

This book has felt at times like a massive undertaking – and as it is my first, also provides a great opportunity to thank all the people that have helped me along the way, both in writing this particular monograph, and on my archaeological journey more widely. I have been helped in writing this book by so many people, for which I am incredibly grateful, and hope one day to be able to return the favour! I probably owe you a collective votive altar in gratitude for everything, but hopefully this will do for now.

To Martin Charlesworth and Julia Clayton, my A-Level archaeology and classics teachers – without you, I might never have taken a degree in archaeology, and none of the amazing things that resulted would ever have happened.

To Phil Freeman, who first introduced me to Varus as an undergrad, introduced me to the team at Kalkriese, and who has spent more hours than either of us probably care to think reading and listening to my thoughts on Varus, I owe a huge debt of thanks.

Huge thanks to all my friends in archaeology who have helped me along the way both in terms of Varus and Greek/Roman archaeology more widely. Especial thanks go to: Boris Burandt, Jon Coulston, Pablo Fernández-Reyes, Simon James, Peter Norris, Matthew Ponting, Owen Rees, John Reid, Andrew Rich, Achim Rost, Guy Stiebel, Anna Walas, Martijn Wijnhoven, Susanne Wilbers-Rost, Nina Willburger. I owe each of you several beers next time our paths cross! And to Rachel Plummer, who has been my friend since we were MA students together – thanks for all the archaeological adventures, garden centres, Greek food, and Gerard Butler movies.

Thanks also to everyone I have met and talked to over Twitter – the archaeology community there has been amazing over the last few years, and has developed some of my thinking about Varus enormously. Also to everyone at *Ancient Warfare Magazine* for getting my popular history writing career going, especially Jasper Oorthuys and Murray Dahm, you have been great writing mentors, and Lindsay Powell, whose work showed me how it was done. Thanks also to Philip Sidnell at Pen & Sword for editorial help with the book, and for letting me extend my deadline when needed. Lots of encouragement and chocolate was provided by my bookshop friends – Gill, Jo, Kate, Laurie, Louise, and Monica – looking forward to hearing them try and sell it to everyone who enters!

Finally, thanks to my family for putting up with me while I wrote this book – not an easy task at times! To my mother Christine, for her constant support and encouragement, and many hosted Friday evenings de-stressing from writing. To my father John, for introducing me to the wonders of history as a child, and for many debates since. To my sisters, Judie and Vicky, for caring about the book and I despite having no real interest at all in the Romans, and to my nephew Thomas and niece Emily for making me laugh and giving me hugs throughout the difficult times. Finally, thanks to my partner Lee, for everything he did while I was writing this book, this, from listening to every new thought I had about Varus to reading through the text to make sure it made sense – I could not have done this without you.

Introduction

Some events in Roman history had such an impact that those perceived to be their architects are forever defined by their connection to them, relegating everything else they might have done or been to a position of unimportance. Despite his long and distinguished military and political career, Publius Quinctilius Varus will always be remembered for one thing above all else – the defeat in the Teutoburg Forest (Germany) in AD 9. The scale of the defeat was sufficient that Varus' reputation was destroyed, and he would thereafter be inescapably associated with the defeat that was soon after given his name – the *Clades Variana*, or 'Varus Disaster'.[1] Were it not for this defeat, Varus would likely have been just another fairly anonymous Roman politician, whose name would only be known to specialists working in his historical period. But instead, Varus became one of the most notorious figures of the early Imperial period, whose name and reputation is known far beyond the small circle of researchers who work on early Imperial Rome.

This book is the culmination of almost twenty years of fascination with Publius Quinctilius Varus, ever since I first learned about the Battle of the Teutoburg as an undergraduate, and subsequently chose it as my BA dissertation topic. While researching it, I became increasingly bemused by the treatment of Varus in both ancient and modern historical sources. He seemed to be almost universally blamed for the disaster – but, no matter how many times I revisited the evidence, I could not see why. The conviction steadily grew that Varus had been blamed for a defeat that he could have done little to prevent, a position which I still hold today. Increasingly, I am not alone in holding this opinion. New research on the battle itself (particularly archaeology at the likely battlefield), as well as into the attitudes of Julio-Claudian emperors to military defeat, have provided new evidence into why Varus was blamed so mercilessly for the events in the Teutoburg. To an increasing number of scholars, Varus is no longer necessarily seen as a complete incompetent who somehow found himself holding one of the most important military commands in the Empire. His reputation is slowly being redeemed, at least in the context of the Teutoburg battle itself. However, until now there has never been a comprehensive biography which explored Varus' entire life, contextualizing the defeat in

Germany through his distinguished and varied career. This book addresses this oversight, reconstructing Varus' biography as completely as possible from surviving evidence, including historical references and archaeological material. The aim is to present a more complete picture of exactly who Varus was when he entered the Teutoburg in AD 9 with his legions. What emerges is a portrait of an experienced and capable individual, far more so than many previous studies would suggest. It provides a detailed insight into the life and career of a figure who operated close to the heart of the early Imperial regime, and who met his end in one of the most well-executed ambushes in military history. This book hopes to complement the various volumes which have been written about the Teutoburg battle itself, and provide new perspectives on one of the main protagonists in that engagement by telling his full life story. It has been a fascinating and rewarding task to do so.

The Infamy of the Teutoburg

The events in the Teutoburg have gone down in historical infamy as one of the greatest military defeats in antiquity (if not of all time). It took place in the late summer/early autumn of AD 9, when Varus was governor of Germany and in command of five legions on the Rhine. A three-legion force, supplemented by nine auxiliary units, was ambushed in the depths of a German forest, whilst on the march to deal with a supposed uprising in a more distant region of Germany. Over the course of a three- or four-day running engagement, three Roman legions (mostly likely the Seventeenth, Eighteenth, and Nineteenth) were almost completely annihilated, along with their commander, Publius Quinctilius Varus, and most of his staff. Most of the Roman soldiers caught in the attack were either killed or captured, and the eagles and other military insignia of all three legions were lost to the Germans. For a while after the battle, the Germans threatened to cross the Rhine and continue their offensive further into the interior of the Empire, provoking widespread alarm and panic that reached as far as the city of Rome itself. The attack had been led by a German chieftain named Arminius, who had been raised in Rome and had served in the Roman army prior to his defection back to his native people; he would go on to cause future problems for the Empire until he was murdered by his own men more than a decade after the Teutoburg. The battle has been seen as a turning point in European history for several centuries – as 'the battle that stopped Rome'.[2] It is portrayed as having permanently ended Roman hopes for the territorial acquisition of Germany into the Empire, although periodic military campaigns were undertaken in the area in the centuries afterwards.[3] As will be seen later in thus book, the reality was not so simple.

The dramatic nature of the events in the Teutoburg in AD 9, and their longer-term potential impact on both Roman and European history, have long made Varus a figure of fascination. Yet, in many discussions of the battle, both ancient and more modern, very little is said about Varus himself, or his earlier life and career – he has become an almost peripheral figure even in the context of an event named after him. But while Varus has become a poorly understood individual, he was clearly once an important one, whose role in the early Imperial period extended far beyond the Teutoburg. Born into relative obscurity as a fairly minor and impoverished member of the Roman aristocracy, Varus rose to become one of the most accomplished members of the Imperial circle under Augustus. He became wealthy and well connected, even marrying into the Imperial family, and was likely a close friend of both Augustus and Tiberius. Varus' appointment to the command of the Rhine legions in AD 7 was the culmination of a rich and varied career. He had served in various administrative and military capacities in both Rome and the provinces – including a consulship, at least two governorships, and one or more legionary commands – as well as twice marrying into the Imperial family. Varus was clearly an experienced and capable individual who was valued and trusted by the Imperial regime.

However, this is not the portrait of Varus that is put forward by the historical record, both ancient and modern. Instead, he is often portrayed as an ineffective, corrupt, and highly flawed individual, who brought down the destruction of the legions through his mismanagement of Germany as provincial governor, and his wilful negligence of warnings about a German conspiracy. He was, so these sources say, an administrator who was unsuited to military command, who was vastly out of his depth in Germany, and entirely unequal to the role of governor and commander on the Rhine. More modern historians have typically followed the ancient assessment of Varus, judging him as 'a competent lawyer and administrator but not an accomplished commander', consistent with the ancient verdicts.[4] The problem with these assessments is that they do not judge the veracity of the ancient opinions about Varus with the evidence from his earlier life and career – a trajectory which has been little-examined in the past, and which is rarely even alluded to in many modern assessments.

Varus in the Roman sources

Varus is a poorly documented figure by modern standards; no biographies of him were written in his own time, and he survives mainly through accounts of the disaster in the Teutoburg, although most of the surviving accounts lack detail, and contain no real insight into Varus as a historical character. Much of his earlier life and career is only known through archaeological discoveries, some of them made fairly recently, including previously unknown military postings, civic appointments, and marriages. From these discoveries, Varus is beginning to emerge as a much more rounded and developed individual, and his role in both Augustus' administration and the Imperial family are becoming much better understood. It is becoming clearer why Varus was appointed to be the governor of Germany in AD 7, and why the defeat in the Teutoburg was an even greater shock to Augustus and the Roman world than had previously been realized.

Varus' life and career before the events in AD 9 are little documented by the historical sources, and his early life and career has to largely be extrapolated from incidental references within the available evidence. The exception is one incident in the client kingdom of Judaea, at that stage under the rule of King Herod, when Varus was governor of the neighbouring province of Syria. He was called upon to mediate a familial dispute in the later stages of Herod's reign, and soon after to subdue a large-scale Jewish uprising which began soon after the king's death. His actions in Judaea were recorded by the Romano-Jewish historian Flavius Josephus in two works – the *Antiquities of the Jews* and the *Jewish War* – both written in the later decades of the first century AD. Although he plays a relatively small role in the overall narrative of Judaean history, Varus appears to have had an impact on the kingdom during his time in Syria. As a sign of his involvement in events, the uprising which he suppressed was referred to in Talmudic sources as the 'War of Varus'. The only other source to mention Varus' time in Syria is Velleius Paterculus, and it is only raised to make accusations that Varus embezzled money while governor there, an accusation not mentioned by any of the other sources.[5] Otherwise, his career prior to the Teutoburg can only be reconstructed through a handful of archaeological references, including several inscriptions on statue bases, and some coin issues bearing his name and/or likeness.

It is through the battle in the Teutoburg that Varus is best documented in history. Varus is mentioned in four main surviving narratives by (in order of composition) Velleius Paterculus, Tacitus, Florus, and Cassius Dio.[6] All but Tacitus focus on the events in AD 9, while Tacitus approaches the events of the battle during a revisit to the site in AD 15 by Germanicus and another Roman army. Each makes a different contribution to the historiography of the battle, and from them a composite image of the battle can be created, although even then what emerges lacks detail in a lot of senses. Between them the sources do not even make it clear where the battle took place, beyond a forest east of the Rhine that was a fair distance from any Roman settlement or military outpost, and which the Romans referred to as the *Teutoburgensis*.[7] The level of detail that they contain about the actual battle, or indeed about Varus himself, varies significantly.

The account by Velleius Paterculus was the earliest of the surviving sources to be written, composed within two decades of the Teutoburg battle taking place. Velleius was a Roman aristocrat, a career soldier and politician, drawn from the same background as Varus, although two decades or more likely separated the pair in age.[8] Early in his career Velleius served as a military tribune in the eastern provinces (under Gaius Caesar), and as a cavalry commander under the future Emperor Tiberius in Germany from around AD 4 to AD 12.[9] He was close to the Imperial regime, as someone who had benefitted greatly from its patronage, and was evidently both loyal to and protective of it. The future Emperor Tiberius emerges particularly well in Velleius' narrative, particularly in the aftermath of the Teutoburg where he is presented as the person who 'rescues' Rome from the danger created by Varus.[10] Velleius' narrative of the Teutoburg is part of a two-volume universal history of Rome, which spanned the entirety of Roman history from the end of the Trojan War through to AD 30, the point at which Velleius is presumed to have died; however, the period between the death of Caesar (44 BC) and the death of Augustus (AD 14) is the most detailed and useful part of the work. It is not certain what the original title of this work was, but it is usually referred to as the *Historiae Romanae,* or the 'Roman History'. Velleius may have intended this work to be a precursor to a much larger and more detailed historical work, although it is unknown whether he ever completed this before his death. The account of the Teutoburg given by Velleius is particularly useful because it was composed within living memory of the event. He would potentially have been able to consult surviving combatants from the battle about their experiences, particularly as some remained in military service for some years afterwards. As a serving military officer at the time of the battle, he may have been privy to more details about the battle than the average civilian in Rome. As it spans the period within which the battle took place, Velleius' narrative also provides context for the Teutoburg – it is the only connected narrative of events in this timespan, making it especially useful to understand the causes and impact of the events in Germany more widely. That said, his narrative of the Teutoburg battle itself is not particularly detailed, especially when compared to that of Cassius Dio, written almost two centuries later. It does not provide any details about the length of the battle, or many of the actions taken by the Romans once the attack began. It also contains little information about Varus himself beyond a few accusations about his earlier career and his failures in Germany, which were almost certainly intended to make Varus look culpable for the defeat. These contribute to a generalized bias against Varus that runs through

Velleius' account of the battle, which may have distorted his presentation of the evidence and its interpretation. Whether this bias was the result of Velleius' intense loyalty to Tiberius and the Imperial regime, which affected the way that he presented the evidence, or the result of a personal dislike of Varus, is unknown.

Next chronologically comes that of Publius Cornelius Tacitus, contained within the first two books of the *Annals*, a narrative account of the years between the death of Augustus (AD 14) and the death of Nero (AD 68). It was likely written in the early second century AD, around a century after the battle, during the reign of Trajan or Hadrian. Although Tacitus had a greater historical perspective on the events than Velleius, his account suffers from his inability to question any survivors of the battle. Whether Tacitus brought any personal biases to his interpretation of the battle is unclear. His early biography is not well known, although he clearly came from a wealthy family, and enjoyed a prominent political career in Rome. Most details of his life refer to administrative and political appointments, and it is not clear whether Tacitus ever served in the Roman army. He was the son-in-law of Gnaeus Julius Agricola, an accomplished military commander and politician whose biography Tacitus later wrote.[11] As a prominent political figure in Rome, Tacitus is thought to have had access to the *Acta Senatus*, the official record of Senate meetings that was kept but not made public.[12] The level of detail throughout the *Annals* suggests that Tacitus was able to access this archive. However, as his narrative only begins in AD 14 with the death of Augustus and the accession of Tiberius, Tacitus does not give an account of the Teutoburg battle itself. Instead, he recounts the visit of another Roman army, commanded by Germanicus, the nephew and adopted son of Tiberius, to the battlefield in AD 15. The passage on the Teutoburg is one of the only times that Tacitus refers to events which happened prior to AD 14 and is the lengthiest example of 'flashback' in the *Annals*.[13] It provides a detailed and often graphic description of the battle's site six years after it was fought, strewn with the skeletal remains of the dead, and the crumbling earthworks of Roman defences. The passage offers some incidental insights into what happened at the battle, particularly through the recollections of Roman survivors who returned with Germanicus, who point out the locations where particular events took place. However, the majority of the narrative information given by Tacitus pertains to the final stages of the battle, with no real discussion of what happened in the rest of the engagement. Varus himself is a largely marginalized figure, who appears to have little agency in the battle, but this presentation may reflect the fact that Germanicus was intended to be the sole focus of attention in this passage, and reference to Varus would have detracted from that.

The wider discussion by Tacitus of Roman campaigns in Germany under Germanicus does help in reconstructing the events of the Teutoburg. The tactics which had proved so effective against Varus were used again by Arminius and the Germans, with the result that the Teutoburg was essentially re-fought several times again, albeit each time resulting in a (sometimes narrow) Roman victory. These details can supplement the accounts of the Teutoburg battle to fill in the gaps in the narrative, particularly where it is made clear that the same tactics were being reused. Tacitus makes little reference to Varus as an individual and does not offer any insight into either his character or his actions during the battle. On the surface, he presents a far more neutral portrait than Velleius had done almost a century earlier. However, Tacitus too had some shortcomings in his historical neutrality, in particular a hatred of perceived tyranny and oppression, resulting from having lived through a 'reign of terror' under the emperor Domitian (AD 81–96).[14] Perhaps for this reason, he expresses more empathy, even sympathy, for the Germans who felt themselves to be unjustifiably oppressed by Roman occupation.[15] Tacitus also very briefly referred to the Teutoburg in the *Germania*, a historical and ethnographic work about the region and its peoples. In discussing the martial ferocity of some of the German tribes, Tacitus lists some of the losses sustained in the Republican period at German hands, going on to describe how this continued into the Imperial period, noting that 'they robbed even a Caesar of Varus and his three legions'.[16] The reference is made in a casual way, without any historical context or explanation. The presentation suggests that the battle was still well known by the early second century AD, and that Tacitus expected his readership to be familiar with what had happened. The *Germania* goes into no further detail about the Teutoburg.

Written around the same time as Tacitus' *Annals* was a work attributed to Lucius Annaeus Florus named the *Epitome of the Histories of Titus Livy*, in tribute to the first century BC/AD historian Titus Livy. Florus' text was a wide-ranging, two-volume historical sketch, and contains a short but colourful narrative sketch of the Teutoburg. The first volume covered events from the foundation of Rome to 25 BC, roughly the same timeline as that of Livy. It was later supplemented by a second book, which covered some later events through to Florus' own lifetime. It is in this book that Florus' brief account of the Teutoburg was written. Unfortunately, the account lacks much in the way of substantial detail, focusing mainly on the fates of Roman soldiers captured by the Germans. Beyond these gory snapshots, it offers little insight into the course of the battle, and reveals nothing of any real use about Varus. The account is useful in terms of graphically illustrating Roman attitudes to the Germans at the time, and if even a fraction of the claims he made about the tortures Roman soldiers were made to suffer were true, it provides a chilling insight into what these unfortunate captives went through.[17] Florus clearly relied on at least one source composed during living memory of the event (not that of Velleius). He refers to the legionary eagles still being lost or in enemy hands, even though they had been recovered within several decades of the battle, the latest in AD 41. It is difficult to say whether this is an argument in favour of Florus' accuracy or not in the events he discusses; the facts in his source(s) may have been gathered from contemporaries of, even combatants in, the Teutoburg – but the fact that Florus repeated lines about the eagles remaining in German hands when they had been recovered more than 60 years earlier suggests he may not have been overly-vigorous in his fact-checking. Although not as hostile towards Varus as Velleius was, Florus was writing in a context where Varus' culpability for the battle had probably been long established, and he makes no effort to re-examine the governor's reputation with the benefit of historical perspective.

The latest account chronologically of the Teutoburg is also the most detailed one – that of Cassius Dio, written in the early third century AD. Dio was a Roman senator and historian of Greek descent, who wrote an extensive eighty-book *History of Rome*, which covers a period of around 1,400 years, from the arrival of Aeneas in Italy through to his own day, ending in AD 229. Unfortunately, not all of the work has survived – some books are entirely missing, others only survive in fragments, or through an abridgement made in the eleventh century by the monk John Xiphilinus. Dio did not have an extensive military background, although he had a prolific political career, which included serving as governor of Smyrna, and proconsulships in Africa and Pannonia. His account of the Teutoburg is the most detailed description of the battle, and it is the only one to mention that the engagement was fought over several days. Dio is also the only one to try to break down the Roman actions on those individual days to produce some clarity on what actually happened. He is also the only one to describe the terrain of the battle's landscape in any detail, and to comment on the weather conditions at the time of the engagement. He does appear to miss a day out of the account – the narrative jumps from the second night to the fourth day – but otherwise it is the most detailed historical source currently available on the battle. It is maddening, therefore, that the very end of the battle's narrative is lost. Dio began to address the last stages of the Roman disintegration, only for the account to then break, and resume again only with the Imperial response to the disaster.[18] What that missing section contained is unclear – perhaps a more detailed discussion of the aftermath of the battle, and the treatment of the captured Romans, which is not mentioned anywhere in the surviving portions of the text. Dio adds little new information about Varus as an individual, although he is not as condemnatory of his actions as Velleius was.

Unfortunately, one source which cannot be discussed in the context of narratives about Varus and the Teutoburg is that of Pliny the Elder, who wrote a twenty-volume history of Rome's wars in Germany, the *Bella Germaniae* ('History of the German Wars'). Likely written in the mid-first century AD, within living memory of the battle but not in its immediate aftermath, the work would undoubtedly have discussed the events in the Teutoburg at length, providing the detail that is sorely missing from most of the surviving accounts. Pliny had personal experience of military service in the German region, serving during a campaign against the Chauci in AD 47 and the Chatti in AD 50. During the latter campaign a small number of Roman survivors of the Teutoburg were discovered still living as slaves in German captivity, and freed.[19] This episode may have offered Pliny the opportunity to speak directly to participants in the battle, although how accurate their recollections would be of a battle fought four decades earlier is questionable, especially given the trauma they may also have gone through as slaves. Unquestionably, the *Bella Germaniae* would have offered unparalleled insight into the Teutoburg battle and may well have contained more biographical detail about Varus than any of the surviving sources. However, the work appears to have been difficult to find even towards later antiquity, and to date, no trace of it has been found.[20] The writing of subsequent historians, particularly Tacitus and Cassius Dio, were likely heavily influenced and informed by the *Bella Germaniae*, which may account for some of the detailed discussions of the battle and battlefield in their works.[21]

The surviving narratives focus almost exclusively on the battle, and of Varus' personal responsibility for the disaster. Only Dio makes any attempt to provide a detailed breakdown of the events of the battle, and even then an entire day of the battle is seemingly missing from the narrative. Where any reference is made to his governorship of the province, it is only to 'explain' the events of AD 9, through emphasizing Varus' ineffectiveness, cruelty, and corruption. He is characterized as the incompetent, corrupt, even naïve commander who led his men into a disaster, despite numerous signs, and even direct warnings, of the plot against Varus and the Roman presence in Germany. The battle is overwhelmingly seen as a Roman defeat rather than a German victory, masterminded by a highly competent commander (particularly in English scholarship). Even where Arminius is given some credit for the battle – and this is not common in either ancient or modern scholarship – Varus is still cast as an incompetent figure, one who allowed his German companion to plot against him, and ignored warnings that Arminius could not be trusted.

Varus and the Teutoburg are further referenced, however briefly, in a number of other sources, including Strabo, Manilius, Frontinus, Seneca the Elder, and Pliny the Elder, each in the context of the AD 9 battle.[22] In these cases, there is no real discussion of the events of the Teutoburg beyond its occurrence, they do not provide a narrative of the battle, nor any discussion of the events – but they do suggest that it had become a 'popular culture' reference within Roman literature, that could be referred to freely in a text without further explanation to the readers about what it meant. If nothing else, this demonstrates the notoriety of the battle for decades, even centuries, to follow.

The *Varusschlacht* Battlefield

Until the late 1980s, the ancient historical sources, flawed as they are, were the only basis on which Varus and the Battle of the Teutoburg could be reconstructed and studied. All analyses of the battle and Varus' actions within it were based on the same narrow range of writings, and there was little prospect for independent reconstruction of the engagement. The situation changed in the late 1980s with the discovery of an early Imperial Romano-Germanic battlefield at the site of Kalkriese in Germany, located just over 15km north of the city of Osnabrück. An extensive battle-related archaeological assemblage has been recovered from the area, providing a key source of new information about what happened in the ambush and running engagement which followed. Most of what has been learned in the years of study since had never even been hinted at by the historical record, and perspectives on the Teutoburg have been substantially changed as a result of the discoveries made around Kalkriese.

For over two centuries historians had attempted to locate the Teutoburg battlefield based on the geographic and topographic descriptions in the various sources, without conclusive success.[23] By the mid-nineteenth century, it had been widely (if almost certainly wrongly) accepted that the battle was fought somewhere near Detmold, some 70km east of Kalkriese. The supposed battlefield was marked with a large monument to the German victory – the Hermannsdenkmal, which towers over the surrounding landscape. The Hermannsdenkmal features a large statue of Arminius (or, as he has been dubbed by later German historians, Hermann), brandishing a sword atop a large classical-style building. Construction began in 1838 in a wave of nationalist enthusiasm and hopes for a united Germany, although funding soon dried-up in the fact of political and social angst. It was eventually completed in the 1870s as victory in the Franco-Prussian War led to renewed enthusiasm for the monument, and the statue was inaugurated in 1875 by Kaiser Wilhelm I. While the location of the Hermannsdenkmal was thought to mark the most likely position of the Teutoburg battlefield, not everyone was convinced by the hypothesis. Towards the end of the nineteenth century, the German historian Theodore Mommsen suggested that the battlefield actually lay nearer to Kalkriese, based in part on reports of gold Roman coins being found by farmers in the region.[24] However, his hypothesis found little favour, no doubt in part because the Hermannsdenkmal gave the impression that the matter of the location was already settled.

Almost a century later, Mommsen's proposal for the battlefield's location would lead a British army officer stationed at Osnabrück to look for the battle in the region around the city through metal detection. The officer's name was Tony Clunn, and his metal detection surveys brought rapid results. In 1987, he located the periphery of a battlefield centred around an area now known as the Oberesch, finding high-denomination coins and, more significantly, lead sling-bullets (*glandes*), a find which indicated a definitively military presence in a region within which the Romans were not historically known to have campaigned.[25] The discoveries were reported to the local archaeological authorities, and intensive excavations in the area have been carried out from 1989 through, with some brief gaps, to the modern day.[26] The site was soon identified as that of an Imperial-period Romano-Germanic battlefield, dating to the first few decades of the first cetury AD, based on the use-dates of the military equipment found at the site, and the coin assemblage. The military equipment at the site clearly points to an early Imperial date – and even then, was innovative for its time, with Kalkriese producing the earliest known evidence for the use of *lorica segmentata* by the legions. None of the coins found in the Kalkriese area have a mint date post-dating AD 9.[27] Several examples from Kalkriese are marked with a VAR countermark, suggesting an association with Varus' time on the Rhine.[28] They could have been used to pay Roman soldiers, suppliers, or the local German population.[29] The countermark would have reminded the recipients of Varus' authority on the Rhine, and may have been intended to help cultivate a sense of personal loyalty among his soldiers, and perhaps the German population as well. Scientific analysis of the VAR marks has found signs of use-wear and re-cutting on the dies used to make the countermarks, suggesting that they were used over a significant period of time, or on large batches of coins at a time – or indeed, both.[30] Varus would have had the authority to countermark coins during his time on the Rhine, whether to pay his soldiers, military suppliers, or even the Germans. Varus would likely not have had the authority to mint coins under his own authority while stationed on the Rhine, as he had been able to in Africa and Syria. Countermarking was the next-best option. However, his activities in Germany no doubt necessitated the use of increasing quantities of coins, potentially creating problems in regions where there was little pre-existing tradition of them being used.[31] The coins alone do not conclusively prove that the Kalkriese battlefield should be associated with Varus, but taken alongside the rest of the assemblage from the site, the argument becomes more compelling. The range of the assemblage, which included not just Roman military equipment, but also a vast array of luxury camp-goods, leisure and personal items, and various non-weapon tools and fittings, suggested that the battlefield was that of a substantial Roman defeat, in which a baggage-train had been captured and looted.[32] Within a few years, it had become clear that the most likely identification for the site was that of the AD 9 Battle of the Teutoburg.[33]

The discoveries made in the Kalkriese area have been substantial. The battle-related assemblage identified extends for some 15km, in places up to 2km across, as befits a running battle fought over multiple days. But while artefacts were deposited throughout this area, the vast majority (more than 90 per cent) were recovered from the Oberesch, which appears to mark a place where the Roman army lost combat cohesion and suffered severe casualties, likely at a late stage of the battle. Excavations at the Oberesch have uncovered a series of eight pits which contain disarticulated human and (a smaller quantity of) animal bones. These are likely the remains of casualties from the battle who were unceremoniously buried after a period of between two and ten years of surface exposure. Skeletal remains of horses and pack-mules have also been discovered at the site, reflecting the presence of cavalry and a large baggage-train within the Roman marching column.[34] During excavations in recent years, Roman military artefacts have also been recovered from German settlements around the Oberesch, widening the conflict landscape far beyond its original boundaries.[35] However, although the conflict landscape around Kalkriese and the Oberesch is extensive, it may in fact only be part of the Teutoburg battlefield, where a section of the Roman marching column was ambushed, with other sites of fighting still to be found nearby.[36]

There are some dissenting opinions on the identification of the area around Kalkriese as the site of the Battle of the Teutoburg, most of which suggest the battlefield should be associated with the slightly later campaigns of Germanicus in the same region between AD 15 and AD 17.[37] Popular candidates for the alternative identifications include a near-disaster for several legions under the command of Aulus Caecina Severus and, more recently, the Battle of the Angrivarian Wall, due to the presence of earthworks at the Oberesch.[38] These engagements saw the Romans once more engage in combat with Arminius and his allies, who attempted to reuse the tactics which had proved so successful at the Teutoburg. Their methods proved less effective in these later battles, however, no doubt in part because the Romans were more prepared than Varus had been for the attacks.[39] The engagements were similar enough in their nature for Tacitus to suggest that Arminius drew direct comparisons between the situations while the engagement against Caecina was being fought.[40] There are some strong proponents for assigning Kalkriese to the campaigns of Germanicus. One proponent has even accused excavators and scholars – whom he dubbed the 'Kalkriese-Kartell' – of deliberately hiding artefacts which would associate the site with Germanicus, including artefacts inscribed with references to the First and Fifth legions.[41] This was done, so he claimed, because authorities were keen to exploit the 2009 anniversary of the battle. No evidence has been found to substantiate these claims.

The coins discovered at the site have also been used to suggest that it should be associated with AD 15–17 rather than AD 9. To those who support a later date, the coin assemblage from Kalkriese, with a mint-date range ending in AD 9, is interpreted in a different way. Most of the coins were minted in Lugdunum, Gaul (modern Lyon, France), and it is argued that it would have taken months, if not years, for most issues to enter general circulation, and that coins minted in AD 9 would not have been in use so soon on the German frontier.[42] It has been further suggested that these coins were used by Germanicus' army, who would not have had access to any other cash money on their campaigns a few years later.[43] However, there is nothing to definitively say that recent coin issues could not have travelled from Gaul to the Rhine in the same year of minting, and others remain convinced that the coin assemblage does support the AD 9 date.[44] Roman coins are not uncommon finds from Germany covering the period from around 12 BC to AD 9, and are recovered from both Roman military installations and Germanic settlements. But following circa AD 9 they become increasingly rare, and even the subsequent campaigns of Tiberius and Germanicus appear to have had little impact on their spread.[45]

A further clue to the date of the battlefield may come from the coins, albeit in a more unusual way. A significant number of the coins from Kalkriese show signs of deliberate defacement, including slashes and piercings over the face of Augustus. It was initially suggested that these marks were made by Roman soldiers to express their discontent with Augustus and the Imperial regime at the time.[46] However, others have suggested that the marks were made by victorious Germans in the aftermath of the Teutoburg, who defaced a symbol of Roman power and then deliberately left it on the battlefield in rejection of what it stood for.[47] None of the coins that were treated in this way were high-denomination, with the majority of them bronze *as* coins, making it a pragmatic way to symbolically signal contempt for the Imperial regime without actually costing a lot. If this was the mechanism by which the defaced coins entered the archaeological record, they strongly point towards Kalkriese being associated with Varus. In neither of the later examples under Germanicus did the Germans gain the victory that would have allowed them to control the site to the degree that they could collect and process coins in this manner.

The nature of the assemblage also supports an association with Varus rather than a later campaign. Many of the arguments associating Kalkriese with Germanicus rely on a reconstruction of how coinage issues spread in the Roman world, without considering the nature of the assemblage as a whole.[48] The range of artefacts, particularly the presence of camp-goods, strongly suggests the looting of a Roman baggage-train, which is strongly indicative of a comprehensive Roman defeat on a scale that does not appear to have taken place under Germanicus. Even some who are uncertain that Kalkriese should definitely be associated with AD 9 acknowledge that the composition of the assemblage is more indicative of a Roman defeat than a victory.[49] Although Germanicus' later campaign suffered some difficulties on the battlefield at times, there are no documented losses on the scale seen at Kalkriese. The historical sources also suggest that Germanicus recognized the potential danger of taking an extensive baggage-train with him on campaign against Arminius. Dio says that Varus was accompanied by a baggage-train which was excessively and problematically large for an army operating in potentially hostile terrain. He states that it was the same size as a train used during peacetime, with the implication that under the circumstances Varus faced, it should have been much smaller.[50] Learning from Varus' errors, Germanicus appears to have made a concerted effort to reduce the burden of his baggage-train while conducting the campaign. He reduced the limit of what could be transported, ensuring the load was kept to a minimum, and inspecting the wagons himself.[51] His aim was almost certainly to ensure that his baggage-train did not become an unwieldy burden.[52] Even with the lighter weight, the baggage-trains threatened at times to become liabilities, again getting stuck when the Romans were moving through muddy and marshy terrain.[53] Given that several Roman historians note the care which Germanicus took over his baggage, it seems unlikely that the decorative statues, ornate furniture, and luxury camp goods found at Kalkriese could belong to his pared-down train.

Although only the discovery of an artefact clearly linked to Varus or one of his legions has any chance of formally ending the debate, the current state of the evidence still suggests that Kalkriese should be taken as a site associated with Varus in AD 9, rather than a later action under Germanicus. This book proceeds on the basis that the site of Kalkriese can be associated with the AD 9 engagement under Varus, albeit potentially only one of several within the wider conflict landscape.

The excavations and subsequent analysis of the assemblage around Kalkriese has benefitted significantly from the application from the earliest stages of investigation of methodologies adapted from battlefield archaeology, originally developed to study nineteenth century battlefields in the United States but increasingly applicable to other time periods; battlefield archaeology particularly emphasizes the importance of recording spatial data during excavations, which allows for detailed analysis of the assemblage's distribution, which greatly assists reconstruction of the event's narrative.[54] The discoveries at Kalkriese have been particularly useful for reassessing the Battle of the Teutoburg as an actual historic event, into which Varus' actions as an individual commander can be contextualized and reinterpreted where appropriate. The archaeological record from the battle site has already provided a lot of new information about the battle, which has significantly altered the interpretation of the events of the running engagement. If Varus is to be remembered for one single – if admittedly catastrophic – event in a long and distinguished career, at least he can be remembered for what *actually* happened at the battle, not what a handful of surviving sources *said* happened.

Aim and Structure

The aim of this book is to draw together all the fragments of evidence about Varus' life and career to produce the first dedicated biography of this often-misunderstood individual. It will look at the overall trajectory of Varus' career development to explore the skills he developed, the Imperial connections he made, and the experiences he went through to better understand his evolution as an administrator, a military commander, and an individual. Ultimately, it hopes to contextualize the events in the Teutoburg, and the judgements made about Varus in Germany, providing a detailed explanation for why he was appointed to such an important command, and contradicting popular perceptions which see him as an incompetent administrator, hopelessly out of his depth in one of the most militarily challenging provincial governorships. This book divides almost naturally into two parts – the first covering Varus' life up to his appointment to Germany/the Rhine in AD 7, the second focused on his time in Germany leading up to and culminating with the battle in the Teutoburg in AD 9, and its aftermath. The two parts are not evenly weighted in time. The first half spans more than five decades, while the second concentrates on a period less than three years long – a fitting structure for a man whose entire life has been characterized by an event that only lasted for three or four days at the end of it.

The book starts with a discussion of the Quinctili Varii family history more generally, in as much as it can be reconstructed (Chapter 1). The following chapter looks at Varus' immediate family background, from his ancestral family to his parents and siblings, alongside an exploration of his early life (Chapter 2). This moves on to a discussion of Varus' early career, from his service as a military tribune in his early twenties through to his consulship in 13 BC, including all his appointments in-between (Chapter 3). This chapter encompasses discussion of Varus' growing prominence within the Imperial regime, and considers the development of his professional and personal relationship with the emperor Augustus, and with Tiberius, Augustus' stepson. This section also includes discussion of Varus' familial life during this period, including his own marriages and those of his sisters, and the political connections which these relationships brought. The next chapter moves on to the middle years of Varus' career, as he began to take on more senior roles, including governorships of the provinces of Africa and Syria, and the experiences he had in these respective positions (Chapter 4).

The second part of the book opens with a chapter looking at Varus' governorship of Germany, including an overview of Roman involvement in the area in the previous decades, and a discussion of what policies Varus pursued while in office (Chapter 5). It considers the events which led to the Battle in the Teutoburg, and explores the impact of Roman provincial administration in creating the discontent which led to the attack. The next chapter addresses the battle in the Teutoburg, looking at the narrative of the conflict, its causes, and Varus' personal actions during the fighting (Chapter 6). It also addresses the aftermath of the battle, discussing why it became such a significant event in early Imperial Roman history. This is followed by a chapter looking at the creation of the 'Varus Disaster', exploring how and why Varus was blamed for the events of the battle, and for wider mistakes in the administration of Germany (Chapter 7). The final chapter explores Varus in wider history, looking at how his reception has changed – or not – in the millennia since the battle, and how he is still portrayed in popular culture and history today (Chapter 8).

A Note on Names and Places

Roman naming conventions were complex in their simplicity.[55] Fathers and sons often shared the same names, as did sisters and female cousins – meaning that in some cases it can be difficult to ascertain exactly which individual is being discussed by a source, or the relationships to one another. In this book, where possible different related individuals have been identified through use of 'the Elder', to indicate the more senior, and 'the Younger' for the junior, usually following similar usage in the ancient sources. Where this is not possible or practical, individuals with the same name will be denoted by brackets giving their respective hierarchical numbers, which were not used in antiquity but are employed here for the sake of clarity. In most cases, individuals will be introduced to the text with their full name, and thereafter be referred to mainly by their cognomen, unless they are more commonly known by another. Most individuals will retain the same name throughout the text, with the exception of Augustus, who is referred to as Octavian for any events that happened before 27 BC, when he was given the title of Augustus, which is used for years after it was given.

In most cases, places mentioned in the text are referred to by either their ancient or modern name, depending on which is known; if both are known and the identification is certain, then both are used where the place is first mentioned and the modern name used from then onwards. Similarly, the Rhine is referred to by its modern name, as are most provinces where the modern political entity broadly synchronizes with the ancient boundaries (e.g. Spain, Britain). Only in cases where there are substantial differences between the two territories, as in the case of Gaul/France, will the ancient name be preferred. 'Germany' is used instead of Germania to indicate the territories beyond the Rhine that Varus was sent to govern, to distinguish it from the two later provinces of Germania Superior and Germania Inferior, which did not exist at the time of the Teutoburg.

Addendum

After the submission of this manuscript, news came out from Germany about new metallurgical research into some of the metal artefacts from Kalkriese, which sheds new light on the identification of the site. Mass spectrometric analyses of *c.* 550 pieces of metal kit from seven different military sites in Germany, including Kalkriese, has been conducted, and although not yet fully published, has produced some interesting results. The metallurgical fingerprint of the sampled artefacts from Kalkriese closely resembles that from the site of Dangstetten, a legionary base occupied pre-AD 9 by the Nineteenth Legion, one of the units destroyed in the Teutoburg; there are no such similarities between the Kalkriese material and that from the other sites included in the study. The results indicate that the military kit found at Kalkriese once belonged to the Nineteenth Legion, strongly suggesting that the site can indeed be associated with AD 9 and Varus, rather than later campaigns conducted by Germanicus.

Chapter 1

The Quinctili Varii Family

Publius Quinctilius Varus was born into the *gens* (clan) Quinctili Varii, an aristocratic Roman family of patrician status. The family was part of the ruling class, and male members had the nominal right to sit in the Senate, as well as the ability – or duty – to pursue a career in public life. The patrician classes were originally thought to comprise the oldest families in Rome, who had been part of the city since its semi-mythical foundation in 753 BC. Romulus, the founder of Rome, was said to have appointed 100 men as *patres* ('fathers'), who became the first senators of the city; their descendants became the patricians, inheriting their political power.[1] Throughout the early Republican period (*circa* 509–264 BC), the patricians evolved into a group of the wealthiest and most influential families in the city. They were functionally in charge of the city, holding the governing and administrative offices which ran it, and had rights and privileges that were not extended to the rest of the population. Below the patricians were the equestrians ('knights'), who were wealthy members of Roman society. Their name reflects their origin as those wealthy enough to afford cavalry equipment during times of war, and like the patricians they were said to have originated in the earliest days of Roman history.[2] Equestrian rank could be passed down from father to son, but it was necessary to maintain high levels of wealth to keep the status, and if a census found that a family no longer satisfied the requirements they would usually be stripped of their status. They could be elected to high political offices, particularly when their wealth was sufficient to buy influence in Rome. Below the equestrians were the remaining plebians, who made up the majority of the freeborn population of Rome. Most came from families without wealth or power, and although they were theoretically able to hold some of the civic positions in the city, rates of social mobility were low.

The fortunes of many of the patrician families in Rome went into decline over the course of the Republican period, with many losing their wealth and importance, while maintaining their theoretical status within the Roman elite. While all patrician families still had the same theoretical rights and privileges, actual power and influence was determined both by the pedigree and history of your family name, and the past achievements of those who bore it. Some families became relatively obscure, with their members no longer holding, or even competing for, the highest political appointments, losing any political influence they once had. Varus' family was one of the patrician clans affected in this way.

By the Late Republican period the Quinctili Varii had become a 'famous rather than a high-born family', with members having largely failed to make any significant political or military impact over the previous centuries.[3] The family was evidently distinguished in terms of longevity, according to some sources dating back to the times of Romulus and Remus, and known as one of the oldest families in Rome, although their glory days were seemingly far behind them. Members of the Quinctili Varii had consistently failed to hit the heights of political power, throughout the duration of the Roman Republic.[4] As members of the patrician class, the male heads of the family had the right to sit in the Roman Senate, the main decision-making body in Republican politics, but appear to have done little of importance while there. The family lacked the highest status because members of the family consistently failed to ascend to the higher offices of the Roman political system. In particular, members of the Quinctili Varii consistently failed to hold the consulate, which was one of the main ways that a family could demonstrate its importance. By the time that Varus was born, it had been over four centuries since a member of the family had been appointed consul.[5] Although the family still had an important and respected name, they were no longer a political force to be reckoned with by the Late Republic, with few prominent ancestors whose fame could be called upon to bolster the reputation of the family. However, male members of the family were likely still involved in the political scene in Rome, despite not holding the higher positions of state, and the heads of the family retained their right to sit in the Senate, the executive arm of Roman government. The clan was also sufficiently important that the men were required to play an active role in Rome's internal conflicts. Sextus Quinctilius Varus, Varus' father, would demonstrate the ongoing activity of the Quinctili Varii during the wars of the Late Republic by playing a part in the conflict between Caesar and Pompey, and later, between Brutus and Cassius against Octavian and Mark Antony.

Ancestral Quinctili Varii

Family background was important in ancient Rome, and ancestors played a significant role in public and private religious practice, particularly from the Late Republican period onwards.[6] Relatively little is known of the generations of the Quinctilii Vari family who came before Publius Quinctilius Varus – although this is not unusual for a minor patrician family who lived largely on the margins of political power. They were clearly, however, a family with a long history, and could be counted among the oldest families in Rome.[7] The Quinctili Varii first appear in the historical record in 453 BC, when a Sextus Quinctilius Varus was elected to hold the Roman consulship, at that time the highest political office in Rome. It was often the high point of a career in public life. The consulship was the highest rank on the *cursus honorum*, the pre-sequenced series of military appointments and political magistracies which dictated the career path of patrician males, and was the ultimate career aim of any male Roman aristocrat. Males would enter the *cursus honorum* around the age of 30, before which they would be expected to complete military service, often on the staff of a commander who was a member of their family, or a family friend. This service would provide individuals with around a decade of military experience before they entered political administration. They would then work their way through a series of administrative appointments of different ranks (*quaestor*, *aedile*, *praetor*) before becoming eligible for the consulship at the age of 42 or 43. Two consuls were elected each year, drawn from the ranks of eligible patricians, who would by that point have served in several different roles within the Roman government, giving them – at least in theory – a good, generalized overview of the workings of the state. By the time of his birth, none of Varus' family had held the consulship in more than four centuries. The males of the family – as patricians – had, presumably, followed careers within the general boundaries of the *cursus honorum*, but failed to excel sufficiently enough for their careers to leave much of a mark on the historical record. The few mentions of them show members of the Quinctili Varii family serving in minor magistracies, and occasionally in military commands, but without making much impact on the wider Roman political sphere.

One potential ancestor of the Publius Quinctilius of note is another Publius Quinctilius Varus, who was a praetor during the Second Punic War. This Quinctilius Varus served in the Republican army, and in 203 BC co-commanded in a battle against a Carthaginian force led by Mago Barca, brother of Hannibal.[8] As a praetor, he was a magistrate who could wield military power (*imperium*) in the field when required, and in this particular engagement, was commanding alongside a proconsul named Marcus Cornelius.[9] In theory, during this battle Cornelius was the higher-ranking individual and should have been in command, but Livy's narrative suggests that it was Quinctilius Varus who took the lead role. When the battle looked as though it might turn against the Romans, Quinctilius Varus determined that a sudden cavalry charge was the best chance of breaking the Carthaginian lines. He offered to lead the attack, or to allow Cornelius to do so. The proconsul left the decision to Quinctilius Varus, who elected to lead the attack, alongside his son, Marcus, who was evidently serving in his father's legion. However, the cavalry charge failed to break the attack as the horses were frightened by the elephants brought up into the Carthaginian lines, and the battle nearly descended into a disaster for the Romans. One of the Roman legions (the Twelfth) suffered significant casualties, and was close to breaking until bolstered by reserve troops. These fresh troops mounted a new assault on the Carthaginian lines, focusing on throwing spears at the elephants, which provoked them into a retreat (although the Carthaginians continued to hold, not least because of the determination of their commander, Mago). It was only when Mago was wounded in the thigh and suffered massive blood-loss that the Carthaginian lines gave way. The Carthaginian casualties were said by Livy to have numbered around 5,000, although Roman losses were placed at around 2,300 men, mostly from the Twelfth Legion, which had particularly suffered during the battle. While not necessarily the most noble ancestor our Quinctilius Varus could have had, if they were related it demonstrates that the Quinctili Varii were involved in at least middle-ranking roles in the *cursus honorum*. However, it is unclear whether this Quinctilius Varus was directly related to the later Varus, or from a different branch of the same family.

In the later years of the Roman Republic, several other members of the Quinctili Varii are mentioned in the historical office, albeit largely on an incidental basis.[10] One member of the family served as a *pontifex* between 73 and 69 BC, one of the highest-ranking priests in the state religious system. Another served as a praetor in 57 BC, and in 56 BC was sent to Hispania Ulterior as a proconsul. The exact relationship of these individuals to Publius Quinctilius Varus is uncertain, although they do not seem to have been part of his immediate family line. None of Varus' other older relatives can be identified in the historical record – although, as one historian notes, this is not particularly unusual for individuals of his position at the time.[11]

Varus' Parents

The status of Varus' parents may give a better indication of the fortunes of the Quinctili Varii at the time of his birth – although unfortunately, we know relatively little about them. It is not known who any of his grandparents were, on either side of the family – the only comment about them which exists in the historical record refers to Varus' (paternal) grandfather, who is said to have committed suicide, although the reason for this is not given.[12] His father was named Sextus Quinctilius Varus, and, like most of the previous Quinctili Varii, appears to have climbed relatively slowly up the *cursus honorum*. He was appointed to the rank of quaestor in or by 49 BC, the first stage of the senatorial career ladder, and a prerequisite for further service – although his future career was disrupted by the outbreak of civil war between Caesar and Pompey. The minimum age requirement for a quaestor was 30, so Sextus must have been born around or before 79 BC, meaning he was entering early adulthood at a time of great political upheaval in the late Roman Republic – and, as will be seen, he did not hesitate to choose a side.

The identity of Varus' mother is uncertain. There is no definitive reference to her name, or even her family, in any source connected with Varus, making it difficult to be certain of her identification. She almost certainly also came from an elite Roman family, likely from the patrician class. It is not known when she was born, or when she married Sextus Quinctilius Varus, although she was probably in her late teens when she married sometime in the early 40s BC, suggesting she was most likely born in the early-to-mid 60s BC. Some suggestion has been made that Varus' mother was a daughter of Gaius Claudius Marcellus Minor, from his first marriage to an unknown woman; if so, her name would have been Claudia Marcella.[13] Marcellus would later marry Octavia by 54 BC, the sister of Octavian/Augustus, making any children of previous marriages – including, in this scenario, Varus' mother – the step-children of Octavia, and step-nephews/nieces of Octavian. They would also be step-siblings to the children of the marriage between Octavia and Marcellus, including Marcus Claudius Marcellus, the nephew of Augustus and for a time his son-in-law and potential heir. Depending on when she was born, theoretically Varus' mother could have lived for a time in Octavia's household as her step-daughter, and presumably Marcellus and Octavia would have arranged her marriage in the late 50s/early 40s BC, evidently to Sextus Quinctilius Varus. In this scenario, the marriage would have been an advantageous one for Sextus Quinctilius Varus, coming as he did from a relatively obscure background. He may have had high hopes of what this marriage could do for his political prospects going forwards – and, as will be seen, Sextus did play a role in some of the tumultuous events which heralded the end of the Republican period.

This identification for Varus' mother is a tempting one, not least as it suggests that Varus had a connection with the Imperial family – albeit a slightly tenuous one – from early in life, even if they had not yet come to the prominence which they would later achieve. *If* this identification is correct, Varus' maternal grandfather, Gaius Claudius Marcellus Minor (who died in 40 BC, during Varus' childhood), had been Octavian/Augustus' brother-in-law, and his mother the step-daughter of Octavia, and the step-niece of Octavian/Augustus – and therefore Varus, in his earlier childhood, the step-grandson of Octavia. Varus would therefore have been born into the fringes of Octavian's family, a connection which may explain his rise to prominence in the early

Imperial regime, and the patronage he received early in his career once Octavian had become Augustus.

Sextus Quinctilius Varus in the Civil Wars

The only member of Varus' direct family who is documented in any detail in the historical record is his father, Sextus Quinctilius Varus, largely because of his (admittedly fairly marginal) involvement in the civil war between Julius Caesar and Gnaeus Pompey – although his presence in the historical record of the conflict is largely incidental.

Tensions had long been building between Caesar and Pompey, two of the most prominent political and military leaders in Rome approaching the middle years of the first century BC, spilling out into open conflict in 49 BC. Caesar had spent much of the previous decade in Gaul, following his consulship in 59 BC, during which period he had made an informal alliance with Pompey and Marcus Licinius Crassus, known as the First Triumvirate, through which each member agreed to use their respective influences to support the actions of the others.[14] After his consulship, Caesar was appointed proconsul in Cisalpine Gaul (in northern Italy, on the Italian side of the Alps) in 58 BC, and in the following years launched a series of campaigns of conquest in Gaul that would see him conquer much territory, up as far as the Rhine, and acquire a lot of wealth, as well as the devoted loyalty of his soldiers. During this time, although Caesar remained ostensibly in alliance with Pompey, the loyalties between them began to decline, a process only exacerbated by the death of Crassus in 53 BC at the Battle of Carrhae. By 51 BC, with the conquest of Gaul largely complete, concerns were growing in Rome about the level of power that Caesar had built up, and what his intentions would be when he returned to the city.[15] An 'anti-Caesar' faction began to develop in Rome, in which Pompey was a prominent figure, along with many of the more traditional members of the Senate, who disliked the way that Caesar conducted both the war in Gaul and his wider political affairs; many were concerned that Caesar would use his military power to invade Rome. But while Caesar was disliked and feared by much of the Roman elite, he was intensely popular with the ordinary people of the city, as well as with his soldiers – 11 legions strong by 49 BC – who were seemingly willing to fight with him for almost any cause. Rome began to split into two factions – the *optimates*, who supported the traditional political order and rule of the Senate, who took Pompey as their nominal leader, and the *populares*, who were seen as being more 'rulers for the people', who coalesced behind Julius Caesar. In mid-January of AD 49 (probably the 10th or 11th), Caesar infamously crossed the Rubicon into Italy with the Thirteenth Legion, starting a chain of events which would lead to a brutal civil war that lasted for more than four years.[16] Many of the aristocratic families living in Rome at the time would have to pick a side – including the men of the Quinctili Varii.

Sextus Quinctilius Varus, like many members of the Roman Senate, was a supporter of the more traditionalist Optimates faction, which opposed Julius Caesar and the Populares. He was present at several military operations against Julius Caesar, including at the siege of Corfinium in 49 BC, one of the first armed engagements of the conflict. Caesar had crossed the Rubicon into Italy with his legions in January 49 BC, and the rate of his advance through Italy had shaken many of his enemies in Rome. Alarmed at his approach, they elected to flee the city, and made for Corfinium (modern Corfinio), which lay approximately 150km east of Rome. Corfinium was a deliberate choice for a second base – during the Social War, fought between the Romans and their Italian allies several decades earlier (91–87 BC), the Italians had designated the city as a rival capital, renaming it Italica and making it the centre of their operations.[17] Although the city was never to become a permanent capital, it maintained a strategic importance through to the outbreak of the civil war, making it an ideal, and symbolic, bolt-hole for the senatorial Optimates – one of whom was Sextus Quinctilius Varus. The city was armed and garrisoned, against the wishes of Pompey, by Lucius Domitius Ahenobarbus, who requested reinforcements from Pompey once Caesar and his army had arrived to lay siege to Corfinium, which was ultimately denied. On discovering this, parties within the city decided to surrender to Caesar rather than face an extended siege, throwing themselves on his mercy. Caesar agreed and requested that the following day all of the senators and their sons be brought before him, so that he could chastise them for their actions and demonstrate his clemency, before dismissing them unharmed. One of these senators, mentioned by name, was Sextus Quinctilius Varus.[18] There is no mention of a son of Sextus, who had likely not been born yet.

This act of mercy by Caesar did little to win Sextus Quinctilius Varus to his cause, and he became one of the many recidivists to re-join the war against Caesar despite the generosity with which they had been treated.[19] After being dismissed at Corfinium, Sextus Quinctilius Varus fled to Africa, where he had joined the army of a prominent Optimate, Publius Attius Varus (no relation). Also in Africa were several legions of soldiers who had been present at Corfinium during the siege but later defected to Caesar, and who had been sent to Africa under the command of Gaius Scribonius Curio to secure Rome's grain supply. On discovering that the legions were more or less still constituted as they had been at Corfinium, Sextus Quinctilius Varus attempted to persuade them to abandon Caesar and re-join the Optimates, including by citing the oaths they had sworn directly to him as quaestor:

> Sextus Quintilius Varus, whose presence at Corfinium was mentioned above, was in Attius Varus' army; he had come to Africa after his release by Caesar. And the legions that Curio had brought over were those that Caesar had previously captured at Corfinium, so much so that, although a few centurions had been changed, the command structure and companies were the same as before. Having this rationale for addressing them, Quintilius began to go from one spot to the next on Curio's line and beseech the soldiers: 'Do not discard your earliest memory of an oath, the one you swore in Domitius' presence and mine when I was quaestor, or bear arms against men who have suffered the same misfortunes as you and endured the same things under siege, or go into combat for people by whom you are insulted as "deserters."' To this he added a few words to raise hopes of largesse: 'If you follow me and Attius, you will necessarily have expectations from my generosity.'[20]

The promises made by Sextus Quinctilius Varus caused some disquiet among the soldiers under Curio's command, although they were evidently not immediately won around to his position. Several discussions were held by the soldiers and commanders about how best to respond to his offer. A rousing speech by Curio reaffirmed the loyalty of the soldiers to Caesar, and a battle between them and the men commanded by Publius Attius Varus was attempted soon after, although the latter troops fled before battle could be fully joined, after seeing high casualties sustained in the first advance by their cavalry. They sustained relatively heavy losses given the fact that battle was never actually joined, with further casualties sustained during the retreat and struggle to get back into the camp. Caesar numbers these at 600 dead, and a further thousand wounded, with a single loss on the Curian side.[21] Following this incident, Sextus Quinctilius Varus disappears from the record of the remaining civil war, and it is unknown what other activities he was involved in before the relatively brief cessation of hostilities early in 45 BC – although, from his appearance later in the record, it is clear that he survived the conflict.[22] Following final campaigns in the Near East and Spain, Julius Caesar returned to Rome in September 45 BC, as did many of the patrician combatants from both sides of the conflict – presumably, including Sextus Quinctilius Varus, although he may have returned earlier. It was around this time that his son, Publius Quinctilius Varus – the subject of this book – was born.

Within a year of Caesar's return to Rome, the chaos and conflict which beset the Late Republic began anew when he was assassinated on the Ides of March 44 BC. His murder in the Curia of Pompey, where he had gone to attend a Senate meeting, was planned by a group of around sixty conspirators, many of them senators themselves. Although the main conspirators are known, particularly Brutus and Cassius, the names of many of the other individuals who took part in the plot have not been preserved.[23] It has cautiously been suggested, albeit without any substantial evidence, that Sextus Quinctilius Varus was part of the conspiracy, and may have been present at the assassination, even as one of the senators who struck a blow at Caesar.[24] Whether or not Sextus was one of the conspirators will probably never be known for certain, but it is certainly not impossible, and is perhaps even likely. Sextus' previous actions demonstrate his deep-seated animosity towards Caesar, twice taking up arms against him, even after an unusual show of mercy following his first transgression. There is no reason to imagine that Sextus' politics or opinions about Caesar had softened in the later stages of the civil war, and this would have made him a likely prospect for getting involved in the plot; his actions following the assassination make his involvement appear even more likely.

In the immediate aftermath of Caesar's death, political negotiations within the Senate aimed to create a reconciliation, whereby the conspirators – or the liberators, as they styled themselves – would be granted amnesty for the assassination, and Caesar's political appointments would remain valid. These efforts ultimately ended up unsuccessful, fuelled in no small part by the disapproval of Octavian, who Caesar had named as heir in his will – much to the surprise, and chagrin, of Mark Antony. Brutus, Cassius, and other members of the conspiracy remained in Rome for several weeks after Caesar's death. By September, both Brutus and Cassius had been assigned new roles in the East, where they began to accrue territory, and raise troops to lead against those of Mark Antony and Octavian, making their main base in Greece. In the October of 43 BC, Octavian and Antony, along with Marcus Aemilius Lepidus, another close ally of Caesar, formed the Second Triumvirate, an alliance which aimed, among other things, to destroy the remaining assassins of Caesar, bringing together the combined military forces of all three triumvirs against those gathered by Brutus and Cassius.[25] The triumvirs courted controversy by introducing proscriptions in Rome to raise money to pay their soldiers, and their main targets were those who had allied against Caesar during the civil war – one of the most notable victims was Marcus Tullius Cicero, who had also been a vocal opponent of Mark Antony. The following year, the triumvirs sent twenty-eight legions to Greece to confront the army of Brutus and Cassius, which numbered nineteen legions financed by funds extracted from the populations of the eastern provinces. The two sides met in two battles at Philippi (Greece), fought within three weeks of each other, pitching the army of Brutus and Cassius against that of Octavian and Antony. Cassius committed suicide following the first engagement, wrongly believing that his army had been comprehensively defeated, when in reality, the battle had no clear victor. Things were very different in the second engagement, where Brutus' army became overwhelmed and was unable to either escape or reform. Brutus withdrew from the battlefield and, like Cassius before him, committed suicide.

It is not clear what actions Sextus took in this period of conflict following Caesar's assassination, although his allegiances ultimately remained with the anti-Caesar faction. At some point he left Rome to join up with the forces of Brutus and Cassius; it is entirely possible that he was prompted to do so by the threat of the proscriptions, if he had not left already. He once again took up arms for the anti-Caesarian cause, albeit this time against Caesar's heirs, and fought in the battles at Philippi. Following defeat in the second battle, Sextus followed the examples of Cassius and Brutus and killed himself shortly afterwards – although one ancient historian claimed that he made one of his freedmen carry out the actual act, after dressing himself in the insignia of his offices.[26] Sextus is said to have decided to take his own life without asking for mercy from Octavian and Antony, despite the fact that this was granted to several other prominent figures among Brutus' faction. Perhaps he recognized that, having received mercy twice from Julius Caesar only to take arms up against him at the next possible opportunity, his chances of being granted forgiveness by Octavian and Mark Antony were slight. Sextus was far from the only individual from the defeated side to commit suicide in the aftermath of Philippi, but this would likely have been of little comfort to the family that he left behind. With his father's death, Varus would become the nominal head of his branch of the Quinctili Varii, despite his young age.

While Varus may have come from a patrician family with a long history, the relative obscurity of its members, combined with his father's actions during the conflicts against Julius Caesar, would in many ways have seemed likely to minimize his own prospects going forward. But, as will be seen, Varus does not appear to have been overly affected by the political choices his father made – although he took a very different direction himself. At a young age he would begin a political career that would eclipse those of any other member of his family, largely thanks to the patronage of Octavian, the man who his father had fought to the death to keep from power.

Chapter 2

Varus' Early Life, 46–25 BC

When Varus was born, there would have been little to suggest that anything more than a career of mediocre political service and obscurity lay before him. As seen in the previous chapter, although Varus came from a distinguished and ancient Patrician family, very few of his relatives or ancestors had made much of a mark on the Roman political stage, and it would not have been considered likely that Varus himself would rise to any particular prominence. His father's active alliance with the anti-Caesarian party on multiple occasions would have potentially left the subsequent generation of Quinctili Varii with few friends in the new regime and, after the death of Sextus Quinctilius Varus at Philippi, without an adult head of that particular branch.

Varus managed to overcome the rather negative political reputation of his father, and his less than prominent ancestral background, by allying himself with the new political regime led by Octavian. From early in his life, Varus would have been aware of the likely career that lay in front of him: working in the public sphere, initially in a military and later a political capacity, through the largely pre-determined structure of the *cursus honorum*.[1] As noted previously, members of the Quinctili Varii had not typically advanced particularly far in their careers, either historically or in more recent years. Nevertheless, it would have been expected of the young Varus to at least undertake the early years of a tribuneship when he reached adulthood, a military command required before seeing how much further he could progress along the political career ladder.

Varus appears to have been an exception to the relative obscurity of his family from early in his career, suggesting an ambition that would over time lead him to some of the highest ranks in the Roman political world, becoming the first of the Quinctili Varii to serve as a consul in four centuries – and even a member of the Imperial family by marriage. This chapter reconstructs as far as possible Varus' early life and education, up to the point where he reached young adulthood and began his career in public life. It explores the foundations that were laid in this period, which would come to shape his later life, leading to his appointment to some of the higher military and political offices in the Roman world.

Varus' early life

Publius Quinctilius Varus was born at some point in the mid-to-late 40s BC; unfortunately, there are no records that allow his birth to be more closely dated. He was one of four children, with three sisters, probably all younger than him.[2] The personal name of only one sister has survived – Quinctilia Varilla – with the other two known only by the fairly anonymous family patronyms 'Quinctilia'. These young members of the family grew up in a time of conflict and strife. Given that their father died in 42 BC, an earlier rather than later date is probably to be preferred for Varus' birth, which possibly took place as early as 46 BC, probably while his father was back in Rome during a brief break in hostilities after the end of the Caesar-Pompey civil war, after Caesar had returned to Rome but before his assassination in 44 BC. Sextus Quinctilius Varus does not appear to have suffered any punishment at Caesar's hands after his return to Rome, in common with many of the elite who had opposed him during the civil war.[3] Caesar was evidently inclined to show clemency to his former adversaries in the aftermath of the war, which many found surprising, although some argued that it was done only for Caesar's political benefit.[4] It is unlikely that the family lost property or wealth in punishment for Sextus Quinctilius Varus' role in the civil war on the side of the Optimates. Whether they suffered any loss of prestige is another question, and one that is impossible to answer; however, they would not have been alone in coming from a family whose patriarch had allied with the opponents of Caesar, including far more prominent figures than Sextus.

Whether Sextus Quinctilius Varus was involved in the assassination of Caesar or not, the anti-Caesarian cause once more disrupted the lives of the Quinctili Varii. When Brutus and Cassius, the ringleaders of the assassination, fled to Greece shortly afterwards, Sextus Quinctilius Varus soon followed them. Once again, he had given his support to the party which opposed Julius Caesar, now represented by the forces of Octavian and Mark Antony. Sextus left his young family back in Rome. Varus was probably around 3 or 4 years old when his father committed suicide at Philippi in 42 BC. At such a young age, Varus had likely spent little time with his father up to that point in his life; children were often considered infants until the age of 7, at which point a father would start to play a more substantial role in a son's upbringing.[5] Sextus had likely been absent from Rome for some months before his death, lessening his involvement with his young family even further. Varus and his three sisters may have been left in a difficult position by the death of their father, and may even have been orphaned by his actions – as previously noted, it is not known who their mother was, or whether she was still alive by 42 BC. Even if she was still alive, it would be necessary for a male family member to step in and look after the fortunes of the young Varus until he reached adulthood.

What happened to Varus and his three sisters in their childhood years after the death of their father is undocumented in any of the surviving historical sources. He does not appear in the record until 22 BC, when he was in his twenties and had already embarked on a political career, and his sisters appear only peripherally even later than this. At best, we can try to reconstruct what is likely to have happened to them, extrapolating from better-documented cases. The young children would have needed to be taken in by another household, and to have become the wards of another, preferably well-connected, man, who could oversee their affairs, and particularly Varus' education and entry into public life. Even among the patrician class, personal connections and recommendations were necessary for a successful career, and it would have been vital for the young Varus to secure a well-connected proxy-father who could recommend him to family friends and potential patrons. Varus' mother is unlikely to have been in a position to do much to help in this area, if indeed she was still alive at all.

As a fatherless minor, Varus was theoretically free from guardianship and the *paterfamilias* (head of the household) of his small family, with authority over his sisters. However, boys of his young age would be assigned a *tutor* (guardian), who would, at least in theory, protect the estate until the boy came of age and was able to take up his role more fully; if the father had left a will, the *tutor* might be mentioned in the text, and would often be a member of the paternal family. One modern historian has suggested that Varus and his sisters may have been taken in to the household of a Quintilius Varus, who lived in Tivoli, and may have been their paternal uncle.[6] Little is known about this potential uncle, although he appears to have been connected to the arts, featuring twice in writings by Horace, one praising his abilities as an art critic, the other mourning his death.[7] One villa in particular is strongly associated with Varus, who later in life may have maintained it as a summer retreat, perhaps after inheriting it from his uncle.[8] The modest ruins of the villa traditionally identified as that of Varus lie on a low ridge overlooking the modern town of Tivoli, 5km northwest of the remains of the palace later built by Hadrian in the early second century AD. The road towards the villa from the town is named the Via dei Quinctilio, a more modern nod to Varus' ancient presence in the area. A church, dedicated to Santa Maria di Quinctilio, lies near – and likely over parts of – the villa, the ruins of which are limited. A few foundational walls survive, although the main part of the villa now lies underneath a private olive grove, and access to the site is prohibited by barbed wire. Local archaeological authorities appear concerned that the little stonework that remains from the villa is being removed by the landowners, although without access to the site it is difficult to confirm these concerns at the present moment. A number of artefacts were found at the site, many of which have ended up in the collections of museums in Rome, particularly that of the Vatican. Although the upstanding remains of the villa are limited, their situation alone gives an idea of the landscape panorama the villa would have enjoyed, overlooking the Aniene River (a major tributary of the Tiber), as well as the Roman settlement below the ridge. Although Hadrian's famous palace would not be built for more than a century, Tivoli was already well-established as a retreat from Rome for the city's elites. The ruins of the villa were the subject of a work by Joseph Turner in 1819 ('View of Tivoli from the Ruins of the Villa of Quintilius Varus'),[9] as part of his artistic exploration of the area around Tivoli. Tourist groups visiting Tivoli are still shown around the ruins of the 'Villa of Varus', the delights of which have, to some, provided a moving contrast to the readily imagined horrors of the Teutoburg Forest.[10] Although there is little direct evidence for the relationship between the Quintilius Varus of Tivoli and the fatherless Publius Quinctilius Varus, the synchronicity in both *nomen* and *cognomen* suggests some family connection, at least, backed up further by mutual links to Tivoli. Certainly, local tradition is firmly in the camp of the villa on the Tivoli hillside as belonging to the Varus of Teutoburg infamy – to convince the locals otherwise would be a difficult job indeed.

Sextus' political affiliations could easily have had a damaging effect on Varus' career prospects. At other points in Roman history, Varus might have found his career over before it had even begun due to the disgrace brought on the family by his father – his prospects could have disappeared before he even turned 5 years old. Varus' prospects under the regime of Octavian and Mark Antony, as the only son of a repeated and fervent anti-Caesar activist, may have seemed poor even in the context of his less-than-illustrious ancestry. It would not necessarily have been unusual for a Roman male to grow up without a father, but this situation left the child reliant on members of the wider family stepping into the role of the deceased patriarch. Fortunately for Varus, whether the guardian was his Tivoli-based uncle or someone else, it appears that whoever took on the guardianship of him and his sisters ensured that they were well cared for. They saw that Varus at least received a decent education, one that would benefit him greatly in the future.

Varus would almost certainly have been raised in a way which befitted his family's status, however tarnished their reputation had become in the previous few years through the actions of Sextus Quinctilius Varus. The upbringing of elite males included formal education in public speaking, linguistics, rhetoric, philosophy, morality and other skills which would prove necessary for a career climbing the *cursus honorum*, in addition to more basic subjects such as literacy and (at least basic) mathematics.[11] He may have been taught individually at home, or as part of a small school for the sons of elite families. The aim would have been to prepare the young Varus for a career in public life, during which he would, if his career progressed according to plan, serve in a number of different military and non-military roles.

A childhood in turmoil

While Varus' family had status and some wealth to support them even after Sextus Quinctilius Varus had died, there is no doubt that he and his sisters grew up in challenging times. Varus' childhood and education took place amidst ongoing political turmoil, and his coming of age would have taken place against a backdrop of conflict between Octavian and Mark Antony, who both saw themselves as the heir of Julius Caesar.[12] Although the conflict would end just before Varus was old enough to be called upon to take an active part in the events, he must have been aware as he grew older that it might become necessary to choose a side as the tensions crept closer to open warfare. His family's earlier loyalties would have been of little help – his father would doubtless have hated both sides. Varus would have to decide for himself who to give his support to – or rather, who might prove of greatest benefit to him later on.

The rivalry between Octavian and Antony that would eventually lead to conflict began to emerge in the immediate aftermath of Caesar's assassination, although an alliance for mutual benefit held them together enough to avoid open warfare for just over a decade. With the deaths of Brutus and Cassius at Philippi, most formal opposition to the Populares cause in Rome evaporated, as it became increasingly clear that the dominant political forces in Rome were now Octavian and Mark Antony, who had spearheaded the campaign of revenge against Caesar's assassins. In 43 BC they formed an official alliance, alongside Marcus Aemilius Lepidus, known as the Second Triumvirate; immediately prior to this, they had been at war in northern Italy, with Octavian against Antony and Lepidus.[13] The name of the alliance was derived from the First Triumvirate between Caesar, Pompey, and Crassus which had been formed the previous decade. Unlike the earlier version, however, the arrangement between Octavian, Antony, and Lepidus was a formal and legally constituted alliance, which would last (at least on paper) for over a decade. The triumvirs divided the territory of the empire between them, with Octavian taking the west, Antony the East, Lepidus Africa, and all three collectively sharing Italy. However, Octavian and Antony were never comfortable allies, and it was always unlikely that an alliance between them would last. Octavian had unexpectedly been named as Caesar's heir in his will, a distinction which Antony had expected to come to him. As Caesar's adopted son, Octavian had inherited much of his wealth – and, more significantly, his social power, patronage, and alliances. Supporters of Caesar largely transferred their loyalty to the young heir. Over the following decade there was growing conflict and resentment between the various parties. In 41–40 BC, Antony's brother Lucius Antonius had waged a war against Octavian, known as the Perusine War, aided by Antony's wife Fulvia. After raising eight legions and briefly holding Rome, Lucius Antonius and Fulvia withdrew to Perusia (modern Perugia, in Umbria) where they were besieged by Octavian and eventually starved into submission. Lucius Antonius and Fulvia were both pardoned by Octavian, whereupon Lucius was sent to govern in Spain, while Fulvia was exiled to the island of Sicyon by Antony, dying of mysterious causes the following year. Her death opened the way for the alliance between Octavian and Antony to be shored up by Antony marrying Octavia (the Elder), Octavian's older sister, in late 40 BC. Soon after, the Second Triumvirate was called upon to deal with the impact of piracy against the grain supply, led by Sextus Pompey, Pompey's son, who continued to fight against Caesar's allies. The campaign against Sextus Pompey was led by Marcus Vipsanius Agrippa, a childhood friend of Octavian who had probably fought for Caesar during the later stages of the civil war, and had served as governor in Transalpine Gaul, during which time he had campaigned extensively, including crossing the Rhine.[14] Briefly, the triumvirs were united against a common enemy.

The situation of unity would not last, and the triumvirs soon set about destroying one another – aiming to take more, even sole, power for themselves. In 36 BC, Lepidus made the political mistake of raising fourteen legions under his own authority to fight in the war against Sextus Pompey – Octavian used the opportunity to accuse him of planning rebellion, and stripped him of power. Now Octavian and Antony alone shared power. Both waged wars of their own to raise money and prestige for their respective sides, perhaps anticipating that events would someday come to conflict between the two of them.[15] Antony was spending an increasing amount of time in the eastern provinces he had been allocated, and was openly involved in an affair with Cleopatra, the queen of Egypt, who had been a supporter of the Second Triumvirate in its war against Caesar's assassins. She was, of course, also Caesar's former mistress, and the mother of his only biological child, Ptolemy Caesar Philopator Philometor, or 'Caesarion' ('Little Caesar').[16] The Second Triumvirate expired in 33 BC, which marked the beginning of the end for the alliance between Octavian and Antony. Late that same year, Antony divorced Octavia in order to marry Cleopatra.[17]

In 32 BC, Octavian illegally seized Antony's will and made the contents public, including provisions stating that all Antony's estates would pass to Cleopatra and his children by her, including the provinces he had charge of, and his intention to rule the empire from Alexandria. These revelations turned public opinion in Rome against Antony, and the following year Octavian went to open war with him. Octavian's efforts against Antony and Cleopatra were led by Marcus Agrippa, who was making a significant name for himself in the service of his friend. The war culminated with the naval Battle of Actium in September 31 BC, in which Antony and Cleopatra's fleets were comprehensively destroyed, and much of their land forces deserted. They both fled to Alexandria, where they would each die by suicide less than a year later. As Octavian's forces entered Egypt, each preferred suicide to the public humiliation that would result from being captured.[18] By late 30 BC, Octavian had emerged as the victor of the last round of the civil wars of the Late Republic.

As the now undisputed master of the Roman world, he would soon go on to change everything about the Roman state. In 27 BC, Octavian was acclaimed as the first emperor of Rome, a king in all but name, taking the title of 'Augustus', and taking much of the authority that had formerly been held by the Senate and the consuls. The Roman Republican system would cease to operate on a functional level, although Augustus would make a show of maintaining the traditions of Rome when he felt it was necessary. But from this point, power lay with Augustus, and later with his successors, as emperor. A political career in Rome no longer relied on wider connections with the elite, although they would no doubt help, but on ingratiating yourself with the Imperial regime, attracting the attention of Augustus or one of his relatives. While this was a significant departure from the previous system, it offered an opportunity to young men like Varus, who could hope to win the patronage of the Imperial family and advance themselves through nepotism, and attempt to win one of the positions that were now in the gift of the emperor to bestow.

Varus himself was likely have been too young to take any part in the conflict which erupted between Octavian and Antony – he would only have been around 15 years old when the Battle of Actium was fought.[19] He would have grown up against a backdrop of uncertainty, particularly as the power struggle between the two factions developed into war. As the conflict developed, it may have become increasingly clear that Varus might need to choose a side in this latest civil war, even though ultimately it would end before he was old enough to take an active role. As Varus entered adulthood, Octavian would have been emerging as the sole power in the Roman world, making him someone that a young man with ambitions beyond his familial limits might well have realized it was worth getting close to.

Coming of age

Varus would have reached manhood between the age of 14 and 16 with his career intended to start soon afterwards. Based on a birthdate in the mid-40s BC, this would have been at some point in the late 30s to early 20s BC, making his entry into adulthood roughly concurrent with Octavian taking power in 30 BC, and being made Augustus in 27 BC. The last years of the Republic and the early Principate would have demonstrated to Varus that the best way to advance his career was through Imperial patronage. In his earlier reign, Augustus typically drew his Imperial appointments from individuals that he knew personally, only diverting from this policy after some years due to protests about the monopoly the Imperial regime had on appointments. Varus' prospects would rely on forging a path into the Imperial circle, and he was likely well aware of this from the earliest stages of his career.

It might be thought that Varus' career might be impeded by his father's political enmity towards first Julius Caesar and later Mark Antony and Octavian, but there is little evidence to suggest that this would ever have been the case. Varus was just one of many young men whose fathers had fought against the Caesarian/Octavian cause; to disbar these sons from engaging in public life due to the actions of their fathers would have left Rome short of ruling elites to hold military and political office. But the toll of decades of civil war had severely diminished the ranks of the aristocracy. Many of the families of senatorial rank no longer satisfied the property criteria to sit in that body, and Augustus therefore reduced the numbers of those eligible to hold the position of senator.[20] Some of these families were replaced with wealthy equestrian families, whom Augustus raised to the rank of patricians.[21] Still, there remained a shortage of young male elites to take up the junior positions in the *cursus honorum* and the seats within the Senate. Augustus could potentially not afford to marginalize the youth of the next generation for their father's alliances – better to give them a place within the regime, and hope that this would win their loyalty. Many sons of the 'discredited' would become significant figures in Augustus' reign, with some of the most prominent individuals being the sons of men who had once viewed Caesar and his family as enemies. Even Augustus' step-son and eventual heir, Tiberius, was the biological son of Tiberius Claudius Nero, who despite fighting for Caesar during the civil war had supported Brutus and Cassius following the assassination, proposing that they be publicly rewarded for opposing a tyrant. He later joined the cause of Mark Antony against Octavian, only returning to Rome on the declaration of a general amnesty; Augustus possibly never fully forgave Tiberius Claudius Nero, with Pliny the Elder suggesting that when

Tiberius became his eventual successor, he found that he had made 'the son of his own enemy his heir'.[22]

Augustus also made the early stages of an elite career easier through a series of policy decisions aimed at getting more senator's sons through the system – a way to replenish the elite ranks thinned by the losses incurred by all sides during two decades of civil war, as well as potentially securing the personal loyalty of many of these younger men. Young men were able to start attending political meetings, including those in the Senate, as soon as they had reached adulthood, giving them experience of public life at a much earlier age than under the Republic.[23] Augustus also doubled the number of senators' sons appointed to military tribuneships, to give more individuals experience of campaigning and camp life. It also increased their levels of responsibility, giving them personal command of a cavalry *ala* in addition to their responsibilities within the legion. This approach served several purposes. It widened the pool of career elites available for Augustus to deploy in key roles later, which was a pressing concern given the high rates of mortality over several decades of near-constant conflict in the Roman world. The appointments also potentially gave these individuals a firmer sense of personal loyalty towards Augustus, which would prove valuable as he attempted to draw the Roman world together under his new regime. They may have been intended to show that he could be merciful when called upon, as Julius Caesar had been. Further, they would also have reassured the young men that they would not suffer for the political choices of their parents, which had been made when most of them were young children. This avoided creating a situation in which a generation of ambitious Roman young men had no choice but to depose the current ruler if they wanted to have a career. Augustus was attempting to secure the future prospects of the Imperial regime as well as dealing with the immediate problems he faced – and he did so with great foresight and skill.

Varus was another individual who, like Tiberius, would flourish under Augustus. He benefitted from Augustus' pragmatic decision to allow the sons of his former enemies to play a part in the new regime. At the same time, in the name of 'restoring the Republic', Augustus attempted to revive the fortunes of some of the more distinguished Patrician families, who had over time fallen into obscurity – and the Quinctili Varii were a perfect candidate for this. Whether the young Varus took advantage of this opportunity is unclear, although the speed with which his career advanced in its early years suggests that he may well have done. Varus may even have joined Octavian's forces at Actium, when he would have been around 15 years old – a little young, but perhaps not impossibly so amidst the chaos and manpower shortages of the Late Republic. It is unlikely that any definitive evidence will ever emerge that could prove this, but the suggestion is an intriguing one. There is certainly the possibility that as a teenager Varus had turned his back on his father's anti-Caesar policy, and wholeheartedly embraced Octavian and his regime. If Varus had fought for Octavian, it would go a long way to explaining why Augustus appears to have taken an interest in Varus' career from a relatively early point (as will be seen in the next chapter).

Individuals such as Varus were exactly who Augustus wanted as part of the Imperial circle going forwards: talented young men of patrician status, with wealth and an established aristocratic background, whose fathers had been against the Caesarian cause during the last days of the Republic, but who themselves were reconciled with the new Imperial regime. The stage was set for Varus to enjoy a prominent career under Augustus – and it would not be long before he made his mark on the political scene in Rome.

Chapter 3

Varus' Early Career, 25–13 BC

As a young aristocrat entering public life in Rome, Varus would have aimed to establish himself on the lower rungs of the *cursus honorum* as quickly as possible. Based on both his family's generalized history of underachievement, combined with the misjudged political decisions of his father, it might have been expected that the young Varus could expect a modest career at best – but he developed into an ambitious young man, and it would not be long before he made his presence felt among the ruling elites in Rome. His career would be shaped particularly by the connections he made with the new Imperial regime, particularly the direct patronage of Augustus, which Varus was to attract at an early age. The course of Varus' early career, up to his holding of the consulship in 13 BC, is not discussed by any single source, but can only be pieced together through a series of almost incidental references in a number of historical works. If any biography of his life was ever written in antiquity it has not survived. It is likely that at least some detail of his life and career was once detailed somewhere, perhaps in Pliny the Elder's *Bella Germaniae*, but little of whatever he may have written was preserved in any of the available accounts.[1] Despite the lack of source material, this period is too central to Varus' personal and professional development to gloss over with vague references to the positions he held, with no further discussion of their wider context. This chapter draws together all the evidence for what we *know* happened to Varus in this time, supplemented where necessary with extrapolations based on the usual career developments for an elite man in his position in the early years of Augustus' reign, and discussion of the significance of his appointments and marriages, particularly with regard to his position within the Imperial circle. It starts, as Roman public careers tended to, with a military tribuneship.

Varus as Military Tribune

The first requirement of the *cursus honorum* was for a young man to spend up to a decade in military service, starting as a military tribune, serving under a more senior patron who was often a friend of the family. The position of military tribune was junior to that of a tribune proper, and appears to have been introduced under Augustus in lieu of the general service in the army which young elites were expected to gain before taking on administrative and political positions back in Rome. To some degree, this meant that young men could be 'fast-tracked' through military service, and they may have spent less than five years in the army as a military tribune, in contrast to the decade of service that had been expected in the Republican period. After serving as a military tribune, he would be eligible to return to Rome and start advancing further up the political ladder. A young man would expect to be appointed as a tribune around the age of 20 years. This experience was seen as a vital part of a young man's training for a political career, giving them personal experience of the military which they could then take into their future career in the Senate – as well as allowing Rome to identify military talents at an earlier age. Given the uncertainties over his birth year it is not entirely clear at what year Varus would have become eligible to serve as a military tribune, but a date in the mid-20s BC, most likely 26/25 BC, seems likely. It is not clear which province Varus was sent to as a tribune, but there is one particularly obvious posting based on the military situation in the mid-20s BC. At the time, the major ongoing Roman conflict was the Cantabrian War in Spain, in which Augustus aimed to finish the two-century long conquest of the peninsula. It took him a decade to do so (29–19 BC).[2] This is the logical place for Varus to have served as military tribune as it was where manpower was most needed at the time. The conflict would have provided an excellent opportunity for a young man embarking on the initial stages of the *cursus honorum* to get experience of what it was like to take an army on campaign. Several other up-and-coming elite men (including Tiberius, his step-son, and Marcus Claudius Marcellus, his nephew and closest male blood relative) served as tribunes in Spain during this conflict, suggesting that this was a priority posting at the time.[3] Although the Cantabrian Wars are not well documented historically, archaeological exploration of the regions impacted by the conflict suggests that it was an extensive and difficult campaign.[4] The manpower needs of the conflict would have been substantial. At least seven legions (and possibly eight) were sent to the war, alongside additional auxiliary and naval units, with some suggestion that between 50,000 and 70,000 Roman troops were deployed in Spain at any one time during this period.[5] A large number of military tribunes would therefore have been needed in the region to help manage the military situation, and Varus was likely one of them.

Augustus' Cantabrian Wars focused on the last areas which still lay outside Imperial rule, in northwestern Spain (the modern regions of Cantabria, Asturias and León).[6] Although confined to a relatively small area, the conflict was extensive in scale, and required the attention of seven legions to eventually eradicate local resistance. Augustus claimed that he wanted to secure and pacify the provinces which had been put under his command, suggesting that there was a real risk of problems arising among the unconquered tribes.[7] It was important to Augustus that he was seen to have justification for his actions in Spain, as he claimed to have never fought an 'unjust' war.[8] But at the same time, a campaign in Spain was probably very convenient politically, removing him from Rome just after he had been made Augustus with far-from-universal approval – he perhaps aimed to impress and placate the Roman people with new military accomplishments.[9] The Cantabrians were said to be fierce warriors, who would have tested the fighting ability of the Roman legions. The writer Strabo even claims that so hardy were the Cantabrians that captives would continue singing songs of victory, even to the point where they were being crucified.[10] Although hostilities had begun in 29 BC they appear to have intensified several years into the conflict, leading to Augustus travelling to Spain to personally supervise some of the conflict. He went to Spain in 26 BC and spent more than a year in the field before ill health forced him to withdraw,[11] making the Cantabrian Wars the only campaign that Augustus conducted in person after the defeat of Mark Antony.[12] By 25 BC, Augustus evidently felt that the main bulk of the war was over and returned to Rome, although it would be another six years before the main resistance could be considered over. Despite the war itself not being particularly glorious – and not being over by 25 BC – Augustus was voted a triumph on his return to Rome, although he turned the honour down.[13] Nevertheless, the war does seem to have been commemorated in Rome as a significant victory for the emperor, as is reflected in the iconography of victory monuments during Augustus' later reign, which frequently depicted Cantabrian-type weapons in reference to the conflict.[14]

Varus' presence in Spain would also help to explain some developments in his career immediately after the period where he held a tribuneship, which suggests that at some point in these years he came to the attention of Augustus personally, making it likely that their paths crossed in the mid-20s BC. The only place this could have happened was in Spain. If Varus was sent to Spain as a military tribune around 26/25 BC, it would not have been an easy posting, but it was a logical place for him to go – this was where the Imperial regime's next generation of capable and trusted commanders needed to be assessed. It is by no means implausible to suggest that the young Varus served as a tribune in Spain during the period when Augustus was there in person, and thereby came to the attention of the emperor at an early stage of his career. This situation becomes even more likely when Varus' potential family links are considered.

As discussed in the first chapter, Varus' mother may have been a daughter of Gaius Claudius Marcellus Minor, who was the father of the aforementioned Marcus Claudius Marcellus, who accompanied Augustus on the campaign – and who would have been Varus' step-uncle. As part of Augustus' attempts to reinvigorate noble Roman families who had fallen into obscurity he may have looked to take on men like Varus – particularly when their wider/maternal family links associated them, even distantly, with the Imperial regime.

If Varus did serve his tribuneship in Spain, it would have provided him with useful military experience. It was not an easy campaign. Strabo recounts how the Roman army struggled to move supplies through the mountainous terrain, leading to scarcities at times, and suggests that they were plagued with mice and other pests who tried to eat what foodstuffs they did manage to procure.[15] But the conflict would also have provided Varus with first-hand experience of how the Roman army could and should fight against an indigenous population. He would have seen how the numerical and technological superiority of the Roman army could be neutralized by an enemy who knew their landscape, and who employed irregular tactics such as raids and ambushes. Unsurprisingly, native forces were often reluctant to engage with the Romans in pitched battle, where they would almost certainly be defeated, relying instead on guerrilla-type ambushes and raids to try and wear down the invading force.[16] The archaeological record suggests that the Cantabrian wars contained numerous instances of this type of conflict, in what became an intensive war.[17] In most cases, the Romans were victorious, despite the effectiveness of the guerrilla-type actions which were used against them. The Roman army adapted to the situation they faced in Spain by employing their own irregular tactics against the enemy, launching attacks on defended settlements,[18] and creating numerous small installations for small garrisons of Roman soldiers, which were intended to monitor the landscape and control the native population.[19]

However, the Roman army did not have everything their own way in Spain, and those posted to the war would also have had the opportunity to see the dangers of provincial conflict, including instances of ambush on the march. Although not documented in the historical record, archaeological excavation has revealed at least one Roman defeat to ambush, at Andagoste (Navarra) in northern Spain. In this engagement a small Roman marching column of about a thousand soldiers suffered a bloody nose at the hands of a Cantabrian force, who ambushed the Romans in the open field. The engagement is not documented in the historical record, but has been identified archaeologically through the physical remains left by the fighting, the spatial distribution of which can be used to partially reconstruct the events of the battle.[20] The archaeology indicates that in this incident a group of Roman soldiers, probably numbering around 1000 men, were attacked unexpectedly while on the march by a Cantabrian force of unknown size or leadership. The Romans heavily resisted the attack, engaging in fierce combat with the attacking Cantabrians, and attempted to build a field-camp within which they could shelter from the attack and establish a plan of action. They appear to have been overwhelmed before the fortifications could be finished, however, leaving traces of battle within the half-constructed boundaries of the makeshift camp. There were likely few Roman survivors of this attack, and the incident would have served as a reminder of the dangers posed by native forces and irregular tactics.

Whether Varus served in Spain or elsewhere, his tribuneship would have been a useful learning experience, where he would have had the opportunity to observe how campaigns were organized and fought, from the logistics off the battlefield to the active combat on it. The lessons he learned as tribune would have been taken forward to his later career, particularly to subsequent military postings – if he did serve in Spain, his exposure to guerrilla-type warfare would have been particularly useful when transferred to active service elsewhere in the Empire. Varus emerged from his tribuneship with his future career prospects not only intact, but showing great potential. When he returned to Rome, it would be with a successful military posting behind him – the first step in climbing the *cursus honorum* had been taken. He likely also married for the first time soon after his return to Rome around 25/24 BC. Unfortunately, there is no record of who his first wife was, and the fact of the marriage has to be extrapolated from other facts in the historical record. This would have made Varus in his early 20s when he married – on the younger side for an elite male in the Roman world more generally.[21] However, Augustus was known to favour early marriage as part of his plan both to boost the population of Rome, and to encourage better 'morality' among his people. Varus may therefore have chosen to enter a marriage earlier than was customary to curry favour with Augustus; given the Imperial favour which would soon be shown to him; if this was indeed the plan it seems to have been successful.[22] The suggestion of a marriage in the mid-late 20s BC rests on an incidental reference by Josephus to a son of Varus serving alongside him in Syria around 4 BC, who was old enough to be given command of a unit of soldiers, placing his birth around 24 BC.[23] This son would therefore have to be the child of an early marriage between Varus and an unknown woman in the mid-20s BC. However, it is not certain that Josephus was referring to Varus' son. An earlier parallel narrative by Josephus about the same events does not mention a son of Varus, with the command of the troops instead being given to a friend named Gaius.[24] Several explanations have been offered for this discrepancy, from Josephus making an error to an issue with the transmission of the text, but there is no solid ground for rejecting the idea that Varus had an early marriage and a son in the 20s BC. There is no later mention in the historical record of either the wife or the son, but this is not particularly unusual for fairly marginal historical figures at this point.[25]

A quaestorship and a tour of the eastern provinces 22–19 BC

Around 22 BC Varus was appointed to be a quaestor, an administrative role that served as the first non-military appointment of the *cursus honorum*. It was also the position that his father had held at the outbreak of the civil war between Caesar and Pompey. Quaestors fulfilled a range of different administrative roles, but were generally responsible for financial affairs, and possessed some limited power. In the Republican period, the minimum age to serve as a quaestor was 30, following a decade of military experience as a tribune, but this limit was lowered under Augustus to 25, reflecting his general flexibility over age limits when it came to talented young individuals. Under Augustus, twenty individuals held the role of quaestor, reduced back to this number early in his reign after having been doubled to forty by Julius Caesar.[26]

Varus would have been in his mid-twenties when he was appointed quaestor, possibly aged 25, exactly the minimum age required to serve in the role.[27] For an ambitious young man, this appointment would have represented a valuable step in his career, making the transition from a basic military role to a civic magistracy. A further mark of progress was soon to follow. Varus was hand-chosen by the emperor as one of only two quaestors to accompany him on a three-year tour of the eastern provinces between 22 and 19 BC. His selection would have been a significant honour, indicating that Varus had already impressed the Imperial authorities.[28] His selection for the Imperial tour may provide further validation for the hypothesis that Varus served as military tribune in Spain under Augustus, where he had caught the attention of the emperor, leading to his appointment for the provincial excursion. Although his previous experience had been largely military, it is likely that Varus was selected for the tour due to his administrative abilities, and he appears to have been particularly involved with financial matters, especially taxation, during his time in the East.

During the trip, Augustus and his delegation visited a number of the eastern provinces, starting in Sicily, and ending up as far east as Syria.[29] The excursion would have given Varus a first-hand look at the inner workings of the Empire, and the role of the emperor and his officials in administrating the provinces. In Sicily he witnessed Augustus make several cities into colonies, rewarding their loyalty and prominence. From Sicily, the Imperial delegation crossed over to Greece, where he rewarded Sparta and punished Athens – the former for supporting Augustus' future wife Livia when she had fled there during the civil war with her then-husband and her son Tiberius, the latter for supporting Antony during Augustus' war with him.[30] The party wintered on the island of Samos, and then continued eastwards, visiting the provinces of Asia and Bithynia (both now part of modern Turkey), and addressing issues in their administration, including the introduction of several reforms, as well as funding particular interests within them (and demanding further tribute from others). Augustus then travelled on to the province of Syria (modern Syria/Lebanon/Turkey), where he dealt with several further problems, including unrest in the cities of Tyre and Sidon, for which they lost the civic privileges they had previously been granted by Rome, reducing them to the status of non-Roman communities in the Empire, which was viewed by at least one Roman historian as akin to slavery.[31]

This trip also saw one of the major publicity triumphs of Augustus' reign: the return of the Roman military standards captured by the Parthians at the Battle of Carrhae in 53 BC, one of the most notorious defeats of the Republican period. The battle had taken place during an invasion of Parthia led by Marcus Licinius Crassus, a wealthy and influential figure in Rome who was a member of the unofficial alliance known as the 'First Triumvirate', alongside Julius Caesar and Gnaeus Pompey. As part of this power-sharing agreement Crassus had been given command of the Roman forces in Syria in 55 BC, from where he launched an invasion of Parthia. The battle saw seven Roman legions – a force of 25–35,000 soldiers, plus thousands of allied light infantry and cavalry – lured into an inhospitable desert area on the direction of Ariamnes, a local chieftain who had once been a Roman ally, assisting Pompey during his earlier campaigns in the area, but who had since defected to the Parthian cause.[32] The Roman army fell to a devastating defeat near the town of Carrhae (modern Harran, Turkey), after being worn out by multiple waves of Parthian attacks, in a terrain that their battle formations were not well suited to.[33] Roman losses in the battle were said to have been 20,000 dead and 10,000 captured, although casualty figures are notoriously unreliable in Roman historical sources.[34] Whatever the exact figures, the manpower loss was significant; Crassus was killed during truce negotiations with the Parthians, although the manner in which he died is not entirely clear. One account suggests that he was killed by a Parthian when a skirmish broke out between the two negotiation parties, while another suggests he may have been killed by a fellow Roman to prevent him from falling into Parthian captivity.[35] The defeat, already a humiliation for Rome, was made worse by the loss of several legionary eagles to the Parthians at the battle. The eagle (*aquila*) was the most important of the military standards carried by a legion into battle – so much so that the *aquilifer* who carried it was a senior officer in the unit, who received double the pay of an ordinary legionary soldier, and ranked just below the centurion. It was a matter of importance that the eagle be protected from capture at all costs, and the *aquilifer* was expected to protect it with his life if necessary. To lose one eagle was a cause for shame; to lose up to seven, as the Romans did at Carrhae, was a disgrace that could only be remedied by the recovery of the lost standards.

It was on his tour of the eastern provinces that Augustus managed to do just that. During negotiations with the Parthian king, Phraates IV, in 20 bc, Augustus was able to secure the return of the Roman eagles lost at Carrhae. Earlier attempts to force the return of the standards and the liberation of surviving prisoners, attempted both by Julius Caesar and later by Mark Antony, had proved unsuccessful, making Augustus' successful return of them even more of a propaganda victory.[36] Dio says that the eagles were returned by Phraates, along with the surviving Roman prisoners-of-war, in order to appease Augustus and prevent him launching an expedition into Parthia.[37] The return of the standards was welcomed by Augustus, who celebrated that he had won back standards lost in war without bloodshed, although the returned standards were seemingly treated as the spoils of war.[38] The reclamation of the standards was listed among the achievements of Augustus' reign on the *Res Gestae*, a monumental biographical inscription erected towards the end of his life, which suggested that he had compelled the Parthians to return the standards, rather than them being offered as a sign of reconciliation.[39] Several coin issues were minted celebrating the return of the eagles, with reverse designs showing them being offered up by a prostrate Parthian, alongside the legend SIGNIS RECEPTIS, 'the standards regained'. In 17 bc, Augustus commissioned the building of a triumphal arch (the now-lost Parthian Arch) in the Forum in Rome, located next to the Temple of Caesar, to celebrate the return of the eagles. This arch was also depicted on coins. The retaken standards were put on display in the nearby Temple of Mars Ultor. Augustus had originally vowed to build the temple over twenty years earlier if victorious at Philippi, but construction works had never started. The temple was eventually built after the standards were recovered. Coin issues celebrated the return of the standards, which were pictured on the reverse. The recovery of the standards was also depicted on the Augustus of Prima Porta statue, one of the best-known depictions of the first Roman emperor, which survives in the form of an ancient marble copy of a lost bronze original, once publicly displayed in Rome. The breastplate design featured several iconographic scenes, including Augustus being presented with the recaptured standards by a submissive Parthian.[40]

Throughout all these events, Varus was present alongside Augustus, observing the emperor's actions and interactions, and learning directly from what he witnessed. He would have seen first-hand how Augustus and his staff managed the provinces, rewarding loyalty and punishing unrest, and how Imperial power was best deployed within the wider Empire. The tour would also have provided an opportunity for Varus to build both professional and personal relationships with other members of the Imperial delegation, particularly Augustus' stepson Tiberius, who was also present. Varus and Tiberius were roughly the same age – Tiberius was born in 42 BC, probably just a few years after Varus – and may already have worked in some proximity to Varus if both had been posted to Spain as military tribunes at the same time. They would later become brothers-in-law for several years, and would serve as co-consuls soon after.

As a quaestor, Varus would also have had a certain number of personal responsibilities and tasks while on the excursion, particularly relating to financial matters in the provinces which they visited. As mentioned previously, Augustus reviewed the finances of numerous cities while in the East, donating grants of money to cities which were in need of it, and asking for additional payments from other cities, presumably those who could pay more than their current share.[41] Varus would have been expected as part of his official role to intercede with councils and civic officials to facilitate these extra payments, likely developing an insight into the administrative processes which kept an empire working. Varus' impact was potentially significant to the civic officials he worked alongside, and there are several fragments of inscriptions dedicated to Varus specifically during his time in the East, at Tenos, Athens, and Pergamon.[42] All the inscriptions are likely to come from bases of statues dedicated in Varus' honour, although the statues themselves are now lost, so it is not clear whether they depicted him, or another Roman-related figure, such as a deity. The Tenos inscription reads:

> The people honoured Publius Quinctilius Varus, quaestor of Imperator Caesar, divine Augustus, patron and benefactor: to the gods.[43]

A fragment of an inscription found in the city of Pergamon (in the province of Asia, now in Turkey) records the dedication of a statue in his honour in 20 BC. Although the fragment is lost, a paper squeeze of it was preserved, and can now be seen in the Westfälisches Römermuseum in Haltern (Germany).[44] The surviving text reads (in Greek): 'The People honours Publius Quintilius Varus, son of Quintilius…', an almost identical wording to the example from Tenos.

These inscriptions represent the earliest archaeological evidence of both Varus' career and his existence. It is not exactly clear what the statues and inscriptions were intending to commemorate – perhaps Varus had done something for the city, or somehow shown it favour or generosity, or maybe they wanted to flatter him in the hope of benefitting from his patronage in the future. But whether the statues marked specific events or were just general honorific gestures, their mere existence suggests that Varus was already becoming a prominent known individual at this early stage in his career. He was evidently far from being just an anonymous official in Augustus' delegation. The statues may even have been intended to curry favour with Augustus by honouring one of his favoured officials.[45]

By the time that Varus returned to Rome in 19 BC, he appears to have created a reputation for himself as one of the officials close to Augustus and the Imperial regime. This would likely serve him well in this still relatively early stage in his career, where he might hope to rapidly continue his progress up the *cursus honorum*, taking on more senior positions – and even one day, he might somehow start to believe, to reach the dizzying heights of the consulship.

Continuing to climb the *cursus honorum* in Rome

After Augustus and his delegation returned from the East in 19 BC, Varus continued to build a public career in Rome. The rigid structure of the *cursus honorum* ensured that Varus' career path was essentially laid out before him, and by this point he would have met the age criteria of both aedile (27) and praetor (30), the prescribed next stages. These roles, like that of quaestor, were both ordinary magistracies filled mainly by the senatorial classes. The position of aedile was much more restricted under Augustus than it had been in the Republican period, when these officials were responsible for the maintenance of public buildings and for regulating state religious festivals. Augustus transferred the religious responsibilities to the emperor, and those of building maintenance to the urban prefect, to some degree relieving the aedileship of any actual authority. Unsurprisingly, it became an unpopular position, and Augustus was compelled at times to force people to take it, with conscripts drawn from the ranks of ex-tribunes and ex-quaestors.[46]

After having served as an aedile, Varus would have been eligible to serve as a praetor, the next role on the public career path. This was a senior magisterial position, and those who held it had *imperium* – official legal power, held in their own right. In civic matters, a praetor was theoretically only outranked by a consul, although in practice, from the time of Augustus onward, praetors largely carried out the will of the emperor rather than any independent agenda.

Like the aedileship, the role of a praetor was much reduced by Augustus, making it more of an administrative position than a magisterial one, although their work was still considered important, despite its shift of focus. The signs of authority were maintained, including the six *lictores* (bodyguards) who would accompany praetors in public, who carried *fasces* (bundles of rods) with them to highlight the *imperium* of the official. This was the first office Varus had held which came with these visible signs of authority – previously, his roles had allowed him a seat in the Senate, and to wear a broad purple stripe on his toga, but no more – and the *lictores* must have been seen as a sign of his growing seniority within the Imperial administration.

Varus' growing prominence may also have been influenced by the marriages of his three sisters, who all married men of some significance in the Roman elite.[47] It is not known exactly when the marriages were contracted, but given the customary age for Roman elite girls to marry, they can most likely be placed in the early-mid 20s BC (assuming that they were all first marriages for the Quinctilias). The marriages would have been arranged either by Varus himself, if he had come of age by the time negotiations were taking place (i.e. by about 32–30 BC), and if not, by whatever guardian had taken the children in earlier in life (most likely a paternal uncle who lived in Tivoli). Roman women could legally marry from the age of 12, although it seems that relatively few did; however, female members of the elite were more likely to get married towards the earlier end of the age-scale. Given that all three sisters were born by 41 BC (as their father died in 42 BC; allowing for the undocumented possibility that their mother was pregnant at the time), they would in theory have been legally able to marry by 29 BC, with at least two of them probably eligible a year or two before this. Given the uncertainty over the age of Roman women when they married, it is probably safest to say that the sisters probably all married at some point in the 20s BC. All married prominent members of the political elite, providing further validation that even at this early stage the Quinctili Varii were seen as a family whose prospects were on the up, and with which it would be beneficial to form an alliance – for more than just the historic name.

One of the Quinctilia sisters married Publius Cornelius Dolabella, a senator who had served as suffect consul (appointed to replace a consul who did not make it to the end of their appointed year) in 35 BC.[48] Although the repeating names used by members of the Roman elite can make it difficult to disentangle the historical record to establish exactly who was who, just belonging to the Dolabella branch of the Cornelii family indicates that he was a man of some prominence. The couple had at least one son, also named Publius Cornelius Dolabella (II), but little else is known of this branch of the family.

A second sister, Quinctilia Varilla (the only sister whose personal name survives) married Sextus Apuleius, another prominent patrician figure. His father was another Sextus Apuleius, and his mother was Octavia the Elder, the half-sister of Augustus and his sister Octavia the Younger, born to Augustus' father Gaius Octavius from his first marriage (to a woman named Ancharia). As such, the Sextus Apuleius who married Quinctilia Varilla was the half-nephew of Augustus, providing Varus' sister (and perhaps Varus himself) with a connection to the Imperial family; Quinctilia Varilla's mother-in-law was the emperor's own half-sister. The Imperial connection certainly appears to have benefitted Sextus Apuleius' career. He became consul in 29 BC, one of the earliest to take the position in the reign of Augustus' (then still Octavian) – Augustus himself served as co-consul with him. The following year, Apuleius was appointed proconsul of Hispania, just after Octavian had launched a campaign of conquest, aiming to bring the entire Iberian peninsula under Roman control, and so making this a significant appointment. His years in Spain are not well documented, but were enough to earn him a triumph back in Rome in 26 BC, suggesting some degree of military success. A proconsulship in Asia followed in 23–22 BC; an inscription found in Ephesus indicates that by this point he was married to Quinctilia Varilla.[49] They would go on to have two children, a son and a daughter. The son, also named Sextus Appuleius (III), was a half-great-nephew to Augustus through his father, and also a nephew of Varus, through his mother. The daughter was Apuleia Varilla, who was a half-great-niece to Augustus, as well as full niece to Varus.[50]

The third Quinctilia sister married a senator named Lucius Nonius Asprenas. Again, this was a marriage which drew the Quinctili Varii even further into the circle of the Imperial family and their friends. Asprenas was a personal friend of Augustus, and a prominent person in the early Imperial regime. He had served as suffect consul in 36 BC, while conflict still raged between Octavian and Mark Antony, putting him in prime position for power under the former's reign. However, in 9 BC Asprenas was hit by a scandal, in which he was accused of a mass poisoning at a dinner party, after which up to 130 people who had attended died. A lawsuit was brought against him, causing a dilemma for Augustus, who was torn between defending his friend and potentially shielding a murderer, or failing to do so, which might lead to condemnation of Asprenas by default.[51] In the end, with wide approval Augustus attended the trial but sat on the observer's benches without making a statement, not even a character witness statement for Asprenas. Nevertheless, the accused was acquitted; one writer suggested that it was perhaps Augustus' *auctoritas*, conveyed merely by his unspeaking presence, that swung the case in his favour. Although found innocent of poisoning, Asprenas' political career never fully recovered – no doubt a blow both to his friend Augustus, and his ambitious brother-in-law, Publius Quinctilius Varus. However, the family was not destroyed by the scandal. Asprenas and Quinctilia had at least two sons, one also named Lucius Nonias Asprenas (II), the other Sextus Nonius Quinctilianus. It has been suggested that the latter was actually a biological son of Varus and one of his wives (probably his second, Vipsania Marcella), taken into the household of his aunt and uncle at some point during his childhood.[52] However, the age of the child makes this hypothesis unlikely, and there is no satisfactory answer as to why Varus would have given away a son to his brother-in-law at this time.[53]

By around 15 BC, Varus was growing in prominence through several different channels. He was personally known to Augustus, having accompanied him on a three-year provincial tour. He almost certainly knew Tiberius, Augustus' stepson, well, and may have served with him during his time as a military tribune, perhaps in Spain. In addition to these professional connections, the marriages of Varus' sisters tied him into a wider political network, and several members of this extended marital network held high office in the Roman political system, including consulships in the late years of the Republic and early years of Augustus' reign. Even better, Varus now also had familial connections – however distant – to the Imperial family through the marriages of his sisters, counting among his brothers-in-law Augustus' half-nephew (Sextus Apuleius II), and a long-standing close friend of the emperor (Lucius Nonius Asprenas). The mother-in-law of one of his sisters was Octavia the Elder, the half-sister of Augustus. Relatives in the Imperial family were being gained by marriage – and increasingly, by a shared bloodline. Varus' own nephew, Sextus Apuleius (III) was Augustus' half-great nephew, meaning that the Quinctili Varii now, by marriage, had relatives born into their family tree that overlapped with that of the Imperial family – something which can only have strengthened Varus' future career prospects.

Legate of the Nineteenth Legion

After several years back in Rome, Varus was probably 30 or 31 years old, and approaching the age where he would become eligible for a consulship – and certainly, the development of both his career and his family network would have suggested that this was no longer an impossibility. However, he would ideally need more experience in the field before his appointment to this position, with military experience being of particular value. This fact, plus the gap in the historical record documenting Varus' activities in this period had long led to speculation that Varus must have held a military command in the years between his arrival back from the East in 19 BC and (see below) his consulship in 13 BC, but there was no historical or epigraphic evidence to place him in a particular province, or with a particular legion, in this period. However, the discovery of a lead disc – probably a luggage-tag – at Dangstetten (Germany) suggests that Varus held a military command in Germany around 15 BC, filling in this important gap in his career history. A scratched inscription on the tag named a Varus as the legate of the Nineteenth Legion, who were at that time stationed at Dangstetten, a base on the Upper Rhine; this was one of the legions that would later fall to disaster in the Teutoburg.[54] The tag makes it almost certain that Varus was in command of the Nineteenth when the legion was stationed at Dangstetten, and presumably with specific cause.[55] When Varus would later encounter the legion again, after being appointed governor of Germany in AD 7, he would have had previous experience with it, and perhaps commanded higher levels of loyalty as a result. Some soldiers in the legion, particularly those at the start of their careers in 15 BC, would potentially have still been in the legion by AD 7, albeit by now as near-retirement veterans of over two decades service.

At the time, the main conflict in the region was centred on the Roman conquest of the Alps, particularly the area that would become the province of Raetia (covering areas of modern Switzerland, Austria, Germany, and Italy). The campaign was led by Tiberius and Drusus the Elder, the two stepsons of Augustus by his wife Livia, one of several military expeditions the two undertook around this time.[56] Tiberius by this stage was an experienced commander, having served on a number of campaigns, including alongside Augustus in Spain ten years earlier. Drusus had less experience in the field, having mainly held administrative positions in Rome previously (for which Augustus had granted Drusus, born in 38 BC, special dispensation to serve five years earlier than usual). The campaign in the Alps would be his first (major) military command. It was expected to be a difficult conflict, and would require experienced commanders in the field to command the large legionary force to be sent against the Alpine tribes.

Varus would have been an obvious choice as one of these commanders. He had some, if limited, experience in the field, accrued earlier in his career during his time as a military tribune – and as discussed earlier in this chapter, he may even have served in Spain alongside Tiberius, who was one of the main commanders in that phase of the Cantabrian Wars. The subsequent tour of the eastern provinces with Augustus would have provided him with valuable administrative experience, which might also prove useful in the field. More importantly, by this point Varus was a known quantity to the Imperial family, including to Tiberius and Drusus, and had likely already been marked out for great things by Augustus. No historical source directly connects Varus with the campaign, but the archaeological evidence for his presence in the region with the Nineteenth Legion suggests that he likely had at least some connection with it. But even if this wasn't the case, the fact that Varus was serving out in the provinces again, in command of a legion, demonstrates that the Imperial regime had faith in his military abilities. Over the following years, Varus built closer and closer links with the Imperial regime, and clearly became someone accepted by the inner circles of the regime.

As Varus' appointment as legate of the Nineteenth Legion is only known through the disc found at Dangstetten, it is difficult to reconstruct his experiences during this time in any great detail. It is necessary therefore to look at the experience of the Alpine war more widely. Legionary legates usually served in command of their unit for three years, so Varus would likely have been present in command for the duration of the Alpine conflict under Tiberius.[57] The campaign was likely in preparation for an expansion into German territory, which began only a few years later. Although the war is not extensively documented in any of the surviving sources, archaeological explorations in the area show that the conflict was far from straightforward, and the Roman army likely met with substantial resistance from indigenous populations.[58] The archaeology suggests that the locals attempted to exploit their knowledge of the landscape to counter the numerical and technological superiority of the invading Roman army, forcing them into narrow terrain points (passes, gorges) where the resisting forces would then attack. These tactics proved effective on several occasions against the Roman forces, particularly around Oberhalbstein, where the Alpine tribes appear to have successfully held off a Roman marching column. Many of the techniques used against the Romans in the Alps would have been familiar to anyone who had served in the Cantabrian wars, as Varus likely had. The war lasted around a year, ending with the (likely grudging) subjugation of the region to Roman rule.

The archaeological record also provides evidence for the direct involvement of the Nineteenth Legion in the campaign. Roman military equipment found at Döttenbichl (Oberammergau, Germany; part of the region under attack in this time), including *pugiones* (daggers), iron catapult-bolts, and a large quantity of iron arrowheads, suggests that a battle took place on the site during the Alpine wars.[59] One catapult bolt excavated from the site bore the stamp of the Nineteenth Legion ("LEG[io] XIX"), suggesting that the legion, or at least part of it, had been present there. In this case, unlike the conflict around Oberhaldstein, the Roman army appear to have been victorious. As legionary legate, Varus would have experienced the Alpine conflict at first-hand, and been witness to the guerrilla-type resistance tactics used, at times to good effect, by the indigenous population. The resistance efforts were ultimately unsuccessful, however. Augustus later (in 6 BC) dedicated a large monument – known as the Tropaeum Alpium – to celebrate the victory at what is now La Turbie in southern France. The trophy did not mark a conflict site from the war, but rather was positioned on an important road in the region, the Via Julia Augusta, consistent with wider Roman practice that victory monuments should be situated in places of visibility, rather than necessarily those connected to the war.[60] Alongside a celebration of the victory, the monument's inscription also named all the tribes subdued during the campaign.[61] The campaign was also commemorated in Augustus' *Res Gestae*, which says that the region was 'brought to a state of peace without waging on any tribe an unjust war'.[62]

Command of the Nineteenth Legion would have given Varus more direct military experience, an area he was probably less experienced in than civic administration. After his short spell as military tribune at the start of his career, Varus appears to have served mainly in civic administrations posts. One of the main benefits of his new position may have been a greater exposure to military life that would serve him well in the future, both in terms of the tactics that could be used by local populations against the Roman army, and the realities of campaign and conflict. It may also have benefitted Varus to serve alongside Tiberius, who was a highly effective commander, and very popular with his men. Roman soldiers could become highly attached to their commanders if they were successful and treated them well. Tiberius, who led the Alpine campaign, was particularly popular with his troops; when he returned to command in Germany after several years away, his men greeted him with an outpouring of affection, calling on him to remember them from past campaigns.[63] A perception of comradeship between the army and its commanders could prove beneficial for morale and ensure greater effectiveness in the field – again, something of which Tiberius was well aware.[64] The only way to achieve this relationship between a commander and his men was through time and exposure. If Varus did serve alongside Tiberius while in command of the Nineteenth Legion, there would have been few better legates that he could learn from. Whatever he learned during this period, it is clear that Varus had far more military experience than historians have credited him with. He would have returned to Rome, after his appointment as a legate ended, with extensive military experience to add to his skills in administration – and with a growing reputation.

Marcus Agrippa's son-in-law

In 14/13 BC, Varus received further confirmation of his status with regards to the Imperial family, when he married a daughter of Marcus Agrippa, the long-standing companion and advisor of Augustus. Her name is not documented in any of the surviving historical sources, but current convention typically refers to her as Vipsania Marcella.[65] The marriage between Varus and Vipsania Marcella is only evidenced by a papyrus document which names Varus, alongside Tiberius, as Agrippa's son-in-law.[66] Until this papyrus was found, it had not been known that Varus had married one of Agrippa's daughters. Her mother was probably Claudia Marcella Major, Agrippa's second wife, who was not without Imperial connections herself – she was Augustus' eldest niece, born to his younger sister Octavia and her husband, Gaius Claudius Marcellus the Younger.[67] She was born sometime between 28 BC, when her parents married, and 24 BC (as she must have been at least 12 years old by 12 BC, when Marcus Agrippa died), most likely around 26 BC, making her twenty years younger than Varus – a substantial age-gap, but not particularly unusual by Roman elite standards.

Vipsania Marcella was probably Varus' second wife, depending on whether he had indeed contracted an earlier marriage in the late 20s BC, as discussed above. It would be surprising if a prominent member of the Imperial administration had remained unmarried well into his thirties (as Augustus evidently favoured early marriages where possible, ambitious young men were wise to marry early where possible). However, whether Varus had been widowed before his marriage to Vipsania Marcella, or had divorced his previous wife (perhaps in order to marry her) is unknown. There is no record of whether Varus and Vipsania Marcella had any surviving children.[68] Varus' marriage to Vipsania Marcella would have marked a significant step up in Varus' social standing, and deepened his links with the Imperial regime. Through her mother, Vipsania Marcella was the great-niece of Augustus, and the granddaughter of the emperor's sister, Octavia. It may also have strengthened the connections between different branches of the Imperial family tree. In the previous chapter, it was mentioned that Varus' mother may have been the daughter of Gaius Claudius Marcellus Minor, who was also the father of Claudia Marcella, Agrippa's wife and Vipsania Marcella's mother. If this were the case, then Varus' mother and Claudia Marcella would have been half-sisters, and therefore Varus and Vipsania Marcella were cousins, and both shared a grandfather in Gaius Claudius Marcellus Minor. Given Augustus' evident fondness for strengthening the Imperial family by marrying cousins to each other, this marriage would not be at all inconsistent with wider marriage policy. The discovery of his marriage to Vipsania Marcella added new clarity to Varus' place within the Imperial regime – not just a supporter of and administrative official within the Imperial regime, but a member of it by marriage, and not just a token marriage to some distant relative, but a bride who was the daughter of Marcus Agrippa, the second man in Rome. The significance of Varus' marriage to Vipsania Marcella cannot be fully understood without considering the prominence of Marcus Agrippa in the Imperial regime. He was a figure so important that for more than a decade, he was likely named in Augustus' will as his heir should the emperor fall victim to an unexpected death.

Agrippa had known Augustus (then Octavian) since childhood, and despite not being from a particularly prominent family, had become one of the most important figures in Rome, accomplished in both military campaigning and civic administration. Agrippa had loyally supported Octavian/Augustus through the civil wars, both against the assassins of Caesar and later against Mark Antony, and played a key role in the victory at Actium in 31 BC. Since then, Agrippa had become Augustus' most trusted and valued advisor,[69] who 'had first place in Caesar's [Octavian/Augustus'] estimation', and was always paid 'exceptional honour' by the emperor.[70] Agrippa was frequently left in charge of affairs in Rome while Augustus was either absent or too ill to govern.[71] Agrippa was appointed consul twice by Augustus early in his reign (in 28 and 27 BC, in addition to an earlier consulship in 37 BC), and on both occasions the emperor himself served as his colleague, emphasising Agrippa's status under the Imperial regime.[72] The governorship of Syria, one of the most difficult provincial commands, was given to Agrippa in 23 BC; he would stay in position for ten years, an exceptionally long governorship (although he was not always in Syria, frequently travelling back to Rome when required, particularly when Augustus was away from the city). Later, Agrippa was given by Augustus 'many privileges almost equal to his [Augustus'] own'.[73] These included tribunician powers – without the need of actually holding the office – which among other things gave him the right of veto over the Senate. Augustus had even brought Agrippa into the Imperial family by marriage, a preferred way to create familial links with prominent figures in Rome.[74] In 28 BC, Agrippa had married Claudia Marcella Major, the daughter of Augustus' sister Octavia and therefore his eldest niece, making Agrippa the nephew-in-law of the emperor. Agrippa was also a very visible presence in the heart of the Empire. Many of the public buildings constructed in Rome during the 20s and 10s BC were financed by Agrippa personally, including the Pantheon, the best surviving example of his building works.[75] The Pantheon is a particularly interesting example as within it a statue of Agrippa stood alongside one of Augustus in the temple's ante-room – a compromise, as the emperor had apparently refused a suggestion that the structure should be named after him, with a large statue of him inside.[76] The dangerous idea that this arrangement reflected that Agrippa saw himself as being the equal of Augustus – or indeed, his rival – had to be refuted, however, with the suggestion instead put forward that Agrippa had instead sought to emphasize his loyalty to the emperor and the Imperial regime.

The prominence of Agrippa in Augustus' regime led to him being considered as a potential Imperial heir, despite his relatively humble background. Augustus had no sons of his own, from any of his three marriages, only a daughter commonly known as Julia the Elder (to distinguish her from her daughter of the same name). In the absence of biological sons, Augustus had the option to nominate a preferred candidate, either drawn from his wider family – his biological nephews, or his stepsons through his wife Livia – or from within the Imperial circle. Augustus would have the option to either marry his daughter Julia to his preferred candidate, making them his son-in-law, or to adopt them directly, depending on age and circumstance, to help bolster their claim to the Imperial power. Given that Agrippa was the same age as Augustus, his prospects as an Imperial heir likely rested on Augustus dying relatively early in his reign, before a suitable younger candidate could be prepared to take the role – but if called upon, Agrippa could have provided stability in the first, untested, transition of Imperial power.

The issue had come to a head in 23 BC, when Augustus had fallen seriously ill, and was widely expected to die. Although he stopped short of directly appointing a successor, Augustus had given his ring to Agrippa,[77] a sign that his long-term companion was his preferred choice as heir, as this gesture of giving rings was typically only given from an individual on their death-bed to the person named in their will as heir.[78] The gesture caused some consternation in the Imperial circles, as it had been anticipated that Augustus would actually nominate a younger alternative – most likely Marcus Claudius Marcellus, his nephew and son-in-law. Marcellus was born in 42 BC, the eldest son of Augustus' sister Octavia and her first husband, Gaius Claudius Marcellus, and he was therefore Augustus' closest male relative. Marcellus had begun a public career in the mid-20s BC, serving as a military tribune alongside his uncle in the Cantabrian Wars around 25 BC. Tiberius, the emperor's stepson, was also present during that campaign, as potentially was Varus.[79] When Marcellus returned to Rome the familial ties between the emperor and his nephew were strengthened by a marriage between Marcellus and Augustus' only child, Julia the Elder. Marcellus was aged around 17 years old when this marriage took place, unusually young for a male member of the Roman elite. Julia was closer to 14 years old, but the marriage of elite women at this age was less unusual. A succession of honours for Marcellus followed, granted directly by Augustus, including a waiving of the minimum age to stand as consul by a full decade, so that Marcellus would be eligible to stand by the age of 22, around 20 BC.[80] With hindsight, it seems clear that Marcellus was being prepared to take on the role of being Augustus' heir, which is perhaps why it was considered such a surprise when Augustus preferred Agrippa over Marcellus in 23 BC, particularly as Augustus appears to have been particularly keen that his successor was a blood relative.[81] The problem for Marcellus may have been that Augustus' illness came slightly too soon for him to be considered ready for the position. Marcellus was only 19 years old at this stage, and relatively inexperienced, with few rungs on the *cursus honorum* behind him. Augustus may have considered that he was just not ready to take on the Imperial role, therefore preferring Agrippa as a safer prospect. Augustus eventually recovered from his illness, but the issue of choosing his heir had provoked disquiet in the inner Imperial circle, with Agrippa and Marcellus angered by Augustus' perceived preference of the other. Agrippa left Rome soon after, which the ancient historians attribute either to Agrippa choosing to leave because Augustus preferred Marcellus, or to Augustus sending him away to avoid a public feud breaking out between the two men.[82] Augustus may even have been concerned that a civil war could break out between the factions of Agrippa and Marcellus, much like the one he himself had fought against Mark Antony.[83] Any rivalry would not be a long-standing one, however, as Marcellus soon after fell ill from the same illness that Augustus had suffered from, and died later in 23 BC.[84]

The death of Marcellus left Augustus with few options for an heir should his death come relatively soon. There were no other young males in the Imperial family approaching adulthood who could be groomed to take Marcellus' place as Augustus' successor. Agrippa appears to have remained the preferred successor, in the interests of which Augustus commanded him to divorce his wife Claudia Marcella Major to marry Julia, Augustus' daughter, in 21 BC.[85] Augustus' most trusted advisor was now also his son-in-law – a move apparently proposed as a political necessity by at least one of Augustus' advisors, who cautioned the emperor that Agrippa's power in Rome had grown sufficient that 'he must either become your son-in-law or be slain'.[86] Augustus evidently chose the latter. The marriage bolstered Agrippa's authority in Rome, granting him 'a dignity above the ordinary, in order that he might govern the people more easily',[87] and Augustus would frequently leave him in charge of Rome for extended periods, particularly when the business of ruling took the emperor into the provinces for months or years at a time. When the marriage of Agrippa and Julia began to bear male children – sons Gaius (born

20 BC) and Lucius (born 17 BC) – it became clearer that Augustus intended his succession to go along this line; he adopted the infant boys in 17 BC, making it widely known that he had a plan for the succession.[88] The adoption of his grandsons would have meant that the Imperial succession stayed within the Augustan blood-line while also incorporating Agrippa, giving his friend and advisor an ongoing stake in the Imperial succession even if he was no longer the heir himself. In 19 BC, Augustus further strengthened Agrippa's links to the Imperial family by marrying his stepson Tiberius to Agrippa's daughter Vipsania Agrippina.[89] Vipsania was born around 36 BC and was betrothed to Tiberius – who was roughly six years her senior – before she was even a year old, although she was 17 when the actual wedding took place. Through these marriages, Agrippa had numerous ties with the Imperial family, and remained a likely candidate to succeed Augustus if he died anytime soon. Even if a younger heir would eventually be sought, it was clear that Agrippa had a place at the heart of the Imperial regime for as long as he lived.

The prominence of Agrippa in the Imperial regime adds an extra layer of context to the marriage between his daughter Vipsania Marcella and Varus, one of the rising figures within the Imperial regime. The fact that Varus was considered, let alone chosen, to marry the daughter of the emperor's son-in-law – and the biological father of Augustus' adopted heirs, Gaius and Lucius – shows his potential importance to the regime. If they succeeded Augustus, Vipsania Marcella would have been the half-sister of the new emperor(s), and Varus their half-brother-in-law – a very close relationship to the heart of Imperial power. Varus had likely been personally chosen to marry Vipsania Marcella, either by Agrippa or perhaps even Augustus himself. Agrippa's family was by that stage sufficiently important that they would not have needed to bring anyone unwanted into the family for the sake of the connections or wealth they could bring, even allowing for the fact that the Vipsanii had previously not been members of the senatorial class. Varus could bring a certain aristocratic pedigree to the family, through his long-standing if not particularly distinguished family name. Nor would it have hurt his prospects that all three of his sisters had contracted marriages with prominent figures in Rome. But these factors alone do not explain the marriage – they would have applied to many other individuals in Rome at the time – so why was Varus chosen? Although it cannot be known for certain, the likelihood is that the marriage resulted from Varus' increasing profile in the Imperial regime, as someone who had been known to Augustus for over a decade, and who had potentially impressed in the civic and military roles he had held during his early career. Varus may have been identified by Augustus and Agrippa as someone who would likely prove loyal to the Imperial regime, particularly when the time came to transfer power to either Agrippa or, if they were old enough by that point, Gaius and Lucius. As one of the more prominent figures from the bridge generation between Augustus/Agrippa and Gaius/Lucius, Varus may have been chosen to marry into Agrippa's family as a way of tying his loyalty to this branch of the Imperial family, and building up a wall of support for the young heirs. Varus was an experienced civic administrator and military commander – like Tiberius, who was put in the same position. Ultimately, Varus must have been judged to be someone whose presence in Agrippa's family would be a benefit rather than a hindrance – an image which contradicts later characterizations of him as a weak, ineffective, and corrupt individual.

Varus' marriage brought him to the heart of the Imperial family, with new connections to multiple branches of the Julio-Claudian family tree. Varus' father-in-law Agrippa was himself the son-in-law of the emperor, married to Augustus' only daughter. Through the marriage of Agrippa and Julia, Vipsania Marcella was the half-sister of Augustus' current heirs, Gaius and Lucius, and Varus therefore directly connected to this next Imperial generation as the half-brother-in-law of the young boys. Nor was Varus' mother-in-law, Claudia Marcella Major, insignificant, being the eldest niece of Augustus, and cousin to his daughter Julia. Varus had also now become the brother-in-law of Tiberius, Augustus' stepson through his marriage to Livia Drusilla. Augustus and Livia had married in 38 BC, but although Livia had birthed two sons from her previous marriage (Tiberius, and his younger brother Drusus), their union did not produce any surviving children. Tiberius had proved himself a capable military commander, and his relationship to the emperor facilitated a quick rise up the *cursus honorum*, which would several times see minimum age requirements for appointments waived as a sign of Augustus' favour. It may also have cemented the links between Tiberius and Varus, who had likely known each other since the 20s BC. As discussed previously, they may have served together during the Cantabrian Wars, and likely fought together during the wars against the Alpine tribes a year or two before Varus' marriage to Vipsania Marcella. Varus was clearly being held in increasingly high esteem by the Imperial regime, and potentially groomed for higher positions in the near future – the first of these appointments would soon follow.

Consul in 13 BC

Varus' marriage to Vipsania Marcella may have paved the way for him to finally reach the pinnacle of the Republican career ladder (and even in the Imperial period, the highest rank short of being the emperor himself) when in 13 BC he was appointed as consul.[90] Varus was the first member of the Quinctili Varii to hold a consulship in more than four centuries, and his appointment reflected the complete turnaround in fortune that his family had enjoyed under Augustus. Varus' colleague in office was his brother-in-law Tiberius – himself the first of his own family to hold the position in over two hundred years. For both Varus and Tiberius, the appointment in 13 BC was the first time they held the consulship. Varus did not hold the position again, although Tiberius would do so on several future occasions, as befitted the stepson, son-in-law, and later adopted son and heir of the emperor. In the Republican period, neither Varus nor Tiberius would have been able to hold this pre-eminent position at the age which they did – Varus was around 32 or 33 years old at most, and Tiberius a little younger at 29 or 30 – but under Augustus the age limit for the consulship had been lowered to 32. Even then, the age limit was waived in the case of Tiberius, and perhaps also for Varus, a prerogative of the emperor in the case of talented or favourite individuals.

In the Republican period, the consulship had been considered the pinnacle of a Roman political career, and the most important position which any individual could hold. In Rome, they acted as legislators, religious officials, and administrators, who were also responsible for organising public works, overseeing elections, and deciding foreign policy, while also being called upon to lead military campaigns when necessary.[91] Two consuls were appointed every year, to avoid power being concentrated with a single individual – otherwise the position would have edged too close to kingship for the comfort of the monarchy-shy Roman state.[92] They served for a single year, in an attempt to minimise corruption, but had near-absolute power during that time, and very few other offices could veto the decision of the consuls. The Republican consulship had also come with a military responsibility, with each consul being given the direct command of two legions. So important were the consuls that years were dated by reference to who was serving in the consulship at the time. During the Republic, the minimum age for a consul was 43 years old, meaning that any individual elected to the office would have spent more than two decades climbing the *cursus honorum*, picking up military and administrative expertise along the way. The consuls for each year were elected by the *comitia centuriata* (Centuriate Assembly), and ratified by the ancient – and largely ceremonial – *comitia curiata* (Curiate Assembly). Although in theory any qualified male could be elected, in practice wider political considerations often influenced the appointments of the consuls in any given year. For most of the Republican period, it had been unusual, if not impossible, to be appointed as consul more than once, and at least a decade was supposed to separate these two terms.

However, since the late second century BC the procedures had begun to change, with high-profile political figures such as Gaius Marius and Julius Caesar being appointed to multiple consulships within a relatively short period of time.[93] Increasingly, the consulship was used as a way to recognize the independent political power of the holder, rather than conferring it on him – or to reward the loyalty of figures close to the power-players in Rome. By the time that Julius Caesar had become the most powerful individual in Rome, the consulship was arguably well on the way to becoming a politically impotent position, with no real suggestion that the consuls – when Caesar himself was not serving as one – would be able to block Caesar's political decisions, particularly once he was declared Dictator in 44 BC.[94] Under Augustus the political importance of the consulship was further reduced. While it remained a prestigious appointment, it no longer came with any real power, becoming a largely ceremonial role through which the emperor could show favour to individuals within the regime.[95] It did however remain an honour, and those who held the position did so largely at Augustus' discretion and preference. Augustus himself had held the consulship eleven times by 13 BC, while Agrippa had held it three times.[96] Individuals could be specifically honoured by being picked to serve alongside prominent members of the Imperial family. It is likely that Varus' consulship was linked to his recent marriage to Vipsania Marcella, which had probably taken place no more than a year or two earlier, conferring a prestigious honour on this new member of the Imperial family, who had been known to Augustus for over a decade by this point.

The appointment of Varus and Tiberius together meant that both consuls for that year were sons-in-law of Marcus Agrippa, at that time effectively the second-in-command of the entire Empire; the timing may not have been a coincidence. It has been suggested that one of the major reasons that Varus and Tiberius were appointed as consuls when they were was to rubber-stamp the award of further political powers to Agrippa. In 13 BC, Agrippa returned to Rome after serving for a decade as the governor of Syria.[97] He was duly granted a five-year extension of his tribunician powers, but also, for the first time, an additional power of *maius imperium proconsulare* ('the greatest proconsular powers), which gave Agrippa authority over everyone in the Empire, barring Augustus himself.[98] The further empowerment of Agrippa in 13 BC was a continuation of a long-standing process by Augustus, likely intended to lay the groundwork for Agrippa to succeed him as emperor. Agrippa had been in effective charge of Rome for the much of the past few years, with Augustus having been absent for several years overseeing the consolidation and assimilations of newer provinces of the Empire, particularly Gaul and Spain. Augustus was initially drawn away from Rome by problems with the Germans, particularly following a severe military reversal at the hands of a raiding Germanic warband,[99] but he would also spend time overseeing operations in Gaul and Spain, particularly the establishment of colonies.[100] Augustus travelled back to Rome in 13 BC, having finished his business in the provinces, while Varus and Tiberius were serving as consuls. To commemorate his safe return, the Senate voted to dedicate an altar in celebration of the Pax Augusta ('Augustan Peace'), on which annual sacrifices would be made by the magistrates, priests, and Vestal Virgins.[101]

The altar to the Pax Augusta – now known as the Ara Pacis – was constructed on the northern outskirts of Rome, in the northeastern corner of the Campus Martius, and dedicated on January 9 BC. The construction was monumental in scale, with the exterior walls decorated with elaborate reliefs depicting a range of religious, mythological, and pseudo-historical scenes, originally painted in bright colour. Of particular interest are the longer north and south faces of the altar, which both contain friezes depicting real-life figures celebrating the peace represented by Augustus' return. The relief may be an artistic depiction of a real parade held to celebrate Augustus' return to Rome and, if so, it is likely that the intention was that these figures should be recognizable to contemporary viewers of the monument. Many of the individuals are now difficult to identify, particularly given the damage and problematic reconstruction which the altar has seen since antiquity, but the clothing and relative position of many of the figures can give some insight into which members of the Imperial family or political elite they are meant to represent. Augustus is identifiable on the southern wall of the altar, surrounded by other figures, with Agrippa pictured a short distance away dressed in his priestly regalia. Two figures standing close to Augustus can almost certainly be identified as consuls – and given that the scene is set in 13 BC, these two figures are almost certainly Varus and Tiberius.[102] The Tiberius figure appears to be slightly further in the foreground than that of Varus, likely reflecting their relative status – as the emperor's stepson, Tiberius just edged out Varus – but the closeness of both figures to Augustus likely reflects their prominence in the Imperial regime. As one historian notes:

> The representation of Varus beside Tiberius would therefore emphasize the special political and familial relationship of these two individuals, while Varus' position in the background would be hierarchically appropriate.[103]

If this figure is Varus, as seems likely, it is the only known stone portrait of him, supplementing a few likely inaccurate images of him on coins (which will be discussed in the following chapter). The depiction on the Ara Pacis is as close as we will likely ever get to knowing what Varus looked like, although the figure itself is fairly unremarkable.

Varus' consulship appears to have been a relatively quiet one, defined mainly by the return of Augustus to Rome, the consequent construction of the Ara Pacis, and the increased political powers awarded to Agrippa. There were some domestic issues to address, including severe flooding of the Tiber, and the commissioning or repair of public works and facilities, none of which are likely to have stretched the consuls overmuch.[104] But the appointment itself was a clear sign of Varus' growing favour with the Imperial regime, likely linked to his marriage to Vipsania Marcella the previous year – he was potentially being groomed for higher levels of authority. Varus was being granted positions equal to those given to Tiberius – marriage to a daughter of Agrippa, accompanied by a consulship – suggesting that a long future at the heart of the Imperial regime was envisioned as being within Varus' future. His position as the son-in-law of Marcus Agrippa was also an important factor – but this relationship would last little more than a year longer.

The Death of Agrippa

In 12 BC, the Roman political world was thrown into chaos by the death of Marcus Agrippa, aged 50 years old. He had fallen ill after setting off on a campaign against the Pannonians, and returned to Campania where he hoped to recover, but instead died. Augustus was said to have been much grieved by the death of his long-term companion and son-in-law, delivering a funerary oration himself, and interring Agrippa's remains in his own mausoleum.[105] For the rest of his reign Augustus never had another advisor as close to him as Agrippa had been.[106] As Agrippa's sons-in-law, both Varus and Tiberius also gave a eulogy at his funeral, as illustrated by the discovery of a papyrus document preserving part of the speech.[107] This very public act would have further underlined the connections between Varus and the Imperial family, particularly in the eyes of the general population.

With the death of Agrippa, Varus had lost his most direct connection to Imperial power and was no longer the son-in-law of Augustus' most favoured advisor and friend. He could now rely only on the legacy of this reputation for his status going forward. The political significance of a daughter of Agrippa was much reduced after his death, as demonstrated by the fate of Tiberius' marriage to Vipsania Agrippina. Tiberius was compelled in 11 BC to divorce his wife Vipsania Agrippina to marry Augustus' daughter Julia, Agrippa's widow.[108] The match was evidently an unhappy one; Tiberius still bore affection for his ex-wife, and had a low opinion of Julia's (moral) character, while Julia hated her new husband, denouncing him in a letter she sent to her father around the time of the marriage.[109] The marriage between Tiberius and Julia was childless, only bearing one still-born daughter, but this was not necessarily a problem for Augustus on a dynastic level, as he likely still intended for Gaius and Lucius, his adopted sons (and biological grandsons) to inherit his position. Tiberius, now married to their mother, would likely have been intended to oversee their succession in the way Agrippa would have done had he still been alive, as there is no indication that Augustus intended at this point for the succession to fall to Tiberius.[110]

Although Varus was no longer the son-in-law of the second man in Rome, he was still in a position of prominence. As long as Varus remained married to Vipsania Marcella he was still the great-nephew-in-law of the emperor, if no longer the brother-in-law of Tiberius. But Varus had not necessarily owed his career progression to his familial relationship with the Imperial regime, but rather had likely gained the marriage through his professional conduct, suggesting that his future was still bright under these changed circumstances. The following years would prove any optimism he felt correct, as he continued to advance with proconsulships in Africa and, more significantly, Syria, one of the most important commands in the Empire at that time.

Chapter 4

Varus as Governor in Africa and Syria, 7–4 BC/AD 1

Having served as a consul in 13 BC, Varus would have been eligible for a number of more senior administrative and military roles, now including several which were typically only open to those who had served a consulship. One of the most desirable roles was an appointment as a governor or proconsul of a province, which could enhance the prestige of the individual appointed there, while also offering them the opportunity for career advancement and monetary enrichment (sometimes illicitly, particularly with regards to the latter). Varus was twice given this role in quick succession, in two of the non-European provinces. These were areas where he had probably not yet held any military commands but did have some experience as a result of his provincial tour with Augustus in 22–19 BC, during which he had visited several of the eastern provinces. Varus was appointed proconsul governor of the province of Africa in 8/7 BC, and soon after completing his time there was transferred to Syria, where he served as governor from 7/6 BC until at least 4 BC. As will be discussed in this chapter, these were important appointments and Varus was challenged by difficult circumstances during his time of service, particularly in Syria. This chapter covers the middle point of Varus' career, as he moved from climbing the *cursus honorum* in Rome to positions of genuine responsibility in the provinces. Although the appointments honoured Varus, they were not sinecures given just because he had known Augustus and Tiberius for a long time, or because he had been Agrippa's son-in-law. There were plenty of easier provincial commands that he could have been given which would have accrued equal prestige for much less work, but this is not what happened – the provinces he governed, particularly Syria, were difficult commands which required experienced and capable men to be put in charge. Varus' earlier career had clearly justified his selection to Augustus – and, largely, the emperor's faith would be rewarded.

The missing years – 12–8 BC

What Varus had been doing between 12 BC, when his consulship ended, and 8 BC when he was appointed as governor, is undocumented, making it impossible to reconstruct his actions during this period, either historically or – thus far – archaeologically. There were a limited number of career options open to ex-consuls – at least, in terms of jobs that would continue to enhance their prestige – and for any individual who wanted to stay in Rome, the choice was often limited to managing the river and aqueducts, or temples and other public works.[1] The best option was to move outside Rome and take a role in the provinces.

It is likely that Varus took a position as a legionary legate (*legatus*) in command of a legion taking active part in one of several conflicts occurring in the northern and eastern fringes of the European Empire. Members of the Imperial family were involved in the command of these conflicts, particularly Augustus' stepsons, Tiberius and Drusus the Elder, who were both heavily active in the field after 12 BC. Tiberius took command in quelling an uprising in Pannonia which had erupted in the aftermath of Agrippa's death, conducting a successful campaign of suppression that saw most of the men in the territory sold into slavery.[2] At the same time, Rome was at near-constant conflict along the Rhine in this period. Between 12 and 9 BC, numerous Roman incursions into German territory had taken place, led by Drusus the Elder, Tiberius' younger brother (these campaigns are discussed in greater detail in the following chapter).[3]

It would not be surprising to discover that Varus had been involved with either of these campaigns in the years following his consulship, particularly given the fact that he may well have built up a steady friendship with Tiberius over the previous decades. A legionary commander in this period was usually appointed for a period of three years, which would suit the time frame where Varus is otherwise 'missing in action'.[4] What Varus was doing between 12 BC and 8 BC must, for now, remain speculative. Unfortunately, no archaeological evidence, such as an inscribed artefact with his name and/or legionary affiliation, has been found to connect Varus to a particular base or legion in this period. Nevertheless, given the trajectory of his later career, it is likely that Varus did serve in a senior military position in the years after his consulship, despite it being unclear exactly where he was deployed. What is known for certain is that by 8 BC, Augustus judged him to be ready for the greater responsibility of a governorship, starting with a year-long appointment as governor of the senatorial province of Africa, and soon afterwards, a longer period as governor of the Imperial province of Syria.

Imperial and Senatorial provinces

Under the Empire, for administrative purposes the provinces were split into two categories – senatorial provinces, and Imperial provinces – by Augustus.[5] The senatorial provinces were located in the Empire's interior, particularly the core Mediterranean heartlands, and were typically pacified areas where there was little immediate prospect of rebellion or invasion. These provinces therefore typically had little standing military garrisoning, beyond that needed for limited policing duties and security for the Roman administrative personnel. These provinces could be safely left to 'the Roman people', and the responsibility for appointing the governor (proconsul) of the province was given to the Senate – although it is almost certain the emperor would in reality have final say over the appointment. The selection was made by ballot, albeit with an attendant, perhaps inevitable, risk of manipulation in the selection.[6] Potential candidates for senatorial governorships had to wait five years after holding the consulship in Rome before they were eligible for a provincial appointment.[7] The proconsular governor chosen by the Senate would serve for a single year. It was not anticipated that the governor would face any military issues during their tenure. Although the position of governor of a senatorial province was prestigious, the lack of a provincial army limited the power – and threat – of the individual in question.

The Imperial provinces were a different proposition. Making up the vast majority of the Empire, these territories were typically on the borders of the Empire, and some were still relatively turbulent and conflict-ridden places. It was necessary to station a standing military garrison in most of these provinces, and for this reason, from 27 bc it was decreed that Augustus, and the emperors after him, were assigned these provinces as their own command. Consequently, the emperor directly appointed individuals to serve as governors in these provinces, referred to officially as the *Legatus Augusti pro praetore* ('Legate of the Emperor with the rank of a Praetor'). As such, they acted as the *de facto* agents of Imperial power in their allotted provinces. Unlike senatorial appointments, there was no requirement for an individual to have spent any time out of office in Rome before being selected by the emperor, and they could even be appointed while still serving in another official role, including consul. By introducing this system, Augustus would be able to limit the length of time any one governor was in position, making it less likely that a provincial garrison would develop greater loyalty to their local commander than the emperor and the state. During the civil wars of the Late Republican period, governors had used the troops stationed in their provinces as their own private armies, giving a military backing to their plays for political power in

Rome – indeed, Augustus' adopted father, Julius Caesar, had done exactly this in Gaul. Augustus was evidently willing to learn from the Republic's mistakes.

So, unsurprisingly, the governorships in the garrisoned provinces largely went to the more trusted figures within the Imperial regime, whose loyalty could be more safely assumed. The governors of Imperial provinces could stay in office for several years at the behest of the emperor, unlike their counterparts in senatorial provinces who were limited to a single year.

The governorship of an Imperial province was ostensibly a greater responsibility than of a senatorial province. In these provinces, the governor was more likely to encounter problems, such as uprisings or invasions, and the position was therefore one of both administrative and military command. The governors of most of the Imperial provinces, especially those on the more turbulent frontiers, were expected to have previous military experience, particularly in legionary command. But this raised a potential problem for Augustus and later emperors, in that these same experienced military commanders posed a security threat, should they turn against the Imperial regime. It was necessary for the emperor to be able to trust – as much as possible – the person appointed to the position, to avoid a repeat of the situation in the Late Republic, where several prominent Roman governors (Pompey Magnus, Julius Caesar, and even Mark Antony) had used their provincial legions as little more than private armies to advance their own political agendas. But it was also necessary for the men appointed to govern these provinces to be effective. Analysis of the appointments made to these provinces suggest that they were made based on previous performance as well as the individual's social standing and connection to the Imperial regime.[8]

The governor himself would not be responsible for determining the policies which would be enacted within the province, but would instead be given a mandate from Rome about what to do during their time in office. This mandate would have been dictated by the emperor in the case of Imperial provinces, and by the Senate for the senatorial provinces, although there is little evidence for how they determined policy or instructed the governors on how to implement it.[9] This is not to say that the governor would have had no autonomy at all, particularly in the day-to-day running of the province, but that his decision-making had to take place in a wider political context. It was mainly the emperor, or less often the Senate, who decided what should or should not be done in each province – something which will become important when considering Varus' actions as governor in Germany. The day-to-day decisions were likely fairly consistent from one province to another – centring on implementing jurisdiction, tax-collection, road construction and public building works, all with the assistance of an administrative staff.[10]

Imperial governors would remain in contact with the emperor throughout their time in the provinces, sending letters to update them about events in the province as required.[11]

Given Varus' evident loyalty to the Imperial regime, he would seem to make an ideal candidate to continue his career in the governorship of a province or two. His past administrative and military experience further suggested his suitability for these more senior provincial roles – and, as will be seen in this chapter, he proved an effective governor in both Africa and Syria, potentially building the reputation for effective governorship that would later see him fatefully appointed to the governorship of Germany.

The Governorship of Africa – 8–7 BC

Varus' first governorship was the province of Africa Proconsularis (corresponding roughly with modern day Tunisia, north-east Algeria, and western Libya). Africa had been a province of the Empire since 146 BC, when it had fallen under Roman control following the end of the Third Punic War, and was one of the wealthiest and most agriculturally fertile regions. Africa was a senatorial province, despite being on the southern frontier of the Empire – Augustus may have made this decision as a diplomatic concession, reflecting the importance of the region to Rome.[12] It was also one of the few senatorial provinces to have a substantial garrison, reflecting its position on the frontier, including a dedicated legion, the Third Augusta.[13] The legion was deployed to Africa in 30 BC, largely to protect the grain supply in the region, and was initially based at Ammaedara (modern Haïdra, Tunisia), close to the northern edge of the Sahara desert, from where the troops could monitor tribal movements in the area. At this time in the late first century BC the legionary soldiers were still recruited from outside the provinces they served in, with most in the Third Augusta at this early stage coming from Gaul. The legion was necessary for the security of the territory, as there were ongoing small-scale outbreaks of conflict in the region throughout the period, particularly when Roman ways of administration clashed with the tenets of traditional nomadic life. Under Augustus, these incidents were kept under control, but early in the reign of Tiberius the Romans would receive a reminder of the potential dangers in Africa, where a revolt led by a former auxiliary soldier named Tacfarinas, who was native to the region, waged a seven-year rebellion that severely threatened Roman security in the region.[14]

Command of the province of Africa was a distinguished appointment, alongside that of the province of Asia. Both of these governorships were typically only given to former consuls and could be the pinnacle of senatorial career.[15] But it was not an empty honour, with the governor charged with real responsibility in the province – particularly to ensure security in the region and maximize the production of the grain supply. Africa was of significant agricultural importance, and exported a substantial amount of grain to the rest of the Empire, including the city of Rome.[16] The distribution of land ownership in Africa had changed significantly as a result of the Roman presence in the province, particularly through the purchase of estates by individual senators, who would function as absentee landlords, the distribution of land to Roman colonists and army veterans, and later, the creation of Imperial estates. The job of the governor in Africa was primarily to ensure the smooth running of the agricultural system, using the Third Augusta where required to maintain the security of the province from raids and rebellion.

Varus probably arrived in the province of Africa in 8 BC, following the required five-year break after holding the consulship before he could be appointed to command a senatorial province.[17] It is not known who he replaced in the role. Varus was around 38 years old when he took the position – still relatively young in the Roman political system, but was already an experienced administrator and military commander, judging even just from the positions that we *know* he had held.[18] Although officially appointed by the Senate, his appointment had likely been at least approved by Augustus, perhaps even strongly influenced by him; appointments as governor of both Africa and Asia seem to have been heavily biased in favour of certain individuals.[19] He would expect to serve for just a year in the province, consistent with customary practice for senatorial provinces.

The overall policies of Varus' rule in Africa would not have been decided by Varus himself, but dictated to him, as consistent with general practice. Keeping the grain supply both secure and bountiful would likely have been Varus' major objective in Africa. As governor, he would also have been responsible for overseeing tax collection, enforcement of legislation, and the administration of justice in provincial disputes – all with the assistance of an appropriate administrative staff. Although there are no detailed accounts of his time in the province, Varus' tenure in Africa appears to have passed fairly smoothly – the absence of any record to the contrary is at least partial validation of this. None of the historians mention any events in connection with Varus' time in Africa, suggesting that nothing of note happened at this time. Given the negative portrayal of Varus by several of these writers, including accusations over his actions in Syria (as will be discussed later in this chapter), it is safe to assume that they would not have hesitated to provide commentary on Africa if it backed up their negative portrayal of him as an individual – leading to the conclusion that Varus' actions in Africa were effective.

In fact, so little impact did Varus' governorship of Africa make on the historical record that it is largely through coins that he can be placed there at all. During his time in Africa, several issues of coins were minted which give insight not just into his spell as governor, but his ongoing relationship with, and role within, the Imperial regime. These coins were not just minted during his governorship for the province, or counter-marked to associate Varus with the coins to those who were using them – on several issues a portrait-bust of Varus featured on the reverse. Using the image of living individuals on coins was still relatively new to the Roman world in the late first century BC (unlike in the Greek world, where it had been happening for centuries). Julius Caesar had been the first Roman to put his own image on coins during his lifetime, on issues distributed by early 44 BC, shortly before his death.[20] Octavian and Mark Antony both embraced the practice following Caesar's death. By the late first century BC it had become increasingly common to see the portrait of a living Roman on a coin, usually a member of the Imperial family (particularly Augustus) or a deity, sometimes supplemented by an additional prominent individual or local political figure on the reverse.

Several coin-types feature the name or portrait of Varus. On one *dupondius* issue, Varus' portrait is shown bare-headed (an inscription below identifies him – P QVINCTILI VARI), as the reverse design of a coin featuring the head of Augustus, flanked by his two adopted sons and heirs, Gaius and Lucius.[21] The two young boys had at one time been Varus' brothers-in-law through his marriage to Vipsania Marcella, and indeed they may still have been; it is unknown whether Varus was still married to Vipsania Marcella at this point (although as he had not yet married for the third and final time, it may be reasonable to suggest they were, as a prompt remarriage would be expected for an integral member of the Imperial circle should they find themselves divorced or widowed). Numerous issues featuring Augustus alongside Gaius and Lucius were minted in the last decade BC, as Augustus sought to promote them as his heirs to the Roman world at large, so it is not surprising to see this issue here. Images of the emperor were common on Roman provincial coinage, and the imagery used alongside it could be an effective way to distribute Imperial propaganda to the wider population.[22] The designs of coins minted during Augustus' reign (and indeed, throughout the Imperial period) were often carefully designed, using images familiar to the populations who would be using them to emphasize the emperor's authority, as well as that of more local Roman officials with closer ties to the region in question.[23] In this context, it would not be particularly surprising to find a provincial governor minting coins bearing his image in a province, even when he was only in office for a single year – if nothing else, it would potentially enhance his wider prestige.

However, given Varus' connections with the Imperial family, this issue may have extra meaning. The image could have demonstrated that Varus continued to play a role in ensuring the successful transition of power to the boys after the death of Augustus. When Varus was Agrippa's son-in-law through his marriage to Vipsania Marcella, it seemed likely that he would be called upon to support the succession of Agrippa, and the same was probably expected with regard to the new heirs. It would therefore have made sense to associate Varus with Gaius and Lucius where possible, with coins offering an ideal medium in which to do so. Other coin issues produced by the African mints dating outside Varus' governorship have a similar design, but with Gaius and Lucius alone on the reverse, opposite a portrait of Augustus on the obverse.[24] This was likely the more common form of the coin, which suggests that in the examples where Varus was pictured, it was not as the result of convention (in showing the portrait of the governor alongside the Imperial family), but a deliberate (propaganda) choice. Varus was also depicted on the reverse of a *dupondius* issue, where his portrait served as the reverse design on a coin depicting the god Sol on the obverse, a deity associated with the emperor in the Imperial period.[25] The message being sent out through these coins was clear: Varus was a powerful man in Roman politics, and closely associated with the Imperial family. The sense of prestige that he derived from them may have been significant.

The year that Varus spent governing Africa would have given him first-hand experience of administrating a province, likely building on skills he had acquired since the late 20s BC when he went on the tour of the eastern Empire with Augustus. There is no evidence to suggest that he dealt with any serious military issues during his year in office, although he was likely constantly aware of the threat posed by the nomadic populations in the region. The impression given by Varus' time in Africa is of an experienced official taking an important but relatively straightforward role, as he began to move into the prime years of his career. In some ways, though, the role in Africa may almost have been below Varus in terms of his experience levels, particularly with regards to military command – but this may be because the governorship of Africa had a wider purpose. It is possible that Varus was appointed to Africa almost as a tedious-but-necessary stepping-stone to the governorship of Syria, which he would be immediately appointed to the following year. Governors of Syria were expected to have both extensive military experience, particularly in legionary command, as well as already having served one term as governor in another province. In 8 BC, while Varus satisfied the former requirement, he lacked the latter. In order to appoint Varus governor of Syria, he would have to serve elsewhere first – the senatorial province of Africa, appointment to which conferred great honour on the holder while only requiring them to serve there for a single year, would be an ideal location. Varus was duly appointed as governor of Syria soon after, likely in the following year. The wisdom of Augustus' decision to appoint him to the role soon became apparent, as conflict spilled out in the region, which required experienced and authoritative Roman leadership to subdue. In Varus, Syria had a governor who would prove more than capable of the task.

The governorship of Syria

In 7 or 6 BC, Varus was transferred to become the governor of the province of Syria, after his year of office in Africa ended.[26] Varus replaced Gaius Sentius Saturninus as governor, who had been in position since 9 BC.[27] He would have been based in the city of Antioch, one of the most important cities in the eastern Empire, although the governorship would take him elsewhere in the region as required. Unlike Africa, Syria was an Imperial province, meaning that Augustus had the choice over who was appointed to the governorship, and hand-picked Varus. It was a more recent addition to the Roman Empire than Africa, having been annexed in 64 BC by Pompey Magnus.[28] Under Augustus, Syria had become one of the Imperial provinces, and was one of the more senior provincial governorships. Syria was a more turbulent province than Africa, and one which required an experienced governor in place, who had 'discretion and guile'.[29] The governor of Syria was responsible for the security not just of the Roman province and its frontier with the Parthian Empire, but of several client kingdoms bordering the province, including Judaea, Cilicia, Emesa, Nabataea, and Commagene. Many of these territories were geographically and politically distant from Rome, running almost autonomously despite Roman oversight.[30] Client kingdoms were technically independent allies of Rome, ruled by kings or chieftains who offered their loyalty and support to Rome, usually in exchange for privileged treatment, military support when it was needed, and the ability to maintain at least a modicum of independence (in comparison to being occupied by Rome).[31] The advantage to Rome was that it gave them a level of influence and control in territories which, for whatever reason, they were not in a position to annex or conquer and rule directly, often because the population was still divided along tribal lines which the Romans would have struggled to manage. The governor of Syria would likely be required to intervene in any problems which arose in the neighbouring client kingdoms, particularly where they threatened the security of allies or Roman territory.

Due to the frontier position of Syria, and the safeguarding responsibilities associated with the client kingdoms, the province had a substantial military garrison of four legions (at the time of Varus' governorship, Third Gallica, Sixth Ferrata, Tenth Fretensis, and Twelfth Fulminata), who were stationed at strategically-significant locations. The governorship of Syria, therefore, was typically given to an individual who had previously governed another province, rather than a first-time appointee, and almost always to an individual with substantial prior military experience, particularly in command of a legion.[32] They were, in the words of one historian, 'extremely distinguished and high-ranking men'.[33] It was a position held by someone experienced, and relatively senior in the hierarchy. The men appointed as governors were also often personally known to Augustus, and they had often previously proved their loyalty to him – most noticeably in the appointment of Marcus Agrippa to the province, who had served as governor for a decade (23–13 BC). The issue of loyalty was a very real concern, given the large military command that came with the governorship of Syria, which could, in the wrong hands, be used to seize power in either the region or the Empire more widely.[34] Varus was only the fifth governor of Syria to have been appointed by Augustus, and his appointment appears to have been consistent with Augustus' earlier practice of appointing capable and loyal individuals, giving some insight into how Varus was viewed by Augustus at this stage in his career.[35] He was clearly judged to be an able candidate, who satisfied the criteria for appointment to one of the most senior provincial appointments of the time.[36]

As Augustus' appointed representative in Syria, Varus would have received his mandate for action directly from the emperor, unlike his previous posting to Africa which had been (nominally at least) controlled by the Senate. Governors in Imperial provinces were expected to act as the emperor's proxy, reporting back to him through letters and then implementing the Imperial policy which was decided based on the reports fed back to Rome. They were not, in most cases, required to decide policy themselves. Although governors in theory had a certain amount of autonomy in how they administered their provinces, they would have to be careful not to invite Imperial disapproval by making 'incorrect' decisions, with the result that many consulted the emperor about issues they could probably have made decisions about themselves.[37] Varus' day-to-day role in Syria would not necessarily have been much different to that in Africa however, at least on the surface, overseeing provincial legislation and jurisdiction, tax-collection, and building works, while also protecting the security of the frontier with Parthia. However, unlike in Africa, where Roman administrative processes had been largely imposed on the province without regional adaptation, Syria had a complex pre-existing political and social structure within which the Roman governor was required to operate, including a number of client kingdoms bordering the province.[38] Much had been inherited from the earlier Greek administration of the region, and the Roman authorities found it necessary to adapt around some of these pre-existing civic systems. Varus would have been assisted in doing so by a small number of lower-ranking officials, including a procurator, who was responsible for financial issues within the province (including the collection of tax), and legionary legates in command of the four legions stationed within the province.

In addition to overseeing the general day-to-day administration of the province, Varus would have needed to remain on top of the specific issues relating to Syria. Perhaps foremost among these was the security of the province, particularly with regard to the Parthian Empire which lay just beyond the Euphrates, and which remained a constant threat. The danger posed by Parthia was not abstract. Just over thirty years earlier, the security of Roman Syria had been severely threatened by a Parthian invasion. In 40 BC, a large Parthian force had invaded Syria, rapidly seizing substantial parts of the province. The Parthians were evidently capitalizing on discontent against the Romans in the area sparked, according to some, by the actions of Mark Antony and Cleopatra. They were also able to ally with the disaffected remnants of the army of Brutus and Cassius who had been defeated in the region only a few years earlier, including a commander named Quintus Labienus, who had fought for Brutus and Cassius against Octavian and Antony.[39] Labienus had persuaded the Parthian king, Orodes II, to invade Syria while Mark Antony was otherwise occupied in Egypt, and he took command of a large part of the army. Once in the region, many other Roman soldiers defected to him, particularly those who had served alongside him for Brutus and Cassius. The Parthian campaign was quick and brutal, and Syria was soon garrisoned against Rome.[40] The Roman governor of Syria, Lucius Decidius Saxa, fled from the province and was soon after captured and executed by Labienus. The Roman troops in the region who tried to resist the Parthian invasion were defeated, and several legions lost their legionary eagles and military standards.[41] A Roman commander named Publius Ventidius Bassus was appointed by Antony to repel the Parthian invasion. Over the next year, Roman troops would fight at least three pitched battles (the Battle of the Cilician Gates and the Battle of the Amanus Pass, both 39 BC; and the Battle of Cyrrhestica in 38 BC), after which the Parthians withdrew from Syria.[42] Labienus was said to have been killed in the final battle.[43] Although Parthian control of Syria had been relatively brief, it had taken Rome several years, and at least three major battles, to fully restore control in the area. Although Syria had been relatively stable since, there was no guarantee that the status quo would continue indefinitely. When Augustus travelled to the eastern provinces in 22 BC, one of his aims may have been to gain a personal understanding of the issues in the area, and to allow him to formulate policy more effectively. Augustus would have been well aware of the potential dangers posed by the Parthians – and others – in the region. As governor, Varus would need to be ready and equal to any military issues which arose during his governorship – Augustus clearly had faith in him as a commander. The threat from Parthia was active rather than dormant, and Augustus would not have had the luxury of appointing someone who was not equal to the job, even if that person was a friend and family member.

Varus' administrative experience would have aided him more widely in managing Syria, particularly regarding financial matters, in which area he seems to have made some changes during his time overseeing the province. When Varus had been part of Augustus' delegation to the eastern provinces in 22–19 bc, he had served in a financial capacity, likely giving him the necessary background knowledge of how money in the eastern provinces worked. The numismatic evidence suggests that Varus had a significant impact on Syria's coinage system. He revived the use of the mint at Antioch, which had been unused for nearly a decade before his governorship, issuing both silver and bronze coins during his time in the province.[44] The imagery initially used on these Syrian issues tied largely into the Greek background of the region, using mythological images rather than Roman political ones. Many examples had the head of Zeus, the king of the gods, on one side; on the reverse, they feature an image of Tyche of Antioch, a cult statue of the Greek goddess of Fortune, alongside the divine personification of the River Orontes, which flowed through the province.[45] These images tied in well to the pre-existing conventions of coinage in the eastern Empire. Later, almost certainly during Varus' governorship, images of Augustus were introduced to the East through the minting of silver tetradrachms, mostly minted in Antioch. The first issues bearing Augustus' portrait featured a reverse design of a seated Zeus, although these were soon replaced with the image of Tyche of Antioch, a change which may have been initiated by Varus in imitation of the coins minted earlier in his governorship.[46] A further, more Imperial issue of coins appeared in the region soon after, almost certainly introduced during Varus' governorship – the SC, or 'senatus consulto' ('by decree of the Senate') type.[47] These were lower denomination base-metal (bronze) coins, which would have been used day-to-day by ordinary people in the province, in contrast to silver and particularly gold coinage, which had much narrower distribution channels. As such, this type of coins is often much more useful for establishing what type of political propaganda messages were being given out to populations at large. As with most Roman coins, the SC issues probably first minted under Varus conveyed a general message about Imperial authority, as most Roman coins did, particularly those which bore the image of Augustus on the obverse. But the SC coins were likely also intended to support Augustus' claims that he had restored Republican values to Rome, and that the Senate still played an important and independent role in the political system (even though it no longer did); the message aimed to further legitimize Augustus' role as the head of the Roman state.[48] The SC coins were widespread in the Empire under Augustus, but had been conspicuously absent from Syria until the time of Varus' governorship – what prompted Augustus to decide that this was the time to expand this numismatic message to the province is unclear, but it might well have been the presence of Varus, his long-term, trusted companion who had some background in the finances of the eastern Empire. However, that Varus was put in position in Syria solely for his financial acumen is debateable. The importance of the military command associated with the province suggests not, as an able commander would be needed on the ground to deal effectively with the regional problems which were always anticipated by the Roman authorities at the time. Varus' skill with economic matters may have been welcomed, but was unlikely to have been the sole reason that he was appointed.

There were rumours that not all of Varus' financial dealings in Syria were legitimate or in the Imperial interest. Velleius Paterculus accuses Varus of some fairly serious financial misconduct during his time in Syria, suggesting that 'he entered the rich province a poor man, but left it a rich man and the province poor', by over-taxing the population and embezzling the money.[49] It is difficult to substantiate the accusation – or indeed, to fully disprove it either. However, it seems unlikely that Varus could have been described as a 'poor' man on his arrival in Syria, perhaps unless Velleius meant this in comparison to some of the very wealthiest people in Rome. Augustus had raised the property qualification for senators to 1,200,000 sesterces (up from 800,000 in the Republic).[50] As Varus was a senator, his personal wealth must have at least met this minimum criterion and may well have exceeded it. Varus had been, and perhaps still was, Marcus Agrippa's son-in-law, a member of the Imperial family by marriage, as well as a long-term associate of Augustus – it seems unlikely that he was ever in any sort of financial penury. If Varus was involved in corruption in Syria, Augustus either failed to hear about it or decided not to take any action, as no charges were brought against him.[51] None of the other surviving historical sources about Varus make any mention of financial misdoings in Syria. It is difficult to know if there was any truth to Velleius' claims about Varus' financial misconduct in Syria, or whether they were invented by the author as a way to illustrate the governor's poor character to his readers, irrespective of the reality. Even if the accusations were true, the actions appear to have done Varus, and Syria, relatively little harm.

But Varus' governorship would actually be dominated and defined not by events in Syria, which was kept under relatively tight control, but by those which took place in the neighbouring client kingdom of Judaea. Varus had arrived in Syria in the final years of the long reign of Herod ('the Great') in Judaea, a Roman ally who had been incredibly influential in the region during the last years of the Late Republic and into the Imperial period. By 7/6 BC, however, it was clear that Herod's long reign was drawing to a close. Varus, as the governor of Syria, was drawn into some of the problems which emerged during Herod's last years, and the events which followed his death. The period was documented by the historian Josephus in two works (*Jewish Antiquities* and *Jewish War*), which is fortunate from the perspective of reconstructing Varus' activities in Judaea, which would otherwise be a complete blank. Josephus was a Jewish military commander and later historian from Judaea who fought in an uprising against Rome in the later first century AD (the First Roman Jewish War, AD 66–73) before surrendering, becoming enslaved and taken to Rome, where he was later freed, becoming a Roman citizen and both a translator and advisor to Emperor Titus. Josephus' narratives on the uprising are the only sources for Varus' behaviour and performance as a provincial governor outside of his experiences in Germany, and provide valuable information on how he responded to a military crisis within his jurisdiction – which will have bearing on later analyses of his actions in Germany. But why was Judaea so important to Roman interests and security in Syria and the East?

The Client Kingdom of Judaea

As governor of Syria, Varus was responsible not just for his province, but for overseeing the neighbouring Roman client kingdoms as well. One of the most significant was the kingdom of Judaea, where at the time of Varus' arrival in Syria Herod had been in power, with Roman support, for over three decades.[52] Judaea had been a Roman client state since 63 BC, when Pompey had conquered the territory. At the time Varus was in Syria, it was not a unified state, but instead comprised of numerous small kingdoms and territories, often divided along pre-existing tribal lines. This was exactly the type of political landscape that the Romans struggled to integrate into the Empire, and consequently, it was decided that Judaea should be administered as a client state for the time being. In theory, Roman oversight of Judaea, and the wider region, should have resulted in relative stability. However, only a few decades before Varus' arrival in Syria, conflict over the Judaean kingship had sparked significant conflict and Rome had intervened to ensure that their favoured candidate emerged as the power on the throne. When making Judaea into a client state of Rome,

Pompey had allowed the incumbent ruling family – the Hasmonean dynasty, who had been in power since 140 BC – to stay in position. Backed by Roman support, the Hasmoneans remained in power for several more decades, until wider problems in the region led to their downfall.

Central to the change in regime was Herod. Herod was not native to Judaea, but from a smaller territory south of Judaea named Idumaea, which had been conquered by the Hasmoneans in the later second century BC, and the population converted to Judaism. When Herod was born, *circa* 72 BC, Judaea and Idumaea were ruled by Hyrcanus II, the Jewish high priest in the region. Herod's father, Antipater I the Idumaean, was a high-ranking official under the Hasmonean rulers of Judaea, and appears to have been a very ambitious individual who exploited the weaknesses of the Hasmonean rule to his own advantage.[53] Antipater later came to the favour of Julius Caesar after assisting him during the civil war against Pompey, and was appointed a procurator in Judaea, tying him in to the governing Roman regime.[54] Within a few years, Antipater had gained enough influence to name his son, Herod, as governor of the region of Galilee, despite Herod only being in his mid-20s at the time.[55] Herod was given further responsibilities in 47/46 BC, when the acting governor of Syria, Sextus Julius Caesar (Julius Caesar's cousin), appointed him a general in the regions of Coele-Syria and Samaria – illustrating the deepening Roman trust of him.[56] Even at this early stage in his career, Herod had shown an astute ability to ingratiate and ally himself with the dominant Roman politicians in the East, which would persist through most of the rest of his life.[57]

When the Parthians invaded Syria in 40 BC, the conflict soon spread to the wider region. Attempting to further weaken Roman control in the area, the Parthians aimed to destabilize the client kingdoms in the region, replacing pro-Roman rulers with others more sympathetic to their interests. In Judaea, they overthrew the ruling high priest and King Hyrcanus II, and installed in his place Antigonus II, also a member of the ruling Hasmonean dynasty. He mutilated his predecessor by cutting off his ears so that he could not be reinstalled on the throne later; only people with all their body parts were eligible to rule in Judaea.[58] Attempts were made to kill Herod during this period, as one of the most important individuals within the Judaean regime, but around 40 BC he was able to escape first to Egypt, and then to Rome.[59] While there, Herod sought out Mark Antony, who in turn presented an account of what was happening in Judaea to the Senate, who decreed – at Antony's encouragement – to name Herod as the new king of Judaea. This was apparently unexpected by Herod, who had intended for his brother-in-law to be named as ruler rather than himself.[60] However, Mark Antony, and the Senate, may have seen Herod, known to be pro-Roman, as a safer choice.

Herod was duly acclaimed 'King of the Jews' by Rome, although it would be some years before he quelled all discontent against his rule.[61] Herod returned to Judaea, where he campaigned against Antigonus II, and also attempted to legitimize his rule by marrying Mariamne (sometimes spelled Mariame), the niece of Antigonus II. By 38 BC, Herod had recaptured most of Judaea except for Jerusalem; it would fall the following year with the assistance of the new Roman governor of Syria, Gaius Sosius.[62] The Roman army which had besieged Jerusalem then attempted to plunder the city, as was customary in Republican warfare. Herod objected as he felt that the city now fell under his jurisdiction, as did its wealth and people. He was only able to prevent the city being ravaged by promising to pay from his personal fortune what the soldiers and their commanders would have taken had they been allowed to loot freely.[63] Antigonus was captured and executed.[64] By this stage, Syria had been brought back under Roman control by Publius Ventidius Bassus. After several years of problems, the eastern region was once again stabilized, with Rome back in control in Syria and Herod now in charge of Judaea in place of the mutilated Hyrcanus II.

Herod may not have had many friends in Judaea in the early years of his reign, either among his family or his population, but he had powerful allies from the Roman world. Herod had been put on the Judaean throne largely through the workings of Antony, and indeed it was Antony who had helped him maintain his kingship during the earlier years of his reign, including through attempts by Cleopatra to have Judaea given to her instead.[65] Antony's patronage of Herod was openly acknowledged by the king, including through public gestures such as the naming of a defensive position in the heart of Jerusalem after him, the Antonia Fortress. Herod strongly disliked Cleopatra, however, and apparently encouraged Antony to put her to death to save his own reputation. The antipathy between the two may have resulted from Cleopatra's earlier attempts to persuade Antony to 'give' her Judaea.[66] Unsurprisingly, Herod gave his support to Antony during the conflict with Octavian, which put him in a potentially difficult position when Octavian emerged victorious. Unlike many of Antony's allies, Herod had not abandoned him in the lead-up to the Battle of Actium in 31 BC, although the troops the king sent to Actium proved largely ineffective. Herod defected to Octavian soon after the battle, taking his army with him.[67] Although Antony was still alive at this point, Herod appears to have decided there was little hope of his former patron's fortunes being revived, and therefore he switched his support to Octavian.[68]

Octavian appears to have been initially unsure about how reliable Herod would be – unclear whether the king's loyalty was to Rome, or to Antony more specifically – while Herod was uncertain about what Octavian's reaction to him would be. Under the terms of Octavian and Antony's now-broken alliance, Octavian had overseen the western provinces while Antony was given those of the East, meaning that Octavian had relatively little experience of the eastern provinces and their rulers. Although it was in the Roman interest to maintain stable rule in their client kingdoms, to avoid the chaos and in-fighting which usually emerged in the absence of a strong king, Octavian needed to be sure that Herod could be trusted. The pair met at Rhodes in 30 BC, where Herod apparently explained his actions to Octavian, emphasizing the loyalty it showed he was capable of – and heavily criticizing Cleopatra's influence over Antony, which would have played well to a Roman audience.[69] Octavian must have accepted Herod's entreaties, as he not only left him in position, but bestowed additional honours and gifts upon the king.[70] As Augustus, the emperor would in 20 BC take two of Herod's sons, Alexander and Aristobulus (by his second wife, Mariamne), into his own household in Rome and see that they were provided with an excellent education, hoping that they would remain friendly to Rome in future. He doubtless hoped that one of the boys would later succeed Herod, ensuring that the next king of Judaea would be an ally of Rome. As long as Herod was in power in Judaea, Rome would have little to worry about from the kingdom. Herod would prove to be the ideal client king – capable, benevolent, and staunchly loyal to Rome. From the perspective of Herod's relationship with Rome, the only difficult moment had come when the relationship between Octavian and Antony had dissolved, leading to open warfare between the two, but he was eventually able to weather that storm.

Herod's reign had brought significant structural and cultural change in Judaea. He instituted large-scale building projects in the existing cities, including the construction of the Second Temple in Jerusalem, as well as several fortress-palaces for himself, at Herodium, Machaerus and Masada. He also oversaw the substantial renovation and rebuilding of a coastal port which was given a Roman makeover, including marketplaces, bathhouses, Roman temples, a theatre, a hippodrome and a substantial palace complex. The settlement was renamed 'Caesarea Maritima' in honour of Augustus.[71] There was also a substantial introduction of Roman material culture to Judaea during Herod's reign, particularly among the elite, suggesting that his friendship with Rome may have set the tone for how the rich chose to present themselves at the time.[72]

Although Herod was a 'good' king by Roman standards, he was not necessarily popular with his subjects. There was some feeling that he had been imposed on Judaea by Rome, and that he was 'King of a Kingdom that no way belonged to him' as a result.[73] The executions of potential Hasmonean challengers to the throne had further alienated large parts of the population.

However, much of the (non-biblical) written evidence for Herod's reign comes from Josephus, who was, for the most part, fairly hostile towards him.[74] This may have led to Josephus exaggerating some of the negative aspects of Herod's reign and the discontent amongst his subjects. But even allowing for this potential bias, there does seem to be some truth behind his suggestion that there were tensions between Herod and his people, who suffered under various aspects of his reign. Herod was said to enforce harsh punishments on those who transgressed the law in Judaea, and to have over-burdened his population with tax and tribute due to the amount of money he needed to raise to buy gifts for his Roman allies.[75] None of these actions would have made him a popular ruler domestically, although they may well have kept his position secure by ensuring an ongoing alliance with Rome. The popular reception of Herod, still widespread today, follows the idea that he was a poor king, and a bad one.[76] In no small part, this was likely due to Herod's role in the New Testament, which saw him attempting to murder the infant Jesus by ordering the wholesale slaughter of the male babies within the kingdom, an event which almost certainly never happened.[77] The image that actually comes through of Herod's reign is of an ambitious, intelligent individual, who ingratiated himself with the Roman political regime to mutual benefit, and who ruled his kingdom effectively, and as ruthlessly as the times demanded.[78]

However, Herod's reign was also beset by political factionalism within the ruling family, and his first decade in power would prove particularly challenging.[79] Herod was viewed by many in Judaea as a usurper, particularly among members of the Hasmonean dynasty who would otherwise have stood in line for the throne. Herod had been externally imposed by Rome, and despite his marriage to Mariamne, which had made him a member of the Hasmonean dynasty by marriage, there had been several attempts to overthrow him in favour of an alternative Hasmonean.[80] Events were not helped by Herod's complicated personal life, which saw him take at least ten wives, several simultaneously, begetting numerous potential heirs, some of whom were later accused of plotting against him. Herod had many of the potential usurpers and their supporters executed – including his brother-in-law Aristobulus in 36 BC, and his second wife Mariamne in 29 BC.[81] Hyrcanus II, despite being in his eighties at the time, was also targeted and executed in 30 BC, on charges of plotting against Herod.[82] These executions should, in theory, have made Herod secure on his throne, but future problems would be encountered when it came to the succession, an issue which would come to dominate Herod's policies in his later years.

Herod and the Roman governors of Syria

Whatever Herod's relationship was with his people, he ultimately had the support of Rome, who likely judged that a loyal and reliable client king was worth backing, as long as he could keep the peace. It was important that the throne of Judaea was held by someone whom the Romans could work with, as the kingdom was important to maintaining the security and prosperity of the region. Unsurprisingly, the governor of Syria often worked closely with Herod to maintain this stable situation. Marcus Agrippa, who had been notionally governor of Syria for ten years (from 23–13 BC), had established a good working relationship with Herod, who travelled from Judaea to see Agrippa on several occasions to offer help and support.[83] In 13 BC, Agrippa had taken Herod's son Antipater to Rome, introducing him to Roman society – Varus, as consul in that year, would almost certainly have met Antipater, as would Tiberius, and probably also Augustus and the wider Imperial family.[84] The Herodian dynasty had learned the value of friendship with Rome – something which Herod, and his sons, would continually renew with gifts sent to prominent figures in Rome, as well as Roman officials in the East, particularly the governor of Syria and his staff.

The governors of provinces could be called upon to help arbitrate political or legal issues in their associated client kingdoms, and Herod called upon the governors of Syria for help at least twice when faced with plots against him. In 7 BC, the then-governor of Syria, Gaius Sentius Saturninus, had been called to assist Herod in deciding what to do about two of his sons, Alexander and Aristobulus, who he accused of plotting to kill him. The two brothers, the sons of Herod's second wife Mariamne, had been raised in Rome from 20–12 BC within the household of Augustus, and had clearly been designated as the next generation of pro-Roman rulers in the region. However, on their return to Rome, aged in their late teens/early twenties, they had become too popular with the people for Herod's liking – and too popular with Herod for their older half-brother, Antipater, who was hoping to be named as Herod's heir and saw in the two a growing likelihood that he would not be.[85] Alexander and Aristobulus were subjected to numerous accusations of plotting against their father, many apparently engineered by Aristobulus, who hoped to get them out of the way.[86] After several reconciliations and rearrests, Herod wrote to Augustus asking for advice on what to do about his sons, receiving the reply that if they were guilty of plotting to kill him they should be executed, but if not they should be treated leniently. Augustus advised that a council be drawn together of different political authorities in the region to decide what should be done with the boys.[87] Saturninus, as governor of Syria, was one of the individuals invited to come and pass judgement on Alexander and Aristobulus. The legates of the legions stationed in Syria, three of whom were Saturninus' sons, were also asked to attend and assist with the proceedings.[88] Unlike many of the others at the meeting, Saturninus advised Herod not to execute his sons, even though he thought they were guilty, advising that it was worse to execute your sons than to be murdered by them. Saturninus' sons agreed with this verdict. Unfortunately for Alexander and Aristobulus, Herod decided with the majority, and his sons were executed soon after.[89] Despite not taking his advice, it was significant that the Roman governor of Syria, and the legionary legates in the province, were called upon to advise the king of Judaea about an internal political issue, for all that Herod had been advised to hold the meeting by Augustus.

Just a few years later, Varus was called upon to advise Herod on a similar issue, when the family once again ran into problems with ambitious members of the younger generation. Varus travelled to Jerusalem at Herod's request to advise him concerning accusations of plotting now made against his eldest son, Antipater.[90] Following the execution of Alexander and Aristobulus, Antipater had become Herod's heir, despite being widely unpopular in the kingdom. He was the only son of Herod old enough to take the position once his half-brothers had been executed.[91] Antipater appears to have been aware that his position was precarious, and spent a lot of money trying to buy support in the region, including sending gifts to potential allies in Rome, as well as to Saturninus the governor and his staff.[92] Antipater himself left Judaea for Rome in 6 BC, remaining there for over a year, during which time a mess of plotting took place back home, in which Antipater was strongly implicated, even in his absence.[93] Shortly before Antipater returned to Judaea from Rome (which Herod had written to urge him to do, concealing his suspicions about his son), Herod consulted Varus about what action he should take against his son – once again deferring to the power of the Roman governor of Syria, and by default, Rome, in the internal affairs of the kingdom. Varus would almost certainly have been aware of the political situation in Judaea and have instructions from Augustus about how to handle this sort of crisis. He would also have already known Antipater, and probably also Herod, from their visits to Rome. Herod summoned a council to hear the evidence against Antipater, for which Varus was appointed judge.[94] Antipater was accused of procuring a potion with which Herod was to be poisoned, which he denied, saying that the potion was harmless. To test this, Varus had a condemned prisoner brought to the court and made to drink the potion; the man died soon after, evidently satisfying Varus that Antipater was guilty of the charges laid against him. Varus then spoke privately to Herod and returned to Antioch. According to

Josephus in one account, Varus then wrote to Augustus to ask his advice about what should be done with Antipater, who was imprisoned by Herod while awaiting the emperor's decision.[95] Although Varus' verdict was not broadcast to the kingdom at large, public opinion appears to have held that Antipater had, on Varus' advice, been spared immediate execution. This incident was the first time that Varus showed the temperance and mercy that would be associated with him throughout Josephus' narrative of his time in Syria.[96] Antipater was taken into custody by Herod, and was eventually executed after reacting a little too prematurely to Herod's death – just five days before his father actually died.[97] Although there was no official confirmation that Varus had approved the eventual sentence of death, it was assumed that his consent had been given to Herod privately, and that the execution met with no disapproval from the Roman side.[98]

By the time that Varus became governor of Syria, it was clear that Herod was likely within the last years of his reign. Aged around 65 years old, Herod had suffered with ill-health for a number of years by this point, and was becoming increasingly difficult to deal with. That Augustus felt Varus was capable of handling diplomatic relations with the king, and potentially also his death and the transition of power, further demonstrates how highly the emperor regarded him. In the last few years of his life, Herod appears to have suffered from a painful and degenerative disease, which likely affected his mental judgement as well as his physical health.[99] Augustus may have grown concerned about Herod's increasingly erratic behaviour, perhaps thinking that the king was going senile; if this was the case, far tighter Roman oversight of the kingdom would be required.[100] Further, there were growing levels of discontent among the population, as well as the growing levels of royal intrigue which had led to the execution of Herod's own sons.[101] As the king of Judaea was still an important political figure in the region, if he was no longer able to adequately discharge his duties this would potentially put additional pressure on the Roman governor in Syria. The governor would have to deal with any discontent provoked by Herod in this period, as well as handling the political landscape of the region without one of Rome's most trusted allies. More than ever, the man chosen to be governor of Syria at this time had to be experienced and capable of handling whatever difficult situations might emerge. The individual appointed to the role would have to oversee the succession, ensuring that Rome's preferred candidate was raised to the throne, and to deal with any civic disorder which followed Herod's death. It was not a time to put in position someone without a proven track-record in managing difficult situations in both a military and diplomatic capacity. That Varus was chosen suggests that he was well-regarded by Augustus and the

Imperial regime more widely. He had not been put in position as a familial honour, hoping there would be no trouble in the region during his time in office – the post was too important, and the potential for unrest too significant, to allow this. Under these circumstances, it is possibly fair to say that Varus was considered one of the most capable and effective figures currently serving in the Imperial administration, felt to be equal to any situation that might develop. As it turned out, there was a substantial Jewish uprising in Judaea when Herod died, and Varus would be called on as governor of Syria to handle the situation as effectively as possible – a task in which, it will be seen, he performed more than capably.

If Varus' time in Syria had only been concerned with the routine administration of the province, little would be known about this phase of his career. When things in the provinces proceeded smoothly, there was little for Roman historians to write about, meaning that periods of relative peace are fairly anonymous in the sources.[102] But the main challenge for provincial governors often came not from the day-to-day running of a province, but in effectively dealing with unexpected problems – ranging from natural disasters to revolts – when they arose. This is where the experience and reliability of the individual was called upon. Many governors would pass their entire time in a province without such issues arising, but Varus would not be so lucky in Syria. He had to deal with a large-scale Jewish uprising in Judaea after the death of Herod. The conflict would prove to be one of the more difficult episodes in Varus' time in Syria, but would also give him the opportunity to demonstrate his military abilities in active conflict. Without the uprising, Varus' time in Syria may have been just as historically anonymous as his year in Africa – but as it is, Josephus provides a detailed account of what Varus did when faced with provincial conflict, in a way that provides a useful precursor to his later actions in Germany.

Herod's death and a contested succession

Soon after the trial of Antipater, Herod died of a long and unpleasant illness which had blighted his final years. He was approximately 70 years old when he died, and according to Josephus, had ruled Judaea for thirty-seven years (since he was named as king by Rome; thirty-four if counted from the capture of Jerusalem).[103] It had become widely known in the preceding days that Herod was dying, hence the fatally over-hasty response of Antipater to the 'news'. The prospect also emboldened the Jewish opposition to the Herodian regime, and gave them time to plan their actions after his death.[104] But in reality, it had probably been suspected for months, if not years, that Herod was terminally ill, which may further have shaped Roman policy in Syria. Augustus must have been aware for some time that the governor of Syria would likely soon be called upon to oversee the succession in Judaea. Although he could not have been certain exactly when it would happen, Augustus would likely have appointed only individuals whom he thought would be sufficient capable, Varus included.

It is unclear how long Varus had been in Syria prior to Herod's death, as it is not known precisely what year Herod actually died, despite extensive research and discussion.[105] In no small part, the attention on the year of Herod's death has been determined by the impact it has on the historical chronology of the life of Jesus Christ, who was born during Herod's reign – therefore, Herod's death provides a *terminus ante quem* for Jesus' birth. The problem with establishing the exact date is that there are a number of inherent contradictions between the sources, which mention multiple events which cannot be easily reconciled to a single year. It is known from Josephus that Varus was the Roman governor of Syria at Herod's death, placing it any time from Varus' arrival in the province in 7/6 BC until he left, which is typically identified as 4/3 BC, but could be any time up to AD 1 (see below). However, this timeline clashes with the Nativity story in the Gospel of Luke which says that Publius Sulpicius Quirinius was the Roman governor at the time of Jesus' birth, probably only a few years before Herod's death – based on the claim that he conducted the census that took Mary and Joseph to Bethlehem.[106] However, other evidence indicates that Quirinius did not become the governor of Syria until AD 6, long after Varus had served in Syria, making his governorship irrelevant to dating the death of Herod.[107] Further adding to the difficulties in determining the year is a statement by Josephus that there was an eclipse of the moon shortly before Herod's death. Astronomical calculations suggest that the main lunar eclipses visible from Judaea in this period took place in 4 BC and 1 BC.[108] Although it is impossible to reconcile all these timeline statements, most modern historians date Herod's death to 4 BC, while a smaller number favour 1 BC.[109] These dates largely satisfy the information from Josephus, if not those of the Bible. The exact year of Herod's death may seem an irrelevance to the wider story of Varus in Syria – and in some ways it is – but it is significant because it feeds into the temporal framework of Varus' time in the East, particularly the date that he left Syria. If Herod died in 4 BC, then Varus could have left the region any time after that year. If, however, Herod died in 1 BC, Varus' tenure in Syria was much longer than most modern reconstructions of his career would suggest (but this is possible, as discussed later in this chapter).

One of the greatest Roman concerns regarding the death of Herod would have been the peaceful transfer of power to an appropriate heir – someone who was pro-Roman, but popular enough among the population of Judaea that they would be accepted as the new king. But there were often problems when the ruler of a client kingdom died, frequently centring around the succession; sometimes because there were rival successors, or on other occasions because Rome had decided the time had come to annex the kingdom and rule it directly. Even when not intending to use the death of the ruler to extend direct territorial control into a kingdom, Rome took a keen interest in any uprisings that took place after the death of a client king, particularly where it threatened to destabilize the region more widely. The Romans also ostensibly had a duty to intervene in the internal politics of a client state to ensure the endurance of the ruling family with which they had made an alliance, if the intention was for them to remain in power for the time being.

Although Herod had tried to make provision for his succession, many of his older potential heirs had been executed for plotting against him, leaving some difficulties about who to appoint as his heir. In his will, adjusted just before his death (immediately after the execution of Antipater), Herod had split his territories between three of his younger sons: Herod Archelaus, who was given the throne of Judaea, Samaria, and Idumea; Herod Antipas, who was made tetrarch of Galilee and Peraea; and Philip, who became tetrarch of the territories north and east of the Jordan.[110] As Judaea was a client state, the dispersal of territory as detailed in Herod's will would have to be approved by Augustus, but there was little doubt that Herod's wishes would be confirmed unless the emperor – or Varus – found a compelling reason to do otherwise.[111] Varus appears to have supported the cause of Archelaus, although doubtless this would not have persisted had Augustus been opposed to this succession.[112] However, Augustus would have had little time yet to form a comprehensive opinion of the Judaean succession, as it had changed just a few days before Herod's death; the news of the execution of Antipater and the new circumstances of Herod's will would not have reached Rome by the time that the king died. Once Augustus had heard the news, he despatched a procurator, Sabinus, to make an inventory of Herod's estate, likely to better inform the Imperial policy in Judaea.[113] Unfortunately for Augustus, Sabinus proved to be a poor appointment, whose actions would cause problems in Judaea down the line.

Meanwhile, increasing discontent was building against Archelaus from within his own family, who began to throw their support behind Herod Antipas, who had been willed the territories of Galilee and Peraea, but not the kingship of Judaea. Antipas wrote to Augustus to put forward a case that he be named king.[114] The emperor was left with a dilemma over who to appoint as king, and sought advice from his closest advisors and friends, including Gaius

Caesar, his adopted son and heir (the biological son of Marcus Agrippa and Augustus' daughter Julia; and thereby Varus brother-in-law). After hearing arguments from both sides, Augustus decided in favour of Archelaus, although still hesitating to make a full public announcement and confirm him as king.[115] Soon after, Augustus received letters from Varus in Rome telling him about a large-scale Jewish uprising in Judaea, but, fortunately for the emperor, it had already been competently handled.

A Revolt in Judaea

It became evident early on that Archelaus was not a popular choice as king among the Jewish population of Judaea, although his succession appears to have been grudgingly accepted in the initial stages after Herod's death – perhaps because, at this stage, he appeared to be Rome's preferred candidate, and had Varus' support.[116] However, the population demanded the removal from office and punishment of many officials who had risen to prominence under Herod, in revenge for the former king's many transgressions against them. Archelaus followed their wishes, although he appears to have been reluctant to do so.[117] Tensions between the new king and his people were already beginning to rise, with mutual mistrust and dislike evident on both sides. The situation soon worsened when a large number of Jews, including some from outside Judaea, travelled to Jerusalem to celebrate the festival of Passover. Archelaus, concerned that the event would encourage discontent against his rule, sent a regiment of soldiers to keep an eye on proceedings and detain any major troublemakers.[118] The pilgrims took exception to the presence of the soldiers and started to stone them. Josephus says that the majority of the soldiers were killed, and the rest ran away, and the Jews returned to the rituals of Passover. Archelaus was infuriated – and terrified – by this turn of events, and sent a much larger armed force into the city. Josephus says that 3,000 Jews were killed by Archelaus' soldiers, while many others fled to the mountains.[119] As well as brutal, Archelaus' act was seen by the Jews as incredibly impious, having taken place during Passover, and because many of the casualties had been injured or killed while on the sacred ground of the temple. The first steps towards revolt had been taken.

Archelaus withdrew from Jerusalem, and met with the procurator Sabinus at Caesarea, the port city which Herod had rebuilt as a tribute to Augustus and Rome.[120] Josephus implies that Sabinus had intended to impound much of Herod's estate, including strongholds and the royal treasuries, pending Augustus' ruling on the succession. However, Varus arrived at Caesarea soon afterwards, having been sent for by Archelaus, who had perhaps perceived

Sabinus' intentions. Varus dissuaded Sabinus from confiscating the property until news was heard from the emperor. As Sabinus was an Imperial procurator, appointed directly by Augustus, Varus technically had no authority over him, but he appears to have attempted to assert his influence anyway. It became evident soon after that Sabinus actually had little intention of following Varus' advice. Following the meeting, Varus returned to Syria, while Archelaus travelled to Rome to put his case for the succession directly to Augustus. Sabinus took advantage of this absence of outside authority to assert his own. He went to Jerusalem, where he occupied Herod's palace, and demanded that various administrators and military commanders come to him and give an account of the royal properties in their possession. The findings were reported back to Augustus by letter. Varus had also written to the emperor to give a financial report alongside his own perspective on the situation in Judaea.[121]

The kingdom had lain in constitutional limbo for months after Herod's death, as the succession was negotiated both at home and in Rome. Archelaus' actions in Jerusalem had only heightened tensions, while Sabinus the procurator's zealous cataloguing of Herod's estate had done little to calm matters. When Varus left Judaea after meeting with Archelaus and Sabinus, he ordered one of the Syrian legions to garrison Jerusalem, in anticipation of an uprising he was expecting to break out in the city.[122] However, Sabinus had used these Roman soldiers as his own personal army, to take custody of Herod's estate by force, despite Varus' instructions that he should leave things alone pending Augustus' decision on the succession. Josephus suggests that Sabinus' actions were entirely motivated by 'his love of gain, and his extraordinary covetousness'.[123] The Jewish population was provoked into resistance, and thousands gathered once more in Jerusalem, during the festival of Shavuot (Jewish Pentecost). They launched an attack on Sabinus, occupying several strategically important positions in the city, and aimed to lay siege to the Roman garrison. Sabinus immediately sent a letter to Varus begging him to come and help – despite the fact that it was Sabinus' actions which had provoked the discontent – emphasizing that it was Varus' soldiers who would be killed if the uprising was successful. The Roman soldiers were commanded by Sabinus to attempt to break out of the siege, although Josephus notes contemptuously that he refused to join in the fight, expecting instead that 'others should first expose themselves to die on account of his avarice'.[124] The Roman soldiers slaughtered the Jewish rebels, although they faced stiff opposition from slingers and archers, who ensured that the Romans sustained a fair number of casualties as well. Eventually, the soldiers set fire to the buildings the Jews were sheltering in and killed anyone who tried to escape, ending the engagement.[125] The Roman soldiers seized the temple's treasury and Sabinus personally received a large chunk of the money.

The battle provoked further discontent among the Jewish population in Jerusalem. A large group surrounded the palace that Sabinus and some of the soldiers were sheltering in and threatened to burn it unless they immediately abandoned the position, promising to hurt neither the men nor Sabinus if they did so peacefully.[126] As a result, most of the soldiers, many of whom had been part of Herod's bodyguard, defected to the Jews, while others remained committed to the Roman side. Sabinus refused to leave the palace, leading the Jews to start preparations to lay siege to it. In anticipation of Varus responding to his letter and arriving with troops, Sabinus made no attempt to prevent or break out from the siege.

The siege of Sabinus in Jerusalem was only one of the problems facing Varus in Judaea. The general rule of law had collapsed across large parts of the kingdom.[127] Whilst there was widespread robbery and murder, often targeted against the unarmed native Jewish population, Roman personnel were also affected at times.[128] In addition, a number of smaller uprisings had broken out across Judaea, provoked by the power vacuum left by Herod's death and the uncertainty of the succession. Numerous small warbands had formed, and numerous 'kings' had been declared. Some of these armed forces began to inflict significant damage on the infrastructure of the kingdom, seizing some palaces, burning others (after raiding their treasuries and armouries, of course) and terrorizing the population.[129] The Roman forces still at liberty in Judaea had to step in and fight against at least two men who had declared themselves king – a former slave of Herod named Simon, and a shepherd named Athronges.[130] Both attracted substantial followings and were causing significant disruption. The Roman response to Simon was rapid, with a group of Roman soldiers led by Gratus, one of the commanders left in the kingdom, meeting him and his men in battle. The Romans were victorious, and Simon was captured and executed while trying to flee.[131] Athronges and his men launched a surprise attack on a Roman force near Emmaus who were out gathering supplies and inflicted heavy casualties, panicking the surviving Romans into an attempted flight, which was halted only by the arrival of reinforcements who turned the fight in the Romans' favour. Athronges survived the battle and would go on to fight small-scale campaigns against the regime for some times afterwards.[132]

Varus had not been idle while these problems broke out across Judaea. It had become clear that the single legion left in Jerusalem would be unable to restore order in the kingdom, and that additional manpower would be required. On receiving Sabinus' letter from Jerusalem, he recognized how dangerous the situation could be, including for the legion he had left in the kingdom, so he made preparations to travel to the kingdom, bringing with him two further legions from Syria.[133] Josephus makes it clear that Varus acted rapidly on hearing the news, responding quickly on the ground to the reports from Judaea – presumably authorized by Augustus at least in an overall sense, although Varus may have been entrusted to respond through his own judgement, perhaps guided by Augustus' principles (there was probably not enough time for Varus to consult with Augustus directly before taking two further legions to Judaea). Varus supplemented his Roman troops with units from client rulers in the region; Aretas, the king of Arabia Petrae, was said to have sent substantial assistance because he wanted to gain favour with the Roman regime.

Varus gathered his forces at Ptolemais, a coastal city in Galilee, and planned his campaign to restore control in Judaea.[134] Part of the Roman force was detached and sent into Galilee, possibly under the command of Varus' son. Josephus is not entirely clear on who commanded this force, stating in the *Jewish Antiquities* that it was Varus' son and a friend of Varus, while in the *Jewish Wars* only the friend is mentioned.[135] This force took control of several cities which had fallen to rebellion, including Sepphoris, which was burned to the ground and its rebellious inhabitants enslaved. The main army was taken by Varus further into Judaea, heading first to the city of Samaria, which was spared destruction as Varus had heard no news of uprisings there. Several other villages and cities were not so lucky, including Emmaus, which was destroyed in retribution for the attack on a Roman foraging party by Athronges and his men – although, Josephus is careful to note, only after the inhabitants had been given the opportunity to leave. Several other settlements lying on Varus' route to Jerusalem were also attacked, leading to 'fire and slaughter', although Josephus is clear that it is the non-Roman allied auxiliary troops who are responsible for this, and that they disobeyed Varus' instruction in order to do so.[136] As Varus approached Jerusalem, where Sabinus and his men still lay under siege in the royal palace, many of the rebels in the city left, leaving the Jewish residents of the city to face the consequences. Perhaps unsurprisingly, the population of Jerusalem blamed the uprising on the non-locals who had flooded into the city to celebrate Shavuot, saying that these strangers were the instigators of the violence, while the resident population had remained unquestionably loyal to Rome. Many of the Romans who had been involved in the uprising came to speak to Varus, including those who had been besieged, and others who had remained free and had fought against several of the pretender-kings. He likely used their testimony to establish what had happened, and to decide what steps to take next. Sabinus was noticeably absent from this period of information-gathering, despite his actions having sparked much of the discontent in Jerusalem itself. Josephus claims that Sabinus slipped away from the city without speaking to Varus, heading directly for the coast. Perhaps

Sabinus was aware of the reception he was likely to receive from Varus should he come into the governor's presence.

Once Varus had restored order in Judaea by force, it was time for the leaders of the uprisings to face Roman justice. Varus sent part of the Roman army across Judaea to seek out the ringleaders and punish them as he found appropriate.[137] Around 2,000 of those judged to be most at blame for the violence were executed by crucifixion.[138] Those who he judged to be less to blame were given their freedom, with no caveats mentioned by Josephus – presented as a further example of the mercy which Varus was capable of, given that there would have been no requirement on him to leave any of the rebels alive. Varus then dismissed most of his allied troops, finding them badly-behaved and insubordinate, only to find that a Jewish force of 10,000 had gathered in opposition to him. Varus and his legions quickly went to meet them in the field but the Jews had little appetite for battle, and surrendered themselves to the Romans. The majority of this last group of rebels were pardoned directly by Varus, but several of the ringleaders were sent to Rome to stand trial before Augustus.[139] Rebel leaders were often sent to Rome for direct trial by the emperor when a provincial governor felt that they posed a wider danger to either the Empire or the emperor himself.[140] Augustus in turn pardoned the majority of the men Varus sent to him, with the exception of those who were directly related to Herod, who were punished.[141]

Relative calm was restored to Judaea for a time following the rebellion, although the question of the succession remained pending. Although it seemed likely that the emperor would have to select an heir from among Herod's sons, there was another potential option – the annexation of Judaea, and its conversion into a Roman province. This prospect would evidently have been welcomed by some even within Judaea itself. So unpalatable was the prospect of Herod's sons ruling the kingdom that a delegation of fifty Jewish delegates travelled to Rome to plead with Augustus directly to annex the kingdom and make it part of the province of Syria.[142] The royal family in Judaea also appear to have supported the idea of coming under direct Roman administration.[143] The wider Judaean elite appear to have been less than impressed by the suggestion, but it was evidently popular with the general population in Judaea – apparently even Roman rule was less daunting a prospect than the continuation of the Herodian regime, or a repeat of the chaos which had so recently overtaken the kingdom. However, Augustus remained disinclined to annex Judaea, likely recognizing that the kingdom was not yet internally organized enough for Roman rule to take over quickly and effectively. Varus still felt that Archelaus was the correct choice for king of Judaea, and commanded Philip, Archelaus' half-brother, to go to Rome and add his support to this judgement.[144] According to Josephus, Varus thought, despite his personal support for Archelaus, that Augustus would likely choose to adapt Herod's will in some way or another and wanted to ensure that Philip would be in place to benefit directly from any changes. Augustus ultimately decided to let Herod's final will stand largely as it had been written, with Archelaus recognized as king, although he was only given control over half the territory Herod had possessed, with the other half split between his brothers Antipas and Philip.[145] This arrangement would last for a decade at most; by AD 6, Judaea had been made into a Roman province, albeit one that did not encompass all of Herod's former territory.[146]

Although the uprising in Judaea was an internal conflict (one modern historian even refers to it as a 'civil war'[147]) which largely failed to threaten any Roman territory or personnel (beyond those in the kingdom), it was nonetheless a significant event, and Varus was inextricably linked to it. In the *Testament of Moses*, the uprising became known as 'the War of Varus', and is mentioned in this source where other Roman interventions in Judaea, including the captures of Jerusalem in 63 BC and 37 BC, were not.[148] The conflict appears to have left a deep impression on the Jewish psyche. The suppression of the Jewish uprising appears to have been significant for Varus and may even have been commemorated on coins minted locally. One issue, minted in Berytus (modern Beirut, Lebanon), bears the head of Augustus on one side, and on the other, two *aquilae* (legionary eagles) between two military standards, below the inscription 'P QVINCT[I]L[I]VS V[A]RVS'.[149] This imagery is distinctively different to that in other coin issues under Varus in Syria, which, as mentioned previously, typically feature mythological scenes. This coin may have been issued to commemorate Varus' success in Judaea, referencing the two legions he led against the uprising through the two eagles and standards displayed on the coin. While it is not certain that this coin was intended to celebrate the ending of the Jewish uprising after Herod's death, the iconography would certainly have supported such a reading.

In what had been a major test of his governorship, Varus had shown himself to be a capable and effective commander under circumstances of discontent and open revolt. Varus was not responsible for any of the actions which had provoked the Jewish uprisings – in fact, Augustus' appointment of Sabinus as procurator in charge of assessing Herod's estate had done more damage than anything Varus did in Judaea. The mistreatment of the Jewish population by Sabinus and his agents, combined with the power vacuum left by Herod's death – and the hatred for the successors the king had named, as well as the Herodian family more widely – appear to have been the main causes of the uprisings, rather than any of the policies enacted by the governor of Syria. Augustus may have appointed Varus governor of Syria to maintain control of

Judaea after Herod's death, should that happen during his years in the East. But there was little Varus could do to keep the peace while the issue of Herod's succession ran on in Rome, beyond responding with necessary military force when needed – and he did so effectively when called upon by Sabinus to break the siege of the palace in Jerusalem. Varus' response to the uprising in Judaea makes it clear that he had far more direct military experience than many historians, both ancient and modern, credit him with. Josephus' account makes it clear that he was directly involved in the campaign in Judaea. He did not stay in Antioch while sending his army out into the field, but went with them, overseeing a two-legion force through an extensive area of hostile territory. His actions appear to have been proportionate and efficient, both in the earlier stages and later on when a resumption of hostilities seemed possible.

A fairly favourable character portrait of Varus emerges from Josephus' narrative of the uprising, and he appears to be portrayed by the historian as the positive opposite of Sabinus the procurator – and, in many ways, as the ideal of a provincial governor.[150] Certainly, in Josephus Varus is a highly effective military commander. He is shown to be concerned about the men under his command, which appears to have motivated his quick response to the news of the legion being besieged in Jerusalem. Varus may have been less hasty had it been just Sabinus who needed his help.[151] Unlike Sabinus, who used the legion for his own purposes and without regard for their safety sent the Roman soldiers out to try and break the siege while he hid in the palace, Varus is shown to care deeply about the men under his command, and he leads them into the field personally, sharing in their privations and dangers. Given the fate he would later lead three legions into Germany, Varus' concern for the survival of the legion he had left in Judaea is all the more meaningful.[152] Where Sabinus is portrayed as weak, sending others out to fight for him, Varus is bold and brave, and his show of power and authority is enough to end the siege, and the widespread rebellion, without recourse to a battle. He was even able to show mercy towards the inhabitants of Jerusalem who insisted that they were caught up in an uprising they did not support.[153] Unlike Sabinus, Varus is not portrayed as being motivated by greed – a complete contrast to his characterization by Velleius – and someone who dismissed his allied troops for being too rapacious in their treatment of the property of the Judaean population. Varus is also portrayed by Josephus as being merciful, showing clemency to many of the Jews who had been involved in the uprisings. The only Jewish city that he commands to be destroyed was Emmaus, in retribution for an attack on Roman soldiers launched from the city. While other settlements were attacked, the blame for this was placed firmly with the allied troops who disobeyed Varus' commands and were sent from his service after the capture of Jerusalem.[154] Punishment for the revolt fell as much as possible on the ringleaders of the uprising, with many others allowed to go free with minor punishment, if any. It might seem odd now to speak of a governor as being merciful when they brutally executed 2,000 rebels, but by Roman standards such clemency was the exception rather than the rule, and in most cases a far greater number of rebels would have expected the ultimate punishment.[155] One modern historian suggests that the crucifixions served to demonstrate how seriously Varus, and by implication Rome, took the uprising, but the fact that mercy was extended to so many who might otherwise have been executed demonstrates that the killings were not just vindictive punishments.[156]

Ultimately, Varus' response to the revolt was effective, with most of the rebels disappearing without even fighting a battle against him. He brought what could have been a bloody and extended conflict to a swift end, without any serious resistance. Although some settlements in the kingdom suffered at the hands of his army, this violence was not sanctioned by Varus, and the perpetrators were dismissed from his service at the earliest practical moment. Josephus makes no mention of Varus allowing his Roman troops to engage in looting, nor of the governor taking the opportunity to add to his personal wealth through confiscations or plunder. The restoration of order across the kingdom by Varus and his army must have been welcomed by the majority of the population. Although the uprising – or 'the War of Varus' – would leave a deep scar on the Jewish psyche, from a Roman perspective it was a textbook case of how to handle a provincial uprising. This situation is not something that would usually be associated with the traditional perception of Publius Quinctilius Varus.

A Corrupt or Capable Governor?

In some ways, because Varus' time in Syria is known only through the context of the uprising in Judaea, it is hard to assess how good a governor he was. Certainly, there were no problems in Syria during his tenure that would suggest he was a particularly bad governor, albeit that he would have received his instruction on what policies to enact from the emperor rather than deciding them himself. While in Syria, Varus would have learned how to balance Imperial expectation with the realities of provincial and client politics on the ground, and how to deal with populations who maintained their own leaderships and a degree of autonomy from Rome.

The problems which erupted in Judaea were not Varus' fault, but he nevertheless dealt with them effectively, without even having to lead his men into battle in order to disperse the large part of the rebellion. In so much as the governor of Syria was required to protect and keep order in the associated client kingdoms, Varus had once more capably completed his task. He was an effective military commander, who when called upon showed good judgement, mercy, and moderation in his treatment of the civilian population.[157] The fact that a delegation of Jews travelled to Rome during Augustus' deliberation over the Judaean succession, asking to be made a province ruled by Rome, probably through the governor of Syria, has been taken by some as further evidence that Varus was a good governor, whose administration offered nothing to fear for the kingdom's population.[158] In allowing them to travel to Rome to plead their case at the same time as Archelaus – Varus' preferred choice to inherit power – was there, attempting to persuade Augustus to let him take the throne, Varus is seen by some as acting with fairness, not favouring his own candidate over the rest.[159] There have been suggestions that the Jewish delegation was not a genuine embassy, but was instead compelled by Varus to go to Rome, to demonstrate to Augustus his effectiveness as a governor in the region.[160] However, Varus would almost certainly not have had sufficient power over the ordinary population of Judaea to explain their enthusiastic support of the idea, suggesting that it really may have reflected popular opinion at the time. Ultimately, Varus is portrayed as a positive character by both Josephus and Nicolaus of Damascus, and while certain elements of the narrative may have been exaggerated for comparative effect (particularly by Josephus to contrast the actions of the Romans in Judaea in his own times), there is nothing to suggest that the texts cover up a raft of negative actions for literary effect.

But Varus' time in Syria is often viewed far more negatively by most modern historians, based almost exclusively on Velleius Paterculus' claims that he was a corrupt governor who embezzled large sums of money from his province. As far as the historical sources go, the claims made by Velleius are completely unsubstantiated. It is possible that there were informal allegations made against Varus during his lifetime with regards to the propriety of his administration there, of which Velleius as a contemporary was aware, but such a claim is pure speculation. Allegations of corruption against a provincial governor were an easy way for historians to characterize what kind of person the individual was – whether or not they were actually true, they indicated that the governor in question was a bad individual, the type who *would* embezzle from his province, even if there was no evidence that he actually had done. Roman historians often looked for these literary shortcuts, so that readers would get the correct impression of an individual's character without an extensive case needing to be detailed in the text.

The circumstances of the revolt would also have provided Varus with useful experience of the potential pitfalls of provincial government – which Roman actions annoyed or alienated the local population, and more importantly, what it could lead to. The actions of Sabinus would have provided a useful caution against financial and material exploitation of subject territories. Josephus had suggested that one of the main causes of the uprising, at least in Jerusalem, had been the greed of the procurator and his men:

> because those foreigners [Sabinus and the Romans], who came to reduce the seditious to sobriety, did, on the contrary, set them more in a flame: because of the injuries they offered them, and the avaricious management of their affairs.[161]

The hatred directed by large parts of the Jewish population towards Herod would have shown how problematic it could be to be seen to disrespect the customs of the native populations – in this case, the Jews – which could lead to rejection not just of one king's rule, but of that of his entire dynasty. He had also seen at first-hand the dangers left by a power vacuum, particularly in the wake of a long-reigning or particularly powerful ruler, and how numerous factions might rise up attempting to fill that space.

When did Varus leave Syria?

Varus had proved a success in Syria, able to administrate his province and deal with problems in the client states that fell under his jurisdiction. Unfortunately, there is little record of what else he achieved in Syria – or indeed, how long he remained in the province after Herod's death. The aftermath of the Jewish uprising in Judaea is the last heard of Varus' time in Syria. Traditionally, Varus' governorship is thought to have ended in 4/3 BC, after he had been in the province for three years.[162] This was a fairly standard length of appointment for a governor at this time. Indeed, part of the reason that Herod's death is dated to 4 BC by many sources is because Varus was clearly governor at the time, and if his tenure ended in 4/3 BC, the king must have died before that date. However, it is far from clear when Varus was replaced in Syria, and who his successor was. The next known governor is Gaius Caesar, Augustus' adopted son (and biological grandson), who was appointed in AD 1. This leaves a gap between 4/3 BC, when Varus is supposed to have left the province, and AD 1, the only occasion in almost five centuries of Roman rule in Syria (in various forms) where the identity of the ruling official in Syria is not known. This blank space may mark a genuine absence of evidence for who took the position between Varus and Gaius Caesar – or alternatively, it may suggest that Varus was retained in Syria for a much longer period than is usually imagined, until AD 1 when Gaius Caesar was appointed.

Although such an extended governorship would be unusual, it was not unprecedented, particularly in the case of Syria. Marcus Agrippa had served as governor for a decade, suggesting that Augustus was open to longer-term occupation of the positions when appropriate. Given the substantial military command that came with Syria, it is likely only those whose loyalty to Augustus was without doubt would even be considered for an extended tenure. It is certainly far from impossible that Varus was deployed by Augustus in Syria for up to eight years (7 BC until as late as AD 1) as a safe pair of hands for the region.[163] If Varus had been in Syria for this extended period, it creates a larger temporal window in which Herod might have died – although 4 BC is the favoured date over 1 BC (the two most likely options), this is largely because Varus is assumed not to have still been in Syria by 1 BC, but it was eminently possible that he was. Such an alteration to the timeline would have little effect on the overall narrative of the revolt, beyond that Varus would be more experienced in the region by the time it broke out, and it remains a viable reconstruction of the chronology.[164]

The main objection to the suggestion that Varus continued as governor of Syria until AD 1 is a fragment of an inscription known as the *Titulus Tiburtinus*, discovered near Tivoli in 1764.[165] It preserves part of the text of an honorific inscription – possibly a funerary epitaph – of a high-ranking figure from Augustus' reign, whose name unfortunately is not included in the surviving section. From the internal dating, the inscription refers to an individual who was honoured with *ornamenta triumphalia*, which only came into existence in 12 BC, revealing that their career must have extended past this date. The inscription was written after AD 14, as it refers to the 'deified Augustus' (i.e. after his death).[166] It also mentions the involvement of the individual concerned with a matter concerning a king. The inscription also mentions that the subject held governorships of Asia and Syria – in the latter case, either with Syria as their second governorship or, in a different reading of the text, that they held the governorship of Syria twice. Debate has been intense over who this individual could be, as it involves reconciling potential gaps in the record of governors of Asia and Syria.[167] The only tenure unaccounted for in Syria is in the potential gap between Varus, if he left in 4 BC, and Gaius' appointment in AD 1. The subject of the inscription is most often identified as Publius Sulpicius Quirinius,[168] although other suggestions have been put forward, including Gaius Sentius Saturninus (Varus' predecessor in the province), Lucius Calpurnius Piso, and Marcus Titius.[169] Discussion of the identity of the inscription's subject waned in the later twentieth century, as no single candidate could be found that satisfied the biography detailed in the text.

It has even been put forward that Varus was the subject of the inscription, which was found near his likely family home in Tivoli.[170] The identification of Varus as the subject of the *Titulus Tiburtinus* is a problematic one, on several counts: he is not known to have been governor of Asia; he is not known to have won the *ornamenta triumphalia*; and he did not outlive Augustus. However, similar problems are associated with most of the other candidates for the inscription's subject, and Varus' career does not preclude him from being the subject – his governorship of Africa would be unknown were it not for the coins he left behind, so even the fact that a theoretical governorship of Asia was not documented in the historical record does not necessarily mean it did not take place. Given the chronology, the only real gap between the Asian governors comes in AD 1/2, when (in no small part on the basis of the *Titulus Tiburtinus*) Quirinius is thought to have been posted to Asia – but, if Varus had only been relieved of service in Syria by Gaius, this time-frame would also suit his appointment to Asia.[171] The rest of the reconstruction is less neat if Varus is the subject, and requires certain stretches of credulity – although, in many ways, no more than have been required for any of the other possible subjects.

If the *Titulus Tiburtinus* is not about Varus, then could he have remained in Syria after 4/3 BC, or not? It largely depends on the interpretation of the text. If the subject was governor of Syria twice, then realistically they must have held the governorship of Syria between Varus and Gaius Caesar, as there is no other window in which the position is not occupied by another known individual. If, however, the inscription refers to someone who held the governorship of Syria as their second command, after Asia, then it is possible that Varus could have remained in position for several more years. Unfortunately, the period is one beset by speculation, in which a number of reconstructions are possible, with the only distinction between them largely what an individual wants to see in the evidence. Varus may have remained in Syria until AD 1, may even be the subject of the *Titulus Tiburtinus*. However, the same evidence (or lack thereof) could be equally used to suggest that he left Syria within months of Herod's death, and was definitely not the subject of the *Titulus Tiburtinus*. Pending a discovery that sheds further light on this period in Roman Syria, all the hypotheses are based on probability and perception, not hard evidence.

Varus' Career after Syria

Whether Varus left Syria in 4/3 BC, AD 1, or somewhere in-between, there is still the question of what he was doing thereafter until AD 7, when he was appointed governor of Germany. The main impact of the year that he left Syria would be in the length of time that elapsed between the end of the Syrian appointment and the beginning of the German – approximately ten years if Varus left Syria in 4/3 BC, reduced to five if he remained until Gaius Caesar took office in AD 1.

The career options for someone who had served back-to-back provincial governorships were limited in terms of promotion – these individuals had largely already reached the highest points a careerist could achieve in the Imperial period. A sideways move into another governorship was one option, although the quantity of suitable candidates would have far exceeded the number of positions available at any one time, and Augustus would have had to carefully balance between the desires of the veteran ex-governors, and the needs of the ambitious young men at the beginning of their careers. One of the most desirable governorships was that of Asia, which, like Africa, was a Senatorial province and appears to be one of the preferred appointments of the Roman elite.[172] However, there is no direct evidence to suggest that Varus ever served as governor in Asia.[173] Indeed, he is not associated with any other provinces, or roles, between Syria and Germany. Once again, he drops out of the historical record.[174] There are two possible explanations for this: either it is a failure of the evidence, or Varus genuinely was absent from the Roman political scene for up to a decade.

Certainly, the quality of the historical evidence for this period is relatively sparse and difficult to work with. In particular, the narrative of Cassius Dio's *Roman History*, a major source for this period, only partially survives – particularly Book 55, which would cover in detail the period following Varus' departure from Syria. But the problem is deeper than damage to a single source. This point in Varus' career also falls into an awkward period in Roman historical writing, where there was relatively little narrative coverage. Tacitus' *Annals*, the major source for early Imperial history, only began with the death of Augustus. Other historical works which do cover this period, such as Velleius Paterculus' *Roman History*, or even Florus' *Epitome of Roman History*, do not address events in sufficient detail. Varus is not mentioned by either writer outside of his time in Germany. However, it is not particularly unusual to find an individual missing from the Roman historical record even for years at a time. Gaps in the biography of even fairly prominent Romans are not uncommon due to the vagaries of the sources – even emperors, as can be seen in the large gaps in the life of Caligula, for example. It has previously been seen that significant other parts of Varus' life and career were not documented in the historical record, and could only be reconstructed from archaeological evidence, and it is not too troublesome – although it is annoying – that this happens again in the later stage of his career. Perhaps he took on another provincial governorship, or military command, or maybe he returned to Rome and focused on domestic politics for a while, without affecting the archaeological record in any way – each possibility is plausible, and yet unprovable.

Usually, an absence of this kind from the historical and archaeological record would be taken as a straightforward omission in the evidence rather than as an indication of something deeper. But in the case of Varus after Syria, political events in the wider Roman world have led some to suggest that there is more meaning to Varus' anonymity at this time – namely, that his career stalled in this period. In this hypothesis, the reason, therefore, that there is no evidence for his appointments in this period is because he did not have any. This seems incredible for someone who had previously enjoyed such favour in the Imperial circle – someone likely patronized by Augustus himself, who married a daughter of Marcus Agrippa, and who was the brother-in-law of Tiberius, as well as probably part of his close circle of friends. It is difficult to imagine an individual this well-connected falling into professional obscurity, even for just a few years – but this has indeed been suggested. Varus' potential fall from Imperial grace has been linked to one event in particular – the retirement of Tiberius from public life in 6 BC.

Tiberius' retirement, which ended up being temporary, is one of the more mysterious political events of the early Imperial period. Following the death of Agrippa in 12 BC, Tiberius had become an increasingly powerful figure in Rome. Augustus had adopted Agrippa's sons Gaius and Lucius (his own grandsons) making it clear that they were his intended heirs in preference to Tiberius (his step-son and later son-in-law). However, neither of the boys would be old enough to take and hold Imperial power should Augustus die soon after Agrippa – in 12 BC, Gaius was 8 years old, and Lucius was 5. Their mother, Julia, had been married to Tiberius after being widowed to add an extra level of protection to the boys, and as discussed in the previous chapter, it is likely that Varus' marriage to Vipsania Marcella had at least partly been intended to bring him into the guarding circle of the young heirs as well. Tiberius' powers had been significantly increased in the years after Agrippa's death, raising him largely to the same status that Augustus' long-term ally had enjoyed; he was appointed consul again in 7 BC, and given the right to celebrate a triumph for his military exploits.[175] Tiberius remained popular with the Roman military, and had proved a more than capable commander multiple times in the field. After the death of his brother Drusus in 9 BC (see following chapter), Tiberius was the best choice for protecting Gaius and Lucius – or indeed, for taking the Imperial throne, on a temporary basis if necessary, if Augustus died before the boys had reached a sufficient age. In 6 BC, however, just as his career was in its greatest ascendancy, Tiberius voluntarily withdrew from public life, and went to live on the island of Rhodes. Why he did this has been the subject of much ancient and modern speculation. Suetonius tells us that Tiberius claimed he stepped back so that he would not overshadow the young heirs, much as Agrippa had done for Marcellus in the 20s BC before the latter's untimely death.[176] This explanation does not seem to have satisfied everyone, including Suetonius, who speculated that it may have been dislike for his wife Julia which drove Tiberius from Rome, or that he hoped to increase his prestige in Rome by leaving.[177] Cassius Dio suggests that there was indeed growing tension between Tiberius and Gaius and Lucius, and that this was the primary reason that Tiberius left Rome, in fear of the potential consequences of such a rivalry – or the suspicions that might fall on him should anything happen to them.[178]

Tiberius' situation changed over the following years. In 2 BC, Julia was exiled from Rome by her father on charges of adultery and treason, and sent to live on the island of Pandateria.[179] Augustus divorced Julia on Tiberius' behalf, writing to him in Rhodes with the news.[180] In 1 BC, Tiberius apparently requested that he be allowed to return to Rome, as Gaius and Lucius were now old enough that he felt he was no longer a threat to them in the succession.[181] Augustus refused. What had started as an apparently voluntary exile had turned now into something forced on Tiberius, although in reality it seems that he remained part of public life in the East, with any Roman dignitaries who passed through Rhodes visiting him.[182] In AD 2, disaster struck when Lucius died of a mysterious illness while travelling to a provincial posting, aged just 20 years old.[183] Soon after, Tiberius was permitted to return to Rome, albeit on the proviso that he did not re-enter political life at that time.[184] The situation only worsened in AD 4, when Gaius Caesar also died, ostensibly from the long-term impact of a wound he had sustained while campaigning in Armenia.[185] Tiberius was now the only real choice for Augustus' heir.[186] He was adopted by the emperor, alongside Marcus Agrippa Postumus, Agrippa's only living son, who had been born in 12 BC after his father's death.[187] But this was not to be a passive role, waiting in safety in Rome for Augustus to die. Tiberius was sent out on active campaign once more, this time in Germany, where it was hoped that he could continue the work of subjugation.[188] Agrippa Postumus did not last long as Tiberius' adopted brother. In AD 6 he was exiled by Augustus to the island of Planasia due to his problematic behaviour, leaving Tiberius, for the time being, as the only realistic heir of Augustus.[189]

The absence of Tiberius from the Roman political scene may have negatively impacted the careers of his closest friends and allies, who would no longer be able to appeal to Augustus for privilege and promotion through Tiberius. If so, Varus may have been one of the ones to suffer. Several modern historians suggest that Tiberius' exile *may* account for what appears to be a severe downturn in Varus' career, as his prospects and interests were closely associated with those of the man who had been, or perhaps still was, his brother-in-law.[190] Alternatively, one modern historian suggests that Varus himself may have gone into semi-retirement, presumably voluntarily, although as he was only aged in his 40s he may have been a little young to have taken this step.[191] However, as mentioned previously, it may rather be a failure of the evidence instead. But there is a neat correlation between Tiberius' return to prominence and Varus receiving provincial command in Germany. Whether this is an example of cause-and-effect, or just coincidence, is difficult to determine. However, it is clear that the Imperial regime was still receptive to Varus, irrespective of what had happened over the past several years, and willing to grant him very high-status roles which once more required significant experience and ability.

A Marriage to Claudia Pulchra

Varus' Imperial links had been further renewed in this period through another marriage, almost certainly his third, in this instance to Claudia Pulchra, a great-niece of Augustus, and a cousin of Tiberius. She was the daughter of Marcus Valerius Messalla Appianus and Claudia Marcella Minor, the daughter of Octavia the Younger, Augustus' sister. Through her mother and grandmother, she was also the cousin of Vipsania Marcella, Varus' previous wife, and of Agrippina the Elder, a daughter of Agrippa and Julia who would soon come to prominence on the wider Roman political scene. The marriage was therefore very much a continuation of Augustus' policy of intra-Imperial matrimony.[192] Whether Varus was a widower or had simply divorced Vipsania Marcella is unknown – there is no record of what happened to her. It is not clear exactly when the marriage took place, although it was almost certainly between 2 BC, the earliest year that Claudia Pulchra could have turned 12, and AD 4, the latest realistic date for the birth of their son, Publius Quinctilius Varus the Younger.[193] Elite Roman women tended to be married earlier than more ordinary Roman women, and it is not improbable that she was only around 12 years old at the time, probably at least a decade younger than Varus' previous wife Vipsania Marcella. Varus would have been in his mid-40s at the time of this marriage, and a prominent figure on the Roman political scene, regardless of whether his career suffered as a result of Tiberius' exile or not.

The marriage was a good match for Varus. It renewed his links with the Imperial family though a member of the younger generation, keeping him at the centre of power in Rome. Claudia Pulchra was likely given no say in the arrangement, but a nuptial alliance to Varus would have seemed a beneficial move for the family at large. The marriage kept Varus within the Imperial family, at more-or-less the same level as he had been before through his marriage to Vipsania Marcella. If the marriage fell within the earlier phases of the date range (2 BC–AD 1), Augustus' willingness to maintain Varus' connection with the Imperial family through marriage suggests that even if Tiberius' exile affected Varus' political standing in Rome, it was not to the degree that he was no longer a welcome member of the Imperial family. If the marriage was towards the later end of the possible range (AD 2–4) then it may possibly be linked to the return of Tiberius from Rhodes, albeit initially as a private citizen, helping to revive and renew the matrimonial bonds which had held the wider Imperial circle together so well in previous decades. The marriage once more tied Varus into the Imperial succession, particularly once Gaius and Lucius were dead, as Tiberius became the most likely heir – and after him Germanicus, who had been adopted by Tiberius at Augustus' behest as his own successor, and who was by AD 5 married to Claudia Pulchra's cousin Agrippina the Elder. As he had once been the uncle of the Imperial heirs (Gaius and Lucius), Varus was now a cousin by marriage to both Tiberius and Germanicus, now the two most likely candidates to succeed Augustus. His support may well have been vital should there be a problem over the succession – but unfortunately, he would not live that long. Within a decade, Varus would receive what would turn out to be his final Imperial appointment, when he was sent to command the legions stationed along the Rhine. His experiences in Syria had prepared him as much as anyone could be for the experience, but it was to prove a challenge unlike any he had ever faced before.

Chapter 5

Varus in Germany, AD 7–9

In AD 7, Varus received what would be his last appointment: the command of the five legions stationed along the Rhine. It was a position of significant responsibility, and made Varus one of the most senior military figures within the Imperial regime. It would prove to be his last appointment; less than three years later his tenure came to an abrupt end when he and three of the Rhine legions were caught in an ambush in the Teutoburg Forest. When he arrived in Germany, Varus was approximately 53 years old, and was likely at the peak of his career. The appointment to the German command recognized his extensive years of experience in both civic administration and military command. What he had been doing between leaving Syria and arriving in Germany, as was discussed in the previous chapter, is unclear but he was obviously still held in high esteem by Augustus, who would not have risked giving the position to someone whose abilities could not be trusted.

The command of the Rhine legions was not given to someone lacking in experience or ability. The challenges were too significant, and the consequences of failure too potentially risky, for the role to be given to anyone in whom Augustus did not have absolute faith. The territories east of the Rhine had yet to be formally organized into a Roman province, and although the Germans were thought to have been subdued and the region increasingly pacified, there was still a risk of unrest which had to be carefully managed. Aspects of Roman public life were slowly spreading as a result of the Roman presence in the region, but their reach remained limited. Security in the region was not assured. The potential dangers still posed by resistant populations was highlighted in AD 6, when a large-scale rebellion broke out across the provinces of Illyricum, Dalmatia, and Pannonia – the Great Illyrian (or Pannonian) Revolt. The conflict absorbed much of Rome's military capacity, from legions and auxiliary units to commanders. With much of the Roman army engaged in suppressing the uprising (regaining control), it was likely considered necessary that other potential fronts be effectively managed to minimize the risk of further rebellions breaking out. In particular, the largely pacified but unsettled region east of the Rhine needed to be kept under control, to avoid placing further pressure on the already overstretched resources of the Roman military. When

Varus was appointed to the Rhine in AD 7, he was likely seen as an appropriate choice for the command – a safe pair of hands, loyal to the Imperial regime, who was able to broadly follow Imperial orders, but able to act on his own initiative when required. While in Syria, he had demonstrated that he was capable of managing diplomatic relations with local rulers, and able to handle localized discontent should the situation arise. His response to the Jewish uprising after the death of Herod had been effective but not overly brutal, and had not created significant resentment among the resident populations that had been caught up in the conflict. Nothing in his previous career would have prompted any doubts about his suitability for the command on the Rhine, particularly given the wider circumstances under which he was appointed.

While on the Rhine, Varus' role was likely relatively simple. His primary aim would have been to maintain security in the region, through diplomatic relations and campaigning in the territories east of the river where necessary. Varus would probably also have hoped to protect and encourage the processes of cultural change in Germany, particularly the development of Roman systems of administration and daily life in the area, which had already been developing for several years before his arrival. It would not have been an easy role, and would have been significantly different to the challenges posed by his earlier governorships. However, as will be seen in this chapter, for much of his time on the Rhine, Varus seemed more than equal to the challenge. This chapter begins with an exploration of Rome's relationship with Germany in the years up to AD 7, including the military campaigns that led to the subjugation of the region, before moving on to consider what Varus did after arriving on the Rhine. Although his time in Germany was to end in disaster, Varus was likely not a poor commander when stationed in the Rhine – but faced difficult circumstances that many others would also have struggled to deal with.

Rome and Germany

Germany had been a mysterious – and often frightening – place on the edge of Roman consciousness for several centuries by the time that Augustus sent troops to try to add it to the territorial Empire.[1] Its territorial boundaries were not fixed in a conventional sense, defined instead by the land claims of the tribes who inhabited the landscape – although from a Roman perspective, the Germanic territories typically lay north and east of the Rhine. A large number of tribes inhabited the region, and the historian Tacitus makes it clear that while the Romans may have viewed them as a homogenized 'German' group, this was far from the reality for the Germans themselves, who only allied under a shared identity when it proved advantageous for them to do so.[2]

The Romans viewed the German peoples as 'Celts', distinguishable from other tribal populations in Europe only in that they were 'wilder, taller, and have yellower hair'.[3] Roman writers marvelled at the strange habits of the Germans – from the fact that the majority lived in small, semi-permanent huts, to the fact that they did not make cheese.[4] More sinister reports, such as claims of human sacrifices made in the cause of fortune-telling and augury, added to the dangerous mystique of the regions beyond the Rhine.[5] The German way of life was clearly significantly different to the Roman style, in common with most of the Iron Age tribal populations of Europe. This does not mean, however, that the German tribal peoples were 'barbaric' or 'primitive', and the archaeological record shows a complex social structure, living in and around population centres known as *oppida*, engaging in manufacturing (iron, pottery, glass) and agricultural activity (including in some areas the cultivation of Mediterranean plants such as plums and figs).[6] Many of the tribes remained relatively unknown to the Romans, particularly those who migrated away from the frontier areas along the Rhine, especially if they moved beyond the Elbe.

Early Roman conquests and campaigns in Germany

It had been barely sixty years since a Roman army had first crossed the Rhine. Julius Caesar was the first Roman commander to campaign beyond the river, leading his troops across in 55 BC as part of the Gallic Wars. His actions were not intended as a full-scale invasion – nor a precursor to one – but to secure the eastern border of Gaul by confronting the German tribes which were crossing the river, some to raid Gallic territory, others to settle in it.[7] He built a bridge rather than crossing on boats, and once the army was in Germany, proceeded to burn the villages and crops of hostile tribes. After eighteen days, he withdrew over the bridge and destroyed it.[8] Caesar crossed the Rhine again in 53 BC, again building a bridge, marauding around the territory for a few weeks, then returning to Gaul.[9] On neither occasion did his army fight a major pitched battle, and there was no attempt to leave a garrison in the region. However, the expeditions were brutal, resulting in high levels of destruction on German territory, and, as attested by archaeological discoveries, at least one massacre.[10] Although Caesar did not overrun Germany at this time, according to Plutarch, he had planned to later return and conduct a campaign of conquest over the river, but was assassinated before he could realize this ambition.[11]

Caesar's actions east of the Rhine had shown that it could be crossed successfully and had theoretically opened the region east of it to Roman territorial ambitions. But in the chaos of civil wars which followed Caesar's time in Gaul, Rome's territorial interest in Germany stalled for several decades.

Roman efforts in the region were reinvigorated by Octavian/Augustus – one historian claimed he aimed to make the area a province in tribute to his adopted father.[12] Marcus Agrippa served as governor of Gaul in 39/38 BC, during which time he campaigned against Germanic tribes on both sides of the Rhine, but again, there was no attempt to establish a permanent Roman presence beyond the river. In the early years of Augustus' reign, Germany appears to have been of lesser concern, with the Cantabrian Wars (29–19 BC) in Spain taking precedence. The Roman system of client kingship appears to have been extended to at least one German chieftain (Maroboduus of the Marcomanni). The elder sons of other leaders were taken as 'hostages' to Rome to ensure the good behaviour of their tribes, with the hope that by being raised in Rome they would be firm allies of the Empire once they returned 'home'.[13] However, once the Cantabrian Wars were concluded in 19 BC, Roman attention turned towards the Rhine.

Augustus' reign was a period of intensive territorial expansion.[14] Literature of the time portrays Rome as the centre of an ever-expanding empire that would one day control the world, with 'no bounds in space or time', an 'empire without end'.[15] So ambitious were they that Livy described Rome as 'the capital of the world'.[16] After securing Spain (29–19 BC) and the Alpine regions (15 BC), the stage was set for Augustus to launch Roman campaigns across the Rhine, and continue his expansion. There were practical reasons to attempt to secure the regions east of the river, particularly that it would provide extra protection to Gaul, potentially freeing it from the periodic Germanic raiding it still suffered.[17] But there may have been little long-term strategic purpose in Augustus' German campaigns beyond the campaigns themselves, resulting from his need for conquest and domination over the known world.[18] Germany offered the opportunity for Augustus to exercise and demonstrate his strength, and to emphasize his connections with his adoptive father, Julius Caesar – although he intended to surpass his achievements.

It is hard to determine whether there was an overarching Augustan strategic plan for Germany beyond conquest and domination, particularly with regards to any intended limits or the establishment of provincial territories. Several modern historians have suggested that Augustus aimed to extend Roman control as far as the River Elbe, which would replace the Rhine as the 'frontier'. Others, however, have questioned whether the contemporary geographic knowledge about the region was sufficiently developed for the emperor to have been able to form this objective.[19] According to the historian Strabo, however, Augustus did consider the Elbe to be the furthest practical extension of Roman command in the region, forbidding his commanders to venture beyond it, even in pursuit of raiding tribes. This was not necessarily a policy in place in earlier phases of his reign, and may have been introduced at a later time.[20] Any 'plan' for Germany that Augustus formulated was almost certainly generalized and fluid, but would aim to expand as far as possible, perhaps to the Elbe, and likely beyond. Germany was not always a priority under Augustus, and could be marginalized at times when matters in other regions drew Imperial attention, such as a pending war against Parthia.[21]

Augustus' ambitions for Germany emerged relatively early in his reign, once it became clear that success was imminent in the Cantabrian Wars. In 22 BC, Gaul had been divided into three separate regions – Gallia Aquitania, Gallia Lugdunensis, and Gallia Belgica.[22] Gallia Belgica was the northernmost of the three provinces, and that which sat along the Rhine; the commander of the Rhine legions fell broadly under the oversight of the governor of the province. Two years later (20 BC), Marcus Agrippa was appointed governor of Gaul by Augustus for the second time, having already served in the role in 39/38 BC. He was likely charged with stabilizing the situation on and over the Rhine and potentially laying the ground for further campaigning in German territory.[23] Agrippa left Gaul in 18 BC, at which point a new phase of Roman military campaigning over the Rhine began, directed towards the conquest of the eastern regions.

Starting in 17 BC, the Romans launched a series of expeditions across the Rhine, claiming initially that their campaigns were conducted as revenge for German raids on Roman territory.[24] Several tribes (the Cherusci, Suebi, and Sicambri) were attacked for allegedly crucifying twenty captured Roman centurions – an action that realistically could hardly fail to bring down Roman vengeance upon them.[25] These tribes, and several others, began raiding Roman territory across the Rhine, making it clear that the river alone was not a suitably robust barrier against German incursion. Gaul would be under constant threat of raids – and potentially worse – until the Germans were subjugated. It was no longer possible for Augustus to ignore the threat posed beyond the river.[26] Roman campaigning in Germany was to begin in earnest soon after – but this would be no small or easy undertaking. All indications were that a major Roman campaign across the Rhine was in preparation, when an unexpectedly and disastrous military defeat demonstrated the still-potent capabilities of the Germans.

The Lollian Disaster – 17/16 BC

It was not be long before Rome faced a severe and unexpected military defeat in Germany – a loss which would likely be seen as more significant were it not to pale in comparison to the Battle of the Teutoburg in AD 9. The defeat saw the ambush and near-destruction of a Roman legion, the Fifth Alaudae, under the command of Marcus Lollius, the governor of Gaul, who had taken position shortly after Marcus Agrippa had left the province.[27] Like Varus, Lollius was an accomplished man in the Imperial regime, having held political office in Rome – including the consulship in 22–21 BC – and several provincial commands, including governorships in Galicia (modern Turkey) and Macedonia.[28] Little personal information about him survives, although the historian Velleius Paterculus was fairly scathing about Lollius' character:

> he was a man who was ever more eager for money than for honest action, and of vicious habits in spite of his excessive efforts at concealment.[29]

Unfortunately, there is no detailed surviving narrative of the engagement itself, just scant references to the loss of close to an entire legion, with few further details.[30] The ancient historians suggest that Lollius and the Fifth Legion were caught in an ambush, probably somewhere in the Meuse valley, and came close to annihilation. The legion's eagle was lost to the Germans, a great source of shame for the Roman army – and indeed, for Augustus, who had only recently extravagantly celebrated the recovery of the legionary eagles lost to Parthia in previous decades.[31] One modern historian suggests that the loss of the eagle may have been an embarrassment for Augustus, not least as the unit had been commanded by someone Augustus had hand-chosen for command.[32] Roman casualties in the defeat were large, and the legion came close to being entirely wiped out. Marcus Lollius himself survived.[33] In fact, he not only survived, but remained in post during the immediate aftermath of the battle, which included being left in charge of other troops soon afterwards.

The defeat was a significant one for Rome. It became known as the *Clades Lolliana*, or 'Lollian Disaster', and alongside the Teutoburg was referred to as one of only two military disasters of Augustus' reign. The emperor felt compelled to travel to Gaul to personally oversee the situation in the wake of the episode, and to coordinate operations against an expected German incursion over the Rhine.[34] However, the Germans were not sufficiently emboldened by their victory, nor did they expect to go without retribution. They withdrew to their tribal territories on hearing that Lollius was gathering troops to return to the field, and that Augustus was planning to join the campaign in person.[35]

Despite its many similarities with the AD 9 Teutoburg battle, the ambush of Lollius and his legion was not as devastating as the later battle. The legion was not disbanded but continued to serve under its previous number and epithet. Lollius, who survived the battle, was punished with little more than the premature cessation of his military career. He faced little public censure, perhaps as a result of his ongoing friendship with Augustus, and the poet Horace even composed an ode to him which, at least on the surface, appears to publicly celebrate Lollius despite his failings in Germany.[36] It has therefore been claimed by some that the Lollian Disaster was seen as more of an inconvenience and humiliation than a serious threat to the Empire, although it is possible that its contemporary significance is overshadowed in the historical record due to the events of AD 9.[37] Nevertheless, perhaps inevitably, Lollius' career went into severe decline after the defeat. His longstanding friendship with Augustus may have kept him from too harsh a punishment, and after more than a decade on the political sidelines was chosen by Augustus to accompany his grandson, Gaius Caesar, on a tour of the eastern provinces beginning in 1 BC. However, he was never again given command of a province or army. Soon after being appointed to Gaius' entourage, accusations of corruption led to Lollius being denounced to Augustus as a traitor, and ultimately, to his suicide soon after.[38] Lollius had survived the disgrace of a military disaster but was evidently unable to weather this later political scandal. However, his name is far less infamous in history than that of Varus, despite their transgressions being little different.

The aftermath of the Lollian Disaster showed the danger the German tribes over the Rhine still posed. It should also have served as a forewarning to the Roman operations in Germany, of the risks of ambush posed by the unfamiliar forested terrain of the regions around the Rhine. Lollius himself was an example of how even an experienced, capable commander could be caught out by these circumstances. Only one legion was lost, and the defeat was more of an inconvenience than a danger, despite the high number of casualties. Although it would be more than twenty years before the next major disaster under Varus, the years between were far from free of threat for Rome.

Subsequent campaigning under Drusus the Elder

While the Lollian Disaster was a damaging and humiliating defeat, it did not dampen Imperial ambitions in Germany in the longer term, and perhaps further convinced Augustus of the need to subdue the German tribes. But while the battle had been an embarrassing defeat for Rome, it also gave Augustus a *casus belli* – a legitimate reason – for going to war with the tribes beyond the Rhine.[39] The campaigns were seen as sufficiently important that Augustus travelled to Gaul to oversee preparations. He would be absent from Rome for around three years, also spending some time in Hispania.[40]

The first phase of campaigning commenced in 15 BC, directed against the tribes in the Alpine regions that would later become the provinces of Raetia and Noricum.[41] There was growing resentment in these areas of Roman encroachment into their territory, and Raetian warbands were raiding into Roman territory with increasing frequency.[42] The campaign was initially led by Drusus the Elder (the younger brother of Tiberius, and Augustus' stepson), who at the time was only 22 years old. It was his first major command. Tiberius later joined the campaign, after he had completed a governorship of Gaul to which he had been appointed in 16 BC, the successor of Marcus Lollius; he had likely been put in the position to maintain the security of the Rhine and northern Gaul. Despite only being 26 years old, Tiberius had more military experience than his brother, having served as a military tribune in Spain during the Cantabrian Wars, and had led an army in the eastern provinces.[43] He brought additional legions to the Alpine conflict. One of those legions was likely the Nineteenth, commanded by Varus, as indicated by the luggage-tag naming him as the unit's legate (as discussed in Chapter 2). This was probably not the first time that Varus and Tiberius had served alongside each other, having likely crossed paths in Spain during the Cantabrian Wars. They may even have been brothers-in-law by this time, depending on whether Varus had married Vipsania Marcella by this point. Augustus' military appointments in this conflict indicate a willingness to entrust command to a younger generation, allowing them to develop their military abilities in the field from positions of leadership, without oversight from more-senior commanders. As discussed in Chapter 2, the Alpine conflict was in many ways a difficult conflict. The local populations attempted to use the topography against the Roman army, funnelling it into areas where the soldiers would be trapped by the landscape. Archaeological evidence suggests that more than once the Roman army was caught in a situation where they could have suffered a comprehensive defeat, but were largely able to extricate themselves; all the identified conflict sites from this war appear to be those of Roman victories. Despite the challenges, the Alpine conflict took a single season to complete. The war provided Varus and his fellow commanders with further experience of dealing with irregular warfare, in which local forces would try and avoid pitched battle at any cost, hoping to wear down Roman resistance by a variety of guerrilla tactics. The campaign had been fought in a hostile territory against an enemy who knew how to use the landscape to their own advantage, although it would ultimately fail to overcome the numerical and technological superiority of the Roman army. Varus also experienced his first command of the Nineteenth Legion, which would remain in the region through to his return in AD 7, taking part in many of the subsequent Roman campaigns against the Germans.

Later in 15 BC Drusus was appointed as governor of Gaul. Alongside numerous civic projects within the province, he also used his tenure to lay logistic and strategic foundations for further beyond the Rhine. Augustus was present in Gaul for some of these preparations, during a three-year absence from the city of Rome.[44] When campaigning in Germany began again in 12 BC, Drusus was appointed to command the invading army. His planning for the campaign was extensive, with new legionary bases established along the Rhine at Vechten, Nijmegen, Xanten, Neuss, Cologne, and Mainz.[45] A significant number of troops were transferred into the region, supplementing the units already stationed there. Drusus led a substantial force in Germany, probably comprising eight legions in total (First Germanica, Fifth Alaudae, Eighth Gemina, Fourteenth Gemina, Sixteenth Gallica, and the Seventeenth, Eighteenth and Nineteenth), supplemented by a large number of auxiliary units.[46]

The expedition across the Rhine in 12 BC was arguably more one of exploration than conquest. Drusus led some of his troops as far north as possible, and may have reached as far as the Baltic region.[47] The following year, Drusus led a campaign against the tribes living in the area roughly delineated by the Rhine and the Lippe. He found his advance was assisted by the fact that the tribes in the region were too busy fighting against each other to mount a serious resistance.[48] He likely reached as far as the source of the Lippe, around modern Bad Lippspringe, which lay in the territory of the Cherusci – not altogether far from where the events in the Teutoburg would take place two decades later. Drusus advanced as far as the Weser but was forced to turn back to the Rhine as winter was fast approaching, and the supplies left to the Roman army would not see them through a winter in hostile territory.[49]

During their return to the Rhine, the Romans received another warning of the potent danger that the Germans still posed. On the way back to the Rhine, Drusus found his army constantly harassed, leading at one point to a situation which could have turned into a devastating defeat for the Roman army:

> For the enemy harassed him everywhere by ambuscades, and once they shut him up in a narrow pass and all but destroyed his army; indeed, they would have annihilated them, had they not conceived a contempt for them, as if they were already captured and needed only the finishing stroke, and so came to close quarters with them in disorder. This led to their being worsted, after which they were no longer so bold, but kept up a petty annoyance of his troops from a distance, while refusing to come nearer.[50]

Drusus found himself the latest victim of a German ambush, which could have had far more devastating consequences than it did. None of the surviving historical sources give much of an account of the attack, and it is unclear how Drusus ended up walking into such a dangerous situation.[51] Despite coming so close to defeat, the battle was referred to as a 'brilliant victory' by Pliny the Elder.[52] It is not clear where the ambush took place, although it was clearly some distance beyond the Rhine. Pliny identifies the location as 'Arbalo', but it has thus far proved impossible to identify where this actually was.[53] It is clear from Dio that it was felt that there had been a very real possibility that Drusus and his men were close to being wiped out, and had been saved not through their own efforts, but because of German mistakes. Had things turned out differently, the defeat would have been devastating to both the Imperial family as well as wider Roman ambitions in Germany. Clearly, although the Romans were well aware of the threat posed by tribal ambushes, they had not yet worked out an effective way to neutralize the danger. As it was, the defeat did not do Drusus much longer-term harm, and soon after he was acclaimed by his men as 'Imperator', although Augustus held off from official confirmation of the title.[54]

In 10 BC, Drusus led yet another expedition across the Rhine, building on the progress made in the previous season. In that year he had left several military installations a short distance into German territory, manned by small garrisons. One of those forts, known as Aliso, was still occupied at the time of the Teutoburg, and would play an important role in the aftermath of the disaster.[55] From this time on, attempts were made to keep a permanent Roman presence, however small, in German territory – a sign that it was intended, over time, to become Roman territory. By early 10 BC, these forts were supplemented by a substantial number of new forts and depots built along the Lippe.[56] This new logistic network may have been created to support Roman campaigning deeper into Germany, potentially aiming to secure territory as far east as the Elbe. A large summer camp was established at Hedemünden, more than 200km beyond the Rhine, from which a large assemblage of Roman militaria has been recovered. By the summer of 10 BC, Drusus left the campaigning in Germany to his subordinates, travelling instead to Lugdunum (Lyon) for the dedication of a temple to the Tres Galliae ('Three Gauls'), and onwards to Rome to oversee political business. The absence of Drusus from the front line means there is little in the surviving sources about this period of Roman campaigning in Germany.

In 9 BC, Drusus was named consul for the first time, but did not stay in Rome for his year in office, departing once more to continue campaigning in Germany. He received reports that the area was relatively calm, suggesting that the military presence of Rome was not, as yet, sparking widespread rebellion among the tribes. Drusus set out from the fortress at Mainz, evidently keen that this year would see the Romans reach the River Elbe.[57] The campaign does not appear to have been an easy one. Although there is no substantial surviving narrative, brief or incidental references to the campaign suggest that Drusus and his men struggled, 'conquering with difficulty the territory traversed and defeating the forces that attacked him only after considerable bloodshed'.[58] Drusus himself was said to have been a brave fighter, eager for glory, who in battle sought hand-to-hand combat with German chieftains in the hope of winning the *spolia opima*, the armour of a defeated enemy leader which could only be taken in this way.[59] The Romans evidently reached the Elbe, but were unable to cross it, leading Drusus to set up victory trophies on the bank before withdrawing. It is unknown which point on the river they reached. Having advanced so far, the Romans turned back towards the Rhine. This move was said to have been influenced in part by a vision Drusus received, foretelling his death if he attempted to enter the lands beyond the Elbe.[60] Nevertheless, the advance was seen as a great achievement, confirming Roman dominance over the barbarian Germans. Most of the tribes were thought subjugated by this point, if not completely pacified.[61] It does not seem to be the case that Augustus intended to establish a province across the Rhine at this time, however, as illustrated by the fact that civic inscriptions at the time still drew a distinction between 'this' (i.e. the Roman) side of the Rhine, and the barbarian 'other' side.[62]

From the earliest campaigns of Drusus, the children of German chieftains were taken as hostages against their tribe's good behaviour.[63] These children – almost certainly eldest sons – were taken to Rome and raised by prominent elite families. Even the Imperial household took in some of these hostages, including (as mentioned previously) Maroboduus of the Marcomanni, who was raised within Augustus' household. The hope was that after being raised from early childhood within a Roman context, as adults these hostages would return to lead their tribes as friends of Rome, familiar with Roman custom and society. The hostages often returned home to their tribes as Roman citizens, further advertising the benefits of friendship with Rome. Many may have served in the Roman army as auxiliary commanders, giving them a further stake in the Imperial system. However, the policy was not without its dangers, and some of the hostages came back to haunt them – none more so than Arminius, the major protagonist against Varus in AD 9. Arminius had been a hostage raised in Rome, also serving as a cavalry commander in the auxilia before returning to Germany as chieftain of the Cherusci. Clearly, the exposure to Rome from an early period in life did not always guarantee enduring friendship.

The situation in Germany changed dramatically soon after Drusus the Elder turned back from the Elbe towards the Rhine, when he died unexpectedly at the age of just 29 years old. The circumstances of his death were mysterious, and no one seems to have been entirely clear on what actually happened. Dio says that he died of an unspecified illness, while Velleius states only that he was the victim of an 'unknown fate'.[64] Suetonius mentions that there were rumours at the time that Augustus arranged for his stepson to be poisoned, ostensibly because of Drusus' well-known Republicanism, although Suetonius was careful to note that he did not believe the allegations.[65] The only detailed reason comes from Livy, who suggests that Drusus died thirty days after fracturing his leg falling from his horse – with the length of time, presumably suggesting an infection/septicaemia or other complication from the break.[66] Drusus' death was evidently a shock back in Rome, and there must have been questions about how and when the German campaigns would continue in the absence of their influential former commander.

Any concerns about the future of Roman Imperial interests in Germany were quickly addressed. On hearing the news of Drusus' injury, Augustus had immediately despatched Tiberius to his brother's side.[67] He arrived shortly before Drusus died, and after his death accompanied the body to Rome for cremation, with the ashes interred in the Mausoleum of Augustus. Prior to Drusus' death, Tiberius had been campaigning in Dalmatia and Pannonia after a localized rebellion had broken out.[68] With this situation stabilized, Tiberius took his brother's place on the Rhine. Although likely prepared for an intensive series of campaigns, Tiberius probably had little to do but consolidate the victories won by Drusus. Velleius Paterculus provides a brief overview of Tiberius' campaigns in Germany:

> The burden of responsibility for this war was then transferred to Nero [Tiberius]. He carried it on with his customary valour and good fortune, and after traversing every part of Germany in a victorious campaign, without any loss of the army entrusted to him – for he made this one of his chief concerns – he so subdued the country as to reduce it almost to the status of a tributary province.[69]

Tiberius was awarded a triumph for his campaigns in 7 BC, and from this time on, parts of Germany beyond the Rhine were likely considered part of the Roman hegemony, their eventual incorporation into the territorial Empire a foregone conclusion. That said, Germany itself was far from pacified, and it is clear that Tiberius' campaigns did not lead to a formal province being established east of the Rhine. Roman influence in the region would grow from this point onwards, but there was ongoing conflict in the area between Rome and German tribes discontented with the Roman presence.

A substantial Roman military presence was maintained in the area, with five legions stationed at various bases along the Rhine, the command of which was given to a succession of senior military figures drawn from the Imperial regime. Despite the heavy presence of Roman troops in the region, Germany was an ongoing source of military problems. These were not dealt with by Tiberius, who 'retired' from public life in 6 BC, and did not return until AD 4. Several other commanders in charge of the Rhine legions were involved in further campaigning in Germany during Tiberius' self-imposed absence. One Rhine commander, Lucius Domitius Ahenobarbus, campaigned throughout German territory between 4 and 1 BC, reaching the Elbe and apparently even crossed it, as Drusus the Elder had held back from doing.[70] Conflict broke out again in the region in AD 1, when Marcus Vinicius was in command of the Rhine legions. Although details of what happened are scant, the conflict was of sufficient scale that Vinicius was awarded triumphal honours for his part in it.[71] In AD 4, after returning to Imperial service – this time as Augustus' heir – Tiberius launched a military campaign against several German tribes (including the Cherusci, Arminius' tribe), advancing as far as the Weser in the first year, and the Elbe in the second (AD 5).[72] Many of the German tribes who faced Tiberius in this period ended up surrendering without much of a fight, seemingly in awe of the power of the Roman army. By the time that Tiberius finished this campaign Germany was largely thought to be pacified, although it had not been organized into a formal province. Nevertheless, the situation in Germany was thought to have been largely stabilized by Tiberius. Velleius Paterculus claimed that after these latest campaigns there was 'nothing left' to be conquered east of the Rhine, beyond one potentially problematic client kingdom, that of the Marcomanni.[73] It was here that Tiberius would next focus his attention.

The Marcomanni, a tribe based in what is now the region of Bohemia, were ruled by a king/chieftain named Maroboduus, who was ostensibly a Roman ally. He had been raised in Rome, likely as a hostage for his tribe's good behaviour, living in the Imperial household and apparently while there had won the favour of Augustus.[74] He had returned to the Marcomanni around 9 BC as ruler, expanding his control to several other tribes in the surrounding area (including the Lugii, the Zumi, the Butones, the Mugilones, the Sibini, and the Semnones), becoming a powerful regional force. Worse, from the Roman perspective, Maroboduus had learned from the example set by the Roman army, and had created a large army – said to comprise 70,000 infantry and 4,000 cavalry – which he drilled to 'almost' Roman standards.[75] While not yet actively hostile to Rome, Augustus grew concerned with the question of *why* Maroboduus had decided to build up such a large, well-trained force. Furthermore, the king had apparently made it clear that he had the resources and will to defend himself against Roman aggression. In the spirit of typical Roman preclusive defence, in AD 6 Tiberius began preparations for a campaign against Maroboduus and the Marcomanni. A massive force of twelve legions was assembled, drawn from numerous provinces, particularly Illyria.[76] Significant logistic plans were put into place to support the army in the field, including the construction of new military installations. In particular, a legionary base at Marktbreit (in Bavaria, on the River Main) was probably established in anticipation of the campaign against the Marcomanni, likely to house the First Germanica and Fifth Alaudae legions ahead of an advance from the east.[77] However, this base, probably like many others, was constructed but never used. At the last minute, Tiberius called off the offensive, when his troops were just five days from Marcomannic territory. A much more pressing military concern had emerged elsewhere, which would need the entire army earmarked for the campaign against Maroboduus – the Illyrian (or Pannonian) Revolt.[78] The Marcomanni, for the time being, would have to wait.

The (Great) Illyrian or Pannonian Revolt – known in antiquity as the *Bellum Batonianum*, or 'Batonian War'[79] – was a serious test of Roman provincial management, and a major threat to the territorial integrity of the Empire.[80] It broke out in the relatively newly formed provinces of Illyricum, Dalmatia and Pannonia.[81] There had been problems in this region before, and Tiberius had previously been called upon to deal with a rebellion there in 9 BC, but this outbreak was on a completely different scale to anything which had been seen before. Velleius suggests that the Revolt provoked widespread fear within the Roman population, to the degree that '… such a panic did this war inspire that even the courage of Caesar Augustus, rendered steady and firm by experience in so many wars, was shaken with fear'.[82] Suetonius adds that the revolt was seen as the most serious foreign conflict since the Punic Wars against Carthage.[83] A large amount of Roman military manpower was required to face the rebels. A significant proportion of the available Roman legions were transferred to Pannonia and Illyria, with apparently fifteen legions and an equal-sized force of auxiliaries required to fight the rebellion. On paper this meant an army of between 100,000 and 150,000 soldiers, although manpower levels likely fluctuated significantly over time.[84] This movement of legions and auxiliary units left their home provinces under-garrisoned and potentially vulnerable themselves to internal unrest – something which indigenous leaders discontented with Roman rule would have been well aware of. Supplementing the legions were veteran soldiers, recalled to service due to the state of emergency Rome faced.[85] Levies of freedmen were also raised, funded by payments demanded from the wealthy. Tiberius was chosen to lead the suppression of the revolt, after the Senate insisted to Augustus that he was the only suitable candidate for the job. Velleius' description of Tiberius' conduct during the war, in which Velleius himself was a combatant, seem to more than justify the decision.[86] However, even with the massive resources allocated to Tiberius, and his abilities as a military commander, it took more than three years to suppress the revolt.

With Tiberius and his army otherwise occupied in Illyria and Pannonia for an indefinite period, Augustus needed a new plan for Germany. Although the region was considered to be largely pacified, a large Roman military presence was still maintained on the Rhine, and was in need of command. Although the planned offensive against the Marcomanni had been abandoned, Rome needed to maintain a readiness for further campaigning in Germany if needed. With much of the Empire's military resources focused on Illyricum it is unlikely that Augustus had any ambitious plans for Germany at this time, but those gains which had already been made would need protecting. The Roman presence east of the Rhine had grown sufficiently that it also needed oversight and management, particularly as more military installations and even settlements were being established.[87] What Augustus needed on the Rhine was a trusted officer who could take command of the legions and maintain the situation in the region until the conflict in Illyricum was over. Varus was an obvious and highly suitable candidate.

Varus' Appointment to the Rhine

Varus was appointed to the command of the Rhine legions at some point in AD 7. He replaced Gaius Sentius Saturninus, who had been in Germany since AD 4, and had served alongside Tiberius while there. This was the second time that Varus had taken a position over from Saturninus, having also succeeded him as governor of Syria; Saturninus had also, like Varus, previously served as governor of Africa. Varus was around 53 years old when he arrived in Germany, and highly experienced in both military and civilian provincial management. He was one of the more senior figures in the Roman administration, having been part of Augustus' professional circle for almost thirty years, as well as being his great-nephew by marriage; Varus was an obvious choice for the appointment. As discussed in the previous chapter, it is unclear what Varus had been doing between leaving Syria (sometime between 4 BC and AD 1), or what role he held immediately prior to his appointment to the Rhine. He may have fallen out of Imperial favour after Syria, perhaps linked to the retirement from public life of Tiberius' – his brother-in-law, and likely close friend – but it is equally possible that Varus held official roles in this period, but that references to them have simply not survived. Whatever other roles he had served, Varus' career overall, particularly his time in Syria, was clearly felt by Augustus to be sufficient experience for command on the Rhine. Varus had demonstrated his ability to cope with challenging situations and would be an obvious and viable candidate for even the most difficult appointments. One modern historian suggests that the marriage to Claudia Pulchra indicates that Varus was once more in the ascendancy, and that the balance of power was once more in his favour, whatever had happened over the previous years.[88]

Augustus had a history of appointing people that he knew and trusted in commands relating to the northern frontier zone – of the Rhine legions, and of Gaul. Tiberius and Drusus were the most prominent such individuals, but many other of the early appointments made to oversee the Rhine legions and the newly acquired German territories were also personal acquaintances of the emperor. In 4 BC, Augustus appointed his nephew-in-law, Lucius Domitius Ahenobarbus, as commander of the Rhine legions.[89] Marcus Vinicius, who had taken the command several years later (AD 1–4), was a friend of the emperor who socialized with him in private life.[90] Gaius Sentius Saturninus, Varus' immediate predecessor on the Rhine, had proved himself an able military commander and civilian administrator who had assisted Tiberius in his campaigns in German territory between AD 4 and 6. He might well have been left in post in Germany for longer had he not been asked by Tiberius to join him in Illyricum. Saturninus had evidently proved effective during his time in Germany and had taken part in the campaigns against several German tribes under the overall command of Tiberius. He had earlier served in the region as a legionary legate during the campaigns conducted by Augustus.[91] Velleius Paterculus was full of praise for him as a governor and a man, stating that he was:

> a man many-sided in his virtues, a man of energy and action, and of foresight, alike able to endure the duties of a soldier as he was well trained in them, but who, likewise, when his labours left room for leisure, made a liberal and elegant use of it, but with this reservation, that one would call him sumptuous and jovial rather than extravagant or indolent.[92]

The bar was evidently set high for those appointed to command on the Rhine.

The outbreak of the Illyrian Revolt was likely a major factor in Varus' appointment to the Rhine. Several legions were transferred from the river to fight in the Illyrian Revolt, meaning that whoever took the position would have to manage the region with a reduced garrison. As a result of the reduced manpower campaigning in the region was paused, likely in favour of consolidation of already-conquered territory and, as will be seen, the advance of Roman formal administration in the region. Despite Varus having a more significant military background than he is often given credit for, Augustus clearly decided that he would be most effectively deployed in Germany than Illyricum. This does not necessarily indicate that Varus lacked sufficient military ability to command in Illyricum, but rather, that the emperor considered him to be of greater use elsewhere. Indeed, as Varus was not appointed to the governorship of Germany until AD 6, it is possible that he even spent some time in Illyricum under Tiberius before being sent to the Rhine.

Varus seemed a natural choice to take on the administration of Germany at a time when conquest began to give way, at least in part, to consolidation. Whoever was appointed would need to maintain awareness of the potential threats within Germany but not be dominated by a need for campaigning, who could contribute to the longer-term political strategy in the region, while also being capable of quick action when required. Although much of his career had been spent in Rome, the eastern provinces, and Africa, he had previously served in Germany as commander of the Nineteenth Legion, giving him experience of the type of guerrilla warfare favoured by the local tribal populations. Although this service was now more than two decades earlier, it may have been sufficient for Varus to be considered experienced in the region. He may also have had further advice from his friend and former brother-in-law Tiberius about how to handle the Germans. Varus had served as governor in two provinces, both of which had come with a military garrison, which he had commanded to excellent effect in quelling the Jewish uprising during his time in Syria. Augustus would have been aware that whoever he appointed would need to have the ability to deal with armed insurrections from the indigenous population. The Roman army had faced several substantial ambushes in Germany, with outcomes ranging from disastrous to a near miss. The Lollian Disaster, and the potential disaster under Drusus the Elder, would no doubt have been on Augustus' mind as he considered who to appoint. The revolt in Judaea would have demonstrated to Augustus that Varus was capable of effectively and efficiently handling medium-level discontent in an effective and diplomatic manner. He had acted swiftly and decisively, and once victorious, had harshly punished the leaders of the rebellion but generally shown mercy to those who had done little more than follow their example. Augustus clearly felt that Varus would be equal to any military challenges raised by the Germans – especially as they were clearly considered on the way to being a pacified population by this point. However, it may not just have been low-level discontent overspilling that Augustus was worried about in the region. There was still the unsettled matter of the threat posed by Maroboduus and the Marcomanni, with an army of approximately 70,000 men theoretically ready to launch an offensive against Rome at any moment. Maroboduus had given the impression that his army was intended to defend his kingdom rather than to launch an attack, but there was no guarantee that the situation would remain the same, and Augustus was not an emperor to take unnecessary chances. Augustus may have considered it possible that Varus would have to act as the 'first response' against a large-scale invasion by the Marcomanni – his abilities as a military commander would certainly have been considered when deciding whether to appoint him to the Rhine.

Although there was a large military element to Varus' role on the Rhine, the strains that the Illyrian Revolt had placed on Rome made it unlikely that Augustus intended him to conduct any large-scale campaigns of conquest. The primary role of the legions would be responsive, rather than offensive. Varus was required to be an administrator and diplomat as well as a military commander, and to maintain the status quo in the region as much as possible. Social and cultural changes were beginning to spread in Germany as a result of the Roman presence in the region, and as the main representative of Rome in the region, Varus would have been involved with the oversight of much of this. Varus had at least some experience in financial administration, developed from the earlier stage of his career when he served as a quaestor during Augustus' tour of the eastern provinces. His time in Syria had also introduced him to the type of diplomacy which was necessary in frontier provinces, particularly dealing with political issues between Rome and client leaders. He would have been more than capable of implementing whatever policies Augustus decided were appropriate for Germany at that time. Varus' career profile largely matched that of individuals sent previously to the Rhine, particularly Gaius Sentius Saturninus, and he had reached a sufficient level of seniority to be entrusted with the role. It cannot have come as a huge surprise when he was appointed to the Rhine in AD 7.

Varus' Role in Germany

It is unclear how developed Germany was in Roman terms by the time that Varus arrived on the Rhine, and how it was being administrated. Some suggest that by AD 7 'Germany was organized as a province, except that regular taxation was apparently not yet imposed',[93] or note that Germany was already being exploited as if it were a province by this period.[94] As such, Varus' role may not have been just that of the military commander of the Rhine legions, as his predecessors had been, but an official who was to take a wider administrative role as well, perhaps even becoming the first governor of a new provincial territory.[95] Others argue that it was not administrated as a province in any form, and fell entirely under the jurisdiction of Gallia Belgica.[96] The ancient sources do not provide much help on this issue. Velleius refers to Varus as 'a general in command of an army' rather than a governor, and criticized almost every activity he undertook that was not military in nature.[97] This would suggest that Varus was not a governor, but just the commander of the Rhine legions. But Dio *does* refer to him as the governor of Germany, and furthermore, to Germany itself as a province.[98] He makes a distinction between the territory which came under Roman control, which he refers to as 'Germania' (Γερμανία) and the unconquered regions, which he calls 'Keltike' (Κελτική). This creates a difficult situation in trying to work out exactly what role Varus was actually appointed to, and whether Germany was considered a province or not at this time. In theory, Velleius should provide more accuracy, with Dio having become confused about the situation at a distance of almost 200 years. On the other hand, perhaps Velleius was trying to minimize the level to which Rome thought it had established control in Germany by suggesting that no attempt had yet been made to make it a province, lessening the humiliation of its subsequent abandonment. The question matters in terms of what Varus' role on the Rhine was intended to be, either purely military, or also involving elements of administrative organization and provincial development. Unfortunately, as there is such uncertainty about the exact status of the territories east of the Rhine at this time, it is difficult to know exactly what Varus' role would have been. He did undertake elements of civic governance while in Germany, it is difficult to know whether this was in his official capacity, or simply as an incidental consequence of being Rome's main representative in the region. What is clear is that Varus' authority, whether as governor or commander, would have varied depending on which region of Germany was concerned. Cassius Dio suggests that Roman control of Germany was only partial even by AD 9, limited to the areas which had been militarily subdued, with other areas still completely independent and hostile.[99] Varus would have to find a way to work with both of these types of region.

Whatever policies Varus carried out in Germany would likely have been guided by Augustus. Trusted officials were often given a large degree of autonomy in how they conducted themselves while in position, particularly during military campaigning in the absence of the emperor, although the degree of initiative permitted may have varied between individuals.[100] But it is likely that the overall direction of their actions was communicated by the emperor, potentially at their appointment and later (see fuller discussion in chapter 4). It has already been seen that while in charge of Syria, Varus was in frequent contact with Augustus, providing him with intelligence from the province, likely to inform the emperor of the 'on the ground' view that could help to shape his decisions. Varus appears to have been a willing agent of the emperor during his governorships, implementing policy as instructed – but capable of acting under his own initiative when events were too rapid for him to consult with Augustus before taking action.

Whether Varus was appointed as a governor or a commander, it is clear that he was intended to undertake a degree of military activity. Velleius Paterculus complained that Varus wasted the opportunity of a summer campaign by holding legal tribunals instead, suggesting that he was supposed to take his army out into the field, at least on occasion.[101] It is unclear whether this wasted summer was in AD 7, 8, or even 9, just months before the Teutoburg took place. Velleius only complains about this happening once though, suggesting that Varus may have led an expedition in the other summer(s) he was present on the Rhine. With the Illyrian Revolt still raging, it is unlikely that Varus was meant to launch any ambitious offensives, and was more likely intended to consolidate recent acquisitions east of the Rhine, and remind the local population of the power of the Roman army.

The command in Germany came with a substantial military garrison. Varus had the command of five legions, each with a main base along the Rhine, from which they could advance during the summer for low-level campaigning, peace-keeping or policing, and diplomatic missions. Three of these legions were the ill-fated Seventeenth, Eighteenth and Nineteenth legions, who were likely stationed on the lower Rhine under Varus' direct command, supplemented by the First Germanica and Fifth Alaudae, who were stationed on the upper river.[102] The First and Fifth were under the command of Lucius Nonius Asprenas, Varus' nephew by his youngest sister and her husband of the same name.[103] The younger Asprenas had previously served with his uncle as a military tribune in Syria.[104] The Seventeenth and Eighteenth legions are likely to have been stationed at either Xanten (Castra Vetera), Oberaden or Haltern (their occupation of whichever fortress was sufficiently time-limited that little record or trace was left). The Nineteenth Legion was at one point posted to Haltern, as evidenced by the find of a lead ingot bearing the legion's mark at the site. It may also have spent some time at Oberaden. The military picture which emerges from this period is of relative flexibility, with legions moving around fluidly according to demand. Due to the exigencies of the Illyrian Revolt, which had taken almost all the available manpower from the province, Varus would have had a lesser force than he might otherwise have commanded in Germany, and a certain part of his army would have to stay on the Rhine year-round, to prevent German raiding parties from crossing into Gaul. He would also have been aware that there would be few reinforcements to call upon if anything went wrong while he was on campaign. Varus, or Augustus, may well therefore have decided to be more cautious in their military ambitions for Germany than they might otherwise have been. However, Velleius clearly saw Varus' lack of campaigning as neglect of his military duty. Further, there is an underlying implication that, had Varus campaigned more vigorously, the Germans may have come to respect and fear him as a commander, and might not have dared to plan the attack at the Teutoburg

In addition to military campaigning, Varus may also have been instructed to oversee the process of developing Roman administration in the region. Even if Germany was being administrated as a provincial territory – and this is far from certain – it was in the very early stages of development. While 'Roman' settlements were beginning to appear, and Roman goods starting to appear on the market, the region still lacked the fundamental infrastructure of a Roman province, particularly a road network.[105] This more civic aspect did not necessarily take precedence over military concerns, but may have been an important facet of Varus' remit in Germany nonetheless. Varus may have been one of the first – if not the first – officials on the Rhine whose role was not exclusively military, for whom at least some of the Germans could have been considered subjects of the Roman Empire. Roman presence east of the Rhine had resulted in significant changes to German life by AD 7.[106] Augustus may not have had a pre-determined strategy beyond conquest and domination in Germany, but the growing pacification in the region which resulted from Roman campaigning began to change the lives of the population. From around 7 BC, some of the regions east of the Rhine were on the way to becoming *de facto* Roman territories, regardless of the position of the Imperial administration.

What is clear is that the German territories were undergoing varying levels of cultural change in the early first century AD, in a process which clearly predated the arrival of Varus on the Rhine. Dio gives the clearest – if still limited – summation of the processes underway in Germany between the conquests and Varus' governorship, and the attitude of the Germans to the changes:

> I shall now relate the events which had taken place in Germany during this period. The Romans were holding portions of it – not entire regions, but merely such districts as happened to have been subdued, so that no record has been made of the fact – and soldiers of theirs were wintering there and cities were being founded. The barbarians were adapting themselves to Roman ways, were becoming accustomed to hold markets, and were meeting in peaceful assemblages. They had not, however, forgotten their ancestral habits, their native manners, their old life of independence, or

the power derived from arms. Hence, so long as they were unlearning these customs gradually and by the way, as one may say, under careful watching, they were not disturbed by the change in their manner of life, and were becoming different without knowing it.[107]

Several important changes in Germany in this early period are highlighted by Dio's brief description. Roman troops were wintering in German territory, rather than returning to the Rhine after the summer, as commanders had been careful to do during periods of conquest and expansion. These actions suggest a certain degree of security, that these territories were no longer considered overly hostile, and that it was not a risk to leave a garrison in an area within which they could easily fall into trouble if the local population turned against them. Other changes likely reflected Imperial policy in the region. In Germany more widely, the indigenous population was seemingly being introduced to the more palatable aspects of traditional Roman life – the holding of markets, and peaceful political meetings in particular. These new ways of living did not immediately supplant the old ways – it seems clear that much of the population remembered life before the Romans arrived – but evidently did not seem overly disturbed or culturally shocked by the changes, which were introduced slowly. The point of Roman policy in Germany at this time was not so much that the Romans would make the Germans into Romans, but that they would let the Germans do it to themselves.[108]

Dio also notes that new 'cities' were developing east of the Rhine. Until relatively recently, it was difficult to verify this claim, as no Roman settlements had been found in the territories beyond the Rhine, but archaeological discoveries have provided some illumination about the creation of new towns/cities soon after the German territories had been conquered. Of particular interest are the remains of a Roman settlement discovered in 1990 a short distance east of the small town of Waldgirmes, approximately 100km beyond the Rhine and some 50km north of Frankfurt.[109] The settlement appears to almost certainly be that of a civilian town, rather than a military installation, the first such Roman foundation beyond the Rhine. A few military artefacts were recovered from the settlement, but these probably belonged to a small Roman garrison sent to the site to survey it and prepare for the construction of the town.[110] However, it was not without military protection, as there was a legionary base nearby at Dorlar, less than 2km southeast of Waldgirmes. However, Waldgirmes does not appear to have been directly related to the legionary base, nor one of the informal civilian settlements which often developed outside Roman military installations, but a purpose-built town which may even have been intended to function as an early administrative centre.[111] The site included a large building in the middle, with an open area at its centre, interpreted as a forum of the type typically found in Roman settlements. The building was constructed from local stone in its earliest phases, almost certainly indicating that the settlement was intended to be permanent. Within the central courtyard, remains of a life-size gilded equestrian statue, almost certainly of Augustus, were discovered, including the head of the horse, and parts of one of the legs.[112] Again, this suggests that the settlement at Waldgirmes was intended to be far more than a temporary position held for a season or two. It seems clear that Augustus intended to develop and maintain a long-term Roman presence in the area, and significantly, that civilian settlements were beginning to develop.

The Imperial authorities had also become aware of the natural resources that could be extracted from Germany, greatly increasing the economic benefits of occupying and holding the regions east of the Rhine. Metals in particular were in demand, particularly lead. There is evidence from the last decade of the first century BC of Imperial control of lead mining areas in what is now the Sauerland region, suggesting that Augustus had authorized the exploitation of these lands for mining operations soon after the conquests of Drusus the Elder and Tiberius.[113] The Romans were aware that there were no significant reserves of gold or silver, noting that perhaps as a consequence the local population little valued artefacts made from such metals.[114] The newly-conquered German territories were evidently being exploited economically from an early period, far in advance of Varus' arrival on the Rhine.

The evidence of the archaeology suggests that there was a significant degree of cultural and material change in the regions east of the Rhine by AD 7, regardless of whether it was being administrated as a provincial territory or not. Most of these developments pre-dated Varus' arrival. In general, the changes do not appear to have met with outright hostility, perhaps because, as Dio suggested, they were so gradual that the Germans did not recognize them. But also, prior to Varus' governorship, many of the changes appear to have been what might be thought of as 'positive' ones – introducing the indigenous population to marketplaces and other Roman amenities, with little demand as yet placed on them as subjects of Rome. In particular, the issue of taxation does not appear to have been raised in these earlier years.[115]

It is likely that Varus was intended to support the pro-Roman cultural change in the region, continuing the process which had emerged over the previous two decades. He may even have aimed to increase its speed and scale where possible. But he understood that any civic administration would have to be balanced against the need to maintain the security of the Rhine, and the Roman territory which lay beyond. Whether by campaigning or diplomacy, he had to balance these two requirements, and act as both an administrator and a commander – a difficult task, but one which he had managed in Syria with great success. But the key thing to note is that Varus was not responsible for the *introduction* of many of these changes, but their maintenance and potential expansion. He was not the first commander on the Rhine to oversee substantial changes in Germany, but was simply responsible for overseeing the next phase of activity. Most of the changes seen thus far had not prompted any negative reaction from the German population. Unfortunately for Varus, the relative peace of his first years on the Rhine would soon be revealed to have masked a growing discontent among some parts of the tribal populations, with devastating results.

A growing discontent?

The changes in Germany which followed the Roman campaigning were not met by universal discontent from the indigenous population. The Germans were, so one Roman historian claimed, 'adapting themselves to Roman ways', as part of a slow-but-steady process.[116] The changes which had started to emerge as a result of the direct Roman occupation of some regions beyond the Rhine did not experience an instant backlash from the locals, and some elements were seemingly not only tolerated, but becoming part of the everyday life of the German population. As discussed previously, it is likely that part of Varus' job was to support and encourage this process, and perhaps to introduce new elements of 'Roman' life to the region.

However, the consensus among the ancient historians at least is that Varus went too far too fast in overseeing the process. Both Velleius and Cassius Dio, the best sources for this period, make the accusation that he mistakenly treated the region and its people as though they had already been completely pacified, which far from reflected the reality.[117] The campaigns in Germany were sufficiently recent that a majority of the population could remember life before the Romans crossed the Rhine. Many of them maintained aspects of life as it had been before Rome had arrived in the region: 'they had not forgotten their ancestral habits, their native manners, their old life of independence, or the power derived from arms'.[118] But Varus, according to Velleius, did not see this, and instead 'he entertained the notion that the Germans were a people who were men only in limbs and voice', whose fighting spirit had been broken and who would pose no further threat to Rome.[119] Dio goes further, suggesting that Varus felt a contempt towards the Germans that saw him treat them as though they had the status of slaves, completely subject to Roman power.[120] Varus' attitudes towards the Germans, so the ancient historians suggest, led him to oversee changes to the region for which the local population was not yet ready. As Dio noted, the Germans were slowly adapting themselves to Roman customs, contented as long as the changes did not become obvious to them – but Varus, the historian suggests, threw a stark light on the process by acting more rapidly than the population was ready for, and in doing so, bred discontent among the people.

Although the specific actions Varus carried out in Germany are mostly not discussed in any of the ancient sources, it is possible to suggest the broad shape of Roman policy in the region during his governorship. Velleius Paterculus suggests that Varus' time in Germany saw an increased use of Roman legal procedures to settle local tribal disputes, replacing the Germanic system of settling such disputes through combat.[121] Velleius argued that Varus became so entangled in introducing Roman law to Germany and arbitrating disputes that he forgot where he was – a newly conquered frontier territory, with a population that was not yet to be trusted – and acted as though he were a praetor back in Rome, 'administering justice in the forum'.[122] On realizing that Varus could be distracted from campaigning by legal procedure, the Germans apparently submitted a continuous stream of fictitious lawsuits which the governor was called upon to address; he apparently did so, lest the Germans slip back into the habit of fighting to settle the issues. In this context, the failure of Varus to campaign over one summer appears almost a deliberate consequence of German action – the governor was kept safely busy and the Germans elsewhere were kept safe.

Dio suggests another potential cause of discontent provoked by Varus – in this case, financial. He suggested that Varus began to 'extract' money from the Germans as though they were part of a 'subject nation', in a way that evidently appears to have gone down badly with the population.[123] It is not clear what payments Dio was referring to. The imposition of tribute payments on newly conquered territories – not a tax – was a normal phenomenon after the completion of a successful Roman campaign. As such, the implication may be that the money Varus 'extracted' from the Germans represented the first attempt to draw a tax from the region, although it could simply have been a higher rate of tribute, perhaps to help pay for the conflict in Illyricum. Whatever it was, it went down badly.[124] For Dio, this financial aspect was the main cause of the discontent which began to emerge:

To this they [the Germans] were in no mood to submit, for the leaders longed for their former ascendancy and the masses preferred their accustomed condition to foreign domination.[125]

Even if the payments demanded were a form of tribute, taxation would likely not have been far behind, leading to the Germans, like other subjected peoples, in effect paying for the very soldiers and administration that repressed them. Velleius does not mention any financial elements to the discontent provoked by Varus in Germany, although it was perhaps to be understood from the comments made immediately prior about Varus embezzling money in Syria that the same might well be the case in Germany, without any explicit accusation being made.

Another perspective on German discontent is provided by Florus, who suggested that it was Varus' moral corruption that particularly provoked problems in the new provincial territories.[126] He accuses Varus of having administrated with cruelty, licentiousness and pride, and of believing that the Germans were sufficiently subdued that they could be completely controlled by the law alone. Florus' account for the reasons behind the battle were popular in the nineteenth century, and Varus' cruel and inappropriate treatment of the Germans was considered a major contributing factor to the building of discontent and the eventual outbreak of revolt.[127] But there is little in the historical record to substantiate Florus' claims of cruelty during Varus' administration, although this does not necessarily mean that it was absent from the Roman regime, perhaps even originating at a lower level than Varus' command. But Florus' account suggests that the German population saw the imposition of any level of Roman law as being crueller than active conflict.[128] By this measure, it is difficult to imagine how any Roman official on the Rhine could have avoided accusations of cruelty. Had it not been Varus in position, the same accusations may have been attached to whoever had been appointed to command in his place. There are even some indications that Varus was responsive to German needs during his governorship, willing to listen to and grant requests and favours, even on issues of security. Cassius Dio recounted that Varus was willing to send detachments of his soldiers to German settlements, where they acted as police or guards as required.[129] Dio saw this as a negative action – that Varus should have kept his legions together rather than weakening them in this way – but it is interesting to note that these detachments were made at German request, rather than the troops being imposed on the communities by the Roman authorities.[130] Although the troops were requested specifically for the hidden purpose of reducing the manpower of the legions, the fact that Varus agreed to the German requests suggests that the remit of the Roman army beyond the Rhine was viewed as encompassing policing and peacekeeping duties in addition to active conquest – but that the presence of soldiers was not necessarily forced on local communities, but granted when requested. Even Velleius, usually hostile to Varus, acknowledged that he acted in Germany with the best of intentions, even if he disagreed with the governor's priorities.[131] It may instead have been generalized disapproval of and scorn for the Roman way of life more generally that the Germans found distasteful, suggesting that they may have responded this way irrespective of who was imposing the changes or how they did it.[132]

By AD 9 discontent with the Roman presence in the region had grown to the extent that some were willing to consider rebellion against Rome. How widespread the discontent was is unknown. None of the written sources give an indication of whether the majority of the population engaged with the movement against Rome or not, and it is unlikely that everyone east of the Rhine turned against Rome in the years preceding the Teutoburg. One modern historian has suggested that it is inaccurate to see the events in the Teutoburg as a general uprising, arguing that it should instead be seen as a mutiny in which only a small part of the German population participated, mostly those who had been recruited into the Roman auxilia.[133] Whatever the scale, internal problems and rebellions were not unusual in recently conquered territories, and they were usually suppressed relatively quickly. Only rarely did they develop into longer-term conflicts; examples like the ongoing Illyrian Revolt were unwelcome but rare exceptions.

The leader of the German resistance against Rome was Arminius, chieftain of the Cherusci tribe, born around 19 BC. The Cherusci had formed an alliance with Rome *circa* 12 BC, when Arminius' father Segimerus (or Sigimer), brokered a peace during the campaigns of Drusus.[134] Arminius was sent to Rome as a young child, probably aged 5 or 6 years old, where he was raised in the household of an unknown elite family.[135] Arminius had a younger brother, known only as Flavus, who was likely also sent to Rome, and was probably raised in the same household as his brother. The brothers were raised as Latin speakers, in addition to their native language. Tacitus noted that Arminius was a capable Latin speaker through to his later years, who used the language even under stressful circumstances.[136] As young adults, both Arminius and Flavus joined the Roman army, likely around the turn of the first century AD. Arminius was promoted to an auxiliary commander, likely leading a troop of Cherusci-recruited cavalry.[137] He may have served on campaign in Armenia – one suggestion for his name is that it is an honorific for an achievement during that conflict[138] – and/or under Tiberius either in Germany, or in Illyricum during the early stages of the revolt.[139] It is possible that Arminius crossed paths with Varus during his military service. At some stage Arminius and his brother became Roman citizens, and Arminius had been granted equestrian rank, making him part of the second-highest social class in Rome.[140] In just over two decades, Arminius had gone from Germanic chieftain's son to part of the Roman social establishment – and would make the reverse journey before too much longer.

Arminius' service in the Roman army was a key factor in the events that would transpire in AD 9. Firstly, it made him a trusted figure, 'part of the club' despite his German background. Roman opinion on Germans was low at this time, typified by Velleius' statement that they were 'a race born to lying'.[141] But Arminius' citizenship, and equestrian status evidently went a long way towards him being viewed by Rome as one of 'us', and no longer one of 'them'. Despite his later actions against Rome, it is clear that he was previously at home in Roman society. But it also had another consequence, deadly and unforeseen. Arminius' service in the Roman army gave him first-hand experience of how the military operated in the field, and how they responded to situations such as ambushes and surprise attacks.[142] This insight into the army's weaknesses, harmless enough in the hands of a loyal ally such as Arminius was thought to be, could be weaponized by an auxiliary who turned against Rome, who could exploit these vulnerabilities to his own advantage. In theory, this was not supposed to happen. The system that Arminius was subjected to – being raised in Rome as a hostage, then serving in the military – was intended to foster a deep-seated loyalty to the Roman state, meaning that the individual would not pose any threat in the future. It appears usually to have worked – indeed, it was even effective for Arminius' brother Flavus, who remained loyal to Rome in AD 9 and beyond, even fighting against Arminius several years later.[143]

Arminius became chieftain of the Cherusci in AD 7/8, when he was around 25/26 years old, returning to Germany at roughly the same time as Varus was appointed governor.[144] As a tribal leader, Arminius may have remained a serving member of the Roman army, serving as an officer under Varus as part of his staff.[145] The two may also have been friends. Dio suggests that Varus and Arminius spent a significant amount of time together during the earlier part of the governorship, calling them 'constant companions', and noting that they often dined together.[146] But at the same time, Arminius was building up support in Germany for an uprising against Rome, despite it not being clear how popular support was among the peoples who lived east of the Rhine. He was evidently well-placed to do so, and was able to unify the Germans to a much greater degree than any of his predecessors. One historian notes that he must have been 'a charismatic leader who took advantage of the confused socio-psychological state of the Germans to build himself a power-position beyond that of customary German leaders'.[147] His leadership qualities no doubt contributed to the devastating impact of the Teutoburg battle. But Varus was as yet unaware of any problems with the man he thought was a friend and ally.

On paper, Arminius would have appeared as a loyal and trustworthy friend of Rome, but the reality would soon be revealed.

Arminius' plot

It is unclear when the discontent provoked by the Roman administration in Germany began to approach the level of open revolt. According to Velleius, Arminius was the key instigator of the revolt, initially only involving a small group of co-conspirators (but later adding to their numbers), convincing them of Rome's vulnerability at that particular moment.[148] Why it was decided to lead an uprising in AD 9 is unclear. Varus' failure to campaign over a summer season (probably in AD 8) may have been used to suggest that he was a weaker leader than most others who had commanded on the Rhine – or a break from hostilities may have blunted the edge of German fear of Rome. However, none of the sources give any indication as to why Arminius was sufficiently discontented with Rome to plot a revolt against their presence in Germany, nor whether he had any ambitions beyond simply driving the Romans back across the Rhine. As such, it is impossible to say whether Arminius had been planning this for years before he was back in Germany, while still on active service with the Roman army, or whether it was something he decided to do only after he became chieftain. Whether there was a single incident which led him to this decision, or a cumulation of outrages is equally uncertain. Certainly, the recent Roman preparations for a campaign against Maroboduus, an ally of Rome raised in the Imperial household itself, would have demonstrated to Arminius that there could be little reward for a chieftain who remained loyal to Rome if the emperor decided that he posed a threat. The Marcomanni may have been spared from the planned invasion by the outbreak of the Illyrian Revolt, but he, and other chieftains in the region, can hardly have been unaware of Roman intentions to invade the kingdom, despite his ostensible alliance with Rome. Arminius may have learned a cautionary lesson from this – that friendship with Rome was conditional on remaining weak enough (militarily) for the relationship to be one of dependence, not of equals. Once your independent military strength exceeded a certain point, you could become a target in the name of defence, without ever having actually directly threatened Rome.

He may have had little difficulty raising support from among the Germans, despite their growing acceptance of some elements of Roman culture. The Roman sources make it clear that the German population had been treated with much brutality in the cause of Roman expansion. Velleius reveals that they had been 'slaughtered like cattle' in the past, with no indication that the Romans had been wrong to treat them this way.[149] It is not difficult to see how resentment caused by this kind of treatment could have been stoked into rebellion by an inspired leader – particularly as the Germans had not, according to the Roman sources, abandoned the militaristic elements of their culture.[150] However, as mentioned previously, it is unknown whether Arminius was leading a popular uprising or a movement more akin to an internal military revolt. If it were the latter, the reasons for Arminius' actions may not necessarily be found in the Roman treatment of the German population more widely, but perhaps over a more localized issue affecting just Arminius and the German auxiliary recruits.

The sources suggest that Arminius was keenly aware that AD 9 was a suitable time for such an uprising, observing that the Roman authorities in Germany (especially Varus) were completely unprepared for any sort of uprising, and were therefore not looking for any signs of it. As mentioned previously, according to the ancient historians Varus appears to have been under the impression that the region had been almost completely pacified and was loyal to Rome, and posed no significant security risk.[151] Arminius evidently decided to capitalize on the governor's complacency. According to Velleius, he judged 'that no one could be more quickly overpowered than the man who feared nothing, and that the most common beginning of disaster was a sense of security'.[152] Varus, as he appears in the sources, was far too complacent. However, there may be other reasons why Arminius decided to launch his attack while Varus was still governor. His relationship with Arminius may also have been a factor in the timing of the revolt. Varus had been in Germany for at least two years at a time when governors usually served for three years, making it possible, even likely, that Varus would be recalled to Rome the next year, possibly before the next campaigning season. Arminius may have felt that his prospects of victory were better against Varus than they might be against someone else, and therefore potentially ensured that the ambush took place while Varus was still in office. The two knew each other well, spending a lot of time together both through work and leisure – the very relationship which would protect Arminius when accusations of plotting were made against him. If Arminius felt that he knew Varus sufficiently well that he could effectively anticipate his response to the ambush and subsequent decisions in the field, this would give him an edge in battle that he would not have against Varus' successor. Arminius may also have felt that he was unlikely to be able to gain the trust of another governor so quickly. On a wider scale, Arminius would also have been aware that while the Illyrian Revolt raged the Rhine army would be as weakened as it ever would be, and that Varus would be able to call on little additional manpower. Staging the uprising while Rome's military attention was distracted may have been an intentional decision, integral to its potential success. He may also have hoped to join forces with the rebels in Illyricum and combine their strength against Rome, which would have presented a far more significant challenge to Rome than facing each force separately.[153] Unfortunately for Arminius, the Illyrian Revolt ended a few days before the attack in the Teutoburg, although the Germans were probably unaware of this at the time of their attack.[154]

The level of preparations suggest that Arminius' plan of action was months, even a year or more, in the making. The conspirators were aware that between the troops stationed in German territory, and the legions on the Rhine, the numerical superiority of the Roman army made open revolt unwise.[155] This is why in advance of the battle Arminius aimed to fragment Varus' army as much as possibly by having him send out multiple detachments to local missions – guarding settlements and provisions, and policing against robbers – the kind of roles that a Roman army often undertook in pacified territories.[156] Based on what happened in AD 9, the plot may always have intended to lure Varus and the rest of his army far from the Rhine, and to ambush them while they were in inhospitable territory. Certainly sufficient plans were put in place to suggest that this was not a last-minute decision.

Although the German plotters no doubt took precautions to keep their plans a secret, rumours of the uprising eventually leaked out, and reached the ears of some Germans who were more loyal to Rome than Arminius had proved. One of these, a prominent member of the Cherusci tribe named Segestes, disclosed the plot to Varus.[157] However, Varus did not heed the warning. Segestes was a reliable source of intelligence, at least in theory. He was a long-term ally of Rome, and like Arminius, had been granted Roman citizenship by Augustus. He did not see his support of Rome as a betrayal of his tribe, and claimed that he was working in the interests of both Germany and Rome by advocating for his home country to be at peace with, and part of, the Roman Empire.[158] According to Tacitus, Segestes warned Varus multiple times about plotting within the province, eventually suggesting that the governor arrest all the German chieftains, including Arminius – and even himself – as this would prevent any immediate uprising. He could then work out who was actually involved in the plot later.[159] However, Varus appears to have paid little attention to the warning; evidently Arminius' loyalty to Rome was not in question. It did not help matters that there was already bad blood between Segestes and Arminius, as the latter had married Segestes' daughter Thusnelda without her father's permission, in spite of the fact that she was already promised in marriage to someone else.[160] Varus appears to have dismissed Segestes' warning as an attempt by the German to make trouble for his hated son-in-law.

It would later become clear that Varus had placed his trust in the wrong man, but it was an understandable error to make. Arminius was a Roman citizen, an auxiliary officer, and likely a member of Varus' staff, as well as a friend and companion to the governor. Segestes, while also a Roman citizen and generally well-regarded by Rome, did not have the same personal relationship with Varus as Arminius did, and was clearly not held in the same regard by the governor. Any doubts Varus had could have been quickly dispelled by Arminius claiming that Segestes' accusations were made out of hatred. But Segestes' warning about the plot was one of the last chances Varus had to avoid disaster in the Teutoburg. Events appear to have moved quickly after Segestes spoke to Varus, and 'after this first warning, there was no time left for a second'.[161] Unfortunately for Varus, and the men of the Seventeenth, Eighteenth and Ninenteenth legions, the opportunity was lost. As a result, at some point in the September of AD 9 they walked straight into the ambush that Segestes had tried to help them avoid. The consequences for the commander and his men would be devastating.

Chapter 6

Varus in the Teutoburg: The Battle and its Aftermath

When Varus set out from the Rhine in the early spring or summer of AD 9, he can have had little idea that he would not live to make the return journey at the end of the campaigning season. He had been warned about Arminius' plotting by a credible source, but chose to disregard this intelligence, and continued to act as though there was no risk posed. In doing so, his fate was sealed, as was that of the legions that would accompany him into the Teutoburg. Arminius' plot culminated in an attack on the Roman marching column as it headed from its summer base back towards the Rhine, at some point in the late summer or early autumn of AD 9, most likely in September. It was not a pitched battle, in which two armies fought by mutual consent, but an ambush of a Roman army on the march, who had not expected to be attacked. The marching column was likely not attacked all at the same time, but in many individual phases, at numerous different locations along its length. As discussed in the previous chapter, Arminius had probably been planning the attack for some time, preparing to use his experience in the Roman *auxilia* to exploit the weaknesses of a Roman army on the march. A running engagement ensued that was fought in multiple episodes across three or four days. By the end, thousands of Roman soldiers lay dead in the Teutoburg, including Varus himself, and Rome would have to cope with the aftermath of a humiliating and potentially dangerous defeat.

The battle in the Teutoburg has become one of the most infamous events of the Imperial period, with far-reaching consequences that will be discussed in detail in the following chapter. This chapter focuses on what actually happened during the battle, using both archaeological and historical evidence to reconstruct the events of the battle over its multi-day run. There is a particular focus on Varus' actions both in the lead-up to the attack and once the ambush had been launched.

Reconstructing the battle – the sources of evidence

There is relatively little historical documentation associated with the battle in the Teutoburg. Only a few sources give any general narrative of the engagement, and most have issues with their reliability that means their accuracy cannot be assumed. As mentioned in the introduction, there is discussion (of varying length) of the events in the Teutoburg in AD 9 in four main sources: the works of (in order of publication) Velleius Paterculus, Tacitus, Florus, and Cassius Dio.[1] Varus and the Teutoburg are also mentioned, but not discussed in any detail, in several other works, including by Strabo, Manilius, Frontinus, Seneca the Elder, and Pliny the Elder.[2] These disparate and often-brief references provide some insight into the battle, but are far from comprehensive in describing what happened in the Teutoburg. In many instances details mentioned in one source are completely absent from others, with no indication of whether their omission should be taken as an indication of their inaccuracy, or that the other author either did not know the information, or chose not to include it. The main account of the battle in antiquity, used as a source by other ancient writers, was probably Pliny the Elder's *Bella Germaniae*, written in the mid-first century AD. Unfortunately, as previously discussed, this work has not survived, although its influence may be seen in the works which post-dated it (every account of the battle except that of Velleius Paterculus).

Velleius Paterculus and Cassius Dio provide the longest surviving accounts of the battle, supplemented by a gloriously gory vignette from Florus, and Tacitus' description of the battlefield six years after the event in his *Annals*. Velleius Paterculus was a contemporary of the events, a military officer himself, and almost certainly knew Varus, and perhaps other higher-ranking officers in his army. He would have been well-placed to provide a comprehensive account of the battle, but unfortunately, his description of events is both brief and biased. In the text, he notes that the passage is intended only to be a lamenting overview of the battle, saying that he has dealt with the engagement in detail in a larger work, which unfortunately has not survived.[3] The account that does survive is dominated by the need to condemn Varus personally for the defeat. Velleius was critical of almost every action that Varus took in Germany, from his interactions with the German people to his response to the threat posed by Arminius and his command once the attack had begun. Varus does nothing except make things worse at every turn. In his narrative, the Romans along the Rhine and in Gaul found themselves in a desperate position in the aftermath of the Teutoburg. Garrisons of soldiers were stranded beyond the Rhine, and there was little standing between the civilian population of the Empire and Arminius' army of terrifying German warriors. The Empire was rescued, however, by the actions of Tiberius, who rushed to the Rhine and stabilized the situation. Once more, Tiberius became the saviour of Roman security, as he had previously done in Germany (when Drusus had died), and during the Pannonian Revolt. It is not surprising to find Velleius eulogizing Tiberius in this way, but unfortunately, it undermines the credibility of his account of the Teutoburg. Velleius was known for a fierce loyalty and devotion to Emperor Tiberius, under whom he had served as an officer in the Roman army at an earlier phase in his career. As such, in Velleius' historical works Tiberius is often portrayed as an almost heroic figure, his qualities universally praised, and his actions never criticized.[4] For Tiberius to be the 'hero' of the Teutoburg, Varus would have to be cast as the 'villain', who had got Rome into the trouble that only Tiberius could rescue it from. As villain, Varus almost inevitably had to be denigrated at every turn, to make the narrative contrast work. While this does not mean that Velleius' account of the battle should be ignored, particularly as it is the only one to be written in living memory of the battle, it also cannot be taken at face value, particularly where Varus specifically is concerned.

The only extended narrative comes from Cassius Dio, who provides much more detail than Velleius, but was writing two centuries after the battle. Dio almost certainly drew on Pliny's lost *Bella Germaniae* in his own account of the battle, which may explain the higher levels of narrative detail – but even so, it gives only a basic overview of the events in the Teutoburg, a sketch from which numerous aspects of interest are unfortunately lacking. Aside from Velleius and Dio, there are few other sources which give much useful or reliable detail about the events of the battle. Florus' brief discourse on the engagement lacks any kind of balance or accuracy, although it attempts to make up for this in entertainment value. Tacitus describes the battlefield when recounting a visit made to the site by another Roman army, this time commanded by Germanicus, on their way to wage war against Arminius in AD 15, but does not particularly mention the events of the battle itself (his work only begins in AD 14 with the death of Augustus).

Part of the issue with these accounts of the battle is that Roman historians did not write military history in the way that we would have liked them to. Military history was a literary genre, with its own set of rules and conventions that dictated how it 'should' be written, for a readership that was almost exclusively wealthy, aristocratic, and based in the Mediterranean. In general, what was wanted was a generalized overview of the battle, contextualized within a generic characterization of the tactically relevant terrain, with the author identifying the relevant elements of the engagement for his readers, and omitting anything surplus to this requirement. The rhetorician Lucian gives further insight into the selective processes used to write military history in antiquity. He recorded the typical formula for a battle-narrative, suggesting that it should focus first on the generals, their speeches, tactics, and troop deployment, followed by a generalized description of the actual fighting.[5] He further advised that narratives should not focus on the actions of an individual unit or soldier without exceptionally good cause – usually when their actions had a direct and specific impact on the outcome of the battle.[6] Most Roman military history follows these conventions when narrating a battle. As a result, most accounts of individual battles are highly episodic, moving from one set-piece to another with no clear indication of how these events were connected in space and time. Although this does not make the narratives useless, the literary conventions of Roman military history do have to be considered when using these sources to reconstruct the events of an individual battle.

Where did the Roman historians get their information from, and how reliable was the evidence that was used as the basis for the descriptions of the battle? This is a difficult question to answer. There were survivors of the battle – discussed in more detail towards the end of this chapter – who could have provided eye-witness accounts, although the nature of the engagement means that each individual would probably only have been present at a small proportion of the overall event, witness only to a fragment of the wider events. Whether any survivors were consulted by historians is unclear. Velleius, as a contemporary of the events, would have had the best opportunity to speak directly to survivors, particularly those who remained in service in the Roman army. He makes no mention of having done so, however, although it is difficult to imagine that he did not pick up on informal hearsay about the events of the battle irrespective of whether he conducted formal interviews with survivors or not. Pliny may also have had the opportunity to speak to survivors who escaped the battle and reached Roman territory, although without the text of the *Bella Germaniae* it is difficult to know whether he did so, or how far these accounts would have shaped his narrative. The level of detail in Dio's account suggests that it was certainly possible that survivors were asked to describe the events which took place, unless the description of events is a fiction on the part of Dio (or his sources), but again, the historian himself makes no reference to participant testimony in his work.

But even if eyewitness survivors were asked to document their experiences at some point in the aftermath of the battle, it is far from guaranteed that these would be accurate representations of events. Battles are notoriously difficult events to reconstruct, even for those who directly participated in them. The traumatic nature of battle, in which the senses can become overloaded and memory fails to function as it normally does, means that even combatants who fought in a battle can struggle to accurately reconstruct the events that took place during fighting, even those which they directly participated in. The Romans were themselves aware of the imperfect nature of memory in extreme circumstances, as indeed the Greeks had been before them. The Greek historian Thucydides noted the narrowness of perception during battle, with combatants aware at best only of events which had happened in their immediate vicinity, and that participants in the same battle frequently gave entirely contradictory accounts of what had actually happened.[7] Aristotle observed that eyewitnesses to certain events could come to believe they had seen things which had not actually taken place.[8] Caesar described a similar phenomenon when recounting a frightened scout returning and reporting having seen things which did not exist.[9] Similarly, Pliny the Elder recounted that people who had been involved in traumatic or frightening events often suffered partial or complete memory loss.[10] Modern psychological studies have backed up the observations made in antiquity about the functioning of memory during battle, including the narrowing of perception, 'weapon focus', and failure to observe details, which often had detrimental effects on performance in battle as well as in remembering it afterwards.[11] So even if survivors of the Teutoburg were questioned afterwards about the events of the battle, their testimony was likely highly problematic, in terms of both accuracy and range – an issue for both Roman historians writing in antiquity, and their counterparts in the more modern world.

Until recently, these problematic historical sources were the only basis that existed for the reconstruction of the events of the Teutoburg. From the nineteenth century onwards, most interpretations of the battle drew heavily on the narrative of Cassius Dio in particular, as the one source to describe events in any real detail. But understanding the events of the Teutoburg is now not reliant on just the historical record, since the discovery of (part of) the battlefield in 1987 at Kalkriese (see introduction for a discussion of its discovery). The assemblage from the running battle, extending over 15km and covering an area of more than 30km², has provided significant insight into how the engagement was fought, how Varus and his army attempted to escape the ambush, and even the state of morale among the soldiers for much of the event. The archaeological evidence will be heavily drawn upon in this chapter in terms of reconstructing the events of the ambush. Although it cannot identify Varus' individual actions during the battle, it is possible to extrapolate some indications of what he did based on the wider battlefield behaviour of the Roman soldiers caught up in the attack.

Varus' Legions – a veteran force?

Three of the five legions that garrisoned the Rhine were ambushed in the Teutoburg – almost certainly the Seventeenth, Eighteenth and Nineteenth.[12] Although they are not named in any of the surviving narratives about the battle specifically, two of the legions can be definitively linked to the Teutoburg: a tombstone from a casualty of the battle records the Eighteenth, while Tacitus names one of the legions involved in the battle as the Nineteenth in a later part of his narrative.[13] There is no direct evidence for the Seventeenth being present in the Teutoburg. Its involvement in the battle is largely extrapolated in that the legionary number was never used again, like those of the Eighteenth and Nineteenth, with the units disbanded in the aftermath of the battle.[14] While it is possible that these were not the legions involved at the Teutoburg, there is no evidence for any other units being there. More comprehensive evidence for the legions involved in the battle would be provided if an artefact bearing a legionary stamp or inscription was found on the site, although unfortunately as yet no such artefacts have been recovered from Kalkriese.[15]

It is possible that the legions at the Teutoburg were not ordinary legions, but were constituted with a dominant leaning towards experienced soldiers, perhaps even some time-served veterans (*evocati*) recalled to the standards due to the manpower crisis resulting from the Illyrian Revolt.[16] Although recalling veterans to active service was not a common action, it was not unheard of at times of crisis – and indeed, it has already been seen that exactly this step was taken at the outbreak of the Illyrian Revolt.[17] Although it appears likely that the majority of these recalled veterans were destined to serve in Illyrium, a number may also have been deployed to other legions in the region, especially if this freed up some younger soldiers to go and fight with another unit on the front line. The Roman sources give some indication that the legions in the Teutoburg were unusual, a cut above the average troops. Velleius describes them as an 'army unexcelled in bravery, the first of Roman armies in discipline, in energy, and in experience in the field', a glowing recommendation from someone who was also serving in the military at the time.[18] Clearly, these troops were thought to be almost an elite unit of soldiers, well-experienced in warfare. Although the potential recall of veterans to serve in Varus' army might seem an odd decision, it makes sense in the wider context of the situation in Germany at the time. Firstly, as discussed in the previous chapter, his governorship took place at the same time as the Illyrian Revolt, a conflict which monopolized the vast majority of available military resources, from generals and manpower to weapons and food. Varus' role in Germany, while not completely without a military character, appears to have been to consolidate Roman control rather than to substantially extend it, avoiding opening another active front for the Romans to fight in. The Romans stationed in the province interior appear to have functioned as guardsmen and police as much as soldiers, and as an occupying force rather than a conquering one. Veteran soldiers, likely already to have experience of military service in Germany, would have been more than equal to this role.

Other soldiers in Varus' legions may have been experienced due to long military careers, some of which may have taken them (voluntarily) long beyond the usual point of retirement. One particular example is Marcus Caelius, a casualty of the Teutoburg who was commemorated with a funerary monument outside the Xanten legionary [base/fort?].[19] The monument bears a portrait of Caelius, dressed in military uniform, flanked by busts of two of his freedmen. The inscription notes that he died in the 'Varian War' (*Bellum Variana*), almost certainly the Teutoburg.[20] This is the only use of the phrase in either an archaeological or historical context, and it is an unusual inclusion, as most Roman tombstones (military or otherwise) do not give a cause of death for the deceased. Caelius himself was not buried below the stone, as his body was never recovered from the battlefield, although the inscription states that the plot could be used by his freedmen should they so desire. It is not surprising that Caelius' body was not recovered, even allowing for the exceptional circumstances of the Teutoburg battle, as Roman soldiers who died in battle were typically not repatriated, even back to a local military base. Their bodies were instead left on the battlefield, receiving varying levels of treatment depending on the time period and circumstances of the engagement. Caelius was the first centurion (*primus pilus*) of the Eighteenth Legion, and the funerary portrait on the stone suggests that he was an individual of prestige. He is shown wearing several military decorations, including a *corona civica*, which was awarded for saving another Roman citizen's life, two gold torques on his shoulders, and five *phalerae* on his breastplate, metal medallions which were often presented to soldiers as awards.[21] He also holds a centurion's *vitis* (wooden staff) in his right hand, further emphasizing his status. Although the inscription does not mention how many years Caelius had served with the army, it does state that he was aged 53½ at his death, around the same age as Varus. Although there was no set age for enlistment, the vast majority of soldiers joined the army between the ages of about 17 and 20, suggesting that Caelius likely enlisted *circa* 27–24 BC, and may have served upwards of 33 years by AD 9. He is unusually old for a serving soldier, and must have either remained in the army long past the usual retirement age, or been someone who was recalled to the legions for further service. Higher-ranking soldiers were typically more willing to extend their service than others, particularly those who became centurions. As Caelius had reached the rank of first centurion, one of the highest ranks a career soldier could achieve, he may well have decided to remain in the army after completing his term of service. His presence would have served as a reminder of the value of experienced soldiers on the Roman army.

The size of Varus' army is an ongoing question. The only source which engages with this issue is Velleius, who says that Varus' force comprised three legions, three auxiliary cavalry units, and six auxiliary infantry cohorts.[22] In theory, a Roman legion at the time comprised of 5,000 men, while auxiliary units comprised either 500 or 1,000 men. Based on this paper strength, Varus' army could have been anything from 20,000–25,000 strong. However, in reality, legion size was likely much more flexible, particularly in times of military crisis for units not themselves stationed within the primary active warzone. The ad hoc composition of Varus' legions, and the potential use of *evocati* troops emphasizes the probability that his army was considerably understrength in comparison to the paper ideal. Potentially, none of the legions or auxiliary units at the Teutoburg were at full strength, making it difficult to know exactly how many soldiers were caught up in the battle. Further reducing the number of troops is the fact that an unknown number of the German auxiliaries appear to have defected with Arminius, joining in the attack on the Roman soldiers once the ambush had begun.

Adding to the question of manpower is Cassius Dio's revelation that in advance of the attack, Arminius had reduced the manpower of Varus' legions as much as possible. Various communities beyond the Rhine asked for Roman soldiers to be detached to them to help with policing and guarding duties, requests which were granted by Varus, a decision which was later condemned as inappropriate in a region as unpacified as Germany turned out to be.[23] Current estimates for the size of the force caught up in the battle range from 10,000 soldiers to around 20,000 at the highest, although this figure usually refers only to military personnel.[24] A significant number of military servants/slaves and camp-followers, including sutlers and the informal families of the soldiers (including women and children), accompanied the army, and would also have been caught in the attack.[25] Whatever the exact numbers, it was a substantial force of soldiers, military personnel, and camp-followers present at the Teutoburg, and most would not survive the battle.

The prelude to battle

In the summer of AD 9 Varus departed from his winter base, probably the legionary fortress at Xanten, into the territories east of the Rhine. Whether he intended to actively campaign against a particular tribe, or whether the mission was more diplomatic in nature – a chance to 'show the flag' to the more remote population – is uncertain. The historical sources do not contain any suggestion that Varus was engaged in any sort of military action in Germany prior to the engagement in the Teutoburg, but even if this was not his primary objective in visiting more distant regions, he would no doubt have been prepared for its possibility.

How far Varus advanced beyond the Rhine is unclear from the sources. The lack of clarity about his area of operations in AD 9 is one reason why the battlefield proved difficult to find for so long, as there was no indication of the likely maximum extent of Varus' movement. Varus almost certainly established a summer base to act as the centre of operations during the summer, likely somewhere along the course of the Weser River. A temporary camp found in 2008 at Porta Westfalica (west of the Weser and a short distance south of Minden) has been cautiously linked with Varus and his army in AD 9. The installation lies *circa* 180km northeast of Xanten, sufficiently in advance of the Rhine to lie within 'summer campaign' distance. Its position fits with the location of the Teutoburg battle at Kalkriese, which lies around 60km northwest of Porta Westfalica. The artefacts from the site include a range of military artefacts, such as hobnails from military sandals, armour fittings, tent fittings, fibulae, surveying plumb-bobs, as well as coins, and the remains of five field-ovens. The assemblage clearly indicates a military presence, and from the dates of the coins occupation of the site can broadly be dated to the Augustan period. Unfortunately, this encompasses any point between the campaigns of Drusus the Elder (starting in 12 BC) to those of Germanicus (through to AD 17), and a firm association with AD 9 cannot be drawn at the moment. It may be that the installation was occupied more than once, if it was found to be a suitable strategic position, which was dismantled and abandoned between the multiple phases of occupation; if so, an association with Varus and his legions is even more likely. Whether Varus' summer base was at Porta Westfalica or another as yet unidentified location, the installation appears not have lacked in comforts. Finds from the battlefield at Kalkriese (see later in this chapter) include ornate furnishings, parts of statues, and leisure-related artefacts, suggesting that Varus transported a significant number of luxury goods with him when he travelled east of the Rhine. Nor is it just in the context of the battlefield that such high-value goods once belonging to Varus have been found. A hoard of ornate silverware found at Hildesheim, the largest hoard of silverwork to be found outside the territorial Roman Empire, has also been associated with Varus in AD 9. The items in the hoard were probably produced in the northwestern territories of the Empire, and it is probable that the hoard was deposited in the Augustan period.[26] The composition of the hoard suggests it was likely war booty rather than a single service of tableware, and was potentially looted from Varus' baggage-train in AD 9 before later being buried at Hildesheim.[27] Varus clearly did not embrace a life lacking in luxuries even when he led an army out in the field.

Arminius would have been under no illusions that a rebellious German force would have had little chance of victory against a Roman army in pitched battle, due to the Roman's superior training, technology, and manpower. Therefore, like any good commander, he aimed to neutralize those Roman superiorities. Firstly, it was decided to attack the Roman army on the march, a time when they were particularly vulnerable.[28] Although the Romans were aware of their vulnerability to ambushes of the marching column, and were aware of the proclivity of tribal armies for using these kind of irregular tactics, there was only so much that could be done to eliminate the risk.[29] Arminius then also aimed to launch the attack in inhospitable terrain, where the Roman soldiers would be unable to adopt a proper battle formation once the attack began. He was undoubtedly aware of the need to prevent the Roman army from being able to launch a counterattack against the ambushers, particularly if they could reach an area of open-ground, where – even after several days of battle – the Romans would likely have the advantage.[30] He was almost spoiled for choice in Germany, which offered a number of wooded, marshy, or hilly areas in which the attack could be launched (the proliferation of these areas in Germany is another reason why it was so difficult to find the battlefield). Varus clearly trusted Arminius to lead himself and the army safely through the terrain, avoiding both hostile communities and unsuitable ground. Arminius was therefore aided by Varus' trust in him, which could allow him to lead the Roman army into the area of his choice, ostensibly taking them through safe and friendly territory, in reality leading them into an area in which the Romans would struggle.[31] Cassius Dio emphasizes that the battlefield landscape of the Teutoburg was dominated by 'impenetrable forest', broken up only by mountains with 'uneven surfaces broken by ravines' – not terrain in which the Roman army would have chosen to fight.[32] This landscape was seemingly selected well in advance of the battle, and was a wise decision – as we shall see, it appears that the Germans may even have prepared limited earthworks, particularly in the Oberesch area, suggesting that the Roman presence in that area was no trick of fate. The stage was set for the battle to begin. Varus' legions had been disadvantaged as much as possible and would be caught in an attack in territory hostile in both population and terrain, launched by an enemy who would appear to be allies right up until the moment the attack began. Varus was not expecting any trouble, despite credible warnings about

Arminius' loyalty. It must have been considered fairly likely that he could be lured into the ambush.

By late summer, Varus would have been preparing to go back to the Rhine, as was usual for Roman armies over a winter. Only once had a Roman army wintered beyond the river, when Tiberius stationed a camp on the Lippe, which was portrayed as an exceptional achievement.[33] Although smaller garrisons were evidently being quartered in German territories beyond the Rhine, it had clearly not yet been decided to leave legions stationed that far out over a winter.[34] All Arminius needed to do now was ensure that Varus entered into the inhospitable territory that had been prepared for the ambush. He did this by creating reports of a potential rebellion further into Germany, which Varus decided to deal with before winter set in, en route to the Rhine.[35] The intelligence was false, created to lure Varus and his army into the inhospitable interior, as far as possible from the safety and reinforcements offered by the Rhine. It is not clear to which tribal territory Varus was lured. Several historians have suggested that it was the Angrivarii who were reported to have revolted, whose territory lay north of Arminius' Cheruscan lands.[36] However, this is far from certain. All three legions went with Varus, which, as others have pointed out, seems a potential over-reaction, although it is noted that Varus could not have known the scale of the supposed rebellion and would find it better to take too many troops than too few.[37] It might also have seemed an unjustified risk to split his army up while travelling towards a potentially hostile landscape, especially as he did not know the scale of the uprising that he was travelling to confront. It may not even have been just military considerations which led Varus to take all three legions with him. Varus may also have seen this quick pre-winter expedition as an opportunity to 'show the colours' in areas the army was not usually seen, reminding the Germans of Roman military strength, whilst also engaging in diplomatic relations with chieftains in more distant territories.[38] The mini-expedition may even have offered his men the chance of a late summer 'adventure' before they returned to the Rhine; this may explain why so many women and children accompanied the marching column.

The Roman army set off with a substantial baggage-train, carrying a wide range of belongings, from military equipment to tools, furniture, dining utensils, and various other camp goods, in addition to food, water, and fodder supplies.[39] Dio suggests that the baggage-train was much larger than one which would usually be taken on a military campaign, further reflecting Varus' obliviousness to the dangers which faced his army on the march.[40] Not only was his train excessive in size, but was also apparently mismanaged, with standards of discipline falling amidst the wagons.

According to the later antique military writer Vegetius, it was recommended to keep the baggage-train in the middle of the marching column.[41] However, Dio suggests that no such discipline could be seen in Varus' marching column in Germany, noting that 'the Romans were not proceeding in any regular order, but were mixed in helter-skelter with the waggons and the unarmed'.[42] He further suggests that the soldiers were mingling with the large group of servants and camp-followers – particularly women and children – who were accompanying the column, rather than staying in their proper place in the line.[43] Tacitus echoes the description by Dio, describing the column as comprising 'three straggling legions', possessing none of the discipline which might otherwise have been expected of an army in potentially hostile terrain.[44] Varus seems to have been so certain that he was moving through friendly territory that discipline on the march was allowed to slip, to the degree that soldiers may have been mingling with their families rather than maintaining a battle-ready formation.

Arminius was with Varus in the early stages of the march as his friend and advisor, and appears to have helped guide the Roman army through the German landscape.[45] The two had likely spent much of the summer together, as Arminius drew together his plans for the attack. Arminius was clearly trusted by Varus to lead the Roman army safely through to their destination. Having a reliable German on his staff may have caused Varus to become complacent about his duties overseeing a marching column. In theory, a commander was supposed to oversee the selection of the route personally, based on a careful collection of itineraries which recorded various topographical features, including settlements, rivers, and mountains, along with the distances between them and the presence or quality of the roads.[46] Varus may have relied on Arminius to provide this information. Although this decision proved unwise in terms of what was later discovered about Arminius' loyalty, it was the convention at the time to gather topographic intelligence, as much as possible, from higher-ranking individuals who knew the terrain well, and Arminius may well have been consulted about the route even had he not been a close advisor of Varus. Similarly, one of the ways that Roman armies on the march were meant to increase their chances of safety was by keeping their route secret from their enemies – something which obviously would not prove possible in this case. Varus appears not to have sent out scouts to check the route ahead for danger, likely as he was in Cherusci territory, which was believed to be fully pacified and friendly to Rome.

With the Roman column marching towards the supposed rebels, Arminius and his allies among Varus' staff excused themselves from the march, claiming that they were going to gather troops from among their allies that would be brought to strengthen Varus' army.[47] They were, of course, instead collecting them to assist in the assault on the Romans. Before launching the main attack, they killed the detachments of troops that had been previously sent to the various German communities, ensuring that they could not re-join Varus' army.[48] This may have been pre-arranged for a particular date, as the date of the ambush itself had apparently been fixed some time in advance by Arminius. The stage was now set for the ambush to begin – Varus had been caught in the trap, and now all that remained to be seen was whether the Romans could escape it or not.

The First Day and Night of Battle

At some point after leaving with Varus' knowledge and blessing, Arminius and his allies launched their first attack on the Roman column. According to Cassius Dio, the ambush began when the Romans were already deep into impenetrable forest, in terrain which the soldiers had already been struggling to move through, requiring them to fell trees, create small bridges, and even lay some basic roads.[49] They were also struggling with the weather, in the midst of an early autumn storm, with heavy rain and strong winds, which made the ground slippery and sent branches cascading down from the tops of trees onto the soldiers below.[50] Suddenly, as if out of nowhere, their German allies arrived, with an unknown number of troops – but instead of rejoining the column, they attacked it. Dio says that the Germans surrounded the column on all sides, using paths through the forest which they knew about but the Romans did not, coming through the most heavily wooded areas which hid their presence until the last possible moment.[51]

The scenes which followed must have been chaotic. Only Cassius Dio gives any sort of indication of how the early stages of the attack unfolded. He describes that once the Germans had surrounded the Romans, they launched volleys of projectiles towards the soldiers stranded amidst the trees.[52] The Roman soldiers initially struggled to mount an effective defence, severely outnumbered at each point and unable to adopt any sort of battle formation due to the dense trees around them. Where exactly on the column the first attacks took place is unclear. Given Arminius' knowledge of how the Roman army operated in the field, he was likely aware that the rear of the column was probably the area best prepared for ambush, and so may have avoided an attack there, hitting elsewhere on the column, possibly in numerous locations at once. In many ways, this would have added to the confusion, potentially leading to some parts of the column being initially unaware of the assault taking place elsewhere. Varus was likely at the head of the column, but it is unclear from the sources whether he was caught up in the first wave of the attack or not.

The fighting from these early stages onwards must have been brutal and highly traumatizing. Not much is known about German fighting styles in this period, although Tacitus gives a brief overview in his ethnographic work, the *Germania*:

> But few [German warriors] use swords or long lances. They carry a spear (framea is their name for it), with a narrow and short head, but so sharp and easy to wield that the same weapon serves, according to circumstances, for close or distant conflict. As for the horse-soldier, he is satisfied with a shield and spear; the foot-soldiers also scatter showers of missiles, each man having several and hurling them to an immense distance, and being naked or lightly clad with a little cloak. There is no display about their equipment: their shields alone are marked with very choice colours. A few only have corslets, and just one or two here and there a metal or leathern helmet. Their horses are remarkable neither for beauty nor for fleetness. Nor are they taught various evolutions after our fashion, but are driven straight forward, or so as to make one wheel to the right in such a compact body that none is left behind another. On the whole, one would say that their chief strength is in their infantry, which fights along with the cavalry; admirably adapted to the action of the latter is the swiftness of certain foot-soldiers, who are picked from the entire youth of their country, and stationed in front of the line. Their number is fixed, a hundred from each canton; and from this they take their name among their countrymen, so that what was originally a mere number has now become a title of distinction. Their line of battle is drawn up in a wedge-like formation. To give ground, provided you return to the attack, is considered prudence rather than cowardice. The bodies of their slain they carry off even in indecisive engagements. To abandon your shield is the basest of crimes; nor may a man thus disgraced be present at the sacred rites, or enter their council; many, indeed, after escaping from battle, have ended their infamy with the halter.[53]

In theory, this fighting style should not have been a match for the numerical, technological, and organizational superiority of the Roman army.[54] Although the Romans had not come out unscathed from their previous conflicts with the Germans, only once – under Lollius – had they faced a situation that they could not fight their way out of. But this occasion in the Teutoburg may have been different, and it cannot even be assumed that all the Germans attacked

Views over the site of the Villa of Varus at Tivoli, Varus' country estate, looking south-east towards the modern town. (*Author's own*)

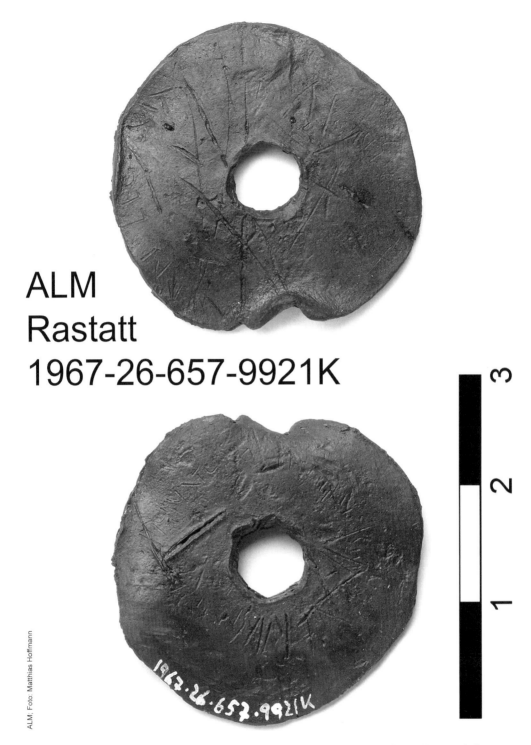

ALM
Rastatt
1967-26-657-9921K

A luggage-tag from Dangstetten (Germany) naming Varus as the legate of the Nineteenth Legion. (*Matthias Hoffmann/Archäologisches Landesmuseum Baden Württemberg*)

Scene from the Ara Pacis in Rome, depicting Varus (left), Augustus (centre), and Tiberius (right). (*Author's own*)

Close-up of Varus on the Ara Pacis. (*Author's own*)

A bronze *as* coin minted under Varus in Africa, with his portrait on the reverse, opposite Augustus (under wheel countermark), Gaius and Lucius. Minted in Achulla 8/7 BC. (*CNG* (*auction 416, Lot 394*))

A bronze *as* minted under Varus in Syria, bearing the image of Varus on the obverse, and two legionary standards on the reverse. Minted in Berytus (Beirut) c.6-4 BC. (*CNG* (*auction 121, Lot 725*))

A bronze *as*, bearing a VAR countermark over a portrait of Augustus. (*CNG* (*auction 116, lot 194*))

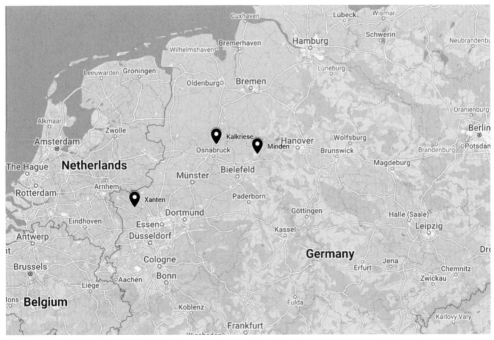

Map showing the location of Kalkriese relative to Varus' likely starting point (Minden) and intended eventual destination (Xanten). (*Author's own via Google Maps*)

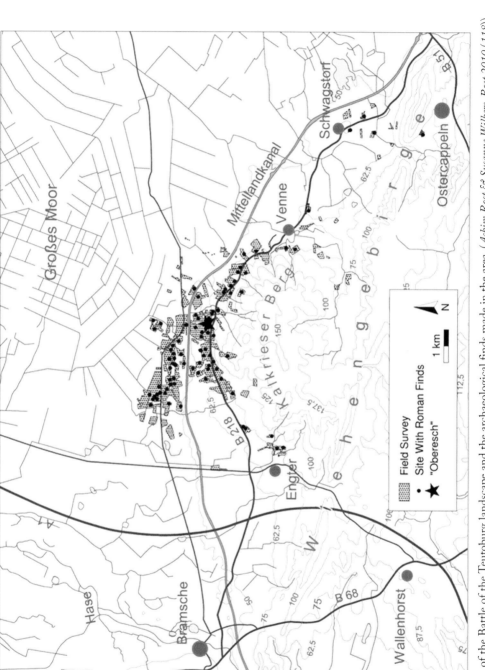

Map of the Battle of the Teutoburg landscape and the archaeological finds made in the area. (*Achim Rost & Susanne Wilbers-Rost 2010 (118)*)

A view over the Oberesch area of the Teutoburg battlefield. (*Author's own*)

A reconstruction of the German rampart at the Oberesch. (*Author's own*)

The 'Der gescheiterte Varus' statue in Haltern-am-See (Germany). (*Fewskulchor via Wikipedia (CC 3.0)*)

using their 'traditional' methods of combat. Many of the German warriors may also have been Roman auxiliaries, who had defected alongside Arminius, fighting with Roman methods and using Roman kit.[55] As an auxiliary commander, Arminius would have been able to deploy these troops far more effectively than previous German leaders had done against the Roman army. Not all the German warriors would have been defected auxiliaries, but they did not have to be, if enough Roman-trained soldiers led the way in the attack. Arminius would have known far more about his enemy than Varus and the Roman soldiers would have known about him and the German warriors, and would use this intelligence to make his attack even more effective.[56]

It is clear from the sources that Varus had not anticipated an attack, and that the Romans as a whole were caught completely unawares by the ambush – something which Varus would later come under strong criticism for.[57] He had therefore evidently failed to make any contingency plans in case of an ambush, an evidently unforgivable error. Ambush was a known danger for the Roman army, and a marching column was, at least in theory, supposed to maintain readiness for attack at any moment. The military was aware of its vulnerability to ambush while on the march. For some, an ambush was the most dangerous situation that the Roman army could face, more perilous even than a pitched battle, as the circumstances of engagement neutralized many of the Roman army's strengths.[58] In theory, Roman soldiers were supposed to be ever-alert for an ambush when they were part of a marching column, keeping their weapons with them at all times and being mentally prepared for an attack at any moment, in the hope that this would help to keep them from panicking if an attack was launched.[59] In anticipation of an attack, the column was supposed to be arranged with the most flexible troops – cavalry and light infantry – at the end of the line, as ambushes were thought most likely to happen towards the rear of the column. However, as mentioned previously, Varus thought himself and his army to be travelling through friendly territory and had consequently allowed the discipline of the marching order to slip, making it difficult for the Romans to mount the rapid and effective response that was their only hope of victory under such circumstances. As a further result of his feeling of security, he may also have neglected one of the key duties of a commander in charge of an army on the march: to identify locations of potential ambush, ensuring that they were scouted properly, and that extra caution was taken while moving through these areas.[60] The ancient sources imply that Varus did not send out scouts to assess the landscape he was moving through, blindly trusting the Germans on his staff to guide him. But although this sounds negligent at first, in reality it likely seemed far more logical and sensible than it appears now. Varus trusted Arminius to lead him through the landscape. How familiar

Varus was with the territories they were passing through is unclear. While there were no Roman roads in the province yet, there were likely established routes through the landscape, some of which Varus may have already used during previous campaigns or other business east of the Rhine.[61] Arminius was leading the Romans through Cherusci territory, an area thought to be friendly to Rome. Varus clearly saw nothing suspicious in the route that Arminius was leading them through, and may even have travelled along these routes before. The commander was content to allow Arminius to lead the way without independently checking the route. But even if Varus had sent out scouts, they would likely have done little to inform Varus about the coming attack. Many of his scouts were probably German auxiliaries, many likely serving in the Cherusci mounted units that planned to defect with Arminius, and thus would not have reported any of the lurking dangers to Varus. Any scouts that were not with Arminius would probably have been killed before they could report anything useful back. Once the attack began, he could no longer trust his guides, and although he could have sent out non-German scouts to try and assess the situation, there is little chance that they would have returned alive. Varus and his army were now blind within a newly hostile landscape.

In the early phases of the battle, the Romans struggled to defend themselves from the attack. Unable to find anywhere they could adopt battle array, they were hit by multiple waves of attack from Germans who loosed projectiles from a distance and disappeared back into the forest. It likely became clear that staying where they were and hoping to wait out the attack would not work. They were sustaining heavy casualties and inflicting few in return, and had no idea of the size of the German force attacking them. The Romans were stranded many days march from the Rhine in terrain they knew very little about, with supplies that would keep them for a while, but not endlessly. Varus had to make a choice about whether to remain in position, to keep moving forward towards the Rhine, or turn back through territory that they had already safely moved through. Continuing forward was potentially hazardous, as they had no way of knowing what dangers lay ahead of them, but they might hope to outpace the Germans and reach the Rhine before being wiped out. If they turned back, they would be passing back through more familiar terrain, but risked the army being trapped even further from the Rhine than they were. Varus elected to push forward towards the safety of Roman territory, moving into the area of modern Kalkriese.

Varus' decision to enter the Kalkriese Pass was likely the most sensible of his options. The ancient historians suggest that the area was very inhospitable, thickly forested, marshy, and isolated, exactly the type of landscape that a Roman army would hope to avoid. However, environmental analysis of the area around Kalkriese suggests that at the time of the battle it was partially cultivated, and populated with a number of German settlements.[62] Even the area around the Oberesch was under management, with areas of open pasture in its western area.[63] Although it was a difficult landscape to move through, requiring the use of sandbars which ran through the marshy areas, it was not as inhospitable as some of the Roman sources suggested. Areas like Germany (as well as Gaul and Britain) were understood by ancient Romans to be barbaric and wild places, contrasted with Roman law and order by characterizations of their terrain as heavily wooded and marshy – areas in which, it was implicitly understood, that the Roman army could not operate at maximum efficiency.[64] This type of terrain became irrevocably entwined with the northern territories in the Roman perception, and 'murky forests and abominable marshes were stock motifs that characterized Germania' in particular.[65] As such, the terrain of *any* event in these areas would be characterized by these Roman preconceptions, regardless of what the reality was. But based on the evidence from around Kalkriese, the reality may have been different in some cases. But even allowing for the terrain not being as difficult as the ancient sources suggested, the Roman army would have struggled to operate effectively within the Kalkriese Pass. Excavations have shown that the assemblage runs through a narrow chain of sandbars running in between a mountain (the Kalkriese Berg) on one side, and a large marsh on the other, which has since been drained. Once caught in this area without friendly guides who knew the terrain, the only hope for the Roman army of getting out would be to chance upon a passage through the marshes.

The shock which Varus must have felt when he discovered that Arminius had indeed been plotting against him must have been both sickening and overwhelming. All of a sudden, all the warnings about Arminius which he had received and refuted were proved to be true. In many ways, Varus had little choice but to have trusted in Arminius, who, at least until proved otherwise, appeared to be an upstanding Roman citizen of relatively high rank, and a fellow soldier. The auxiliary system worked on the basis that enfranchizing provincial non-citizens through their military service would make them loyal to the Roman state, thus neutralizing any threat that they might otherwise pose. In this case, it evidently had not worked, but up until the moment of the attack, Varus would not have known this, having already dismissed the accusations against Arminius. None of the ancient sources recount Varus' reaction to the first attack, if he was even a witness to it, but it must have been an incredibly difficult moment for him.

Exactly where the first attack took place is unclear. It is likely to be somewhere east of the Oberesch, potentially in the area of the landscape corridor where

Roman military artefacts first start to emerge on the route through to Kalkriese. Once the ambush began, there was little time for rest or planning if the Romans were to have any chance of escaping. History had shown that the Roman army often reacted poorly when confronted by ambush, particularly where the terrain and/or encirclement by the enemy meant that they were unable to adopt battle-order.[66] If order could not be established quickly, then a rapid disaster could ensue – when combat cohesion is lost, by any army, a rapid collapse into unpredictable and damaging behaviour often ensues, as soldiers forget their training and make a series of decisions that actually lessen their chances of survival.[67] The Romans were well aware of this potential problem – Tacitus noted that it was to be expected in a sudden attack that 'every man [is] quick to obey his impulse and slow to hear the word of command', which had to be factored in by a commander who hoped to escape a problematic situation.[68] Such a disaster had been seen several centuries earlier, during the Second Punic War, showing how dangerous an ambush could be. When a large Roman army was ambushed near Lake Trasimene by Hannibal and his Carthaginian army, there was near-universal panic among the Roman soldiers, who were unable to either fight or flee, having been tightly caught in a defile between the lake on one side, and hills on the other.[69] The Roman soldiers fell into a state of complete combat disintegration, bunching together when they were unable to form any proper battle formation. Time was wasted while the Romans were deciding what to do, with heavy casualties sustained while deliberations unfolded.[70] Eventually, when it proved impossible to escape, the Roman soldiers had made some attempt to fight their way out of the ambush, spurred on by the words of their commander, but after just three hours, their resistance was broken and the battle over; many of the Romans drowned in the lake.

Although the circumstances they faced in the Teutoburg were likely as challenging as any Roman army had ever faced, and both the terrain and weather were against them, the Romans tried to take the initiative from Arminius and his allies. Varus would have been aware that the time for decision-making was short; the disaster under Lollius in 17/16 BC, and the near-disaster under Drusus the Elder a few years later, would no doubt have been prominent in his mind as he searched for a solution to the problem he and his army found themselves in. Crucially, at this early stage, Varus' army did not descend into a state of combat disintegration, but were able to retain cohesion even as the ambush unfolded around them. This conclusion is based partly on the length of the ensuing battle, which would last for three more days, in contrast to Trasimene where the soldiers, having lost their tactical unity fairly early on, were slaughtered within a few hours.[71] The immediate response was to construct a camp in the area of the initial ambush, which could provide some brief respite while they planned what to do next.[72] Dio suggests that this was quite a struggle, as the forest and sloped ground gave little by way of suitable building locations, but the task was achieved nonetheless.

It was not uncommon during provincial warfare for the Roman army to have to construct a camp in the midst of battle, with part of the army constructing the installation while the rest continued fighting; a similar situation would occur during Germanicus' campaigns in the same region.[73] However, such mid-battle constructions were not always successful. Archaeological investigations at Andagoste (Navarra, Spain) uncovered evidence of a smaller Roman army (around 1,000 soldiers) which had also been ambushed on the march while campaigning in the late first century BC, probably during Augustus' Cantabrian Wars.[74] When the attack began, the soldiers attempted either to construct a new field camp, or perhaps to reconstruct one from which they had recently departed, to take shelter from the attack. Their efforts proved unsuccessful; the interior was breached before the fortifications were finished, and the Roman force likely wiped out. The engagement is not documented in the surviving historical record and may have been a minor engagement that was soon forgotten to Roman military history. But it would have been within living memory at the time of the Teutoburg – and Varus may himself have known of the defeat, having probably served in the Cantabrian Wars early in his career.

Unfortunately, as yet no conclusive evidence has been found for the location of this camp, or any of the others that Varus' army constructed in their attempt to escape the Teutoburg (although see later in this chapter for arguments in favour of a Roman camp at the Oberesch). It must have been of a considerable size to shelter the troops of three legions and nine auxiliary units, however depleted in manpower they might have been going into the battle. Unfortunately, it is hard to detect Roman camps in this region due to the underlying soil conditions which make remote identification (particularly aerial photography) difficult. Although a number of military installations have been identified by other means, many cannot be dated more closely than 'Augustan period'.[75] It can only be hoped that one day remains of this camp, and any others associated with Varus in AD 9, are discovered by some other method.

During the first night, as the Romans sheltered in a hastily-constructed camp, it was evidently decided that the only hope of survival lay in trying to reach the safety of Roman territory along the Rhine. The decision was probably taken by Varus, perhaps in consultation with his officers. As the commander of the legions, it was ultimately his responsibility to decide what action they took in response to the attack. This plan was likely their only option. The dangers that holing up in a military installation (whether pre-existing or constructed after an attack) and trying to outlast the enemy was rarely a workable plan, particularly when there was little prospect of reinforcements arriving to bolster the stricken force. Just over sixty years earlier (in 54 BC) a Roman legion had attempted to do the same, and the outcome had been a well-publicized disaster.[76] While wintering in the territory of the Eburones, the Fifth Legion had found themselves under attack from the tribe, but were offered safe passage to other legionary forces by the rebellion's leader, Ambiorix, as long as they left peacefully. Once the Romans had left the security of the fort they had been ambushed in a ravine, sustaining heavy casualties. Most of the soldiers panicked, and it proved difficult to make an effective defence. A second Eburone attack, while the Roman and Gallic leaders ostensibly negotiated a truce, finished off the majority of the Roman soldiers. Some escaped back to Roman territory, but most of the few survivors fell back to the fort they had recently departed from, and committed suicide overnight.[77] The moral appeared to be that trying to fight your way out of a situation was better than trying to defend an impossible position.

Staying put in the Kalkriese area was not an option for Varus and his army. Winter was rapidly encroaching, and the distance of Kalkriese from any other Roman outpost made it unlikely that any help would arrive in time to save them. Similarly, given the conditions and the effectiveness of the German irregular ambush tactics, it was unlikely that the Romans would be given the opportunity to adopt battle array and fight a quasi-pitched engagement. There is no indication that Varus intended to make a 'last stand' at any point in the battle, although perhaps this reflects the lack of suitable terrain on which to do so rather than a tactical decision on the commander's part. Given the circumstances, a fighting withdrawal was the only option. Given the extensive campaign experience his soldiers already had, as well as their evident resilience to the early stages of the ambush, Varus may well have thought his army was more than capable of withstanding further German attacks and breaking free of the ambush zone.[78] It might not have been the perfect plan but was the best course of action available at the time. At this point the situation may not have seemed as hopeless as it would later become, and Varus may have entertained some optimism about their chances of survival. He had dealt with an insurrection before while governor of Syria, albeit not one directed so brutally towards the Roman army, nor so well-planned and executed. He would no doubt have been aware that Drusus the Elder had been able to extricate himself and his army from a similar attack in Germany two decades earlier, demonstrating that it was possible to survive this kind of situation. Varus would use his experience of provincial warfare, and also his knowledge of how both the Germans generally and Arminius specifically operated to try and formulate an escape towards the Rhine. Their best chance would be to move quickly and try to outpace the German attack – but the day's action had shown that his army in its current state was not well-suited to manoeuvring.

To help the Roman force to move more rapidly through the ambush zone, the decision was made to abandon most of the baggage train, taking only what they absolutely needed to survive the journey to the Rhine.[79] This was a standard military practice in situations where it would prove a severe burden in withdrawing from a dangerous situation.[80] During the Gallic Wars baggage-trains were abandoned on several occasions to allow the army to fight and escape more effectively, as they also were during the desperate retreat from the battlefield at Carrhae in 53 BC.[81] A decision about the baggage was no doubt made more pressing by the fact that Varus' army may have been accompanied by a larger number of wagons than was usual on campaign, as they were travelling back from their summer camp to the installations on the Rhine where they intended to spend the winter. They were likely carrying a far larger load than most armies would take on a dedicated campaign, including the luxury items (tableware, furniture) discussed earlier in this chapter. Dio states that the wagons which were no longer needed were burned, but given the wet weather and lack of preparation it may have proved difficult to carry out, and consequently others were just abandoned. Not all of the baggage-train was abandoned, however, as there is evidence from the Oberesch for both wagons (metal fittings) and mules (metal harness fittings, decorative glass harness beads, skeletal remains).[82] Some of the wagons were probably used to transport the wounded, and perhaps also the dead, while it was still possible to do so.[83]

The destruction of the baggage-train would have made it easier and quicker to move through the difficult terrain, but must have been a difficult decision to make. It would have meant abandoning everything that was surplus to survival requirements, and would potentially have left the Romans dangerously short on supplies, particularly of the food and water they would no longer be able to rely on their German allies to provide.[84] It is likely that Varus himself, in consultation with his higher-ranking officers, was the person who had to make the call on abandoning the baggage train. In reality, he probably had little option but to take this action. The wagons had already proved a problem in terms of the initial defence against the ambush,[85] and in trying to escape the wagons would have slowed the army down significantly, particularly given the wet weather that would doubtless have seen them frequently bogged down in the mud. Given that speed and flexibility would be the Romans' friend in reaching safety, it was all but inevitable that the baggage-train had to be left behind, but it was still a momentous decision to take. It admitted that, in the current conditions, the Germans were likely to win the battle. In this context, Varus comes across as a decisive commander, capable of identifying the army's priorities in terms of survival, planning an escape, and able to take the difficult steps to execute that plan. He followed a military precedent that had proved effective in the past – and indeed, it likely helped the Roman army to get as far as it did in terms of escaping the ambush zone.

The archaeology provides further evidence for the maintenance of combat cohesion in the early stages of the battle. The battle-related assemblage first develops in an area approximately 15km east of the Oberesch, which may indicate that the first attacks took place in this area. Only a few artefacts are found in this area, mainly limited to small artefacts that were lost underfoot in the chaos rather than deliberately abandoned in a panic. Furthermore, although the Romans may have sustained heavy casualties in the attacks here, there is no evidence that the wounded were abandoned at this stage in the battle.[86] The bodies of any soldiers who were killed may also have been transported, although it is difficult to know the scale of Roman losses in this particular phase of the battle. Throughout the engagement attempts appear to have been made to give medical treatment to wounded soldiers, and some of the human remains from the Oberesch indicate that they may have had bandaged wounds at the time of their death.[87] Tacitus recounts how, in a later ambush of another Roman army by Arminius, the unwounded soldiers did their best to hold off the German attack while the wounded and the baggage-train were evacuated, a decision which was put down to the experience and calmness under pressure of the beleaguered troops' commander, Aulus Caecina.[88] A similar scenario can be imagined in AD 9, with Varus the experienced figure attempting to lead his army to safety. That this was done so effectively suggests that the Roman soldiers caught in the ambush evidently planned to fight to the very end for their survival. They did not panic, or fall apart, but remembered their training, and made an attempt to break free of the German attack.

The Battle Continues

The initial ambush launched by Arminius and his allies was just the start of an extended ordeal for Varus and his army. After spending the first night in a hastily-constructed camp and destroying or abandoning the vast majority of the baggage-train, the Romans emerged ready to try and escape their German attackers. According to Dio, they were much more disciplined than they had been the previous day, managing to hold a formation and, for a sort time, escape the forested areas that Arminius had attempted to trap them in.[89] Dio is at pains to note that the Romans still sustained casualties during this second morning, but it is clear that they were much less severe than in the attack of the previous day. At this point, the Romans may have allowed themselves to become cautiously optimistic that they might actually manage to escape the ambush and make it back to the Rhine safely, but their situation would soon worsen significantly.

After a short distance in the open, the Romans were evidently forced back into a forested area, where they once again came under heavy attack. The Roman soldiers attempted to form a battle line amidst the trees, in the hope of mounting a combined cavalry and infantry charge against their assailants, but struggled to do so, finding their order disrupted both by the trees and their fellow soldiers. The Romans sustained heavy casualties in this attack, the heaviest of the battle thus far according to Dio.[90] Thereafter, Dio's narrative becomes more vague. He does not discuss what actions the Romans took that night, whether they built another camp or attempted to press on without one. His narrative reopens on the fourth day of the battle – evidently a day has been lost somewhere – at which point the beleaguered Romans were still attempting to escape the ambush, but evidently growing both weaker and wearier. Although far from annihilated, the Roman force was by this point severely depleted, having sustained significant casualties in the earlier phases of the running battle.[91] Arminius also found his force growing in size, as many Germans who had hesitated to join his rebellion were lured over by the success of the ambush thus far, and the possibilities of looting that it presented.[92] For those Romans who still lived, the weather was still hindering their progress, with rain heavy enough to prevent their weapons being used effectively – their weapons hard to grip, and their shields soaked through – alongside wind violent enough that soldiers struggled to stand in it, let alone march.[93] Dio notes that the Germans were not similarly inconvenienced by the weather, due to their lighter equipment, and the fact that they could withdraw from the front line once their kit was too wet.

The stress of the ongoing battle must have been enormous, from Varus through to all his soldiers, and the many servants and camp-followers who were also hoping that the Roman force could somehow break through the ambush. Until recently, there were few studies which acknowledged Roman soldiers as humans who behaved in human ways, rather than cogs in the 'Roman War Machine'. But in the last few decades, there has been an increased interest in developing an understanding of the experience of battle for the average rank-and-file Roman soldier, adapted from studies in the same area for more recent history.[94] These studies focus on the sensory experience of battle from the perspective of a combatant in the midst of the action, considering the sights, smells, noises, and emotions they would have been exposed to, and assessing how they would have affected the behaviour of the soldiers. While often insightful, most of these attempts have focused almost exclusively on pitched battle, as there are not enough detailed written sources giving sufficiently comprehensive narratives about other types of engagement (e.g. ambushes, skirmishes, raids), despite the fact that these likely offered a dramatically different experience for the soldiers fighting in them. Only recently have attempts been made to engage with the 'face of irregular battle' in the Roman world, and the experience of fighting under these circumstances.[95] They conclude that it must have been a terrifying and daunting experience, in which the usual military conventions for behaviour were constantly at risk of collapse. In the Teutoburg, the Roman soldiers were exposed for days to the constant threat of death and, what may have been worse, the prospect of capture and ensuing torture, enslavement, or painful execution.[96] A recent reconstruction of the experience in the Teutoburg for the average Roman soldier paints a fairly grim picture, from the unsettling feelings they may have had when they realized they could not hold their weapons properly in the rain, to the panic they must have felt with projectiles raining down from all sides, with comrades potentially crushing them from every side as they attempted to escape death.[97] The events in the Teutoburg were likely a test of morale and resolve for even the most-hardened veterans among Varus' army.

Varus must have faced some difficult days during the long-running battle. Leaving aside any feelings of guilt and culpability, the situation would have left him with vital decisions to make, potentially on a continuous basis, as he attempted to break his army through the German ambush when they could flee to the Rhine. With Arminius' defection, he had lost one of his most trusted advisors, who he had likely relied upon for intelligence input on the situation in Germany, as well as his geographic knowledge. Varus hopefully knew in which general direction the Rhine lay, but may have been fumbling blindly through the landscape trying to get there, making the army vulnerable to further pitfalls. Furthermore, Arminius' knowledge of both Varus and how the Roman army operated in the field likely meant that he could anticipate almost every decision that Varus would take as he attempted to escape the ambush, and could make contingencies before the Romans even started to carry out the action. Given the manpower Arminius had, he may even have been able to cover for multiple eventualities at the same time, shifting his troops around with each move that Varus made. There was painfully little that Varus could do to outwit Arminius – none of the decisions that he made were bad ones, but they were just unable to achieve the breakthrough that the Roman army needed to survive.

By the third or fourth day of running battle, the Romans were entering the end-phase of the battle. Despite their efforts, they were no closer to breaking through the German ambush towards the Rhine, nor had they been able to seize the initiative and inflict any real damage on their assailants. After multiple days of marching and fighting at the same time, with little rest or sleep, and likely little food or water, the soldiers must have been both physically and mentally exhausted. None of the surviving sources give a description of events in the Teutoburg at this point, but a potential insight into the experience is perhaps provided by Tacitus, when he describes a similar situation faced by another Roman army in the same region six years later, this time under the command of Aulus Caecina:

> Slipping in their own blood and the marsh-slime, the beasts threw their riders, scattered all they met, and trampled the fallen underfoot. The eagles caused the greatest difficulty of all, as it was impossible either to advance them against the storm of spears or to plant them in the water-logged soil. Caecina, while attempting to keep the front intact, fell with his horse stabbed under him, and was being rapidly surrounded when the first legion interposed. A point in our favour was the rapacity of the enemy, who left the carnage to pursue the spoils; and towards evening the legions struggled out on to open and solid ground. Nor was this the end of their miseries. A rampart had to be raised and material sought for the earthwork; and most of the tools for excavating soil or cutting turf had been lost. There were no tents for the companies, no dressings for the wounded, and as they divided their rations, foul with dirt or blood, they bewailed the deathlike gloom and that for so many thousands of men but a single day now remained.[98]

In this case, the Romans were again fighting against Arminius, in the same general region as the Teutoburg during a putative campaign led against the Germans by Germanicus. Like Varus, Caecina had trouble with his baggage-train, which kept getting stuck in the mud, leading to general confusion among his soldiers, who fell out of battle-order in their efforts to move the baggage, largely ignoring commands given to them in an ever-building panic. Arminius had then attempted to repeat the tactics which had worked so well against Varus and his army – to the degree that Tacitus has himself directly compared the two armies, suggesting that they would share the same fate, as indeed they nearly did.[99] It was likely only the example of the earlier AD 9 disaster that gave Caecina the intelligence to escape Arminius' attack.

By the last day of the battle, Varus' troops appear to have reached a point of crisis, where they could no longer continue to effectively resist the attacks on them. From this point, tactical disintegration was almost inevitable.[100] As their casualties grew, so too did the German numbers, creating an increasing numerical imbalance between the two forces. For a long while – perhaps much longer than Arminius would ever have expected – the Romans had held their combat cohesion, attempting to break free of the German assault and make their way to safety on the Rhine. But there was only so long that the Roman soldiers could last without respite or safety – after three or four days, they were still more than 100km from the Rhine, and growing weaker every day. It is at this point that the hopelessness of their situation may have begun to dawn on many of the surviving Romans. Unfortunately, Dio's account lacks much detail about the final stages of the battle, but the archaeological discoveries around Kalkriese and the Oberesch provide their own account of what happened towards the end of the engagement.

Based on the archaeology, it appears that the Roman army was able to move itself and a limited number of wagons a certain distance westwards of the first ambush – but little did they know that they were only moving further into danger.[101] At the area now known as the Oberesch, a large part of the surviving army appears to have come under sustained attack, leading to the effective destruction as a fighting unit of whatever force had entered the area. Nor was it apparently chance that the Romans ended up at the Oberesch. Excavations in the area, following Tony Clunn's discoveries in 1987, found evidence of an artificial rampart at the Oberesch, seemingly constructed several months before the battle took place.[102] The rampart was about 400m long, and originally stood to a height of around 2m with a width of 4m, with a palisade along at least part of its length.[103] It ran in a zig-zag pattern alongside the path that passed through the pass. The pass was also flanked by a large marsh on one side and a mountain on the other; between these and the rampart, it became an almost inescapable trap for the Romans once they had entered the pass.[104] The Germans could use the rampart to attack the Romans from above, while relying on the structure to defend them from any retaliatory action, and also cutting off the best route for escape that the Romans soldiers would have had. The rampart might well have been Arminius' idea. Throughout the ambush, he would have attempted to use his knowledge of how the Roman army operated under ambush conditions to anticipate Varus' decisions, and take steps to render them ineffective before they had even started. Using a rampart to trap the Romans so that they could neither advance nor retreat was an excellent tactical decision.

Some have argued that the rampart at the Oberesch was not created by the Germans, but is in fact the remains of a Roman camp constructed during the battle.[105] However, it has been noted that Arminius would have been more than capable of ordering the construction of a rampart in a Roman style, given his previous military experience.[106] Its presence would also fit with Arminius' evident preparation of a conflict landscape that was as hostile to the Roman army as possible. However, no Roman finds have yet been found in the area that would have formed the proposed camp's interior, which suggests that the Romans never occupied this space, nor fought in it.[107] Yet at least one side of the rampart was still standing at the end of the battle, as it collapsed over partially looted Roman remains. If the camp had been constructed by the Romans, it would either have been destroyed when they departed from it, in which case the rampart would not still have stood at a later stage in the battle, or they were overrun while constructing or occupying it, in which case it is hard to imagine a complete absence of artefacts in this area.[108] There is, as yet, no good explanation for this absence of artefacts if the rampart is to be identified as a Roman camp.

The Roman army is likely to have sustained sufficiently high casualties at the Oberesch that they were unable to continue functioning as a cohesive force.[109] The soldiers would have been trapped within the pass, unable to move forward or retreat. In many ways, it was a testament to both their experience and will to survive that they made it so far in the face of a relentless attack – the state they were in by this point must have been pitiful. The assemblage from the Oberesch contains few of the artefact types typical of Roman battle sites – lead sling-bullets, iron arrowheads, and iron hobnails from military sandals – suggesting that by this point, most of the soldiers had probably expended any projectile weapons they had, and many may even have been lacking their footwear, lost to the muddy terrain they had crossed. In the last stages of the ambush, many of the surviving soldiers appear to have fallen into a state of combat disintegration, where they were no longer able to maintain combat cohesion or to mount an effective defence against their attackers.[110] This state of hopelessness also appears to have infected the surviving Roman officers, including Varus himself – who had survived up to this point, and who may well have been integral to the maintenance of cohesion within his army. But at this late stage in the battle, Varus was to become a casualty of the battle that had taken the lives of so many of his men. His career, and his life, was to end here in Germany – his ultimate posting in more ways than one.

The Death of Varus

Towards the late stages of the battle in the Teutoburg, Publius Quinctilius Varus met his death. He had survived the first days of the attack, although not unscathed, as Tacitus suggests that he had been wounded at some point in the engagement.[111] How serious the wound was is unclear. But as the Romans reached the end stages of the battle, Varus made the decision to kill himself, alongside several of his officers.[112] In doing so, he hoped to avoid falling into enemy hands, and the pain and humiliation that would almost inevitably result after his capture. None of the sources provide much detail about his death, however. The method used is not recorded in any of the surviving sources, although from references to other military suicides in the historical record, falling on his sword is the most likely probability. Dio calls his suicide 'terrible yet unavoidable' and appears to recognize the act as a brave one, likely the only course of action open to Varus at this time. Velleius, however – a contemporary of Varus – was much more condemnatory of the suicide, saying that Varus had 'had more courage to die than to fight', with the implication that Varus should have avoided taking this action. Presumably, Velleius felt that Varus should have continued to fight alongside his men until the last possible moment, rather than taking an 'easy way out' and leaving them to face the enemy without their commander. Why Velleius felt that Varus' soldiers would be disadvantaged by the loss of a leader who is otherwise characterized as useless and unmilitary is unclear. Perhaps he was better loved by his men than the hostile historian chose to recognize. The location of both his wounding and his suicide were seemingly well-enough known that survivors of the battle were able to point to the locations several years later, although it is impossible to know if they actually did so with any accuracy.[113]

Velleius' condemnation of Varus' suicide appears unfair when it is contextualized against wider military practice, which could often see commanders judged if they *did not* commit suicide in the aftermath of an overwhelming defeat, when they had happened to survive it. Indeed, Varus' father had committed suicide following the defeat at Philippi, as had apparently his grandfather, although it is less clear under what circumstances the latter took place.[114] His action should not have drawn any particular moral censure, even if it was felt by some that it took place earlier than it should have done, and he should have fought on longer before taking his death into his own hands.

Under most circumstances, suicide on the battlefield was not condemned by Roman society, for soldiers of any rank. It was often considered preferable to the alternative – being captured by the enemy, with the pain and shame that this would being on the soldier and his family. Roman citizen soldiers captured by the enemy were stripped of their legal status, essentially making them dead in the eyes of the law, and in most cases, no formal effort would be made by the state to free them.[115] As a result, when defeat on the battlefield was inevitable with no prospect of escape, Roman soldiers of all ranks are frequently documented as having taken the step to end their own lives.[116] Such actions were seen on pitched battlefields, but were particularly common when the Romans were caught in a comprehensive defeat following an ambush. In the late stages of the ambush at Lake Trasimene, the historian Polybius suggests that Roman soldiers even asked their comrades to kill them when they lacked the strength or will to do so themselves.[117] During the Gallic Wars, when a group of survivors from the Fifth Legion was trapped in their camp following an ambush by the Eburones, as mentioned previously, they all committed suicide over the first night.[118] To modern eyes, these cases may seem extreme. But to Roman eyes, the suicides would be much more understandable. Rather than a panicked decision made by frightened men, many of these battlefield suicides were arguably rational responses to the situation they found themselves in, when capture and/or a more painful death was their only alternative; certainly, Roman soldiers largely expected to be treated badly if they were taken prisoner.[119]

Commanders in particular had reason to fear capture by the enemy, with their treatment likely to be even worse than that of the ordinary soldiers, and to involve a large degree of public humiliation. On the rare occasions that Roman commanders oversaw a comprehensive defeat many would kill themselves, particularly when capture seemed inevitable, or brought significant shame.[120] The commander's suicide was not required following a military disaster, as demonstrated by Marcus Lollius who took no such action in the aftermath of his defeat, but many chose self-killing regardless.[121] If pain and suffering were the likely outcome of capture for ordinary soldiers, they were an even more significant threat to higher-ranking figures. Varus must have been aware of the likely fate that awaited him were he to be captured by the enemy – public humiliation, torture, enslavement, and execution were all possibilities. He was likely aware that his own escape was a remote prospect by the late stages of the battle. Arminius may well have commanded his men to try and capture Varus alive. Even had Varus attempted to fight until he was cut down, the numerical superiority of the Germans by this point would likely mean that they could be able to surround and subdue him before this point. Although Varus chose to commit suicide while the late stages of the battle were still being fought around him, which seems at the heart of Velleius' criticism, it may have been the last opportunity he had to do so.

Whatever motivated his decision, Varus now lay dead on the battlefield, alongside many of his more prominent officers. What happened to his body is a matter of debate. Velleius says that the surviving Roman soldiers attempted to cremate him on the battlefield, but were evidently unable to fully conduct the process, likely due to the difficulties of finding both sufficient fuel and time while the battle was still being fought. Sometime later, the partially-burned body fell into German hands, where it was despoiled by several prominent Germans, including the nephew of Segestes, who was fighting as part of Varus' army.[122] Velleius branded the German treatment of Varus' body as a sign of their complete barbarity,[123] although it was not uncommon for the bodies of the enemy dead to be mistreated during Roman warfare more widely. Velleius added that Varus' corpse was decapitated and the head sent to Maroboduus, the chieftain of the Marcomanni.[124] On receiving it, Maroboduus sent the head to Augustus, for an unspecified reason, but clearly feeling it was the best course of action. The emperor would eventually ensure that it received a formal burial in the Quinctili Varii family tomb.[125] The only other account to offer any insight into what happened to Varus' body is that of Florus, who suggests that it was buried by the soldiers, but similarly that it was disinterred.[126] He does not mention an attempt at cremation, but may simply have omitted this detail from the narrative, as it is not precluded by his statement that the body was buried – it may have been so in its partially-cremated state.

The fact that an attempt was made to dispose of Varus' body on the battlefield is further testimony to the combat hardiness of the Roman soldiers. Apparently even at this late stage in the battle they possessed sufficient combat integration that they attempted to protect the body of their commander from despoilment. Their efforts perhaps also provide an insight into how the soldiers felt about Varus. Despite him having led them into an ambush that it was increasingly clear very few of them would walk away from, they still made efforts to keep his body as safe as possible, suggesting that they may have retained respect for him as their commander, and did not bear him immediate anger for the ambush he had led them into.[127] Cremation was the method most commonly used to dispose of the Roman dead on the battlefield, in no small part because the Romans found that if they buried their dead instead, the enemy would inevitably come and exhume the bodies.[128] However, the process was often only partially successful when conducted in a hurry, as was evidently the case with Varus.[129] If circumstances had been better, perhaps they might have tried to return Varus' body home – repatriation of the war-dead was not widely practised in Roman warfare, with the dead customarily left on the battlefield, but exceptions were often made for commanders and other members of the elite.[130] Ultimately, the efforts of the soldiers to preserve Varus' body in death were unsuccessful – like his other soldiers, he faced indignity in death, although his head eventually found rest in the family tomb at Augustus' command.

The End of the Battle

The battle in the Teutoburg ended relatively soon after Varus' death. Dio goes as far as to suggest that the news of Varus' suicide led many of the surviving Romans to give up hope, leading to a complete collapse in unit cohesion:

> When news of this [Varus' suicide] had spread, none of the rest, even if he had any strength left, defended himself any longer. Some imitated their leader, and others, casting aside their arms, allowed anybody who pleased to slay them; for to flee was impossible, however much one might desire to do so. Every man, therefore, and every horse was cut down without fear of resistance.[131]

The situation which Dio describes is one of almost complete tactical disintegration, with many of the Roman soldiers no longer having the physical or mental capacity to continue defending themselves.[132] While many of these soldiers would have been wounded, and all of them exhausted and famished, some still would have had the strength to defend themselves, but no longer the will. Unable to escape, the Romans surrendered themselves to death – and what ensued was a slaughter. Some of the Roman soldiers followed Varus' example and committed suicide, while others dropped their weapons and allowed themselves to be killed without resistance by the enemy. It is difficult to say whether Varus' suicide had such an impact on the remaining soldiers because he himself had been an important factor in their maintenance of cohesion, or because the death of the commander was taken as a sign that the battle was lost.

However, despite the desperate face put on the end of the battle by Dio, it is clear that not every Roman soldier lost their will to live with the news of Varus' death. Indeed, several instances of soldiers acting with clear heads and purpose can be found among both the history and the archaeology. Velleius recounts that one of Varus' cavalry officers, named Vala Numonius, tried to flee the battlefield with his mounted troops, hoping to reach the Rhine.[133] The attempt left the surviving infantry soldiers unprotected by any cavalry, which Velleius strongly condemned. He appeared to feel that justice was done when Numonius was unable to make good his escape, and that he 'did not survive those whom he had abandoned, but died in the act of deserting them'.

Some Roman soldiers were captured by the Germans during the battle. They may have been wounded, taken prisoner rather than slaughtered when they gave up defending themselves, or even just overwhelmed before they had a chance to either escape or commit suicide themselves. Tacitus says that the military tribunes and the most prominent centurions were slaughtered, as human sacrifices at woodland altars close by.[134] He also mentions torture-pits and gibbets, apparently still visible at the site six years later, which had been used against Roman captives. However, Tacitus' account pales in comparison to Florus' brief but gory account of the fate of captured soldiers, although his account may reveal as much about Roman fears as the actual events of the battle:

> They put out the eyes of some of them and cut off the hands of others; they sewed up the mouth of one of them after first cutting out his tongue, exclaiming, 'At last, you viper, you have ceased to hiss'.[135]

Florus suggested that the cruellest punishments were reserved for those Roman soldiers who asked for mercy on legal grounds.[136] So daunting was the prospect of German mistreatment that another Roman taken captive a short time after the battle committed suicide by smashing his head open with the chain he was bound with.[137] Not all the captured Romans were executed, however – which, for all its ritual significance, would have cut into the profits of war – and some evidently ended up in German slavery. A small number of prisoners were ransomed sometime after the battle (it is not clear how long), on a private basis by their relatives rather than the state, although it is unclear whether these were captives taken at the Teutoburg, or in the ongoing military action afterwards.[138] Even private ransom of Roman prisoners of war was unusual, yet clearly permitted on this particular occasion – although it came with the caveat that the ransomed soldiers were prohibited from entering Italy.[139] Aside from those ransomed, it is difficult to imagine that many of the captured Romans lived very long as slaves, but it was possible. A small group of enslaved survivors from the Teutoburg were liberated by another Roman army campaigning in Germany in AD 50, although it had almost certainly not been planned, despite the pride the soldiers took in having done so.[140] However, there is no record of any earlier attempt to liberate any survivors of the battle who were in slavery, despite it being much more likely that they still lived at this point.

An archaeological discovery at Kalkriese made in 2018 provides further fascinating insight into the Roman prisoners taken in the battle, with the discovery of an almost complete piece of *lorica segmentata* armour, and other pieces of legionary kit.[141] A metal-detection survey at the site picked up strong signals from the side wall of an excavation trench, indicating that a large metal object might lie close by. A large block of soil was removed within which the unknown artefact was contained, to ensure it was not damaged during the process of excavation and removal. CT scans revealed it to be a set of *lorica segmentata* armour, heavily compressed but largely complete, down to its fixtures and fittings and even some traces of the leather ties. An iron collar was also found with the armour, such as would be fixed around the neck of a prisoner, which would have connected to cuffs placed around their wrists. No human remains were found in the deposit. That the owner of the armour was taken captive by the Germans is almost certain, but whether he was still wearing the armour when it went into the ground is unknown. The identification of a Roman prisoner at the site provides another clear indication that the battlefield should be associated with Varus and not any later campaigns.

Not every soldier in Varus' army was killed or captured. Some of the soldiers caught in the Teutoburg attack did eventually reach Roman territory. Tacitus says that some of them remained in service in the Roman army, and went back to Germany with Germanicus' army six years later.[142] They led him to the battlefield and then showed him around the site, pointing out where the eagles had been captured, where certain officers had been killed, and where Varus had been wounded and committed suicide. How they had managed to escape is not discussed by Tacitus. Later on, their survival would be used to taunt them, on the basis that 'these were the Romans of Varus' army who had been the quickest to run', although they appear to have remained with the army until a relatively late stage, and were able to point out the place where Varus had committed suicide.[143] The archaeological explorations around Kalkriese further suggest that a number of individuals or small groups were still capable of fighting in areas west of the Oberesch. A number of Roman artefacts have been recovered from German settlements, in an assemblage only increasing in size as excavations in these areas continue. These artefacts were once thought to be part of the assemblage looted from the battlefield by the Germans, but increasingly appear to have been deposited by active fighting. It is possible even that some limited part of the baggage-train made it past the Oberesch, although the majority appears to have been lost.[144] Any surviving soldiers who maintained sufficient individual combat readiness might have stood a chance of survival when the main battle was over, retreating slowly and carefully in small groups once German interest had turned from killing to looting. They may even have faced little resistance, as there would be easier pickings than largely unwounded soldiers who were still willing to fight.[145] Roman weapons have been found in German settlements west of Kalkriese, which may have been deposited by some of these soldiers attempting to make a desperate escape.[146]

The archaeology also shows that attempts were made by the Romans to bury some of their more valuable artefacts in the landscape around the Oberesch, to keep them from falling into German hands. Several caches of precious metals – mainly silver coins, but also silver weapon elements including a scabbard – were found around 2km northwest of the Oberesch.[147] They had evidently been deliberately buried by the Romans, probably to keep them out of enemy hands. Similar hoards have been found associated with the sites of other Roman battlefield defeats, suggesting that this may have been standard practice.[148] The efforts made on these particular occasions were effective, as the valuables buried below were not found until excavations in the modern day. However, the vast majority of the artefacts taken onto the battlefield, from the belongings on the baggage train to the weapons, armour, and even clothing of the Roman soldiers, were in German hands soon after the battle.

Casualties of the battle

While it is clear that there were some Roman survivors of the battle, whatever vestiges of Varus' army made it off the battlefield was likely only a fraction of the army which had walked into the ambush. The human toll of the battle was significant. As discussed earlier in this chapter, it is not certain how many soldiers and camp-followers were caught in the attack, but it was in excess of 10,000. None of the extant sources provide a number for the casualties sustained, but they each make it clear that only a minority of the army survived. The lack of information may be a deliberate omission on the part of the authors, but may equally reflect the fact that there was no reliable information on the human losses of the battle.[149] In an average battle the defeated army would expect to see losses of around 14 to 16 per cent.[150] At the Teutoburg, Roman casualty rates were clearly much higher, although this is not surprising given the circumstances of the battle. It is likely not unrealistic to suggest that casualties could have run as high as 80 per cent or even 90 per cent – depending on how many Romans were there, casualties of 9,000 or more soldiers, in addition to a large but unknown number of camp-followers, would have been lost. Not all would have died in the actual fighting. The descriptions of the German treatment of their captives suggest a significant number of Romans were taken alive, albeit that many would have been executed soon afterwards; many of those taken captive would likely have been wounded and may have died of their injuries soon after the battle anyway. An unknown number would have been sold into German slavery, where their life expectancy would also generally be limited.

As the Roman army did not have access to the battlefield in the aftermath of the ambush it must have proved difficult to create a comprehensive casualty list, as the dead would presumably have to be identified simply as everyone who had not made it back to the Rhine.[151] Few of the soldiers who died alongside Varus in the Teutoburg are known by name. Velleius mentions two camp prefects who perished, Lucius Eggius and Ceionius, the former who died honourably in battle, the latter who proposed surrendering to the Germans and was probably taken captive and executed.[152] Velleius also mentions a cavalry commander named Vala Numonius who attempted to flee with his units and was cut down by the enemy in the process.[153] From the inscribed pieces of kit mentioned earlier in the chapter, two further names can be added – Titus Vibius Tadius, and Marcus Aius, although anything about their fate beyond their presence on the battlefield is unknown. The only other casualty to be known by name is Marcus Caelius, whose cenotaph was discovered at Xanten.[154] Caelius has become perhaps the most well-known victim of the Teutoburg after Varus himself, and his cenotaph is the only tangible link to a casualty of what the inscription called the 'Varian War'. No other inscriptions have been found which relate to the Teutoburg. Whether this is an accident of survival or because they were rare in antiquity is unclear.

When the survivors took stock after the fighting ended, they also realized that the legionary eagles of the Seventeenth, Eighteenth and Nineteenth had been lost – losing the eagle was one of the most disgraceful things that could happen to a Roman legion. All three eagles appear to have fallen into German hands; Florus claimed that one was kept from the enemy when the standard-bearer concealed it in his tunic and threw himself into the marsh – but given what happened with the eagles later on, this either did not happen, or failed to fully hide the eagle.[155] The other sources suggest that all three legionary eagles were in German hands by the end of the battle. Tacitus further suggests that they were put on display by Arminius in the immediate aftermath, alongside other captured military standards, and that they were 'insulted' in an unspecified manner.[156]

Immediate Military Concerns

News of the disaster in the Teutoburg spread across the Roman world, probably arriving in Rome just over a week after the survivors first reached the Rhine.[157] The news prompted fear and distress on the part of those who heard it. The population of northern Gaul appear to have fearfully anticipated hordes of

Germans crossing the Rhine and launching raids of a scale not before seen. Augustus feared that the victory in the Teutoburg would embolden Arminius to push onwards, over the Rhine, potentially advancing deep into Roman territory, maybe even reaching Rome itself. The garrison that would usually protect the Rhine from such incursions had been severely depleted by the defeat. There were probably only two legions remaining in Germany, the First Germanica and the Fifth Alaudae. There was little prospect of immediately replenishing the manpower of the lost legions. Dio suggests that it was hard to find new recruits for the legions in the aftermath of the Teutoburg, as 'there were no citizens of military age left worth mentioning',[158] while the auxiliary troops left in the region had also been depleted. While this may have been an exaggeration, the Rhine garrison had certainly been severely weakened by the battle. It was still under strength more generally as a result of the transfer of legions to fight in the Illyrian Revolt, who had not yet returned from the conflict. If ever there was a time that the Germans could invade the territorial heartlands of the Empire, this was their opportunity. Roman military reactions to the disaster were consequently rapid. The First and Fifth legions were quickly marched to the Lower Rhine by their commander, Lucius Nonius Asprenas, Varus' nephew. This move bolstered the loyalty of the populations living along the Rhine, who had not taken part in Arminius' uprising but were apparently beginning to question the wisdom of their alliance with Rome.[159] Velleius credits Asprenas with saving a lot of Roman lives through his actions, although the historian notes the slightly unsavoury rumour that Asprenas took the opportunity to 'appropriate' the belongings of those who had died at the Teutoburg, later also claiming their inheritances.

In the immediate aftermath of the Teutoburg, the Germans involved in the ambush had begun looting the battlefield.[160] They may also have constructed a Graeco-Roman style victory trophy at the heart of the battlefield, perhaps in mocking mimicry of the practices of their defeated opponents.[161] The looting process was primarily concerned with the most valuable artefacts, prioritizing metal artefacts, particularly weapons, some of which would later be used by German troops against the Romans in another campaign.[162] The assemblage left behind at the Oberesch, where the Germans likely concentrated their processing efforts, provides a detailed insight into the looting of the battlefield. The looting initially prioritized high-value and functional metal artefacts, particularly weapons and metal armour, much of which could be found relatively easily due both to physical size, and its likely proximity to the bodies of the dead. Armour was stripped roughly from the bodies of the dead, depositing small fragments and fittings onto the ground that were not always picked up. The metal binding from shields was ripped away from the wooden bases and crumpled into balls for easier transportation. Precious metals were evidently favoured over base ones, particularly as the Germans largely lacked the ability to re-smelt the iron artefacts. The priorities of the initial looting phase can be seen particularly through one well-known artefact from the site – the mask from a cavalry face-helmet, the image of which is almost synonymous with the site at Kalkriese. The mask was once covered with a silver veneer over the iron base which survives today. The silver was removed, but the iron was not taken in the first phase of looting, and was covered over before it could be taken from the site. Many small items, such as projectiles or metal kit fragments, were deeply embedded in the topsoil during the battle and its aftermath, and there was probably little effort made to recover these pieces. Some pieces were deposited during the looting process itself, including elements of kit which fell off armour as it was stripped from the dead, and pieces of balled-up shield-binding. Other parts of the assemblage were preserved when part of the rampart collapsed, burying a partially-looted assemblage below it. The booty was likely collected together centrally at the Oberesch, probably in front of the rampart, before being transported away. However, the Germans appear to have left the battlefield before the looting was complete, after what appears to have been an initial hurried period of looting, which prioritized the most valuable and most useful artefacts, recognizing that with so much Roman material to choose from, only some of the assemblage could be taken.[163] Why this initial phase was so brief is uncertain. Perhaps the Germans wanted to leave the site in case a Roman army came upon them while they were still looting the field, or they were needed to fight elsewhere.

The booty looted from the battlefield would have been widely distributed among those who had taken part in the battle. Some artefacts ended up in German settlements around Kalkriese, where there is some evidence of iron weapons being repurposed as domestic artefacts.[164] More luxurious items likely went to chieftains or other prominent individuals, although some of it would later be returned to Roman hands during Germanicus' campaigns.[165] Some of the material may have travelled even further afield. The hoard of silverware discovered in Hildesheim (approximately 130km from Kalkriese) has been identified as booty from the battle, as have several depositions of luxury items in bogs and graves in Denmark from this same period.[166] This comprehensive German looting process at the Oberesch is one of the main arguments in favour of the site being associated with Varus rather than Germanicus. The Kalkriese area was clearly in German hands at the end of the battle, by the way that the material was processed. Roman armies collected together deposited metalwork from battlefields and transported it away, whereas there is clear evidence of significant processing on the site itself here. The nature of the entire assemblage is completely different to that of a battlefield where the Romans were the victors. The only example comparable to Kalkriese is the landscape around the battlefield of Abritus (Bulgaria), where the Romans were comprehensively defeated.

Arminius made an almost immediate push towards the Rhine, over-running most of the Roman military installations that lay in his path.[167] The Germans may have hoped to join forces with the rebels in Illyricum, which would have presented a major problem to the manpower-depleted Romans. Fortunately for Rome, the Illyrian Revolt had come to an end shortly before the Teutoburg, although Arminius probably did not know that at the time of the battle.[168] The German advance was then stopped short of the Rhine by fierce Roman resistance at the fort of Aliso, which was held under the command of the camp prefect, Lucius Caedicius, who appears to have taken significant command of the situation in Germany in the immediate aftermath of the Teutoburg.[169] The Germans attempted to capture the fort, and, when this proved unsuccessful, began to lay siege to it. The Roman garrison at Aliso by this time may have included survivors from the Teutoburg who had fled there. They proved able to hold off the sustained assault from an 'insurmountable' number of German attackers, buying time for reinforcements to arrive on the Rhine, and to come to their rescue.[170] The fort at Aliso contained not just soldiers, but also a large number of women and children,[171] who may have taken shelter in the fort when the German uprising began. The garrison may have learned from Varus' recent example that it could be close to impossible to escape an attacking force of Germans in their own terrain, especially without a reliable local guide. They chose to remain in the base, hoping either that the Germans would leave, or a Roman relief force would arrive. Dio suggests that the Romans were able to hold the fort because the Germans lacked the skills to mount an effective siege, and because the garrison included a large number of archers, who were able to inflict heavy casualties on their attackers.[172] Frontinus suggested that they also used a degree of psychological warfare to convince the Germans that their manpower was much more significant than it actually was:

> When the survivors of the Varian disaster were under siege and seemed to be running short of food, they spent an entire night in leading prisoners round their store-houses; then, having cut off their hands, they turned them loose. These men persuaded the besieging force to cherish no hope of an early reduction of the Romans by starvation, since they had an abundance of food supplies.[173]

The tactics employed by the garrison at Aliso were evidently effective, and they survived the German assault. Aliso has been cautiously identified as being located in Haltern-am-See, which lies just under 100km southwest of Kalkriese, and about 50km east of the legionary base at Xanten.[174] Although the identification is not yet conclusive, it remains the most plausible suggestion for the location of Aliso.

While the soldiers already stationed in Germany attempted to hold back the German advance with the limited manpower available to them, re-enforcements were on the way. As the Illyrian Revolt had ended just before the Teutoburg, the manpower which for several years had been diverted to that conflict, could now be redirected towards the Rhine where they were sorely needed. Despite a generalized manpower shortage, Augustus strengthened the forces available by forcing citizens of military age to enlist, first by confiscating the estates of 20 per cent of the men under 35, and 10 per cent of those over. When this still did not prompt the men to sign-up, he had some of them executed.[175] He ended up forcing time-served veterans and freedmen to serve, choosing as many as he could by lot. The extreme reaction of Augustus in terms of recruiting soldiers is a sign of the panic that the Teutoburg defeat had raised in him, to the degree that he was willing to throw every manpower source he could raise at the Rhine, despite the impact it might have on his popularity.

Augustus appointed Tiberius – who was by this point his official heir – to the command of the new army and despatched him immediately to the Rhine. Tiberius had once before been sent to secure a region in the aftermath of a military disaster, having been appointed governor of Gaul after the Lollian Disaster, and was called upon to do the same in AD 9. Once again, as Velleius puts it, Tiberius was called upon to be the 'constant protector of the Roman empire'.[176] His passage through Gaul reassured the population of the province, still awaiting the arrival of a German invasion, that security was about to be reimposed on the Rhine frontier. Tiberius redistributed his army, strengthened the frontier garrisons, and then took the conflict into German territory, advancing beyond the Rhine despite being told by Augustus that he should just hold the river frontier instead.[177]

When the Germans learnt that Tiberius had restrengthened the garrisons on the Rhine, and was now advancing beyond the river, their resolve began to crumble. On hearing that Tiberius was marching towards Aliso, the besieging Germans largely withdrew, leaving only a small number of men there, who nonetheless hoped to find a way to defeat the Roman garrison.[178] They were wary of Roman sallies from the fort, keeping a safe distance away, and evidently hoped to starve the Romans out of the fort, counting on them running out of food before re-enforcements could arrive. The German plan worked, in that the Romans ran out of provisions before Tiberius and his army arrived and decided to break out from the fort, using a stormy night as cover. The Romans managed to advance a certain distance undetected, but their presence was inadvertently betrayed by the women and children who followed them, who kept shouting to the soldiers. The Germans fell on the fleeing Romans, who according to Dio would have been wiped out had it not been for the attackers becoming distracted by plundering the Roman baggage, allowing some soldiers to make a rapid escape some distance from the fort. These soldiers then had their trumpeters play the signal for a double march, leading the Germans to believe that a Roman relief army had finally arrived, under the command of Asprenas. They consequently withdrew, and Asprenas, having learned about the events at Aliso, arrived soon afterwards. Velleius showered praise on the Roman force at Aliso, stating that by

> following a design that was carefully considered, and using a vigilance that was ever on the alert, they watched their chance, and with the sword won their way back to their friends.[179]

After the disaster in the Teutoburg, and near disasters in the weeks following, the Romans were finally beginning to re-establish military control at least as far as the Rhine, while withdrawing their vulnerable garrisons that still lay east of the river. Tiberius had headed off another potential disaster, much more quickly than had been expected, but the consequences of the Teutoburg were far from over.[180]

Augustus' response to the disaster

When he heard about the disaster in the Teutoburg, Augustus is credited by Suetonius with one of the most memorable lines of ancient history – 'Quinctilius Varus, give me back my legions!', which he is said to have exclaimed more than once.[181] This response undoubtedly captures the emperor's feelings towards the defeat. Unfortunately, it is not recorded by any other historian, which undermines its claims of veracity, although it remains a popular way to characterize Augustus' reaction to the news. The emperor does appear to have been thrown into a state of excessive shock and grief by the defeat, tearing his clothes, leaving his hair and beard to grow for several months as a sign of his mourning for the loss, and occasionally banging his head against doorframes while crying out.[182] In doing so, he probably participated in a much wider public expression of grief and mourning for the legions in Rome, and Italy more widely, where many of the lost soldiers would have had families.[183] The anniversary of the battle was evidently treated by Augustus as a day of mourning for the rest of his reign, although it is not clear upon which of the three or four days of the battle the anniversary was marked.[184] Festivals were cancelled, and much of the usual business of government was not carried out during the weeks after the disaster.[185] Augustus also ruled that governors due to leave their provinces should stay in them for the time being, concerned that a change of personnel might lead to discontent among the population, and wanting to leave provincial affairs in the hands of experienced men who already knew what they were doing.[186] He further promised games to the god Jupiter Optimus Maximus in exchange for divine protection of the Roman state.[187]

Augustus was evidently severely concerned that this single defeat could develop into a much larger-scale disaster. As mentioned previously, he compelled men of military age to enlist in the regions, punishing those who refused with disenfranchisement and even death, before settling on the forced recruitment by lot of time-served veterans and freedmen. Germans and Gauls who were currently serving in the Praetorian Guard were dismissed from service and sent away from Rome, as Augustus was concerned that they might start a rebellion in the city, or join the Germans should they arrive nearby.[188] Unarmed Germans who happened to be in the city were also asked to leave. His actions appear to be consistent with the precautions taken when Rome itself had been threatened in the past – Augustus' preparations very much appear to have been those of someone who expected the enemy to appear at his door.[189] They may have also have been intended to limit the outbreak of panic in the city by reassuring the population that sufficient precautionary measures were being taken.[190]

Augustus appears to have remained in a state of shock and agitation until news arrived from the Rhine that the situation had been stabilized – that some soldiers had survived, the Rhine forts still stood, and the Germans had not yet crossed into Roman territory.[191] After hearing this, his mood changed to reflection rather than panic. He apparently came to the conclusion that such a large-scale defeat could only have been brought down by an offended deity who wanted to punish Rome for an unknown transgression.[192] He subsequently sought for possible omens that had foretold the disaster in the days leading up to it, and found them:

For the temple of Mars in the field of the same name was struck by lightning, and many locusts flew into the very city and were devoured by swallows; the peaks of the Alps seemed to collapse upon one another and to send up three columns of fire; the sky in many places seemed ablaze and numerous comets appeared at one and the same time; spears seemed to dart from the north and to fall in the direction of the Roman camps; bees formed their combs about the altars in the camps; a statue of Victory that was in the province of Germany and faced the enemy's territory turned about to face Italy.[193]

Dio does not speculate on what Augustus considered to be the cause of this divine wrath, and evidently the portents had not been recognized as harbingers of disaster in Germany when they happened. The way that Augustus grasped for a supernatural explanation for the event perhaps suggests that he was struggling to find meaning in a terrestrial one. This could not be a normal military defeat, but had to reflect something bigger, something that he could have done nothing to prevent.

Augustus was not accustomed to military defeat. The only major losses he had overseen in his long reign had been in Germany, the Lollian Disaster and the Battle of the Teutoburg. Perhaps more problematically, the latter came when there was no longer much time for new glory to outweigh the shame of disaster.[194] He had turned 70 years old in the month before the Teutoburg, and had for a long time been concerned about his legacy. A defeat on this scale towards the end of his reign was not a welcome addition to the events of his life. The Teutoburg threatened to cast a shadow over his legacy more permanently. It was also a more personal loss. One aspect of Augustus' reaction to the Teutoburg which is not often considered is the fact that it was also a personal loss for him – not of his soldiers, but of Varus himself. Augustus was said to have been intensely loyal to those he knew well and trusted.[195] Varus may well have been part of this small group. Augustus had known Varus for over three decades, since Varus was in his early twenties. He had appointed him to his delegation to the eastern provinces in 22 BC, perhaps after they had already crossed paths in Spain during the Cantabrian Wars, and had taken an interest in his career ever since. Augustus had overseen Varus twice marrying into the Imperial inner-circle, to the daughter of Marcus Agrippa (Augustus' heir at the time) and later to Claudia Pulchra, a marriage which had made Varus an in-law member of the Imperial family. It is hard to imagine that Varus' death, under such brutal circumstances, did not affect Augustus on a personal level, amidst his grief for the defeat more widely. Velleius says that Varus' head was sent to Augustus by Maroboduus after it had been carried to him in turn, and that the emperor ensured it received a proper burial in the family tomb.[196]

Augustus' relationship with Varus may, however, also have heightened his personal feelings of betrayal at the defeat. Not only had Rome been put in danger by a military disaster, but it had been overseen by one of the people most trusted by the emperor. Varus had been appointed to a difficult job, arguably because Augustus felt that he was one of the only people he could trust in the role. With the Illyrian Revolt raging, Augustus had needed someone reliable in Germany, who could support Roman development in the region but above all provide security and stability along the Rhine. Augustus was known to have been fairly cautious when conducting his own military campaigns, and to have strongly disapproved of recklessness in the field:

> He [Augustus] thought nothing less becoming in a well-trained leader than haste and rashness, and, accordingly, favourite sayings of his were: 'More haste, less speed'; 'Better a safe commander than a bold'; and 'That is done quickly enough which is done well enough'.[197]

Suetonius added that the emperor was also said not to have chased after warfare or battle unless the prospects of victory far outweighed the prospects of defeat. Augustus was likely aware of the dangers of irregular warfare on the fringes of the Empire, not least as he had seen first-hand the devastating impact of ambush while on campaign during the Cantabrian Wars, and had witnessed how little even a good commander could do under such circumstances.[198] Varus had likely also served in the Cantabrian campaign, and in many ways was the kind of commander favoured by Augustus, which he had ably demonstrated in Syria, where his approach to the Jewish uprising had secured peace with little Roman loss. Varus had never let the emperor down before – but in Germany he failed to do what was required of him, and had nearly brought down disaster on Rome. Even though the feared invasion had not manifested, the Teutoburg would still have long-term ramifications for Rome – Imperial policy would have to rapidly adjust to the new circumstances.

Avenging the Teutoburg – the campaigns of Germanicus

After Tiberius had secured the Rhine region in the immediate aftermath of the Teutoburg, Augustus withdrew him from the region, and did not initiate any further campaigning east of the Rhine in the remaining five years of his region. On his deathbed, Augustus advised Tiberius not to try and expand into Germany.[199] This was likely not an unpopular decision in Rome, where there was a generalized mistrust, even hatred, of Germany, even going back years before the disaster.[200] This was an extreme departure from Augustus' approach in his earlier reign, which had seen him extend Roman territorial control significantly.[201] Although he did not withdraw troops from the Rhine, Augustus did not attempt to recover the territories east of the river. However, it would have been far from clear at this point that Imperial ambitions for Germany had been abandoned. The territories were not completely forgotten by Rome, although they were seemingly no longer garrisoned by the Roman army, and no campaigning appears to have taken place. But civic settlements such as that at Waldgirmes were not abandoned in this period, suggesting that any Roman withdrawal from Germany was seen as only a temporary measure.[202]

When Tiberius became emperor in AD 14, he could not ignore the problems in Germany. He was familiar with the region, having campaigned in it multiple times, and may have felt that the early years of his reign offered an opportunity to deal with it on his own terms, rather than those dictated to him by Augustus. The Germans still posed an active threat, particularly while Arminius still lived. Just because they had not managed to cross the Rhine in AD 9 did not mean that they would not try again, perhaps more successfully this time. Arminius had become a threat in the region, and threatened Roman security along the Rhine, which Tiberius would no doubt have been keenly aware of. On a more personal level, Tiberius had likely been close to Varus. The two had served as consuls together in 13 BC, and had been brothers-in-law when each was married to a daughter of Marcus Agrippa, and Tiberius may have felt some responsibility to punish those he held responsible for the death of Varus and his men. Consequently, between AD 15 and 17, in the first few years of Tiberius' reign, his nephew Germanicus waged a substantial campaign in Germany, centred around the same territories in which Varus had been active just a few years before.[203] However, his primary objective was not the reconquest of the territory, but 'to redeem the prestige lost with Quintilius [sic] Varus and his army than from any wish to extend the Empire or with any prospect of an adequate recompense'.[204] Essentially, he hoped to soothe the damaged Roman pride, and to send a message to any future rebels about the retribution that would result from such uprisings. At the same time, there was a practical need for someone to weaken, even destroy, the threat posed by the Germans in general, and Arminius specifically.

During the campaign, Germanicus visited the Teutoburg battlefield, guided by survivors of the battle who were now serving within his army. Tacitus preserves a description of the battlefield as Germanicus found it in AD 15, six years after the battle:

There came upon the Caesar, therefore, a passionate desire to pay the last tribute to the fallen and their leader, while the whole army present with him were stirred to pity at thought of their kindred, of their friends, ay! and of the chances of battle and of the lot of mankind. Sending Caecina forward to explore the secret forest passes and to throw bridges and causeways over the flooded marshes and treacherous levels, they pursued their march over the dismal tract, hideous to sight and memory. Varus' first camp, with its broad sweep and measured spaces for officers and eagles, advertised the labours of three legions: then a half-ruined wall and shallow ditch showed that there the now broken remnant had taken cover. In the plain between were bleaching bones, scattered or in little heaps, as the men had fallen, fleeing or standing fast. Hard by lay splintered spears and limbs of horses, while human skulls were nailed prominently on the tree-trunks. In the neighbouring groves stood the savage altars at which they had slaughtered the tribunes and chief centurions. Survivors of the disaster, who had escaped the battle or their chains, told how here the legates fell, there the eagles were taken, where the first wound was dealt upon Varus, and where he found death by the suicidal stroke of his own unhappy hand. They spoke of the tribunal from which Arminius made his harangue, all the gibbets and torture-pits for the prisoners, and the arrogance with which he insulted the standards and eagles. And so, six years after the fatal field, a Roman army, present on the ground, buried the bones of the three legions; and no man knew whether he consigned to earth the remains of a stranger or a kinsman, but all thought of all as friends and members of one family, and, with anger rising against the enemy, mourned at once and hated. At the erection of the funeral-mound the Caesar laid the first sod, paying a dear tribute to the departed, and associating himself with the grief of those around him.[205]

Tacitus paints a grim scene, although the way that he described the battlefield landscape may owe as much to literary convention as a realistic observation of the site.[206] One of the main tasks that Germanicus undertook at the site was the burial of the by-now-skeletal remains of the Roman dead. According to the Roman historians, little effort was made by the Germans to bury the Roman dead, who were instead left exposed for years afterwards. He buried these remains below a large tumulus, although the monument was torn down by the Germans as soon as Germanicus and his army left the area.[207] Tiberius was said to have strongly disapproved of the act, in no small part because he worried about the impact that seeing the remains of the slaughtered Roman soldiers would have a negative impact on the morale of the current army, and instil fear of the Germans among them.[208] However, Germanicus may have felt it worth the risk, and that burying the remains of the long-dead Roman casualties of the battle would reassure his soldiers that they would receive similarly respectful treatment should they die during the upcoming war.[209]

Eight bone-pits have been excavated in the Oberesch area which contain the disarticulated remains of a number of casualties from the battle, which have been linked cautiously by some to the burial by Germanicus, even though there are multiple pits rather than one single large inhumation.[210] The pits vary in size from 30–40cm to 4m², and contain a jumbled assortment of human bones, with a small amount of animal bone mixed in.[211] Most of the bones belonged to men of combatant age – roughly 20 to 40 years old – with one possible female bone among the assemblage. Many of the bones were found in poor condition, with signs of animal gnawing on the ends of many of the long limb-bones, suggesting that they had been exposed on the surface for a period of between two and ten years before burial. A small number of partially-articulated bones were found, which may have been kept in relative position by either the remnants of tight clothing, non-metal armour, or bandages, organic materials which have not survived their time in the ground.[212] There is no evidence for attempts to cremate the remains, which has raised questions from some who suggest this was not consistent with Roman military practice at the time.[213] However, others note that Roman military burial customs were often flexible in the face of reality, and that little should be read into the lack of cremation.[214] The practicalities of cremating skeletal material may not have been considered worth the time and effort, in what was a pressing military situation – especially given that the purpose of that disposal method was to prevent the despoilment of the dead, which had already taken place years earlier. The pits may have been created by Romans present later on the site, alongside the larger mound Germanicus is said to have raised, but may also be the work of Germans living in the area, who wanted to reclaim the land some years after the battle. Although Tacitus' description of the battlefield area suggests that it was abandoned after the ambush, the increasing archaeological evidence for German land-use in the area suggests that this may not have been the case in reality. Much of the conflict landscape, including the Oberesch, lay on one of the main routes through the area, as well as in an area that was under active cultivation prior to the battle. The bones may have been cleared away as an inconvenience once their value as a victory display had worn thin. A similar situation was seen around the battlefield of Arausio following an engagement in 105 BC, in which the bodies of a defeated Gallic and German tribal force were abandoned on the site. The local population ended up using their bones to fence their vineyards.[215] They found that the agricultural fertility of the site was significantly increased in the years following the battle, a phenomenon which had been observed on other battlefields as well (although they did not know why). The people around Kalkriese likely found that the slaughter of the battle was leading to a similar situation, and may have been keen to clear the site after a few years so that they could take advantage of the situation.

Germanicus went on to wage a vicious conflict against Arminius and his allies, in which the German chieftain attempted on multiple occasions to repeat the tactics which had proved so successful against Varus. On one occasion an ambush startled a Roman cavalry contingent, nearly leading to them attempting to flee into a marsh where they would have been easily defeated; Germanicus restored order at the last moment.[216] Another contingent of the army, under the command of Aulus Caecina, was surrounded by the enemy and close to disaster, only just managing to fight their way out of trouble – and arguably only because they had learned from Varus' example about what not to do in the situation.[217] The Romans were well aware of the risks posed by the Germans fighting in their own territory, but were seemingly powerless to do much about it most of the time. Their mere presence put them at a disadvantage compared to the lightly-armed Germans who knew the terrain, and who could melt away into the surrounding landscape whenever they felt under threat.

During the German campaign, Tacitus narrated a set-piece discussion between Arminius and his brother Flavus, through which he explored the two different perspectives of Roman actions in Germany.[218] The two had been raised together as hostages in Rome, and both had served in the Roman army, but Flavus had declined to join his brother in rebellion. The discussion between the two is clearly fictionalized by Tacitus, who cannot possibly have known what was discussed between the two – if the meeting ever happened – but it created an opportunity to set two perspectives against each other: the loyal brother, who enjoyed success in the army, with higher pay and numerous military decorations – but who had lost an eye in service – and the treacherous brother, who claimed that fidelity to Rome was a betrayal of Germany. Tacitus had the brothers almost exchanging blows over the argument before they were separated by another Roman officer, unable to reconcile their differences as Roman and German.[219]

Germanicus eventually gained the upper hand when Arminius and his allies met the Romans in pitched battle, in a plain called Idistaviso, the location of which is as yet unidentified.[220] Roman military organization won the battle, despite Arminius' best efforts to rally his troops amidst the heat of battle. Tacitus described the battle as:

a brilliant, and to us not a bloody, victory. The enemy were slaughtered from the fifth hour of daylight to nightfall, and for ten miles the ground was littered with corpses and weapons.[221]

Arminius was wounded but escaped, possibly with the help of some sympathetic German auxiliaries. Almost immediately afterwards, another battle was fought, known as the Battle of the Angrivarian Wall, where a large German coalition of troops suffered a comprehensive defeat.[222] The Germans were slaughtered by the Romans. However, Germanicus was unable to push the victory any further as winter was approaching and he wanted to withdraw his troops back to the Rhine. He sent a large part of his army by boat and lost a large number of soldiers in a late summer storm which capsized much of the fleet.[223] Germanicus was then withdrawn from Germany by Tiberius, who was said to be growing envious of his nephew's success. In doing so, Tacitus said, he 'withdrew him [Germanicus] from a glory already within his grasp', although Germanicus was voted a triumph for his victories east of the Rhine.[224] It had perhaps never been the plan for these campaigns to restore Roman territorial dominance over the region. Although there were several good reasons for a punative campaign, including avenging the humiliation of Rome and weakening Arminius' power-base, it may also have been planned simply to give the Rhine legions something to do. When Tiberius had become emperor they had mutinied, protesting their low pay, poor treatment, and the fact that they had been kept in service long after they should have been allowed to retire.[225] The disaffected troops attacked their centurions, beating them and throwing them out of the camp or into the Rhine. Discipline broke down, and the soldiers were no longer observing all their military duties. Germanicus had to personally intervene to end the mutiny. When he arrived, the soldiers had confronted him, listing their grievances, and graphically demonstrating some of them. Some soldiers, complaining that they had not been discharged from service, used the gesture of kissing Germanicus' hand to thrust his fingers in their mouths to feel the toothless gums within, as a sign of their age.[226] Germanicus was eventually able to end the mutiny, with the main instigators executed by the other men of the legion, and others dishonourably discharged from the army.[227] Although the immediate danger was over, it was clear that there was a problem with the soldiers on the Rhine. One of the best ways to deal with such an issue was to keep the soldiers busy, directing their energy and frustration against the enemy rather than Rome, and this may have been one of the reasons that Tiberius ordered Germanicus to lead a campaign into Germany the following year.[228] The campaign would have addressed several imminent problems for Tiberius, but did not necessarily ever aim to restore Roman dominance over the region east of the Rhine.

Germanicus had successfully avenged the Teutoburg, inflicting heavy defeats on many of the tribes who had contributed warriors to Arminius' force, and had gone a long way towards neutralizing the threat to Rome from east of the Rhine. However, his campaigns had another achievement, a more unexpected one. During the campaign, Germanicus oversaw the recovery of two of the legionary eagles lost in the Teutoburg, first that of the Nineteenth Legion, which was being carried around by the Bructeri tribe, and another which was found buried in woodland in the territory of the Marsi.[229] An arch was dedicated in the Roman forum to celebrate their return.[230] The third eagle would not be recovered for several decades, eventually returning to Roman hands during a campaign early in the reign of Claudius, Germanicus' younger brother.[231]

Germanicus' campaign had broken the resistance of the Germans and destroyed much of Arminius' power. Relatively early in the campaign the Romans had taken Arminius' wife, Thusnelda, into their custody and promised her their protection at the request of her father, Segestes, in recognition of the loyalty he had shown them.[232] Thusnelda was pregnant at the time, and later gave birth to a son, Thumelicus, who was taken hostage by Rome and raised in Ravenna.[233] Arminius was said to have been 'driven frantic by the seizure of his wife and the subjugation to slavery of her unborn child', motivating him still further to make war against Rome.[234] What happened to Thumelicus in later life is unclear.[235] Arminius was still alive when Germanicus was withdrawn from Germany, and according to Strabo the war was not considered to be 'over' when the Romans left the region in AD 17.[236] But after the defeats at Idistaviso and the Angrivarian Wall, Arminius' power was broken and he never challenged Rome significantly again. Instead, he waged war on Maroboduus, his main rival for power in Germany, in a conflict that ended without a clear victory for either side. Arminius was later murdered by his own men in AD 21, when he laid too bare his ambitions to become a 'king' in Germany, prompting rebellion from his fellow countrymen who did not want to be ruled that way. While some had proposed to poison Arminius, in the end he was openly attacked and killed, aged 37, by his own relatives. Tacitus painted a relatively flattering portrait of Arminius – certainly a better one than Varus ever received – despite the damage he had once done to Rome:

> Undoubtedly [Arminius was] the liberator of Germany; a man who, not in its infancy as captains and kings before him, but in the high noon of its sovereignty, threw down the challenge to the Roman nation, in battle

with ambiguous results, in war without defeat; he completed thirty-seven years of life, twelve of power, and to this day is sung in tribal lays, though he is an unknown being to Greek historians, who admire only the history of Greece, and receives less than his due from us of Rome, who glorify the ancient days and show little concern for our own.[237]

Arminius had done well to remain out of Roman captivity, but could not escape the German elite in-fighting that would lead to his death at the hands of kinsmen who should have been his allies. It is almost fitting, given his actions in the Teutoburg, that his death should have come at the hands of those whom he should have been able to trust. But ultimately, even with his life cut short, he achieved much of what he had seemingly hoped to when he began to formulate a plot against Varus: he drove the Romans back to the western side of the Rhine. Although Roman armies would periodically cross the river to campaign against particular German tribes, there was never again a concerted effort to establish permanent dominance over the region in the way that there had been during the reign of Augustus.

Germanicus may have avenged the Teutoburg, but it would be a long time before the battle was forgotten. It would go on to be blamed for the seeming abandonment of Roman Imperial ambitions east of the Rhine, and has subsequently been viewed as a 'turning point' in European history in a way that it did not inevitably have to be. Varus would remain inextricably linked with the battle in a way most defeated commanders were not, and would be comprehensively blamed for the defeat. Over the following decades, the battle in the Teutoburg would transform into the 'Varus Disaster', and Varus' reputation would be lost in the process.

Chapter 7

Creating the 'Varus Disaster': The Legacy of The Teutoburg

Roman losses in the Teutoburg had been significant. Three legions and an unknown number of auxiliary units had been lost, along with their eagles and other insignia. Varus was dead, along with many of his soldiers. Most survivors of the battle had either been executed by the Germans or sold into slavery; very few made it back to the safety of the Rhine. The news had quickly spread to Rome, leaving Augustus in shock and fear about an imminent German invasion. Arminius had hoped to lead his troops out of Germany into Gaul, and was ultimately held back only by desperate defensive actions on the part of the garrison at Aliso. The situation was stabilized soon after by Tiberius, although there was no attempt to re-establish Roman dominance east of the Rhine. When he became emperor in AD 14, Tiberius sent Germanicus to campaign in Germany for several years, to break the power that Arminius had developed in the region, and to avenge the Teutoburg. Although successful, these campaigns did not lead to any attempt to permanently restore Roman dominance on the areas of Germany that lay beyond the Rhine.

The defeat in AD 9 alone did not need to end Roman Imperial ambitions east of the Rhine. The situation was grim for Rome, but it was also far from unrecoverable. Large-scale military defeats were not usual for the Romans, and complete disasters even rarer, but they were not without precedent.[1] Rome had sustained greater casualties than those of the Teutoburg and gone on to win the war. Legions had been wiped out before and been reconstituted, and territorial dominance re-established in regions from which the Romans had been driven. Recovery from the defeat was far from impossible. But for some reason, this did not happen after the Teutoburg. Many things damaged by the battle were not restored to their previous state in the years following the engagement. Once Tiberius declined to restore Roman control east of the Rhine during his reign, the events of the Teutoburg took on a much greater historical significance. As a result, it became a much more damaging defeat for Rome than it might have initially seemed, and with hindsight looks like a much more definitive turning point in history than it probably was in the immediate aftermath of the battle. Now it would prove necessary for someone to be blamed for the defeat, and it was evidently decided soon that this person would be Varus.

None of the written sources on the battle predate the end of Germanicus' campaigns. It is therefore impossible to gauge how Varus was judged in Rome during the first years after the battle, before it became evident that Tiberius was not going to send further campaigns of conquest over the Rhine. By the AD 20s, just over a decade after the battle, Varus was being blamed for the defeat. He was held culpable on a variety of levels: that long term, he had not seen how Roman policy in Germany would provoke discontent; in the mid-term, that he had ignored rumours of plotting by Arminius and his allies; and in the short-term, that he had made all the wrong decisions once the ambush had been sprung. These accusations do not tell the full story of Varus' culpability. As we have seen, he was a capable, experienced military commander and administrator who faced a difficult situation in Germany, and one who coped with events as well as anyone would have done in his position. But the reaction of Augustus as transmitted through the sources (whether accurate or not) made it clear that Varus was to be held as the primary facilitator of the defeat, irrespective of how much he had actually contributed to it. The achievements of his earlier career were forgotten in the wake of the Teutoburg. Many would be written out entirely of the mainstream historical record, surviving only in Josephus' brief account of his time in Syria, and in a small number of archaeological finds. It is almost as though Varus' life up to the Teutoburg was censored in the interests of serving a historical narrative that developed to blame him for the defeat, to the exclusion of others. In particular, Augustus and the Imperial regime were shielded from any culpability for the defeat, while Arminius was deliberately marginalized to lessen the achievement of his victory. These aims necessitated a certain characterisation of Varus that was not accurate, but it was the only way to shape the narrative in the way that the Romans wanted it. This chapter explores the creation of the 'Varus Disaster' in Roman historiography, considering how culpable Varus actually was for the events in Germany, and exploring how his presentation in the ancient sources was adapted to show him in the worst possible light. It offers a reconsideration of the evidence as transmitted from antiquity, and suggests that Varus was scapegoated for the defeat to protect Augustus and the Imperial regime from any negative association with the defeat.

From defeat to disaster

Following the campaigns of Germanicus, Tiberius appears to have decided to abandon any immediate plans to re-establish Roman territorial control in the region. Settlements such as that at Waldgirmes were finally abandoned, with their buildings carefully dismantled and the remains set on fire by the departing Romans.[2] While Roman campaigns did still periodically campaign east of the Rhine under subsequent emperors,[3] Roman territorial dominance was never established in the region to the degree that seems to have been desired under Augustus. By the second century AD the Rhine had become an increasingly permanent linear boundary between the Empire and the German territories beyond, garrisoned in parts by forts, watchtowers, and a wooden palisade. However, Roman armies periodically continued to cross the frontier, sometimes advancing deep into German territory, for several centuries. A Romano-German battle site discovered at Harzhorn (only about 70km south of Hanover) dating to the mid-third century AD demonstrates the range of some of these campaigns, as it lies in excess of 300km in advance of the frontier at that time.[4] The engagement was entirely undocumented, but based on the assemblage appears to date to the reign of Maximinius Thrax (AD 235–238). Thrax was known to have campaigned in Germany, but until the discovery of the Harzhorn, was thought to have stayed much closer to the Rhine.[5] In this battle, the Germans once again ambushed a Roman marching column in an inhospitable wooded area, occupying the ridges of a narrow pass as the soldiers moved through. However, the archaeology indicates that this time the Romans were the victors.

With Tiberius' abandonment of Germany, the defeat in the Teutoburg suddenly took on new meaning. It was no longer a temporary setback in Roman Imperial expansion, but had instead changed the relationship between Rome and Germany forever. But this shift in the Imperial attitude towards Germany was not an inevitable consequence of the defeat in the Teutoburg. It was not a large-scale popular uprising, but at worst was limited to a small number of participating tribes,[6] and may initially have been more on the scale of an internal military mutiny.[7] The loss of the legions was problematic in the short-term, but the men could always be replaced, despite allusions in the sources to difficulties with legionary recruitment at this time. Rome had suffered worse defeats than the Teutoburg before and survived. Further, the campaigns of Germanicus had demonstrated that Roman armies could still be effective in Germany, and with Arminius dead, would potentially cause little problem in the future.

But after the Teutoburg, neither Augustus nor Tiberius wished to restore Roman control over the territories east of the Rhine. The impetus for their decision has subsequently been traced back to the Teutoburg, despite the fact that the 'abandonment' of Germany would not happen for almost another decade. Augustus' motivation appears to have been prompted by caution, and a fear of further military disaster in the closing years of his reign. Tiberius' decision is more difficult to fathom. He knew the region well, having campaigned there multiple times, including in the aftermath of the Teutoburg battle. The reconquest of even some of the German territories would have provided him with a propaganda-friendly victory, potentially early in his reign had he let Germanicus continue the campaigns he had started in AD 15. But for some unknown reason, Tiberius recalled Germanicus, and the following year sent him to command the Roman army in Asia. He was not replaced on the Rhine. Why Tiberius decided to end Roman campaigning in Germany is unclear, but it may have been as simple as general disinterest. He did not particularly want to be emperor, and undertook many of the tasks associated with the role only grudgingly.[8] He may simply have had little motivation to launch new campaigns in Germany to try and restore the region to Roman control and restart any moves towards making it a province that there might have been under Augustus. Germanicus had secured the Rhine, but would not be allowed to reconquer the region.

But at the point where Tiberius withdrew Germanicus from the Rhine and ended campaigning east of the Rhine, the Teutoburg battle suddenly took on a greater historical significance than it had possessed in the immediate aftermath.[9] The historiography would thereafter have to reflect the new circumstances, and the Teutoburg was now not just a single military defeat, but the beginning of the end for Roman Imperial ambitions east of the Rhine. The defeat suddenly had new meaning, as one of the worst Roman military disasters of Augustus' reign, if not of all Roman history. Blame would have to be allocated, and the majority of it would fall onto Varus. The process by which Varus would be held culpable for the Teutoburg began under Augustus, and continued into the longer-term historical record as represented by all the surviving sources; the creation of the 'Varus Disaster' had begun.

Blaming and Shaming Varus

Soon after the battle, the question of who or what was to blame for the defeat began to circulate in Rome. From the earliest points, Varus appears to have been held almost solely to blame. No fault was attached to the legions, and even Arminius avoiding much condemnation for his actions, possibly because he had acted no differently to how the treacherous Germans were expected to behave. Although it was not customary for Roman defeats to be named after the commander, it was not uncommon for them to receive at least some of the blame. Varus was far from the only general whose recklessness and incompetence was seen as a key factor in a battlefield loss.[10] But his treatment at the hands of the historical record was markedly different, even down to the fact that most forms of referring to the engagement featured his name. The Romans did not appear to call the defeat the 'Battle of the Teutoburg', but as either the 'War of Varus', or the 'Varian Disaster'. The cenotaph of Marcus Caelius refers to the 'War of Varus', which was consistent with wider historiographical practice when it came to referring to individual conflicts,[11] but the phrase is not found in any of the historical sources. They typically refer to the battle as the *Clades Variana*, or 'Varus Disaster', the word *clades* indicating an event much more damaging than a normal scale military defeat.[12] It continues to be known as such even today, although there has been a shift in some sources towards the 'Battle of the Teutoburg (Forest)' in more recent decades. For an engagement to even be given a formal name was in some ways unusual, as Roman writers tended not to allocate formal battle names in the way that more modern military history does.[13] Very few military disasters in the Roman world earned the distinction of being a *clades*, even engagements such as the battles at Trasimene or Cannae, where far larger numbers of Roman soldiers were lost, were not called 'disasters' as such. In the Republican period, Roman defeats had tended not to be named after their commanders, even if they were felt to be at fault. But under Augustus, two large-scale reverses were referred to as 'disasters', that of Lollius, and of Varus, in a practice of associating Roman defeat with the losing commander that would become more common in the Imperial period.[14] Every time that the *Clades Variana* was mentioned, Varus' culpability was reaffirmed. Thus it became a disaster that he had not just experienced and died in, but one which he had created, and was held solely and personally responsible. This clearly also reflected the view of Augustus on the battle, as encapsulated by Suetonius' record of his lamentation: 'Quinctilius Varus, give me back my legions!' It was not Arminius who had 'taken' the legions, but Varus, and Varus who was implored to reverse the defeat.

All the surviving historical sources follow Augustus' line in blaming Varus for the defeat. Each narrative contains a negative characterization of Varus, focusing on his flaws and unsuitability for the role. In Velleius the description crosses into outright hostility, which the others largely fall short of, while maintaining a critical attitude to him. Their boundaries of blame extended far beyond just the battle itself, to include most of Varus' time on the Rhine, and the way he conducted his affairs in Germany generally. This process encompassed several timeframes: in the longer-term, he was blamed for how he administrated the province; in the middle-term, that he ignored warnings that an attack was imminent and did nothing to verify the reports of rebellion; and in the short-term, that when the ambush began he mismanaged the situation, leading his army further into problems instead of away from them.

Several of the sources suggest that Varus was the wrong choice for Germany, and that he was not suited to the command of the Rhine legions. None of the writers make reference to his earlier career apart from Velleius, who mentions his governorship in Syria – but only so that he could make accusations of embezzlement against him. Varus' consulship, governorship of Africa, and numerous other military commands were completely left out, making Varus seem much less experienced than he actually was. He is characterized as being an administrator rather than the warrior that Germany needed at the time, who lacked the toughness, mental acuity, and brutality required of an effective Roman commander. The criticism is particularly well summarized by Velleius:

> [Varus] was a man of mild character and of a quiet disposition, somewhat slow in mind as he was in body, and more accustomed to the leisure of the camp than to actual service in war.[15]

Velleius chose to portray Varus as someone who liked the easy life and enjoyed a bit of luxury, who was not as experienced in military campaigning as might be expected from someone in his position. The characterization of Varus sits in contrast to Velleius' comments on other commanders who operated on the Rhine, such as Gaius Sentius Saturninus,[16] and particularly Tiberius, although in the case of the latter this says more about Velleius' personal relationship with him than it does about Varus.[17] Velleius appears to criticize Varus for not being as dynamic a military commander as he seems to feel he should be, although he makes no mention of when Varus acted in just that way while governor of Syria. Indeed, Varus was far more experienced in warfare than Velleius suggested, having likely campaigned in the Cantabrian Wars and the Alpine campaigns of Drusus and Tiberius, in addition to the suppression of an uprising in Judaea. Perhaps Velleius intended to convey that Varus lacked the instinct for campaigning that someone like Drusus, Tiberius, or Germanicus had. Nevertheless, he had faced his fair share of conflict in the past.

The way that Varus chose to run his administration in Germany was strongly criticized by several of the Roman historians, as was his apparent naivety in terms of how to treat the German regions which lay east of the Rhine. Both Velleius and Dio were critical of the fact that he acted as though he were in a pacified province, such as he had governed in Africa and Syria, rather than the semi-conquered frontier region that he actually commanded.[18] As discussed in Chapter 5, the status of Germany at this time is unclear, with some indications that it was being administered at least partially as a province, others that it remained outside the Empire. Velleius referred to Varus being put in command of the army in Germany (i.e. commander of the Rhine legions),[19] while Dio called him the governor of Germany.[20] The distinction is important, as Varus was accused of impropriety in acting as though Germany was a settled province, and it would be helpful to know for certain whether it was actually a province or not at this point. That said, the distinction between an unsettled region and an unsettled new province is likely to be negligible in contrast to a 'settled province'; what matters is that whatever the status of the German territories, their security should not have been presumed. Varus was accused by both Velleius and Dio of failing to take the proper precautions appropriate to the situation he had been sent to oversee. It was suggested that he failed to recognize the still-potent military capacity of the German population, and to have ignored the fact that they remained open to armed insurrection against Rome. Velleius suggests that Varus' overconfidence in the pacification of the Germans made him incredibly vulnerable to betrayal and attack, calling Varus 'negligent' in his duty.[21] The implication in the sources is that Varus should have approached his role in Germany as a military duty rather than one of civilian administration. Consequently, his policies also come in for some criticism. Dio suggests that he disrupted a natural process of cultural shift by forcing change too quickly on the German population, highlighting how quickly their lifestyle was changing. Velleius also highlights Varus' overreliance on the power of Roman law as a problem, suggesting that Varus thought the Germans would now act as obedient subjects, with the result that he conducted civic tribunals instead of military campaigns.[22]

Most of the sources, however, hold short of suggesting that Varus treated the Germans badly on an objective scale. Roman officials were not particularly known for their restraint in dealing with tribal populations. One of the leaders of the Illyrian Revolt blamed the Romans for bringing the uprising on themselves through their poor treatment of the region, claiming that 'you send as guardians of your flocks, not dogs or shepherds, but wolves'.[23] But few accusations of poor administration of this type were levelled at Varus. Only Florus claimed that Varus ruled with 'cruelty', although he did not actually provide any examples of such behaviour. Similar statements are absent from the other sources. Even Velleius, Varus' biggest critic, admitted that he had good intentions while serving in Germany. The overall impression is of a man who acted in a way that would have been more than acceptable in a more settled territory, but which was inappropriate for the Rhine region at that time, regardless of whether it had yet been designated a province or not. Either way, Varus is shown to have misjudged the situation, and to have failed to adapt his behaviour to the unique circumstances he faced in Germany. His policies were portrayed as being too radical for the period, and the historians again emphasize that while there was nothing *innately* wrong in what Varus was doing, his actions were not suited to Germany at that point. This was not unique to Germany at that time, however, with Roman misjudgements about regional pacification also contributing to the outbreak of the Illyrian Revolt. The first century AD saw several instances of 'general tensions that were the result of the transformation from native to colonial rule'.[24] After the outbreak of the Illyrian Revolt Augustus may have been more aware of the potential pitfalls than he had been before. Varus could have been appointed in the hope that his career experience would make him better suited than most to negotiate the difficulties of increasing the level of Roman administration in a region. That he was unable to do so is unlikely to have been just Varus' fault.

Unsurprisingly, the sources were also generally unsympathetic towards Varus' response to the warnings he received about Arminius' planned treachery. Varus is portrayed as being generally unwilling to recognize the duplicitousness of the Germans, particularly those he felt were friends and allies of both Rome and himself personally. His unwavering trust in Arminius drew particular criticism, although the judgement of Varus on this issue would almost inevitably have been coloured by hindsight. Velleius said that Varus acted as though he was blinded to Arminius' proposed treachery, but hints that so great was his negligence that it almost seemed divinely inspired:

> fate now dominated the plans of Varus and had blindfolded the eyes of his mind. Indeed, it is usually the case that heaven perverts the judgement of the man whose fortune it means to reverse, and brings it to pass – and this is the wretched part of it – that that which happens by chance seems to be deserved, and accident passes over into culpability. And so Quin[c]tilius refused to believe the story, and insisted upon judging the apparent friendship of the Germans toward him by the standard of his merit.[25]

Velleius writes almost as though the defeat was pre-ordained by the gods – a perspective seemingly shared by Augustus – but this does little to exonerate Varus. Varus' negligence in following up the intelligence he received from Segestes about Arminius is portrayed as one of the key factors in the defeat, and there are some hints that his unilateral decision to trust Arminius, potentially against the advice of his staff, was considered partly to blame. There is no suggestion in the sources that Varus made any attempt to verify or disprove the accusations made against Arminius, nor that he consulted any of his staff about the best course of action – further, he seemingly then allowed Arminius to retain the same level of seniority and trust in his staff, allowing him to direct the Roman marching column to the alleged area of discontent. One source suggests that when Germanicus was campaigning in the same region, he realized that the defeat in the Teutoburg had been down to Varus' 'rashness and lack of care', rather than any factor innate to the landscape or the German force.[26] Germanicus therefore consulted a council when making decisions during the campaign, evidently contrary to his usual practice, where he would rely on his own instincts and judgement alone – a lesson that he learned from Varus' example.

In terms of the engagement in the Teutoburg, Varus from the very start is portrayed as both culpable and incompetent, and completely ignoring the dangerous situation building up around him and his army. None of the sources mention him sending out scouts to explore the territory ahead, as should have been done, no matter how friendly the area they were moving through was thought to be. Once the ambush began, the initial impact was worsened by the fact that the Roman column had not maintained discipline while on the move. They had not remained ready for attack at any moment, as they should have done, and the soldiers had been allowed to fall out of any kind of battle-ready formation, mixing instead with their families and friends amidst the wagons of the baggage-train. The absence of discipline is characterized as a gross negligence on Varus' part, and illustrative of his general lack of military instincts. Velleius further implies that Varus ordered his men not to engage with the Germans in the initial stages of the attack, going so far as to censure those who attempted to fight back:

> nor was as much opportunity as they had wished given to the soldiers either of fighting or of extricating themselves, except against heavy odds; nay, some were even heavily chastised for using the arms and showing the spirit of Romans.[27]

Velleius' statement implies that the Romans would have been able to extricate themselves from the initial ambush, and potentially avoid the entire disaster to follow, had they been allowed to fight in the early stages. Varus comes across as an ineffective and potentially cowardly commander, who would prefer to run than face the enemy. This impression is only heightened when Velleius soon after describes how the soldiers at Aliso managed to escape the Germans through cunning and brute force.[28] Varus' actual actions during the battle are not described in any of the sources. Even in Dio's account, the most complete narrative, Varus is not mentioned between the moment the attack began and his suicide in the late stages of the battle. This served to make Varus a marginal figure in the defeat that would come to bear his name. In reality he was likely highly active throughout the battle, issuing orders on the direction of march, the construction of camps, and the destruction of the baggage-train, although he is not associated in the narrative with any of these actions. Varus' absence from the narratives was perhaps intended to suggest that his actions were of little significance during the running battle. If the purpose of the accounts was to blame him for the failure to escape the battle, it would little help their purpose to show him as an effective hands-on commander, helping to formulate an escape plan that might have come close to working.

Varus' eventual suicide towards the end of the battle drew censure from Velleius, who suggested that it was a cowardly act of deserting his men, although Dio presents it simply as a predictable inevitability. Varus' death is portrayed particularly by Velleius as his final insult to his soldiers. Velleius implies that through negligence Varus had stirred unrest in Germany, and had ignored warnings of Arminius' betrayal, leading to the ambush in the Teutoburg – and he then betrayed his men a final time by abandoning them to a miserable fate by his suicide. None of the other sources condemn Varus' suicide, although Dio does link it to the tactical disintegration of much of the remaining Roman army, suggesting that with the death of their commander the remaining survivors gave up hope.[29] However, he does not condemn Varus for this, only noting that the two were linked.

Other contributory factors

There are few attempts in the sources to find anyone else to blame for the defeat except Varus. However, both the terrain and the weather conditions are raised as contributing factors, acknowledging the increased difficulties Varus faced because of them. It was common in Roman history to blame a military disaster at least partially on the terrain.[30] The ancient accounts of the Teutoburg all emphasize the underlying problems posed by the terrain, almost as though the beleaguered Romans were fighting two battles at once – one against the Germans, the second against the landscape.[31] Although environmental analyses have suggested that the battlefield landscape was not as thickly wooded as the sources suggested, conditions were still clearly far from ideal.[32] Arminius was able to use the forests to obscure the collection of his troops, who lay unseen while waiting to launch their attack. It was as though the 'treacherous enemy worked with its hidden forests to bring Rome down', with the trees cast almost as co-conspirators in the attack.[33] When Tacitus described Germanicus' later journey through the same landscape, he also emphasized the hostility of the German terrain, in contrast to the civilized landscapes of the Empire.[34] However, these topographic descriptions may have served a wider purpose in the narratives of the writers.

When describing the terrain, there may have been a tacit understanding between the writers and their readership that Varus should not have entered this landscape without misgivings. They implied that a commander who led his troops into such unsuitable landscapes shouldered the blame for any consequences which resulted from his army being caught in inhospitable terrain. On some occasions, Roman soldiers had expressed their anger when they were placed in this sort of situation by their leaders. During the Samnite Wars, a Roman army was caught in the Caudine Forks (321 BC), unable to escape an area surrounded by mountains as both defiles exiting it were held by the enemy. The troops had no choice but to surrender. The soldiers were angry at their commanders who had led them into the situation, to the point of almost physically attacking them, despite the fact that no Roman lives were lost.[35] There is no mention in any of the surviving sources of a similar reaction from Varus' men – and indeed, as previously seen, they went to significant efforts to try and keep his body from being despoiled by the enemy.

Another factor which counted strongly against the Romans during the battle was the weather conditions. There was an autumn storm which brought strong winds and driving rain, which made the inhospitable terrain even harder to deal with from the earliest stage of the battle.[36] The Roman troops were badly affected by the weather conditions, in a way that the Germans were not, as described by Dio:

> a heavy downpour and violent wind assailed them, preventing them from going forward and even from standing securely, and moreover depriving them of the use of their weapons. For they could not handle their bows or their javelins with any success, nor, for that matter, their shields, which were thoroughly soaked. Their opponents, on the other hand, being for the most part lightly equipped, and able to approach and retire freely, suffered less from the storm.[37]

The storm made it much harder for the Romans to fight effectively. The weather was probably not unusual for the Rhine region, but the soldiers may nevertheless have been unaccustomed to fighting under such conditions. Usually, the campaigning season would be over by the time that autumn storms began to set in. However, the Teutoburg took place relatively late in the year, after Varus had departed from his summer camp and was moving the legions back towards the winter bases on the Rhine. His intention was to confront a localized uprising on the way, likely not expecting to fight a large-scale engagement, let alone an ambush on the scale that unfolded. Arminius could not have predicted the weather when he set the date for the attack, although he may well have hoped for it. The wind and rain did nothing to help the Romans make their escape, and hindered their ability to fight effectively, compounding the difficulties they were already facing from the terrain. The storm no doubt had a significant impact on the battle, but it is portrayed only as a contributing factor in the Roman sources. Weather was often raised in Roman military narratives as a causative factor in a defeat, although it was rarely seen as the only factor.[38]

The legions themselves attracted little censure in the narratives of the Teutoburg. They are characterized as a highly capable and experienced force who were let down in the field by their commander. Velleius suggests that once the attack began, they were betrayed once more, this time by Varus' incompetence in leading them out of the attack. The legions are described by Velleius as 'unexcelled in bravery, the first of Roman armies in discipline, in energy, and in experience in the field'.[39] He added that Varus lost his 'magnificent army more through lack of judgement in the commander than of valour in his soldiers',[40] suggesting that under better command, they could have extricated themselves. Velleius suggests that under better command the soldiers at the Teutoburg would have been able to fight their way out of the German attack, as those caught up in the later engagement at Aliso had been able to do under the leadership of Lucius Caedicius, the camp prefect.[41] Yet Dio also makes it clear that the Roman soldiers were apparently willing to take advantage of Varus' laxity in standards on the march, mingling with their families and the baggage-wagons rather than maintaining formation and combat readiness, and later states that this indiscipline contributed to chaotic scenes at the start of the battle. However, the soldiers themselves were not blamed for their lack of discipline on the march, with Varus instead held to account, as though the writers accepted that even the best Roman soldiers could not be expected to self-impose discipline on the march. There was no suggestion that the soldiers at the Teutoburg had not fought well, aside from the problems using their weapons which resulted from the weather, nor that they had failed to obey any of his commands. The fact that they managed to withstand over three days of German attack suggests that the soldiers maintained their discipline for an astonishing period, perhaps reflecting their experience and status. Soldiers did not always escape being blamed for battlefield defeats, but in the case of the Teutoburg, they were not held responsible for the outcome of the battle.[42]

Perhaps surprisingly, there was not much condemnation of Arminius in the ancient sources. He is not characterized as a typical 'barbarian', perhaps due to the fact that he grew up in Rome, had become a Roman citizen and equestrian, and had served in the Roman army. He had betrayed Roman trust, but perhaps it was felt that at this stage, little else could be expected of a German; his brother Flavus' loyalty served to remind readers that there was hope for greater fidelity in the future, however. Despite his war against Rome, Arminius comes across as a noble and almost dignified figure, his portrayal almost sympathetic at times, particularly in Tacitus' account of the war with Germanicus. His military abilities are mentioned but not overstated, as though a German could not be credited with too much in the way of advanced strategic theory, whilst it was also stretching credulity too much to imagine that someone completely unskilled and ignorant could have masterminded the victory in the Teutoburg. The accounts stop short of giving Arminius full credit for the victory, however, strongly implying in all cases that the battle was lost through Varus' mistakes, rather than won by Arminius' tactics. Underlying all the ancient accounts of the battle is the message that Varus and his legions *could* have fought their way out of the ambush, but were prevented from doing so effectively.[43] That they failed to was put down to the incompetence of Varus, not the tactical plan devised by Arminius, although as seen in the previous chapter, the archaeology from the battlefield, particularly the construction of the rampart at the Oberesch, suggests otherwise.

The overall impression of Varus transmitted by the Roman sources is not necessarily of a *bad* man, but of the wrong man in the wrong place at the wrong time. His personal decisions and judgement, on everything from policy in Germany to the decisions made when the ambush started, are collectively blamed for the defeat in the Teutoburg as well as for why it happened. His personal culpability for the defeat was further emphasized by Tacitus' description of the campaigns later conducted in the same region by Germanicus, in which both he and Aulus Caecina faced attacks similar to that of AD 9. Both were able to escape the situation, implying that even the situation in the Teutoburg would not have been a lost cause in the hands of a better commander.[44] Based on his characterization in the ancient sources, Varus should never have been posted to the Rhine in the first place – and yet he was. The problem with the impression given by the ancient sources is that it does not match up with what is known of Varus' political and military career. He did not lack military experience, and had faced German tribes on campaign before, as well as leading an army to put down an armed insurrection among a non-Roman population. He also had an extensive background in provincial administration, having governed some of the most prominent provinces in the Empire. It seems difficult to imagine that he could have made some of the fundamental errors that he is accused of by the sources. Which leads to the question – was Varus really as culpable as the Roman historians made him seem, and if not, then why was he portrayed in this way?

Reassessing Varus' culpability

One of the problems with blaming Varus for the defeat in the Teutoburg is the prerequisite to believe in the flawed character portrait transmitted by the ancient sources, without wondering exactly how someone so unsuited to the role could have been appointed to the Rhine command. Varus was almost certainly not as incapable a figure as the Roman sources suggested that he was, and his appointment to the Rhine should not be considered an error. Varus was an obvious choice for governor, and Augustus would likely have had few reservations about his suitability for the role. He was a senior figure in the Imperial regime, with almost three decades of service behind him when he was appointed, although this was not highlighted in the historical record. The ancient sources on the Teutoburg mention little of his earlier career, omitting his consulship in 13 BC, his governorship of Africa, his campaigning in Judaea (his time in Syria is only mentioned in the context of embezzlement). There is no mention of his relationship with the Imperial regime, including the fact that he had been Marcus Agrippa's son-in-law, Tiberius' brother-in-law, and, by AD 9, Augustus' great-nephew by marriage. Varus' career may not have been as accomplished as that of some of his contemporaries, Tiberius in particular, but he was still a distinguished careerist with a decent track record behind him. He was perfectly capable of dealing with military problems and civilian unrest, and had previously done so in Syria and Judaea, where his proactive and decisive response had probably shortened the conflict, and saved much bloodshed. In the aftermath of the Jewish uprising Varus won praise for his response, particularly for his decision to execute the ringleaders to set an example to the kingdom at large, while sparing the followers who had been led astray. Varus had also coped well with the delicate diplomacy required towards the end of Herod's reign, where as governor of Syria he had been drawn in to arbitrate on the legal aspects of the struggles between Herod and his sons. He did so impeccably. It is easy to see why Augustus felt secure in appointing Varus to the Rhine, especially if he hoped to increase Roman influence in the region in an attempt to either create or consolidate a province east of the river.

One of the major factors cited in the lead-up to the Teutoburg is that the changes introduced to Germany from AD 7 onwards were ill-judged, imposed too soon on a population that was not yet ready for them. But Varus was not directly responsible for the overall direction of Roman policy in Germany. Even as governor, he would not have had the authority to decide how ready Germany was for certain aspects of Roman rule. The broad direction of Roman action in Germany would be decided by Augustus. It was Varus' job to realize the will of the emperor, not to make any of the big policy decisions himself. He would likely have had a large degree of autonomy in actually carrying out Augustus' will, as was often given to trusted commanders in more distant regions,[45] but his role would largely be to determine *how* certain policies were to be enacted, rather than what they should be. He would probably have stayed in regular communication with Augustus, as he had done while governor of Syria, providing more detailed intelligence on the reality on the Rhine that Augustus could use to inform his policies. But ultimately, it was the emperor who remained in charge of what happened in the province. The Roman policies which were followed in the region would have been dictated by how pacified Augustus thought Germany was, not Varus. Ultimately, it would have been the emperor who decided whether the time had come to begin administrating Germany as though it were a province, even moving towards formally annexing the region to the Empire. Varus may have been appointed because he was particularly qualified for this remit, able to handle the growing introduction of Roman civic administration in the region, while also able to deal with any military problems which resulted.

Yet it is Varus who is accused by the sources of introducing too many changes too quickly, of thinking that the territory was more pacified than it was, attracting hostility and ultimately rebellion amongst the Germans. He oversaw the increasing use of Roman legal procedure to settle tribal disputes, ostensibly at the request of the Germans themselves. In theory Roman law should not have been a major source of justice in the region at this time, regardless of whether Germany was being administrated as a province or not. Roman law only applied to Roman citizens, and most of the Germans living in the Roman-influenced regions would not yet have gained citizenship. Non-citizens remained under the authority of whatever conventions had been in place before their conquest.[46] So either the impact was limited to the few high-status Germans who had been made citizens (including Arminius and Segestes), or Varus was extending the remit of Roman law beyond its usual parameters, although there is little precedent for governors having the power to undertake such a decision. According to Velleius, Varus was enthusiastic about the introduction of Roman legal proceedings to Germany.[47] However, he does not give the impression that this was forced on the Germans by Varus, suggesting in fact that they deliberately called him in to settle tribal disputes, to lull him into a false sense of security. Varus may initially have been asked to adjudicate in local disputes where it was not strictly necessary as a recognition of Roman power in the region, only for his enthusiasm for the process to be used against him.

Varus may also have overseen the introduction of at least the start of a formal taxation, which was always likely to provoke ill-feeling among the population. Tribute was already being taken from the Germans as a result of their subjugation. It was known that tribute payments were a cause of discontent for subject populations and had been one of the contributing factors in the outbreak of the Illyrian Revolt in AD 6.[48] Despite this, payments were collected in Germany, but by AD 7 Augustus may have decided that the time was right to replace them with a tax. However, the extent to which this is a possibility depends on whether Germany had by this time been claimed as a Roman province or not, so it is difficult to say for certain whether moves were made to introduce taxation to the region. Dio implies that attempts to collect a tax were made, saying that Varus 'exacted money [from the Germans] as he would from subject nations'.[49] Taxes were a necessary contribution towards the high costs of maintaining a military presence in a frontier region, despite the controversy that their introduction no doubt provoked. Augustus may not have felt he had much choice, particularly with regards to the introduction of a tax, as the Empire was phenomenally expensive to run, and there had been high military expenditure in recent years when dealing with the Illyrian Revolt, for little material return.[50] It is difficult to say how far Varus went in the process of introducing taxation to the eastern Rhine communities, but had the Roman dominance of the region persisted, it would inevitably have been introduced at some point.

Varus himself probably had little agency in the introduction of these policies. Instead, he likely carried out decisions which had been made by Augustus, albeit potentially using his intelligence and input. It was the emperor, not the governors or commanders, who decided when a territory was ready for certain aspects of Roman administration to be introduced. Thus if there was a misjudgement over the readiness of the Germans to accept these policies, it was made by the emperor, not Varus himself. The worst that Varus could have done is have been clumsy or inept in his execution of the policies, but there is no real indication of this in the sources. He was implementing potentially unpopular policies, but there is little room to see how he could have done this much differently to the way he did. The introduction of taxation and the use of Roman law were always likely to cause problems in a subject territory, and Varus may have been appointed specifically because Augustus felt that he could cope with this difficult transitional period. The decision to implement these policies was made by Augustus – Varus was just the representative of his will in the province, and did not bear much responsibility for the discontent provoked by the direction of Roman rule during his time as governor. None of the Roman sources particularly suggest that it was the *way* that Varus implemented the changes that caused problems, but the nature of the changes themselves. If the introduction of more aspects of Roman public life were at the heart of the rebellion, then it was Augustus who was to blame, not Varus.

In reality, Germany had already seen the introduction of a number of aspects of Roman life in the years prior to Varus' arrival in the region (see chapter 5 for more details). Roman towns were being established, as evidenced at Waldgirmes, mining operations had been introduced in certain areas, soldiers were being garrisoned in German settlements, and Roman-style material culture was beginning to spread. Some of these changes were not necessarily the result of a formal Imperial policy, but an organic process encouraged by the relative peace that Roman dominance in the region had brought. Others, such as the building of settlements like Waldgirmes, suggest a more official involvement. The laying-out of Waldgirmes suggests that it may have been intended as a Roman administrative centre from early in its foundation, possibly even as a provincial capital.[51] Some elements of typical Roman infrastructure had still not been well developed, most notably permanent roads which were still largely absent, to the degree that Varus' army was said to have been constructing temporary roads as it marched before being attacked.[52] The process of introducing changes to the German territories pre-dated Varus, and all had seemingly been previously accepted by the local population. While Dio suggests that this was because they were introduced so slowly that the people did not notice them, it is difficult to imagine that they can have been completely ignorant of Roman towns being constructed, Roman soldiers being garrisoned in their settlements and campaigning in their landscapes, and of Roman goods entering their communities.[53] To imagine that the Roman influence suddenly became both noticeable and unacceptable under Varus, when it had been growing since the campaigns of Drusus the Elder almost two decades earlier, is unrealistic.

Perhaps the Germans lost their fear of consequence under Varus' governorship. He appears to have been a less forceful military figure than some of his predecessors, although whether that was by choice or Imperial command is debatable. Velleius criticized Varus for not campaigning enough during his governorship, as if Varus felt that the military element of his role on the Rhine was over. As he does not mention Varus coming under any sort of official censure for this decision, his actions may have been tacitly approved of by Augustus. There are several reasons why holding back from campaigning might have been a sensible decision. Firstly, with the Illyrian Revolt still raging, Varus would have been aware that there were no additional resources available to him should something go wrong. He and the five Rhine legions were the only thing standing between German invasion and the Empire, and Varus potentially felt it better to play things conservatively in terms of military action, lest a disaster take place that he could stop. The Lollian Disaster, and the near-disaster under Drusus, would have served as reminders of the dangers that lurked in Germany, and Varus may have decided not to risk himself, his legions, and the Empire by campaigning on the limits. Varus may have been aware that his regime was introducing some controversial policies, and did not want to provoke further discontent by making them also seem like the 'enemy' – which, if taxation was to be introduced, would essentially be making the Germans pay for their own repression by the Roman army. Perhaps Varus felt that by exacting taxation from the Germans, 'as he would from subject nations', meant that it was no longer acceptable to campaign against them in the same way as previous years.[54]

There is more substance to the accusation that Varus was over-trusting of the pacification of the Germans, and of the loyalty of Arminius, but even this merits revisiting. Although the Germans may or may not yet have been provincial citizens of Rome by AD 7, it had been several years since they were simple 'enemies' of Rome. The territories east of the Rhine had been subjugated to the level of paying tribute, and a sufficient level of peace had developed that new civilian settlements were being developed in the area. The process implies that events were moving towards the Germans becoming part of the Roman Empire, rather than enemies of it. If and when parts of Germany were made into a province, the resident population would not automatically gain many more legal rights than they did before, as these were restricted to those who held formal Roman citizenship, they would become *peregrini* ('foreigners'), and the prospect of becoming more integrated in the Empire in the near future, particularly as citizenship began to spread. Many elite individuals such as Arminius and Segestes had already been given Roman citizenship. More would follow, including through service in the Roman army. There was at least one Cheruscan cavalry unit, which had previously been commanded by Arminius, and likely other tribal auxiliary units, who all would have returned home if they survived twenty-five years of service as Roman citizens, with the full protection of Roman law behind them. Slowly, the status of the Germans beyond the Rhine was changing from hostile enemies of Rome to friendly allies, and eventually loyal subjects. That this may have affected Varus' perspective on the Germans themselves is only to be expected, especially those he was working closely with on a daily basis. This may also explain why he agreed to detach soldiers to German communities – again, potentially something that he should not officially have done, but which makes sense in the context of the friendlier allied Germans now being treated as quasi-subjects, rather than enemies, of Rome. While Varus clearly did fail to anticipate the disloyalty of his German allies, it is not entirely surprising given the context that he primarily looked for danger coming from outside his own camp, not within. Perhaps Varus felt that the loyalty of the Germans had already been proven beyond doubt, and did not think to question it further.

But Varus' friendship with certain members of the German elite did not necessarily blind him to his responsibilities, even when they required an armed response. Varus had demonstrated previously that he was capable of confronting an uprising with a heavy military response if required. Indeed, this is exactly what he was doing when the Teutoburg ambush took place, reacting to intelligence of discontent in a further reach of Germany. Although the report came at the end of the campaigning season, when a campaign would not usually be undertaken, Varus chose to confront the discontent immediately, rather than let it worsen unmonitored over the winter months. By taking three legions with him, he made a show of force, and theoretically at least was ready for the uprising to be much bigger than his intelligence had reported. It also avoided splitting up his legions completely in what he knew would eventually become hostile territory as he went further. Varus did not refuse to believe the reports of German rebellion, and indeed responded in what would have been an appropriate manner, had the rumours of uprising not actually have been part of the plan to lure him into the ambush. But this kind of decisive action, confronting uprisings with force and speed, had proved highly effective for Varus in Judaea. Had the situation he faced matched what was reported to him by Arminius, his response might well have been the best way to handle the situation. His error was perhaps in assuming that the Cheruscan territory which he had to pass through to reach the rebelling community was friendly, at Arminius' assurance. Varus should perhaps have been more ready for an attack in this area, even if he did not think it would come from his allies.

More than anything, Varus' blind trust in Arminius was blamed by many of the ancient writers for the disaster. If this had not been the case – if Varus had listened to the warnings, had arrested Arminius and his allies pending investigation, even if he had not allocated Arminius responsibility for guiding the Roman column – then, the sources suggest, the entire disaster could have been avoided. There is some truth to this. Had Arminius been in custody, he would not have been able to give false intelligence about an uprising that needed to be confronted, or to lead the Romans into the ambush. Further investigations might have revealed the scale and the nature of the plot. But were there sufficient grounds to take such action against Arminius?

The report of his disloyalty came from one source, Arminius' father-in-law Segestes, who was known to bear significant animosity to the man he felt had abducted and forcibly married his daughter, Thusnelda. In this context, the accusation made against Arminius could come across merely as infighting, of a disgruntled father trying to make trouble for his hated son-in-law. Varus had come across such familial infighting in Syria, where he had refused to arbitrate in the dispute between Herod and his sons, and evidently decided that the same policy should apply in Germany. Segestes, like Arminius, was an elite member of the Cherusci and a Roman citizen – but it was his word against Arminius', and Arminius was evidently more trusted by the Imperial authorities than Segestes. Arminius had been raised in Rome, had served in the Roman army, and had given Varus no other reason to distrust him. Varus had to choose between the two testimonies he was given. If he detained Arminius pending further investigations that then found him to be innocent, he might potentially have damaged both Arminius' loyalty towards Rome, and his personal relationship with the German who had become one of his closest advisors. Varus may have judged that this was the greater risk.

While governor of Syria, Varus had become adept in the delicate diplomacy required to deal with the kings and tribal leaders who fell broadly under his jurisdiction. He may have been attempting to do the same here, dealing with an internal dispute provoked by personal enmity between two members of the elite, which threatened to destabilize security in his province. It is of little surprise that Varus wanted time to think about his response before acting. Unfortunately, this was a luxury he did not have. Velleius suggests that the warning from Segestes arrived very soon before the attack took place, saying that 'after this first warning, there was no time left for a second'.[55] Varus apparently did not have sufficient opportunity to make any investigation of the allegations against Arminius, whom he still needed to guide his army to the Rhine. With hindsight, Varus' slip in intelligence seems problematic, and his failure to follow up on the warning given by Segestes verges strongly towards the negligent – but if he is understood as a Roman official attempting to arbitrate what appeared to him to be a feud between the two men, his actions become more understandable. Had Arminius and other potential members of the rebellion been arrested then the battle would not have unfolded in the way that it did, although if the level of discontent was sufficiently high in the region it may have manifested in some other form of uprising. The battle in the Teutoburg would nonetheless have been avoided.

The final accusation often levelled at Varus is that his actions were generally ineffective once the ambush had begun. But again, when Varus' actions are looked at in detail, there appear to be few grounds for this accusation. He is accused of allowing, even encouraging, ill-discipline among his marching column, allowing his soldiers to abandon their proper positioning and instead mingle with the camp-followers amidst the baggage-train, because he thought them to still be within friendly territory. But the Roman soldiers nevertheless possessed sufficient discipline not only to deal with the initial attack, holding off the Germans long enough for a camp to be built, and to maintain their combat cohesion for three more days. These were hardly the actions of an army which lacked discipline. Varus was considered marginal to this combat hardiness by the ancient historians, who emphasized the sterling qualities of the legions involved independent of their commander. But it is likely that Varus acted as a figurehead for the soldiers, to the degree that when he finally committed suicide in the late stages of the battle, many of his men followed his example, feeling that hope was truly lost.[56] That some of his surviving men attempted to keep Varus' body from being despoiled by the enemy suggests that they maintained a level of respect for him as their commander.

The decisions that Varus appears to have made following the start of the attack were actually appropriate to the situation, and appear to have followed what protocols there were for ambushes. He ordered the construction of a camp to shelter in overnight, which was one of the priorities in such a situation, and then ordered the baggage-train to be made as light and portable as possible. This was a sensible action, and consistent with wider Roman practice in ambush.[57] Varus also made the decision to try and break out of the ambush, rather than sitting around hoping for a rescue, or retreating back the way he had come, which would only have taken the Romans deeper into unfriendly territory. Undoubtedly he would have preferred to face his attackers in open battle, but this would never be willingly offered when their hit-and-run tactics were proving so effective, and the terrain was sufficiently restrictive that the Romans found it impossible to adopt battle-array anyway. A rapid attempt to escape towards the Rhine, fighting where necessary, was the best option, and this was clearly the choice that Varus made. Having destroyed much of their baggage-train, the Romans hoped to move more quickly and flexibly, hoping to outpace the Germans and escape the ambush, although even so, it would likely have taken a week or more to reach even the closest Roman installation, likely the fort at Haltern.[58] As a result, the Roman army entered the Kalkriese pass.

The archaeological discoveries around Kalkriese add a further element to the assessment of Varus' actions during the ambush. His decision to enter the narrow valley between the Kalkriese Berg and a bog, an area traversed only by a small number of sandbars, resulted in a large part of his army becoming trapped and slaughtered at the Oberesch. There is no mention of Varus sending scouts ahead before moving the army forward, an oversight which has drawn strong condemnation from some modern scholars.[59] However, there may have been little realistic prospect of scouting once the battle had begun, not least as Arminius and his men were likely the scouts for Varus' army. Such was the German control of the terrain though that even had Varus sent out scouts, they were unlikely to return, leaving Varus aware that danger from the enemy lurked in the pass, but no better informed about the terrain that lay within.[60]

Even had he known about the treacherous topography of the pass, Varus may have felt he had little choice but to take it, as the route still offered his army the best chance of a successful escape from the ambush. The terrain was less than ideal, but the pass was the only way to reach the Rhine without passing back a long distance through terrain they had already covered – and it is likely, with the abandonment of the baggage-train and the lack of supplies from their allies, that the Romans did not have enough food to take anything but the most direct route to the river.[61] Any other path that he took would have been too long, or potentially, no safer. There was no better option available to him. Perhaps had the scouts been able to reconnoitre the pass as far west as the Oberesch and report back their intelligence this might have made Varus think twice about his decision, particularly if the rampart built there was German work, but even had he sent scouts there was little chance they would return. The Romans went into the Kalkriese defile unaware of the extent of the preparations the Germans had made for their presence, particularly the earthworks constructed at the Oberesch, but likely confident that they could fight or force their way through any opposition. Unfortunately, Arminius had engineered a trap in the area, with the rampart construction at the Oberesch that created a 'kill zone'. Varus was no doubt aware of the danger he was marching his column towards, but there was no other realistic option. Thus he took what one modern historian deemed a 'calculated risk', unaware of the scale of preparations which had been made, and likely not expecting as intensive an attack as ensued, perhaps hoping that the Germans would be unable to maintain the pressure on the Romans.[62] However, the Romans were entering an area prepared to ensure that there was no realistic prospect of escape.[63]

Whatever mistakes Varus might have made while on the Rhine, which were fewer than the ancient sources suggested, once the attack in the Teutoburg began, he made a series of relatively good decisions from a poor range of options. From the earliest stages, he appears to have been confident that the Romans would be able to escape the attack, and to reach safety on the Rhine. He undertook a series of actions to make this easier: lightening the load of his soldiers, choosing the most direct route to the river, and making a fighting retreat as they went. He does appear to have underestimated the strength and organization of the Germans, perhaps not factoring in that they were now led by Roman-trained officers and perhaps also contained auxiliary soldiers, but otherwise did little wrong. But if Varus had made a series of correct decisions, why did the ambush still end in disaster, and the almost complete destruction of all three legions?

The problem Varus had was that Arminius was in a position to anticipate all his decisions, and to take pre-emptive action against them. Having served as an auxiliary commander, Arminius was aware of the inherent vulnerability of the Roman army on the march to ambush, and the procedures they would attempt to follow should such an attack take place. He was therefore able to adapt his tactics accordingly to fully exploit this weakness of Varus' army. It was this that allowed him to identify the best way to attack the Roman column. Arminius was likely aware that the Roman army was particularly vulnerable to being caught in narrow passes and defiles – and these could even be artificially prepared, as with the rampart at the Oberesch.[64] It would have been difficult for the Roman soldiers to escape from the Oberesch area once they had arrived there.[65] As a member of Varus' staff, Arminius may even have been briefed by Varus about what actions the army would take should they be ambushed on the march once they were closer to the unfriendly territory, giving him a detailed insight into what he intended to do should the column be attacked. Up until the night before the attack, Arminius would have been present in the Roman camp(s), able to listen to everything that was going on.[66] He could even have discussed the dangers the Romans were facing with soldiers in the camp. Varus was facing an enemy who knew him and his army as well as anyone, and who knew just how to exploit its vulnerabilities whilst lacking the respective evidence about the Germans.[67] On paper, Varus did everything right once the attack began, everything he should have done, but in this unique case, his experience was working against him. Arminius, it seems, had covered every contingency before Varus had even thought of it, making Roman victory in the attack almost impossible.

It is clear that Varus did make some errors that indirectly contributed to the disaster in the Teutoburg, particularly his decision to trust Arminius when accusations of disloyalty were made against him. But this was an understandable error given Arminius' background and role in the Imperial system. Varus was not responsible, however, for the underlying policy changes which were blamed strongly for inciting rebellious feelings among the tribes. Nor, once the battle began, did he make any particularly glaring errors. Even had he correctly understood the scale of the challenge he faced, there was still likely no other option for escape than the one that he attempted to take.[68] The battle in the Teutoburg was a disaster for Rome, but it does not appear to have been one of Varus' making – so why did he receive all the blame?

Imperial policy and the Teutoburg

If Varus was not to be held accountable for the defeat in the Teutoburg, then the blame lay somewhere else, or rather with *someone* else. No other persons are held responsible for the defeat by the ancient sources, but there are two other figures who each bear a significant degree of responsibility for the defeat: Augustus and Arminius. But it was not a simple matter to blame either of these individuals for the defeat. The consequences of their actions were therefore shifted onto Varus, who was dead and could not defend himself against the accusations.

Augustus' decision to expand Imperial control east of the Rhine had been a bold one, attempting to do something which no Roman leader had ever seriously tried to do before, even Julius Caesar, his adopted father. As discussed in the previous chapter, the Roman army had faced substantial difficulties campaigning in Germany, with one serious disaster (under Lollius) and one near-disaster (under Drusus the Elder) already under their belts by the time that Varus was appointed. It was not unusual for provincial acquisitions to take a long time – Augustus' Cantabrian Wars had ended a 200-year process of conquest in Spain – and to face resistance from local populations as they went. As mentioned previously, it is far from clear whether Rome had formally annexed any territories east of the Rhine by AD 7, and thus what level of jurisdiction Varus actually had in the region. Although some aspects of Roman life were being adopted, much of the German population maintained a largely 'non-Roman' daily life. They were only slowly warming to aspects of Roman culture, and as it turned out, were still far from ready to accept the less favourable aspects. Perhaps German society was itself not developed enough to be integrated into the Roman Empire. Generally, the process worked best when the target populations were already functioning in a manner at least complementary to the Roman system, so that the Romans could integrate themselves into a pre-existing framework, working with elites who were pro-Roman but also maintained strong control over their populations. While Rome had begun this process in Germany, as evidenced by the raising of hostages in Rome, and making members of the elite Roman citizens, it had clearly not advanced as far as Augustus appears to have thought. In the aftermath of the Teutoburg, Augustus likely came to the conclusion that the expansion into Germany was a step too far, at least at the time. If so, the blame for this could only fall on Augustus, who would have been the one to make the decision to launch campaigns of conquest beyond the Rhine. After the Teutoburg, Augustus did not send further campaigns into Germany, either to reconquer the territories or even to take revenge on Arminius. While it is too much to say that the Teutoburg defeat prompted a wholesale reversal of Augustus' German policy (as discussed previously, it was not decided to 'abandon' Germany until the reign of Tiberius), it might nevertheless have suited the Roman historians to suggest that it did. Augustus' subsequent decisions about Germany, and indeed those of Tiberius, could that way be presented as being a direct result of the Teutoburg disaster, rather than a wholesale reversal of a premature Imperial policy in the region. Augustus might have wrongly judged Germany ready for a certain level of cultural change, but if the changes to his policy could be blamed on the battle, and therefore Varus, the emperor would avoid culpability, as long as he stayed clear of any responsibility for the battle itself. Substantial effort was seemingly made by the Roman historians to ensure that no blame attached itself to Augustus over the actual disaster in AD 9, steering clear of any suggestion that the emperor made mistakes in either appointing Varus or the mandate he provided to the new governor. Augustus is instead portrayed as an unwitting victim of the disaster, left mourning his lost legions and searching for the cause of the divine ill-will that had brought down such misfortune on his regime. Yet Augustus had clearly made some errors in his German policy that at least contributed to the disaster.

The emperor might have faced some questions over his appointment of Varus to the Rhine. If Varus was the wrong man for the job, as several of the ancient sources suggest, then it was the emperor that had made a severe error in judgement by appointing him. The descriptions of Varus' character in the ancient sources, as incompetent, unmilitary, and perhaps corrupt, might have left their readers wondering why he had been appointed in the first place, as he seemed so unsuitable for the job. The character flaws mentioned by the sources were not portrayed as only developing once Varus was installed on the Rhine. These negative aspects of Varus' personality were almost certainly exaggerated, even created, to help draw the blame towards the unwitting governor. But once this character portrait had been made, it threatened to implicate Augustus in the disaster as the man who had placed Varus in position. In reality, Varus was much more capable and experienced than the sources suggested, and was probably not the wrong man for the job. But if he had been, it would have been down to Augustus. Likely for this reason, more emphasis was put in the sources on the discontent being provoked by the way that Varus acted in Germany – but here too, Augustus, bears some responsibility. The policies which Varus followed on the Rhine were almost certainly guided by Augustus, as they had been under previous commanders. It was Augustus who had decided that Germany was ready for Roman settlements to be established, and for markets, taxation, and Roman law to be introduced, and potentially that this process should be intensified by Varus.[69] If this was the case, it is unsurprising that the sources generally stopped short of saying that the policies being introduced were wrong. Rather, they suggest that it was that Varus was introducing them too quickly, not that he was introducing them at all.[70] In doing so, accountability was shifted from the emperor to the governor, even though the pace of change was likely also dictated by Augustus. If Varus had seriously diverted from the timetable he was given by Augustus, he would likely have been subject to serious censure, even withdrawal from the province – otherwise the emperor would stand in line once more for criticism, for not sanctioning Varus for disobeying him. In this light, it has to be assumed that everything Varus did as governor he did with the full approval of Augustus. It should also not be forgotten that Varus, in the earliest days of his career, had learned about provincial administration directly from Augustus, during the tour of the eastern provinces – it is difficult to imagine that he did not follow these lessons in his later postings.

In reality, a wide range of factors contributed to the defeat in the Teutoburg – some lying at Varus' feet, others at those of Augustus, and likely a number of other Imperial functionaries in between. Mistakes were undoubtedly made. It is clear that the level of danger posed by Germany had been seriously underestimated, an error likely first made by Augustus and compounded by Varus. The policies introduced in Germany were not unusual, and in the early stages had not provoked any significant discontent. Perhaps Varus could have reacted better to the intelligence he received about Arminius, but he had reasons to respond in the way he did. It was certainly understandable that he would trust a fellow officer above a potentially hostile German, even if that German was also a citizen. Any mistakes Varus made once the ambush had started are understandable under the circumstances, but the overall logic of his decision making during the battle was sound, and he potentially got further towards an escape than others might have done in the same situation.[71] In many ways, it is strange that there are still attempts to establish 'blame' for the Teutoburg, when it is clear that there were so many contributing factors that no one single mistake can be isolated as the 'reason' the battle happened. Even if perhaps one different decision on Varus' part might have avoided the disaster, this does not mean that he was to 'blame' for the disaster. However, as a concerted effort was made by the ancient historians to ensure no fault attached to Augustus over the defeat, it was almost inevitable that Varus would be held accountable.

An Imperial scapegoat?

Why was it so important that Augustus be absolved for the events in the Teutoburg? Much of the reason lies in the self-image that Augustus had cultivated and promoted over his decades in power. Over his long reign, Augustus had become almost synonymous with the state, to the degree that he was inextricable from the events, both triumphs and disasters, which occurred. How Augustus presented himself and his regime was important to the maintenance of his authority, because his claim to power was actually tenuous, and the Imperial system that he had built up around him was genuinely fragile. Augustus had been able to take power as a result of his connection to Julius Caesar, which had given him the legitimacy and wealth to pursue the political ambitions he had likely harboured since childhood. After the civil wars, he had become the unquestionable leader of the Roman state. But it was initially a precarious position, as the powers that Augustus took had made him a king in all but name – and the Roman people were traditionally hostile to the very idea of monarchy. However, they were also tired from decades of conflict, and perhaps willing to accept Augustus' power-grab in exchange for the security and stability that his regime appeared to guarantee.[72] As part of this 'deal', the military integrity of the territorial Empire had to remain secure at all times, and the emperor himself had to appear as an infallible authority, who could be relied upon to preserve the safety and prosperity of the Roman people. At the centre of this system was Augustus, who as emperor was treated with an almost quasi-religious significance, as befitted the adopted son of the god he had declared Julius Caesar to be.

Military defeats did not sit well within the Imperial power system, and emperors from Augustus onwards would often do whatever they could to avoid being blamed for a military defeat.[73] Through their position, emperors were effectively the 'commander-in-chief' of the Roman army. They were able to claim the victories of the legions as their own, but this left them in a less desirable position in the case of defeat. A substantial reverse could seriously damage the image and reputation of the emperor.[74] The practical elements of Augustus' response in the aftermath of the Teutoburg doubtless went some way to re-establishing him as a figure who offered safety and security to the people of the Empire, although the reports of his emotional response may have undermined this to a degree, depending on how widely they were reported or believed.[75]

Augustus could not have been unaware in AD 9 that the regime was approaching a potentially dangerous moment – the first succession, when Augustus would attempt to bequeath the power he had won to his eventual chosen heir, his step-son Tiberius. Augustus appears to have been especially concerned that the Roman people would reject the new system when it came to transfer his power to a successor, potentially sparking off another period of devastating civil war. His attempts to find a supernatural cause for the disaster, to identify which deity had been offended, and soothe them, may betray a genuine worry that the divine powers had turned against him. Alternatively, Augustus may have taken advantage of a widespread popular belief in the revelatory power of omens to further divert blame away from himself, although this may have led to questions about what exactly he had done to bring divine wrath down upon Rome, or why he had been unable to divert it.

The later years of Augustus' rule were beset by widespread problems, including natural disasters, economic crisis, and grain shortages in Rome, in addition to the recent military problem of the Illyrian Revolt.[76] The disaster in the Teutoburg made the Imperial regime seem weak just at the moment it could not afford to appear this way. Augustus had partially established his power on the promise that his regime would provide security and stability. The events in Germany threatened to compromise this position, even to expose it as an illusion. They also potentially highlighted the risk of relying on the judgement of a single man. Augustus and his Imperial regime could not be associated with any responsibility for the disaster, but had to be portrayed as unwitting victims of fate. Augustus may therefore have allowed the blame to fall on Varus for the sake of his own reputation, and perhaps even to protect the regime. Far better to shift the blame on to Varus, who was unable to defend himself, and let all the Roman hostility fall on his reputation, and not that of the emperor. The official position was that Varus had caused the disaster, not the Imperial regime.

A glimpse of this is seen in Velleius Paterculus' account of the Teutoburg, as the only 'living memory' source that survives, probably written in the AD 20s, less than two decades after the events. The text is particularly hostile towards Varus, reflecting Velleius' professional and personal perspectives, and perhaps also wider public opinion at the time.[77] The Imperial regime would likely not have welcomed anything which contradicted this account, which may explain why ransomed survivors were not allowed to enter Italy after they had been freed and their rights restored.[78] As with the Lollian Disaster, the Teutoburg was deliberately distanced from Augustus. It was better for the emperor, and so the Empire, for such defeats to be rendered 'the responsibility of incompetent generals'.[79] Naming these defeats after the defeated commander further helped to establish distance between the battle and the emperor.[80] By the creation of the 'VARUS Disaster', Augustus was divested of any responsibility or blame, despite the fact that it was his policies in Germany which had helped to provoke the discontent that had led to the attack.

Fear of the Germans

It may also have been necessary to ensure that Arminius did not receive too much credit for the defeat in the Teutoburg, for the sake of the people of the Empire, particularly in Rome and Gaul. The battle had to be presented as a Roman loss rather than a German victory, despite the humiliation that might come attached to that decision. While Arminius' betrayal of Varus was perhaps only to be expected in the Roman perception of the 'barbaric' Germans, it also represented another potential danger to the Imperial regime, one which Augustus needed to distract his population from.

Arminius represented a new kind of threat in the early Imperial period. Although he was born outside the territorial Empire, from a young age he was raised in Rome, rising to become a citizen and a member of the aristocracy. He also served with seeming distinction in the Roman *auxilia*. He spoke Latin fluently, to the degree that he was known to speak in that language when agitated.[81] This upbringing was intended to inculcate a 'Roman' way of life in Arminius (and his fellow hostages), making them not just allies of Rome, but part of the system. They could then be used to support Imperial ambitions in their homelands and beyond. In some, perhaps many, cases the process was successful from a Roman perspective. It certainly worked with Arminius' younger brother Flavus, who remained loyal to Rome in the face of his brother's conflict, even when invited by Arminius to join him.[82] But Arminius was the dangerous result of what happened when the process failed. He was an enemy who as an 'insider' knew the workings of the Roman state and the Roman army, who knew its weaknesses and how to exploit them, and who could gain the trust of key figures to maximize their vulnerability, and who could do all this while looking innocent and trustworthy. The rewards of loyalty and service to Rome listed by his brother – increased pay and military decorations – were scorned by Arminius.[83] When Flavus could not be lured over to Arminius' side through reminders of their shared heritage, and appeals over their mother, and Flavus' German wife, the pair almost came to blows, prevented only by the intervention of their comrades who dragged them apart.[84] But although Arminius had failed to persuade his brother to join his war against Rome, he managed to bring many other Germans into the conflict, with a degree of unity that had not been anticipated by the Roman authorities. The German tribes had previously failed to ally together against Rome during the original campaigns of conquest, continuing to fight amongst themselves rather than fight a common enemy.[85] Arminius was able to change that.

There is no doubt that Arminius used his knowledge of how the Roman army worked to exploit its vulnerabilities to his own gain, nor that he abused his trusted position to maximize his chances of success in the Teutoburg battle. Arminius was an excellent leader, who managed to channel dissatisfaction in Germany into a full-scale rebellion against Rome. Dio suggests that it was not the changes themselves that provoked discontent, but a feeling among the Germans that their old way of life was being lost, apparently provoked by Varus moving too quickly in his agenda of change.[86] It may well have been Arminius who stoked this discontent far beyond the level it might otherwise have reached. He made an error in allowing plans of the plot to spread widely enough that they reached the ears of his father-in-law Segestes, who hated Arminius and would almost certainly report the intelligence to Varus. It is difficult to know how concerned Arminius would have been about Varus' response, and whether he would now reconsider allowing Arminius to lead the army through Germany. If he entertained any worries, they soon disappeared. Varus disregarded the warning and took no action against Arminius or the other members of the plot. He was still asked to lead the Roman column towards the supposedly rebellious tribal areas. Once the Roman army was on the march, the attack could be launched on the planned day, the landscape of the route already having been prepared to maximize the damage inflicted on the unwitting Roman soldiers.

This kind of insider infiltration would not have been possible under the Republican military system, where non-citizen troops fought as allied units but were not a regularized part of the Roman army – but it became possible with the introduction of the auxiliary system, developed by Augustus as part of a wider reorganization of the Roman army early in his reign. He increasingly professionalized the army, recruiting soldiers for extended terms of service rather than for individual campaigns, as had been Republican practice. As such, under the Imperial regime soldiering became a career. Only citizens could be recruited into the legions, initially for a period of sixteen years, later increased by Augustus to twenty.[87] Non-citizen troops were also recruited into the Roman army from this point as auxiliary troops.[88] The units were smaller than legions, approximately 480–1,000 men (on paper), and could be infantry, cavalry, or a mixture of both. The auxiliary units supported the legions in battle, often using combat methods not used by the legionaries, such as archery and slinging. Most cavalry were auxiliaries as well, and were often used as scouts. Although the auxiliary system had not reached the same level of development under Augustus that it would in the 'High Empire', it was doubtless already clear that the auxiliaries would be an important source of manpower for the Roman army going forward. Rome would increasingly rely on these troops. In exchange for twenty-five years of service, an auxiliary would retire with full Roman citizenship for himself, his wife, and any children they might have. The system relied upon the fact that the material rewards of service, such as regular pay, food, campaign booty, and citizenship on retirement, would be enough to buy the loyalty of auxiliary soldiers for long enough for it to become an ingrained habit. To help with the process, auxiliary units might be commanded by several officers from the same background as them, albeit usually from the elites, who could serve as transitional figures between their old tribal identity and their new one as a Roman soldier. As well as boosting the number of troops available to fight for Rome, the system helped to spread Roman citizenship in the provinces, gradually enfranchising a larger and larger group of people. The *auxilia* would become a cornerstone of the Roman military system in the early Imperial period, without which the army might well have struggled to function. Although it is not made overtly clear in the sources, there is enough evidence to suggest that some, even many, of the (German) auxiliary troops in Varus' army defected to Arminius and joined in the attack on their fellow soldiers.

The Teutoburg had exposed a dangerous flaw in the auxiliary system: that commanders and soldiers who would ultimately not be loyal to Rome would be trained by the Empire, and then be able to use their skills in fighting their former comrades. Arminius and the Teutoburg was a perfect illustration of where this path could lead. But Rome needed the manpower provided by the recruitment of non-citizens to maintain an effective military force. It was better if questions were not asked about the wisdom of the system by the Roman population at large. It was therefore important to ensure that the events in the Teutoburg did not make the wider Roman population aware that in training auxiliaries, they were perhaps training their own enemies to fight more effectively against them. An effective way to do this was to minimize Arminius' role in the Teutoburg defeat by suggesting that Varus had been negligent and naïve, and had fallen into traps that no one else would. The threat posed by future ex-auxiliary rebels had to be neutralized by making it seem as though any half-decent commander would not have ignored rumours of plotting, and further, would be able to fight his way out of an attack. Had Arminius been presented as an accomplished commander in his own right, against whom any Roman governor would have struggled, the threats of raising and training potential enemies might have become apparent to a wider part of the population. Although Germanicus was eventually able to defeat Arminius, it took several years of campaigning and was only achieved when the Romans managed to face Arminius in pitched battle.[89]

The Teutoburg would not be the last time that Rome faced problems from auxiliaries who 'betrayed' and attacked them, using skills developed in the *auxilia* to wage an effective campaign.[90] In AD 17, a deserter auxiliary named

Tacfarinas would begin a guerrilla campaign against Rome in North Africa that would last for almost seven years, using his knowledge of the army in the same way Arminius had.[91] Like Arminius, Tacfarinas was negatively characterized by the ancient sources as a barbarian, despite the fact that he too was apparently an excellent military commander, who trained a hand-picked unit of recruits into a force that could rival the Roman army in obedience and discipline.[92] Rome also faced problems in AD 69–70 when Julius Civilis, a Batavian auxiliary officer, led a Batavian uprising against them. Tacitus described Civilis as 'cunning beyond the average barbarian', and he caused significant problems for the Romans before his uprising was subdued.[93] In Tacitus' narrative of the uprising, it is clear to see how Civilis' Roman military training assisted in his conflict against Rome.[94] There were real dangers posed by Roman-trained rebels.[95] But in the aftermath of the Teutoburg, the important thing was not the reality of the threat that they posed, but how it was seen by the Roman people. They could not be allowed to know the innate risks of the auxiliary system in its early phases, and so the successes against Rome of individuals the state had itself trained had to be minimized. No credit could be given to Arminius, or indeed the Germans, for their victory in the Teutoburg. The battle *had* to be Varus' loss, not Arminius' victory.

Perhaps more worryingly for Rome, the Teutoburg also revealed that the Romans could not only be beaten in an individual battle, but also cast out of territory that they had previously conquered and dominated. As discussed previously, although the abandonment of Germany had not been an inevitable consequence of the events in AD 9, by the time that the histories were written, it was becoming clear that there was no Imperial impetus to reconquer the territories east of the Rhine. It could easily have seemed as though the Germans had driven the Romans out by their victory, and this was a dangerous precedent to set. It demonstrated to the entire world that the Romans could be forced to withdraw from a province if the armies were given a sufficiently bloody nose. How far the news of the Teutoburg spread in the Roman world (through both provinces and unconquered territories) is unknown, but it was likely far and wide. The poet Ovid heard about the battle relatively soon after it took place when he was exiled in Tomis (modern Constanta, Romania), suggesting that it likely became common knowledge even in remote parts of the Roman world. If other would-be rebels were to hear of the success, either in its aftermath or years afterwards, it could lead them to realize that Rome was not invulnerable. It is not difficult to imagine future rebels like Boudica drawing inspiration from the Teutoburg, particularly once it had become clear that Rome did not re-launch extensive campaigns of conquest in the German region. It had to be emphasized in the historiography of the battle that this was a one-off event due to the incompetence of the commander, rather than any inherent Roman weakness. Varus' reputation was sacrificed in the hope of avoiding similar disasters in the future. Augustus may not have personally censored the works of individual historians, but the potential impact to both a writer and his patrons of displeasing or alienating the Emperor may have led many to compose their works within the boundaries of what would be deemed acceptable to the Imperial regime.

Forever Lost Legions

The legionary eagles of two of Varus' legions may have been recovered by AD 17, but by this point their units no longer existed. The legions which had been defeated in the Teutoburg were not reformed after the battle, despite there being a small number of survivors, suggesting that the legions had not been entirely destroyed. These men were instead absorbed into other units. They became almost 'ghost' units, an impression intensified by the fact that none of the surviving sources name any of the legions in their narratives of the Teutoburg, and the Nineteenth is only mentioned in the context of Germanicus recovering its eagle. The numbers of the Seventeenth, Eighteenth and Nineteenth were not used again.[96] At first the lost units were not even replaced by newly-raised ones, briefly reducing the number of legions from twenty-eight to twenty-five.[97] There were survivors of the Teutoburg who could have been used as a basic force to reform at least one of the lost legions, but while some of them do appear to have stayed in service with the Roman army (some were present on Germanicus' campaigns) they were evidently redeployed to new units. The disbandment of a legion, however compromised by defeat, was an unusual event, one which is not extensively documented in the surviving sources covering this period.[98] It is not clear what criteria determined whether a legion would be disbanded – certainly a single defeat would not justify such an extreme decision.[99] Although it had been a humiliating defeat, the sources are united in claiming that the soldiers had not disgraced themselves in the battle, but had fought bravely to the end. It would not have been clear for almost a decade that the German territories were to be left unconquered, and so it cannot have been the shame of ending Roman presence in Germany that led to the legions being disbanded. Although the legions had lost much of their manpower, their levels could have been restored through additional recruitment. It has been suggested that the loss of a legionary eagle was the determining factor, but this had not been true even of another instance of loss during Augustus' own reign. When the Fifth Legion had been almost wiped out in the disaster under Marcus Lollius, it remained in service, despite the fact that it lost its legionary eagle.[100] So Augustus' decision to disband the Seventeenth, Eighteenth and Nineteenth legions was a contrast to his earlier actions. It was also surprising given the reputation for pragmatism that the emperor had built up. In his earlier reign, Augustus had been known for being able to move past military losses. When the emperor was once consumed with sorrow over the deaths of friends earlier in his reign, one writer expressed surprise at his inability to move on, commenting that 'When his legions were slaughtered, new ones were at once enrolled'.[101] This suggests that Augustus had not always seen a battlefield defeat alone as enough to disband or not replace legions. So why were things so different for the legions lost in the Teutoburg?

Sadly, there is no satisfactory or conclusive answer to the question. The legions in question did not have a particularly long or glorious history. All three had likely been raised relatively recently, probably during Augustus' civil wars, but had evidently not won any particularly famous victories or honours, and as far as we know, lacked any official titles.[102] Their only historical impact of any note would have been the Teutoburg. The lack of distinction may have made it easier to abandon the numbers of the now-blighted legions, particularly given the paucity of survivors, but it does not explain *why* this happened. The loss of the eagles, which remained in enemy hands for nearly a decade, may have been a factor. Augustus was keenly aware of the symbolic value of military eagles, and (as discussed in an earlier chapter) had extensively celebrated his recovery of the standards and eagles lost to the Parthians in the 50s and 40s BC (at Carrhae and during Mark Antony's Armenian campaigns). To now find himself in the position of the ruler who had overseen the loss, rather than recovery, of standards may have been a source of embarrassment. He may not have wished to draw further attention to the fact by recruiting to the affected legions, particularly as none of the eagles had yet been recovered. The legions themselves may have become an inherent and dangerous reminder of the defeat. Augustus appears to have been fairly unforgiving when it came to perceived failures on the part of his legions. During the Cantabrian Wars, he had stripped the honorific title 'Augusta' from one of his legions because they had been involved in multiple defeats, although the unit itself was not disbanded.[103] Perhaps Augustus considered it too risky to restore the Teutoburg legions. As one historian notes, 'certain legionary designations became disgraceful or dangerous if they recalled defeat and internal strife instead of success and stability',[104] and those commanded by Varus would certainly do so for decades to come.

But it may have been the scale of the defeat at the Teutoburg that was the deciding factor in withdrawing the legionary numbers. It is possible that the numbers were felt to now be 'unlucky', or there were concerns that soldiers would be reluctant to serve in these units. Soldiers have traditionally been a superstitious group. Indeed, Augustus himself perhaps had his own misgivings about the legionary numbers. The emperor was known to be superstitious. Suetonius noted that 'certain auspices and omens he regarded as infallible'.[105] If he put his left shoe on before his right, he considered it a bad sign, while if it rained when he set out on a journey, it was a good one. The Roman sources suggest that Augustus at least partially believed that the Teutoburg disaster had been brought down by divine wrath (as discussed in the previous chapter). It would not be surprising if he considered the Seventeenth, Eighteenth and Nineteenth legions themselves to be tainted, with the result that they should be immediately withdrawn from use lest they attract any further misfortune. That this decision persisted may have been because 'the designations themselves became a painful memory to the imperial house, ill-omened and to be avoided even centuries later'.[106] To reconstitute the legions, or even reuse the numbers, would remind both the Romans and their enemies of Rome of things that the regime would prefer remain forgotten. However, efforts were seemingly not made to erase all trace of the legions having ever existed, despite them not being named in the historical narratives. There was no attempt to erase the mark of the Eighteenth Legion on Marcus Caelius' tombstone, and the inscription even mentioned that he died in the 'Varian War'. Ultimately, all that is known for certain is that these legions never again appeared in the historical or archaeological record.

Varus' Family after the Teutoburg

Perhaps Augustus had some sense that he was being unfair to his old friend in allowing his reputation to be destroyed, even if it was for a good reason. When he was sent Varus' head by Maroboduus, Augustus ensured that it received a respectful burial in the Quinctili Varii family tomb, the only funerary honours he could be offered by that point. The emperor also appears to have disapproved of the German treatment of the rest of Varus' body. At a later date, when considering granting a pardon to Segestes' son he hesitated, as the son was accused of despoiling Varus' body, in contrast to his father Segimerus, who was pardoned without delay.[107] Varus was not condemned to *damnatio memoriae*, meaning that his name and image was not struck from the public record, nor was his estate forfeit to the state.[108] Elite individuals could be subjected to this process if it was felt that they had betrayed the emperor, and by implication Rome itself, making them a traitor and a public enemy. Augustus must not have felt that Varus' actions required this extreme punishment.[109] Varus' image was not removed from the frieze of the Ara Pacis and his name was still included in Augustus' *Res Gestae*, as one of the consuls in 13 BC when the emperor returned from Spain and Gaul and the Senate voted to consecrate the altar to Peace in thanks.[110] When Josephus wrote decades after the Teutoburg, he did not find it necessary to minimize or remove the portions of the narrative relating to Varus, and did not mention the disastrous events in the Teutoburg, despite the fact that his readership would almost certainly have made the connection. Varus' son was able to inherit his estate in the normal way, which evidently left him a wealthy man, and the family was allowed to continue living in Rome and participating in public life.

While the Quinctilii Varii were not censured as a result of the events in the Teutoburg, the defeat began the start of a rapid decline in their fortunes. Within two decades almost every member had fallen from prominence. With Varus dead, their main connection to Imperial power and prestige was lost, and no one emerged to take his place under either Augustus or Tiberius. We know little of what happened to the family in the first years after AD 9, but by the AD 20s several of them found themselves falling foul of the political regime. In AD 26 Tiberius withdrew from Rome to the island of Capri, absenting himself from most aspects of public life from that time onwards. Affairs in Rome were increasingly managed by his Prefect of the Praetorian Guard, Lucius Aelius Sejanus, an ambitious individual who had gained Tiberius' trust alongside the hatred of most of the Imperial family. Sejanus oversaw a period of brutality directed towards the Roman elites, which led to many of them facing financial proscriptions, exile, and even death, often fuelled by personal grievances. Varus' family were among his many victims. Perhaps they had been protected until then by Tiberius through a lingering loyalty to his friend and former brother-in-law, but with Tiberius now absent from Rome, it was possible for enemies of the family to move against them.

Sejanus moved against the Quinctili Varii relatively quickly. In AD 26, Varus' third wife, Claudia Pulchra, became one of his first victims. She was prosecuted by Gnaeus Domitius Afer on charges of unchastity and adultery, practising poisoning, and using magic to endanger the life of Tiberius.[111] The accusations were almost certainly fabricated, used as a pretext to attack Claudia Pulchra because she was close to Agrippina the Elder, her second cousin. Agrippina was one of the most powerful members of the Imperial regime, the granddaughter of Augustus, and the widow of Germanicus.[112] She was also a bitter enemy of Sejanus, who used his influence in Rome to prosecute many people because of their links to Agrippina.[113] Agrippina pleaded directly to Tiberius for mercy for Claudia Pulchra, saying that she had done nothing wrong and that Sejanus' accusation was merely a smokescreen through which she herself was being attacked. This evidently fell on deaf ears.[114] Claudia Pulchra was condemned, along with a man named Furnius who was said to be her lover. After this she disappears from this historical record, but she was probably exiled from Rome, and died soon afterwards.[115]

Domitius Afer also attempted to prosecute Publius Quinctilius Varus the Younger, Varus' son by Claudia Pulchra, in AD 27. Varus the Younger was one of the wealthier men in Rome at the time, likely due to the inheritance of his father's estate.[116] Afer was joined in his accusations by Publius Cornelius Dolabella, which seems remarkable given that he was probably Varus the Younger's cousin, the son of one of Varus' sisters.[117] Tacitus found it difficult to understand Dolabella's decision to get involved with the prosecution against Varus the Younger, noting that 'with his high descent and his family connection with Varus, he was now setting out to destroy his own nobility and his own blood'. The charges of which he was accused are not documented, but in most of these cases men were accused of *maiestas* – treason, or plotting against the emperor. Varus the Younger may have been another victim of Sejanus' feud with Agrippina. He was connected with Agrippina not just through his mother, but had also been engaged to Agrippina's daughter Livilla, although a wedding never took place.[118] The outcome of the trial was delayed due to Tiberius' absence, and what happened thereafter to Varus the Younger is unclear. He disappears from the historical record at this point, leading some to suggest that he was condemned and either exiled or executed. However, an incidental reference by Seneca suggests that he may have survived, and gone on to practice law. During one court trial, an opponent was said to criticize what he saw as an oversight on Varus the Younger's part by saying 'It was by that sort of carelessness that your father lost his army'.[119] But Varus the Younger played no further role in the surviving historical narrative, and his fate is unknown. However, it seems unlikely that he survived much past AD 27.

The fortunes of Varus' relatives through the marriages of his three sisters varied in the years following the Teutoburg. None were excluded from public life as a result of Varus' very public fall from grace, but several may have been impeded in their career by the removal of a relative who had been so close to the Imperial regime. One sister had married Publius Cornelius Dolabella (I), and had a son of the same name, Publius Cornelius Dolabella (II). Although the repeated names make it particularly difficult to distinguish members of this family, the son of Dolabella and Quinctilia appears to have had a prominent senatorial and military career, serving as consul in AD 10. He may also have been proconsul for Africa in AD 23/24. A Publius Cornelius Dolabella served in this role, but it is uncertain whether it was the one who was the son of Quinctilia or not.[120] This Dolabella would go on to end the long-running conflict against the rebel Tacfarinas in AD 24.[121] If he was the son of Quinctilia, and thus the nephew of Varus, this victory perhaps takes on new significance. The victory over a former auxiliary rebel may have provided some redemption to the family, more than a decade after the defeat in the Teutoburg, if a different threat to Rome had been neutralized by Varus' nephew.

Another Quinctilia sister had married Sextus Apuleius (II), a union that had produced two children. However, this branch of the family would die out within a few decades. One child was a son, also named Sextus Apuleius (III). Not much is known about him, although he evidently served as consul in AD 14, the year that Augustus died. In keeping with Augustus' tradition of creating firm links between the more distant branches of the Imperial family, Sextus married Fabia Numantia, whose mother was Augustus' step-sister Marcia.[122] Their marriage produced another Sextus Apuleius (IV), who died young, under unknown circumstances. On his tombstone, found in Luna (modern Luni, Italy) he was described as being the last of his family line.[123] Sextus Apuleius (II) and Quinctilia also had a daughter, Apuleia Varilla, who was a half-great-niece to Augustus, as well as full niece to Varus. She came to a less-than-happy end. In AD 17 she was accused of adultery, insulting the deified Augustus and his widow Livia, and by extension, treason.[124] She was exiled from Rome, and ordered to stay at least 200 miles from the city, and her family were charged with enforcing the punishment. Her lover was exiled from both Italy and Africa. Nothing more is known of Apuleia Varilla.

Varus had possibly been closest to the family of his third Quinctilia sister, who had married the suspected poisoner Lucius Nonias Asprenas. One son, also named Lucius Nonias Asprenas (II), can be tracked at multiple points in his public career, and is found under his uncle's command several times. Asprenas (II) had served as a military tribune in Syria in 4 BC while Varus was the governor of the province.[125] Potentially by this point in his career Varus was able to use his influence to raise the status of his family members. Asprenas (II) would soon go on to serve as a suffect consul in AD 6, before rejoining Varus in provincial service, in this case in Germany as a consular legate. Although he was in Germany at the time of the Teutoburg, Asprenas (II) was not caught up in the ambush, as he was stationed at the legionary fortress of Mainz. In the aftermath of the disaster, Asprenas (II) led troops from Mainz along the Rhine to protect the frontier and potentially rescue any Roman survivors. The act partially backfired. While he was credited with saving the lives of some soldiers who had survived the Teutoburg, he was also later accused of looting the property that officers killed in the Teutoburg had left in the Rhine bases.[126] This potential scandal did not hurt his career for long, if at all, and by AD 14/15 Asprenas (II) had been appointed proconsul of Africa. Almost immediately he had to deal with a delicate situation. In AD 14, a Roman named Sempronius Gracchus was murdered under Asprenas' jurisdiction. Gracchus had been in political exile from Rome for fourteen years, having been sent to the Kerkennah Islands (off the coast of Tunisia) on accusations of adultery with Julia the Elder during her marriage to Marcus Agrippa.[127] Gracchus was killed by a group of Roman soldiers who had been sent to murder him.[128] Most people believed that Tiberius was responsible for the assassination, but rumours spread that it was actually Asprenas (II) who had despatched the soldiers, although the reason why he would have done so is unclear. Again, there seem to have been no major negative consequences to this act. Asprenas was back in Rome by AD 20, when he spoke in the Senate asking why the future emperor Claudius had not been included in an official list of thanksgiving for those who had avenged the death of Germanicus.[129]

Lucius Nonius Asprenas (I) and his wife Quinctilia also raised another son, named Sextus Nonius Quinctilianus. His unusual cognomen has led some to suggestion that he might not have been the biological son of Asprenas (I) and Quinctilia, but rather that of Varus and his wife (most likely Vipsania), but who was then adopted by his aunt and uncle. Quinctilianus also enjoyed a distinguished early career, serving as a *triumvir monetalis* (an official overseeing the minting of coins) in 6 BC, and probably serving as a military tribune with Varus in Syria, alongside his brother/cousin Asprenas (II). He was a consul in AD 8, hand-picked by Augustus after the elections descended into chaos. After several years of anonymity, Quinctilianus was appointed proconsul of Asia in AD 16/17. At some point he married Sosia, the daughter of Gaius Sosius, a prominent military commander and politician in the late years of the Republic, who had supported Mark Antony against Octavian but been rehabilitated by the Imperial regime. Quinctilianus and Sosia had at least two sons. One of these sons, also named Sextus Nonius Quinctilianus (II), had a public career and served as a suffect consul in AD 38 in the reign of Caligula. Again, nothing further is known of him after this point.

The fortunes of the Quinctili Varii family had risen spectacularly through Varus' connection with Augustus and the Imperial family. They would never rise so high again. Within one lifetime, the family was rescued from obscurity and raised to the outer level of the Imperial circle, becoming one of the best-connected families in Rome, something that could scarcely have seemed possible following the suicide of Varus' father after Philippi. But once Varus was dead, and his name disgraced for the good of Augustus and the state, the family struggled to maintain its political significance. The family name may even have died with Varus' son, Publius Quinctilius Varus the Younger. The decline in fortunes of the Quinctili Varii may have contributed to the denigration of Varus in the historical record. There was no one in the family of sufficient importance to prevent the sources writing whatever they wanted about Varus, or to influence the development of the flawed character portrait which emerged in the aftermath of Germanicus' campaigns. It was a significant fall from grace for a family who had enjoyed prominence in the reign of Augustus. If it were not for the Teutoburg, the family may well have continued to be one of the more important families in Rome, although Varus himself would likely be known as just another obscure career politician who held a handful of provincial commands and did little with them. The event which was the biggest disaster of his life is also the reason that he is still remembered more than two millennia after his death. Despite being for a disastrous reason, Publius Quinctilius Varus is still one of the most recognizable names from Roman history, and one of the few non-emperors to achieve such notoriety. His legacy may be a complicated one, but at least he has one.

Chapter 8

Varus in Later History and Culture

T he battle in the Teutoburg is certainly one of the better-known events from Roman history, if not as infamous as events such as the assassination of Julius Caesar or the destruction of Pompeii. It has been seen as a turning point in European history that prevented Germany from being incorporated into the Roman Empire, albeit erroneously, as the battle itself was not the sole catalyst for the abandonment of Roman imperial ambitions east of the Rhine. In the Roman world, the historical records give an insight into the attempts made by the historians and regime to rationalize the defeat, and to be able to cope psychologically with its aftermath. The battle was mentioned in numerous contexts in the first century AD but diminishes after this point, appearing mainly only in historical narratives, as though a century of perspective had enabled Rome to get over the shock.

In the post-medieval world there has been a significant amount of interest in the Teutoburg battle, particularly in Germany, with it being used as the subject matter for everything from political propaganda to providing the plot of operas. But much of this has centred around Arminius, who has frequently been used as a symbol of German unity and nation-building in Germany. Varus has been almost a peripheral figure in this subsequent use of the Teutoburg, representing the cruelty and weakness of Rome, often as an allegory for whomever Germany felt was their enemy at the time.

Over time, the way that the battle has been characterized has changed, and perspectives on the contributing roles of the various individuals have evolved. Even the name of the battle has changed. In Anglocentric scholarship the battle was once almost universally known as the 'Varus Disaster', but is now equally if not more likely to be referred to as the 'Battle of the Teutoburg' or 'Battle of the Teutoburg Forest'. In German scholarship, the battle remains named after the Roman governor at the heart of it (but in a less accusatory way) as the *Varusschlacht* ('Varus Battle'), but is also referred to as the *Schlacht im Teutoburger (Wald)* ('Battle in the Teutoburg (Forest)', the *Arminiusschlacht* ('Arminius Battle') or *Hermannschlacht* (Hermann's Battle). A lot more is now known about the battle, mainly as a result of the archaeological excavations at Kalkriese, which have shed light on many aspects of the engagement which were not documented in the surviving historical sources. What is now gradually emerging is a much more nuanced narrative of the battle, which offers a different perspective on Varus and his military abilities. Archaeological discoveries more widely have revealed more than was previously known about Varus' earlier career, demonstrating how experienced he was when he arrived on the Rhine, in contrast to the portrayal of the ancient sources. Further, the discipline of ancient history now no longer takes as verbatim the narratives transmitted by the sources, but critically assesses them and questions their reliability and potential motive.

As such, it is no longer necessary to believe that Varus was an incompetent at fault for the Teutoburg just because Velleius Paterculus said so. Until relatively recently, the historical assessment of Varus followed almost exactly what was transmitted through the ancient sources, casting him as a reckless and incompetent governor and commander who had single-handedly led his army to defeat. However, in more recent decades Varus' reputation has begun to be restored to some degree, although many still do not recognize him as an entirely competent and reliable figure. Some historians still follow the interpretation of his character and actions transmitted by the ancient sources, but perspectives are slowly changing. Varus' actions in Germany can now be neutrally assessed using a wide range of evidence, but it has been a long process to get to this point. This chapter explores the historiography of the Teutoburg battle from antiquity to the modern day and explores how Varus was marginalized in the post-medieval period, ending with an exploration of how Varus is portrayed today.

Commemoration in Roman culture

In the immediate aftermath of the Teutoburg, the battle may not immediately have been seen as the disaster it later became in the historical record. It was a shock, certainly, and a humiliating defeat that initially sparked panic in Rome, both with Augustus and the people more widely. But defeat in Germany was not something that Rome was entirely unfamiliar with: the defeat under Lollius and the near-disaster under Drusus the Elder were within living memory. The scale of the Teutoburg in terms of the lives lost was more dramatic than that of the previous engagements. It would have affected families living in Rome, and in Italy more widely, on a personal level, as legionary recruitment at the time was still largely drawn from the Italian peninsula. All the known casualties of the Teutoburg came from an Italian background, including Marcus Caelius, whose cenotaph reveals he was from Bononia (modern Bologna, Italy). Many families in Italy would have lost a relative in the Teutoburg, or have known someone who had. Thus it was a very personal defeat for those at the heart of the Empire. Even those who did not suffer personal losses in the battle would have experienced the psychological shock of the battle. It may have been comparable to the World Trade Centre attacks of 9/11, an event whose impact was felt by far more people than were personally affected by it. The fact that Arminius' rebellion against Rome was ultimately successful, in that Roman dominance was not restored over the region, would have contributed further to the feeling. This was the only time in the first century AD that the Romans did not recover territories which had been lost to rebellion. In the first months, even years, after the battle it may not have been clear what a long-term impact the defeat would have on Roman policy in Germany – the battle may have been seen as little more than a setback, from which Rome would emerge triumphant once more. The recent Illyrian Revolt would have reminded the Romans of the inherent dangers posed by the non-Mediterranean provinces, whilst also demonstrating to the people at large that Rome always emerged victorious in the end. It would be several years, past Augustus' reign and into that of Tiberius, before the reality of the long-term situation in Germany would emerge.

It is difficult to know how Varus was viewed in the years immediately after the battle – whether the reputation he would later gain as an incompetent who was almost entirely to blame for the defeat was already being sown, or whether he was regarded more sympathetically than the later reception would suggest. Once the Germans had been held at the Rhine and the Empire kept safe, the defeat became much like any other – an inconvenience, but nothing that the Romans had not experienced before, and emerged from triumphant. There is some indication that he may have been seen as a relatively innocent victim in the initial period after the battle. Strabo's *Geography* provides one of the earliest mentions of the battle, written at some point between AD 9 and AD 21, and presents Varus as a victim of German treachery, rather than an incompetent commander who should have seen the betrayal coming:

> Against these people [the Germans] mistrust was the surest defence; for those who were trusted effected the most mischief. For example, the Cherusci, and those who were subject to them, amongst whom three Roman legions with their general, Quintilius [sic] Varus, perished by ambush, in violation of the truce; nevertheless all have received punishment for this perfidy, which furnished to Germanicus the Younger the opportunity of a most brilliant triumph, he leading publicly as his captives the most illustrious persons, both men and women, amongst whom were Segimuntus, the son of Segestes, the chief of the Cherusci,

and his sister, named Thusnelda, the wife of Armenius [sic], who led on the Cherusci when they treacherously attacked Quintilius [sic] Varus, and even to this day continues the war.[1]

Strabo portrays the Teutoburg as being almost an inevitable consequence of the poor morals of the Germans, but does not indicate that Varus was in any way to blame, even in not recognizing the capacity of the Germans for betrayal. He emphasizes that there was a truce between Rome and the German tribes that Varus should have been able to rely on to keep the peace. The passage concentrates more on the Germans who were held responsible for the attack, and the efforts made by Germanicus against them – focusing on the consequences of betrayal for the enemies of Rome, rather than looking to blame Varus. Perhaps in these early years after the Teutoburg Varus' personal actions were felt to be irrelevant, because he was operating in a context where peace had seemed to be secured. It was not his place to question the assurances he had been given about the pacification of the territories east of the Rhine. Irrespective of what Varus had or had not done, ultimately he may not have been held culpable because it was clearly a German action that had led to the disaster. Without the machinations of Arminius and his allies, nothing would have happened, making them, not the Romans, entirely to blame. Rome had been similarly betrayed by other partially acculturated natives in the past, including during the Illyrian Revolt, and the officials in charge of those regions had not been censured in the way that Varus later was.[2] It was an unfortunate truth that some allies would be loyal and reliable while some would not, and it was impossible to tell which was which until something happened. For a while, Varus was apparently not blamed just because he had made the wrong call on Arminius.

This neutral, even supportive attitude towards Varus was not to last. By the AD 20s, as seen in the previous chapter, the Imperial perspective on the Teutoburg had changed, and wider Roman attitudes towards Varus appear to have shifted significantly. This was likely as a wider realisation dawned that there would be no more German campaigns after that of Germanicus, and that the German territories east of the Rhine should now be considered lost.[3] Augustus had not launched any military campaigns to try and retake the lost territories, sending Tiberius to secure the Rhine frontier and no further. There is no indication that the emperor intended to ever send troops beyond the river again, although this did not equate yet to an abandonment of the region. Roman settlements in the region, such as Waldgirmes, were still occupied in this period. But Tiberius replicated and thereby ratified Augustus' decision not to restore Roman dominance over the region. He despatched

Germanicus to secure the region, to punish the Germans for the defeat, but not to reconquer them. Once a conclusive victory had been won against Arminius in AD 17, the Romans withdrew from the eastern Rhine. At this point, Waldgirmes was systematically abandoned, as doubtless were other settlements that had persisted in the interim period between the Teutoburg and Germanicus' withdrawal. Only at that point did the Teutoburg become a significant defeat, and a turning point in the history of Rome and Germany, in a way that had not been inevitable when the battle was fought. It evolved over time into the 'battle that stopped Rome' – and a much bigger historical problem. As discussed in the previous chapter, much of the historical record from that point onwards was concerned with ensuring that blame for this defeat, and subsequent abandonment of Germany, did not fall on Augustus and the Imperial regime.

Such factors were likely heavily in play by the time that Velleius wrote the earliest known narrative of the battle, likely in the AD 20s. At this stage, the immediate aftermath period where it was less important to allocate blame had passed, and what resulted is an account strongly influenced by Tiberius' policy decision to abandon Imperial ambitions east of the Rhine. Velleius appears to have had a particular dislike of Varus, whom he likely knew personally, and which comes through strongly in his writing. It may be that something specific had happened between the two to cause Velleius to take against Varus, or that they were rivals, both serving in the Roman army at the same time. Alternatively, Velleius' intensive loyalty to the Imperial regime, particularly under Tiberius, may account for his strong dislike of the man who had led three legions to a costly and humiliating defeat. As discussed previously, Velleius was close to Tiberius, serving much of his military career under the future emperor, and was strongly biased towards him in his written work.[4] It is perhaps unsurprising that in this earliest narrative of the Teutoburg, Varus was portrayed as the villain – not least, as it allowed Tiberius, who stabilized the situation on the Rhine in the aftermath of the battle, to appear the hero.

Whether Velleius reflected the wider consensus of the Roman people at the time he wrote is difficult to assess – but certainly, the way that he portrayed Varus seems to have defined later interpretations of the governor, with only Dio presenting a more sympathetic perspective (and even then, only relatively). A passage in Seneca the Elder's *Controversiae* suggests that by the AD 20s Varus was becoming more widely accepted as being to blame for the defeat. In a court case *circa* AD 24–26 where Publius Quinctilius Varus the Younger was acting as a lawyer, the opposition claimed that he had been careless over a matter, taunting him that 'It was by that sort of carelessness that your father lost his army'.[5] Clearly by this point the narrative that Varus' actions had brought down the events of the Teutoburg upon himself was beginning to take hold, to the degree that it could be weaponized against his son. Interestingly, however, Seneca adds that the comment was met by general disapproval, particularly in how it 'slandered' Varus in the cause of chastising his son, which was 'something we all disapproved [of]'. So while it was becoming increasingly common by the AD 20s to blame Varus for the defeat, as illustrated by this incident as well as in Velleius, it was still not universally accepted that Varus should be characterized this way. The AD 20s therefore probably marks the period where blame started to fall on Varus for the defeat, but the process was not yet complete.

A short time later (*circa* AD 30–40), the poet Marcus Manilius wrote the *Astronomica*, a work which discussed celestial phenomena and related them to cultural and historical events from the Roman world. In one passage, the poem mentions how strange lights in the sky were thought to foretell devastating events, and links one such occasion to the disaster in the Teutoburg:

> Wars, too, the fires portend, and sudden insurrection, and arms uplifted in stealthy treachery; so of late, when in foreign parts, its oaths forsworn, barbarous Germany made away with our commander Varus and stained the fields with three legions' blood, did menacing lights burn in every quarter of the skies; nature herself waged war with fire, marshalling her forces against us and threatening our destruction.[6]

Manilius' description of the omens which foretold the battle link into the superstitious approach that Augustus took after hearing of the defeat, in which he assumed that unknown gods must have been offended by something that the Romans did, linking other portents to the defeat. The fact that the battle was now being mentioned in a more popular cultural context suggests that its impact had been deeply felt within the Roman world. But again, Varus is not portrayed in this passage as being responsible for the defeat. Like Strabo, the blame is deflected onto the Germans who betrayed their oaths, rather than Varus for not recognizing their disloyalty in time.

References to the battle in the later first century AD reveal new insights into the Roman perspective on the defeat. Although Pliny the Elder's account of the battle in the *Bella Germaniae* was lost, he does refer to it in the *Natural History*, published *circa* AD 77, noting that it caused significant problems for Augustus, and led to some challenging his authority.[7] The references note the potential damage that the defeat could have done to Augustus' regime, and perhaps illustrates why historians of the time took such care to shield the emperor from any responsibility for the battle. Pliny referred to the battle as the *'Variana clades'*, the first known use of this particular term for the battle (Velleius had referred to it as a *clades*, but did not include Varus' name as part of it). It is likely that his larger work on the German conflict would have referred to the engagement in similar terms. By the second half of the first century, Varus was being included in the name of the disastrous battle and, it can be assumed, was being fairly universally blamed for it, in contrast to the earlier sources which had largely held the Germans responsible. The shift between the two appears to have happened at some point in the AD 40s-70s, a generation on from the defeat. By this point, few of the survivors of the battle would have been alive to present an alternative narrative to that being disseminated by the historical sources, to defend either themselves or Varus. Those who had been involved in the background of the battle, if not actually during the engagement itself, would similarly be dead. From this point, it would be much easier to shape or distort the historical record, as there would be few left who could provide a credible contradiction. Even the Quinctili Varii would not have been able to intervene to prevent the denigration of Varus' legacy, as most of them were already dead by this point, and those who survived did not have the influence to protect his reputation. The narrative that would be followed going forward was likely laid out in Pliny's *Bella Germaniae*. Although the work itself has not survived, its influence can be seen in the works of Tacitus, Dio, and even Florus. Despite discrepancies between the sources on details within the engagement, they all present the case that Varus was to blame for the disaster, which almost certainly originated with Pliny. It may even have been the *Bella Germaniae* that changed Roman public opinion on Varus, causing him to be held responsible for the defeat in a way that he had not been before. A keen motivation for this was likely the protection of the Imperial regime, which was a matter of concern for the historiography of the battle going back to Velleius. But it was not until the mid-first century AD that it properly took hold, and changed Varus from an unlucky official betrayed by Arminius, to a commander who had almost single-handedly lost three legions and destroyed Roman imperial ambitions east of the Rhine.

The social importance of the battle appears to have severely declined after the first century AD – it was still mentioned in major historical works and occasional military treatises (although none of the latter ever seriously engaged with what had gone wrong before and during the battle), but was not referenced in wider Roman culture. Cassius Dio's account of the battle, written in the late second or early third century AD, is the latest known references to the battle. After this, it was no longer mentioned by any subsequent historians or other writers – and it would only continue to decline in cultural importance in following decades.

Although it was generally agreed in the Roman world that the defeat in the Teutoburg had been a tragedy no matter who was to blame, one individual saw things differently. Emperor Gaius (Caligula) is said to have regretted that no such disaster had happened in his reign to make his rule more memorable.[8] He appeared to be almost envious of the defeat, craving the notoriety that the battle seemingly bestowed on Augustus' reign – and in some ways, he was right in his assessment, as the battle remains one of the better-known engagements from the Roman world.

Medieval rediscovery of the Teutoburg

In the later Roman period the battle in the Teutoburg appears to have been almost forgotten. This would not be unexpected in the case of an engagement that had been fought centuries earlier, and which had since been superseded in the disaster stakes by more recent – and more serious – military reverses.[9] Many of the historical texts composed earlier in the Imperial period became hard to access later in the period, even for historians with links to the Imperial regime. In the chaos which followed the collapse of the western Roman Empire in the fifth-century AD, the histories of Velleius, Pliny, Tacitus, Dio, and others became functionally lost for almost a millennium. By the later medieval period, the battle had largely been forgotten, its memory preserved only in a handful of obscure German chronicles, which supplemented a few historical references with a lot of conjecture supplied by the author.[10] At this point, the association of the battle with the 'Teutoburg Forest' had also been forgotten, and attempts to locate the battle were largely random, including a hypothesis in the eleventh century that placed the battle at Augsburg in Germany.[11] The significant change happened in the later-fifteenth and sixteenth centuries, when a number of Roman-period texts were 'rediscovered', including the relevant works of Florus (printed 1471), Tacitus (printed 1515), Velleius Paterculus (printed 1517), Suetonius (printed 1520), and Cassius Dio (printed 1548).[12] Not all the sources survived, however, with Pliny's *Bella Germaniae* lost in this period. Even the texts that did survive were not always in one piece, which has had an impact on the study of the Teutoburg. Cassius Dio's account of the battle trails off into nothing just after the death of Varus and the disintegration of the remaining Roman soldiers: 'Every man, therefore, and every horse was cut down without fear of resistance, and the…'.[13] It only resumes again with the Germans having been prevented from crossing the Rhine. Clearly some important parts of the narrative are missing, but there is no way to know what they are. Our knowledge today of the Teutoburg relies solely on these chance survivals from antiquity, and is undermined by those works which have been lost.

But with the rediscovery of these surviving ancient texts, for the first time in centuries scholars had access to a wide range of sources about the battle – and could approach the events from a far different perspective than that of the Romans who had originally written them. The battle in the Teutoburg became of growing interest to scholars, particularly (and unsurprisingly) in the German world, and it was increasingly used as a connection between the disconnected contemporaneous 'German' world of the medieval period, and the idealized unified 'Germany' that was seen to have existed in antiquity. Much of this was transmitted through political imagery, more suited to conveying a message to the largely non-literate contemporary society, in which Arminius was increasingly mythologized, if often also portrayed in anachronistic clothing.[14] Arminius was sometimes shown holding the severed head of Varus (not mentioned in any of the sources, although Velleius does mention Varus being decapitated), in an allusion to the Biblical story of David and Goliath. Even the non-literate would have understood who the hero of this scene was.

The way that the key characters in the narrative were received was particularly different in the medieval period. Where Varus had previously been the villain and Arminius an almost peripheral bit-part player, now Arminius was cast as the hero, and Varus increasingly both vilified and marginalized. The characterization of Varus portrayed in the ancient sources was never really questioned at this early stage of historiography, and Velleius' portrait of a flawed, corrupt, and incompetent governor and commander was largely accepted at face value; it would be several centuries before classical scholarship developed to the stage where the accuracy of ancient historical texts would come under any serious scrutiny. By contrast, a significant amount of focus was now cast on Arminius, and he was being cited as a figure of German national identity and unity as early as 1520.[15] He was renamed 'Hermann' (in spite of the 'Hermann the German' appellation that this would lead to) as early as the first half of the sixteenth century, the German theologian Martin Luther providing an early example of the name change. In 1543, Arminius was included in a list of twelve ancient German heroes, in which he was referred to as both Arminius and Hermann.[16] There was no real attempt in this period to interrogate the reputation or actions of Varus in the Teutoburg – he was a convenient villain of the story, and it was in the interests of no one to explore the reality further. Varus was the face of Rome, of the enemy, but he personally was unimportant; any other faceless 'Roman' would have served just as well in his place.

Varus and Arminius in the nineteenth century

Varus was far from rehabilitated by the nineteenth century historians, even those whose sympathies ostensibly lay with the Romans. One particularly vicious character assassination suggested that Varus was not just a corrupt governor, but one who actively mistreated his provincial population, in the manner of all Roman aristocrats:

> Varus was a true representative of the higher classes of the Romans; among whom a general taste for literature, a keen susceptibility to all intellectual gratifications, a minute acquaintance with the principles and practice of their own national jurisprudence, a careful training in the schools of the rhetoricians, and a fondness for either partaking in or watching the intellectual strife of forensic oratory, had become generally diffused; without, however, having humanized the old Roman spirit of cruel indifference for human feelings and human sufferings, and without acting as the least check on unprincipled avarice and ambition, or on habitual and gross profligacy. Accustomed to govern the depraved and debased natives of Syria, a country where courage in man, and virtue in woman, had for centuries been unknown, Varus thought that he might gratify his licentious and rapacious passions with equal impunity among the high-minded sons and pure-spirited daughters of Germany.[17]

The same text goes on to condemn Varus as a 'contemptible' general, who was in no way equal to the task that he had been given. The author's sympathies appear to have lain strongly with Arminius, of whom he later writes that 'an Englishman is entitled to claim a closer degree of relationship with Arminius than can be claimed by any German of modern Germany', due to the Saxon migration to England in the early modern period. He also argues that Arminius should be counted among the English national heroes – an idea which never seemed to gain any traction, perhaps because England had its own figurehead from antiquity in Boudica, despite the fact that she was a woman and ultimately unsuccessful.

Far more attention was given to the character of Arminius in the nineteenth century, who was used as a symbol of German unity and nationalism through to the end of the Second World War.[18] He became a 'symbol of nostalgic longing, of a proud, free Germany',[19] a German hero (from a time before 'Germany' existed), whose resistance of Rome marked out the superiority of his descendants. Arminius – or Hermann, as he was almost universally referred to by German writers – was the subject of more than a dozen operas written in the first half of the nineteenth century, which increasingly cast him as a German national hero.[20] Varus, in contrast, was little more than the stock 'bad guy' whose presence was necessary only so far as he allowed for the hero to shine. Arminius was depicted in art as a liberator, the person who had freed Germany from subjugation to Rome – and Varus as the pantomime villain, little more than a caricature. He was the Roman commander who happened to be there, rather than someone who was an architect of the battle in any way. On the rare occasions that any attention was given to Varus, it was usually to subvert his role in the engagement. In the 1808 play *Die Hermannsschlacht*, written by German playwright Heinrich von Kleist, Varus is portrayed as intending to secretly attack Arminius under the guise of allying together against one of his enemies. On learning of the intended betrayal, Arminius does what Varus in reality did not do, and recognizes the threat as a real one, and launches the attack in the Teutoburg. This portrayal addressed the fact that Arminius had broken the oath of loyalty he had taken to Rome, by suggesting that Varus had broken it first in planning to attack him. There was no real positive portrayal of Varus in this period within the German cultural sources.

Despite the quasi-mythical status of the battle, the growing national significance of the Teutoburg meant that there was a strong desire to find the actual location of the battle. However, none of the ancient texts preserved anywhere near enough geographic detail to locate the site. Tacitus' comments that it was in the Teutoburg, and that the Teutoburg was somewhere between the Ems and the Lippe, was all that there was to go on. Unsurprisingly, hundreds of different hypotheses for the location were put forward from the sixteenth century onward.[21] Although none could be verified as the 'real' location (and no attempts were made to do so through archaeological evidence), towards the mid-nineteenth interest in Arminius/Hermann and the Teutoburg had grown to the degree that a monument to the victory was to be created. This provided the impetus for the battle site to be definitively located, so that the German victory over Rome could be commemorated there. It was decided that the area around the city of Detmold was the most likely position for the battlefield, and consequently between 1838 and 1875 a large statue of Arminius – the *Hermannsdenkmal*, or Hermann's Monument – was constructed on the Grotenburg hill, a short distance southwest of the city.[22] In reflection of the 'new' enemy at the time of construction, the figure is orientated towards France rather than Italy.[23] The monument consists of a large statue of Arminius, shown raising his sword atop a large pedestal. The statue is nearly 25m tall, while the monument itself stands at a height of just over 53m. It dominates the surrounding landscape and became a tourist destination in its own right – and it remains one of the most popular sights in the region, attracting hundreds of thousands of visitors a year. In 1909, the *Hermannsdenkmal* was the centre of celebrations marking the 1900th anniversary of the Teutoburg, with a nine-day schedule of events including parades and re-enactments of the battle, and a keynote speech from the military historian Hans Delbrück, at that time considered one of the foremost experts on the battle.[24]

The *Hermannsdenkmal* became a tourist destination under the Weimar Republic, and an increasingly well-known part of the nationalist landscape. It also became a location where discontent with the ruling regime could be expressed during the 1920s. Celebrations in 1925 to mark the fiftieth anniversary of the monument's dedication were used as an opportunity to attack the Treaty of Versailles, and the *Hermannsdenkmal* would be increasingly exploited by the far-right over the following decade.[25] Adolf Hitler visited the monument in 1926, and from 1930 the Nazis began to hold assemblies at the site, although its relative remoteness meant that it was never among the most favoured rally locations. Hitler was said to have been an admirer of Arminius, seeing him as a 'freedom fighter who had liberated the pure Aryan German peoples from the yoke of Rome',[26] although it is possible that Hitler simply recognized in him a convenient historical figure who could be subverted to support the Nazi cause.[27] The *Hermannsdenkmal* would feature in Nazi propaganda in the 1930s and 1940s, including one scene where Hitler was shown in the foreground of the monument, imitating the statue's pose. Rallies would also be held there, particularly those of the Hitler Youth, who posed for group photos in front of the statue. However, Arminius was never central to the Nazi regime, despite the perceived importance of the Teutoburg. Nazi use of Arminius/Hermann in their propaganda declined after Hitler became chancellor in 1933, perhaps because he wanted symbols that were exclusively Nazi, and which could not be claimed by any other group.[28] It would also have proved increasingly politically inexpedient, given the alliance between Hitler's fascist regime in Germany and that of Benito Mussolini in Italy, to the point that the *Hermannsdenkmal* was omitted from a sightseeing itinerary when Mussolini visited Germany in 1936, despite it being one of the most prominent tourist destinations in the country.[29] In the aftermath of the Second World War, however, the use of Arminius and the Teutoburg by the Nazi regime meant that they fell foul of the anti-Nationalist ideology, and fell into obscurity for several decades. It would not be until the late twentieth century that Arminius, Varus, or even the Teutoburg would become of widespread interest again, motivated by the archaeological discoveries at Kalkriese, and the looming 2,000th anniversary of the battle.

Rehabilitation of Varus in the twentieth and twenty-first centuries

Varus is notable in his absence from much of the attention focused on the Teutoburg in the nineteenth and earlier-twentieth centuries. Unlike Arminius, he did not serve any purpose as a convenient and unifying political leader, and there was little impetus to re-examine his role in Germany. In more recent decades, Varus has been slightly rehabilitated, as a more critical attitude towards the ancient sources developed in the later twentieth century and into the twenty-first. The political currency and emotional significance of the battle in German national consciousness had begun to lessen by this point, particularly in the aftermath of the Second World War, with the result that more-objective study of Varus, Arminius, and the Teutoburg is becoming increasingly possible.[30] Of even greater benefit is the fact that scholars are now more willing to review and challenge the narratives transmitted by the ancient sources – the opinions of a handful of Roman writers no longer entirely shape the discourse on Varus and the Teutoburg. Their accounts of the battle are no longer taken purely at face value, with questions posed about the accuracy of their own sources, the impact of literary convention and agenda, and any personal biases they brought to their writing – particularly in the case of Velleius Paterculus, who was recognized as being particularly hostile to Varus.

Some still follow the line that Varus was 'a competent lawyer and administrator but not an accomplished commander' who should not have been sent to the Rhine.[31] But others increasingly recognize that Varus was not as inexperienced as the ancient sources suggested, as demonstrated by archaeological finds about his earlier career. The discovery of Varus' connections to the Imperial regime, particularly his marriage to the daughter of Marcus Agrippa, have also led some to challenge the way that he was characterized in antiquity. There is a growing recognition that Varus was scapegoated by an Imperial regime unwilling to accept any association with the defeat, either in the policies implemented in Germany or the man chosen to carry them out. For many, Varus was just an average member of the Roman elite, no better or worse than anyone else, who did little to bring the battle upon himself.[32] Other factors which contributed to the disaster are now being recognized, many of which were outside of Varus' control, from wider-scale problems such as the failure of Roman intelligence in Germany more widely,[33] to more localized issues such as the weather at the time of the battle.[34] He was not solely responsible for the circumstances under which the rebellion in Germany developed, and did little wrong in the battle itself. Varus faced a disciplined, well-trained commander who had anticipated his actions once the ambush was launched, and even then, managed to keep his troops fighting for more than three days under episodic attack. If the Romans had been able to escape the ambush, Varus might have been celebrated as a great military commander; it was just unfortunate for him that in Arminius, he had run up against a better one.

The gradual change in Varus' reception is reflected by the fact that he now has at least one statue dedicated to him. In 2003 a more than life-size (2.3m) bronze statue of Varus was dedicated in Kardinal-von-Galen-Park in Haltern am See, the town believed to mark the modern location of Aliso, the fort so successfully defended in the aftermath of the Teutoburg. The piece, sculpted by Wilfried Koch, is entitled *Der gescheiterte Varus*, or 'The Failed Varus', and depicts Varus in semi-skeletal form, unarmed, barefooted, and dressed in rags – but with his helmet still on. An inscription alongside the statue explains the context of the piece through reference to the Teutoburg and Arminius, accusing the latter of treason against Rome due to the fact that he broke an alliance with them.[35] It is a surprisingly moving sculpture which presents Varus as a victim of Arminius, reminding the viewer that he lost his life in the attack when circumstances forced him to commit suicide. It is one of the only times that Varus has been depicted in modern sculpture. Its presence suggests that the perceptions of Varus are beginning to change in the modern day, albeit slowly.

There is still a widespread fascination with Varus and the events of the Teutoburg among those with an interest in Roman (military) history. Any online search will reveal dozens of message-boards dedicated to discussion of the battle, while articles both re-entrenching and refuting common misconceptions about Varus, Arminius, and the Teutoburg abound. No doubt in part this is influenced by the scale of the defeat, as well the allure of unanswered mysteries surrounding the exact events of the battle, and what exactly happened to the soldiers who fought in it.[36]

It may take a while longer, however, before Varus is completely rehabilitated, at least in terms of his reception by the wider public. Varus is a character in the video game *Total War: Rome II*, in which players can game the Battle of the Teutoburg, attempting to reach safety before the Germans overwhelm them. If Varus is killed in the engagement, the battle is lost; to the disapproval of some, in the gameplay Varus has a tendency to try and flee the battlefield, leaving his soldiers behind, despite there being no suggestion that he did this in reality. Gamers can also play as Arminius in *Total War: Arena*, as one of the few 'barbarian' commanders. Many modern media portrayals still depict Varus in the same light as earlier sources – as an incompetent commander completely to blame for the battle. Among the most recent offers is the Netflix show *Barbaren* ('Barbarians'), which recounts the story largely from the perspective of Arminius and the Germans. Some significant liberties are taken with the known historical record: that Arminius was raised in Varus' household in Rome, for instance, as well as implying that the battle was over in a single attack, in which Varus died relatively early on. It also takes for granted that Varus' administration in Germany was brutal, with severe punishments being visited on those who protested against them. But for all its inaccuracies and speculations, *Barbaren* does also highlight some of the more interesting angles to the story. It addresses that the feud between Segestes and Arminius may have led to Varus dismissing the intelligence he received as unreliable. It also deals with the dual identity of Arminius as both a Roman soldier and a German chieftain, and his struggles to reconcile the two, particularly when he is called upon to take action against individual Germans. In the series, Arminius only abandons his former identity when he felt that Rome had transgressed too significantly the boundaries of acceptable behaviour. Up until this point, he had not only stood by and watched as Rome inflicted cruelty on the Germans, but actually participated in it. Arminius is the central figure of the series; although Varus' actions are discussed and, to a degree, rationalized in the context of the situation in Germany at the time, he still comes across largely as a generic Roman official with little regard for the native people of the region.

Varus may never be completely rehabilitated – the scale and consequence of the defeat may prove too significant to completely overcome – but he is being recognized as a more complex character than many of the ancient sources had suggested. That it is slowly being acknowledged that he may not have been as culpable for the defeat as has previously been suggested is a step forward – although it is unlikely that he will ever be considered blameless for the defeat.

The 'Varusschlacht' at Kalkriese

The archaeology of the Teutoburg battle has completed revised the way that the engagement is interpreted, and has inspired excavations at a number of other Roman battle sites.[37] As discussed in the introduction, it is not accepted by everyone that the Varus battlefield is to be found here, but the on current evidence, it is far more likely that it is the site of the AD 9 battle. New discoveries, such as the *lorica segmentate* discovered alongside an iron prisoner collar, only serve to emphasize the identification. The finds from the site have provided new insight into the events of the battle, and have provided some basis for reconstructing what the events were like for the soldiers that experienced them. Kalkriese was the first Roman conflict landscape to be excavated with methods developed specifically to explore battle sites. The assemblage of 6,000+ metal artefacts grows with every new excavation.

The discovery of the Varus battlefield at Kalkriese prompted a new wave of interest in Varus within the region, particularly as the archaeological insights came just a few decades before the 2,000th anniversary of the battle – 2009 was consequently a busy year for commemorations of the battle. It was decided that there should be a permanent home for the many finds from the site to be presented, within which the battle as a whole could also be presented. A museum and archaeological park – the Museum und Park Kalkriese – opened on the battlefield in 2002.[38] The archaeological park covers an area of approximately 20 hectares, in the middle of the German countryside just over 15km north of the city of Osnabrück. It includes the area of the Oberesch, where a large number of Roman casualties fell in the last stages of the battle, potentially even Varus himself, as his suicide was said to have immediately preceded the tactical collapse of the Roman army. The area is still undergoing excavation. Visitors are given short talks about the results and are able to question the archaeologists as they work.

Significant effort has been expended in linking the historic events of the battle to the landscape of the park. The presumed route of the Roman army through the area that has become the archaeological park is marked by metal slabs in the ground. Some are inscribed with short quotes from the ancient sources about the battle, others with the names of individuals known to have died in the engagement. These panels have apparently evoked strong responses from visitors, some of whom see them as representing gravestones, others the lost shields of Roman casualties of the battle.[39] Panels around the park contain passages from the ancient historians about the battle, and mark where key artefacts were discovered, cross-referenced to their location in the on-site museum. Effort has been made to represent different aspects of the battlefield landscape in AD 9 throughout the park. Part of the site has been given over to forestation, which has been deliberately left without interference as much as possible, to give some impression of how the site might have looked in antiquity. A section of the rampart has been rebuilt along the line of the original structure; on some days, groups of schoolchildren visiting the site can be seen 're-enacting' the battle in this area.

Some of the finds from the battlefield are presented in the on-site museum. The building evokes the form of a Roman watchtower, albeit at 37m it is much taller, and is constructed out of rusted steel panels overlaid on a steel frame, in reference to the corroded state of many of the finds from the battlefield. Emphasis in the museum space was on not just displaying the artefacts from the site, but in reconstructing at least some part of the sensual experience of the battle for visitors, who follow a route that takes them through a narrow space where they are suddenly surrounded by a chaotic multi-media presentation.[40]

Interestingly, the perspective that visitors are invited to empathize with is that of a Roman soldier caught up in the attack, not one of the victorious Germans. The displays aim not to put too much focus on Varus or Arminius, or to ask visitors to judge who was at fault for the defeat, but to concentrate on what the battle was like for the Roman soldiers who were caught up in it, and to explain clearly why the battle unfolded in the way that it did. In developing the museum and park complex at Kalkriese, it was considered important that the site not have echoes of the former far-right exploitation of either Arminius or the Varus battle, and it was never suggested that it become a place of national commemoration.[41] The site is known as the 'Museum und Park Kalkriese', avoiding any mention of the Teutoburg, and the battle is referred to as the *Varusschlacht*, avoiding overt reference to Arminius/Hermann. The symbol of the museum and park is the cavalry face-mask base found at the Oberesch – an artefact which belonged to an unknown Roman combatant in the battle.

The fame of the battle is also visible in the wider landscape around the battlefield. The area around Kalkriese and the city of Osnabrück has utilized the infamy of the Teutoburg by citing Varus in numerous ways, from the 'Golfclub Varus' which lies a short distance from the battlefield, to the 'Varus burger' that could be purchased from an eatery in the city in the months before the 2009 anniversary. A 'Varus and Arminius' chess set has been made, in which Romans and German are pitted together in the classic strategy game. The battle has become part of the inherent culture of the area. The Google Maps directory for the Teutoburg Forest even contains a number of 'reviews' that refer to the battle, including one from the username Publius Quinctilius Varus: '0/10 would not go through again'. The cultural impact of the battle is still being felt in a variety of ways.

Final Thoughts

Publius Quinctilius Varus was not a Roman hero. He led three legions into an ambush that he could well have avoided, starting off a chain of events that would lead to the almost total Roman abandonment of Germany beyond the Rhine. Many Romans were bereaved as a result of his actions, the inherent dangers of Augustus' auxiliary system were exposed, and Rome was shaken by learning that a determined 'barbarian' force was capable of overthrowing provincial rule. There were seemingly many moments that Varus could have changed history by doing something different – from different policies in the province to believing the reports about Arminius' plotting – but these opportunities were not taken. For a long time, Varus was held solely to blame for the defeat that came to bear his name – the Varus Disaster.

Varus is remembered for the final and most notorious event in a long and varied political and military career, and has become defined by it, despite the fact that in reality, he likely did little wrong. He had very few options other than to act as he did, given the socio-political constraints within which he was operating. He was not a perfect governor or commander – and such status by then was likely limited only to beloved members of the core Imperial family – but he was experienced and competent in both civic and military affairs. Much about his earlier life and career is forgotten – but exploring where he came from and how he ended up in command at the Teutoburg only adds to our understanding of this often-demonized figure from Roman history. Ironically, had the disaster been avoided – had Varus made different choices, or Arminius remained loyal – then he would likely be a forgotten man of history, known from a few random inscriptions as another unremarkable Roman bureaucrat. Instead, his name is still recognized today, and the events of his life inspiring books still, including this one. Doubtless Varus would have preferred to be remembered for something positive than for the disastrous military defeat that his name has become synonymous with – but we can at least try and understand him as the complete individual that he was, not just the villain of the Teutoburg. If he is still then found wanting, then so be it – at least the judgement would be based on who he really was, not what some hostile historians claimed him to be.

Notes

Introduction

1. The earliest surviving reference in a historical text to the battle in the Teutoburg as a *clades*, or 'disaster' comes within two decades of the engagement (Velleius Paterculus 2.117.1), although it is not described as the '*Clades Variana*' at that point. Pliny the Elder referred to the '*Variana clades*' in the *Natural History* (7.46), written before AD 77. Tacitus (*Annals* 1.10.4) similarly uses the phrase when writing in the early second century AD, suggesting that the characterization had persisted.

2. Wells 2003.

3. Although others (e.g. Abdale 2016: 216–217) suggest that the importance of the Teutoburg to Roman history may have been overstated, noting that numerous campaigns were conducted in the area over following decades and centuries, suggesting that the Roman military presence never entirely disappeared. However, they would never result in the Germanic territories becoming a permanent province of the Empire. While hindsight might suggest that the gradual evolution in Imperial policy towards the territories east of the Rhine after AD 9 is indicative that the area was to be 'abandoned' as far as permanent acquisition is concerned, this indicates a sense of inevitability that is almost certainly inaccurate. It is unlikely that AD 9 marked a point at which Imperial ambitions for Germany were shelved, and contemporaries likely still viewed these territories as being part of the wider Roman hegemony. There was probably never a point at which the Roman authorities decided that the annexation of Germany was off the table, despite the fact that it was never attempted again.

4. Todd 2004: 48; this assessment is particularly strange given that at no point in his career is Varus known to have worked as a lawyer.

5. Velleius 2.117.2.

6. Velleius Paterculus, *Roman History* 2.117.1–2.119.5 (hereafter 'Velleius'); Florus, *Epitome of Roman History* 2.30 (hereafter 'Florus'; Cassius Dio, *Roman History* 56.18–24 (hereafter 'Dio'); Tacitus *Annals* 1.60–1.61 (the disaster is also referred to in 1.55, about Varus being warned ahead of time about Arminius' coming betrayal; 1.65, where Caecina had a dream of Varus while under attack by Arminius in the same region; and 2.45, on the 'butchering' of the legions and the spoils they had taken from them).

7. The modern area referred to as the 'Teutoburg Forest' is not necessarily an example of the name surviving from the Roman period to now. The forest area (running from Paderborn in the south to the western periphery of Osnabrück) was renamed in 1616 by the historian Philip Clüver to reflect the fact that it was thought to be the Teutoburgensis of classical history. It had previously been known as the Osning Forest. Clüver believed that the Teutoburg battle had been fought somewhere near

Detmold, based in no small part on the presence of a mountain there traditionally known as the 'Teutburg' [sic], but there is no obvious connection beyond the name.

8. Velleius was likely born *c.* 19 BC, while Varus was probably born *c.*46 BC.

9. Velleius 2.111.3. Velleius implies that his posting to Tiberius' military staff as a *legatus Augusti* came after he gave up the opportunity to have a province allocated to himself.

10. Velleius 2.120.1–2.

11. Tacitus, *Agricola* 9. Agricola was heavily involved in campaigning in Britain, both as a tribune AD 58–62 (during which time he likely took part in the suppression of the Boudican revolt in AD 60/61), and as governor of the province AD 77–85, during which time he campaigned extensively in Scotland. Even if Tacitus himself lacked first-hand experience of provincial conflict, Agricola's experiences may have influenced his thoughts on the subject.

12. Apparently as the result of a decree passed by Augustus (Suetonius, *Life of Augustus* 36). An individual senator was appointed to keep the records (Tacitus, *Annals* 5.4), which were made available upon request to some favoured individuals.

13. See Pagán 1999: 303–304 for discussion of the Teutoburg 'flashback' scene in the *Annals*.

14. Mellor 1993: 8–9.

15. E.g. Tacitus, *Annals* 2.9–10.

16. Tacitus, *Germania* 37.

17. Florus is not the only one to claim that Roman soldiers were tortured by the Germans – Tacitus (*Annals* 1.61) does mention the same, but not in the same detail.

18. Dio 56.21.1: 'Every man, therefore, and every horse was cut down without fear of resistance, and the . . .'

19. Tacitus, *Annals* 12.27.

20. Pliny the Elder's *Bella Germaniae* may have been difficult to source even in later antiquity; a letter from the historian Symmachus in the late fourth century AD refers to the difficulty of accessing a copy of this work, unlike those of Livy and Julius Caesar, which were readily available (*Letters* IV.18).

21. For Pliny's influence on Tacitus' works see Sallman 1984.

22. Strabo, *Geography* 7.1.4; Manlius, *Astronomica* 1.898–901; Seneca the Elder, *Controversiae* 1.3.10; Pliny, *Natural History* 7.46; Frontinus *Stratagems* 3.15.4, 4.7.8. Ovid may also have referred to the disaster in the *Tristia* (2.165–178, 2.225–231) in two passages that may allude to the defeat in Germany, although the dating of the poem is not certain, and it may have been composed several months before the battle took place, or in its aftermath (see Thakur 2014 for a discussion of the date). There is also some suggestion that Seneca the Younger may have referenced Varus in a letter (*Epistles* 47.10) – the text is traditionally read as referring to a military disaster under Marius, with a date in the Republican period (probably the catastrophic defeat at Arausio in 105 BC), but some have hypothesized that the text should be read as 'Varus', not 'Marius' (see the LOEB edition of Seneca's *Epistles*, volume 1 pp. 307). Quotes reads: 'As a result of the massacres in Marius's [Varus'] day, many a man of distinguished birth, who was taking the first steps toward senatorial rank by service in the army, was humbled by fortune'.

23. For a discussion of attempts and proposed locations see Derks 2017 (170). Hypotheses for the location fell into four main geographic areas: around the Lippe, around the city of Münster, somewhere south of Münsteraner Bucht and around

Wiehengebirge/Weserbergland. All attempts were made on the basis of reconciling the topography as described in the ancient sources with that of the contemporaneous landscape, supplemented by 'common sense' approaches in which the researcher in question determined what they would have done under the circumstances.

24. Mommsen 1885.
25. For Clunn's discovery of the battlefield see Clunn 2005.
26. For English summaries of the battlefield and finds from Kalkriese see Schlüter 1999 and Moosbauer 2020, as well as the wide range of English-language articles published by Achim Rost and Susanne Wilbers-Rost both separately and together, many of which are referenced in the bibliography.
27. Wigg-Wolf 2007.
28. On the coins see Murdoch 2006: 187–188.
29. Although this is not definitive – it is possible that the VAR refers to a different individual, possibly in the reign of Tiberius, as some examples appear to have the VAR overlaying a Tiberian countermark, suggest it post-dates Tiberius' accession in AD 14.
30. Tolksdorf et al. 2017.
31. One numismatist suggests that prices of goods in Roman coins were likely much cheaper on the fringes of the Empire than they were in Rome, noting that more lower-denomination coins proliferate in these areas (see Reece 1981).
32. On the complete assemblage from Kalkriese, see Harnecker & Franzius 2008 and Harnecker & Mylo 2011.
33. Schlüter 1992.
34. Wilbers-Rost & Rost 2009, Rost 2017.
35. Rost & Wilbers-Rost 2019.
36. Not least as it is likely that Varus' army would have been marching in more than one column, to reduce its length – with three legions in tow, the line may have been inconveniently extended if deployed in a single length. As such, the area around Kalkriese may be the location where one column was attacked, with the sites of other ambush sections still to be found nearby.
37. See particularly Wolters 2008: 150–173, who argues strongly against the identification, based particularly on the coin evidence from the site.
38. Caecina – Tacitus, Annals 1.63–65; Battle of the Angrivarian Wall – Tacitus, Annals 2.19.
39. Tacitus, Annals 1.65 recounts that Caecina was visited in a dream by the ghost of Varus, who appeared 'blood-bedraggled, from the marsh, and [Caecina] heard him calling, though he refused to obey and pushed him back when he extended his hand.'
40. Tacitus, Annals 1.65.
41. Kehne 2000.
42. See Chantraine 2002.
43. Burmeister 2015: 19–20.
44. Wigg-Wolf 2007.
45. Wigg-Wolf 2007: 132–133.
46. Berger 1996: 55.
47. Kemmers & Myrberg 2011: 98–99.
48. Wilbers-Rost 2003: 138.
49. E.g. Burmeister 2015: 21.
50. Dio 56.20.2.

51. Suetonius, *Life of Tiberius* 18.1.
52. Even with the lighter weight, the baggage-trains threatened at times to become liabilities, again getting stuck when the Romans were moving through muddy and marshy terrain (Tacitus, *Annals* 1.65). The Germans under Arminius were apparently still able to move much more fluidly around the landscape, which sometimes allowed them to seize a tactical advantage by working out where the Romans were marching to and getting there first (Tacitus, *Annals* 1.63).
53. Tacitus, *Annals* 1.65.
54. Battlefield archaeology has particularly been developed since excavations at the Little Bighorn battlefield in Montana, the site of Custer's final defeat; on these excavations, and discussion of the methodologies used at the site, see Scott *et al.* 1989 and Scott 2011. For the use of the methodologies of battlefield and conflict archaeology in other periods, see Freeman & Pollard 2001, Scott & McFeaters 2011; for prehistory and the ancient world more specifically, see Roymans & Fernandez-Götz 2018.
55. Male citizens usually had a three-part name comprising a praenomen, nomen, and a cognomen, roughly equivalent to a personal name, a tribal family name, and a more personal family name usually referring to a characteristic or achievement of a previous member of the individual branch of the family. Daughters received their name as a feminized version of their fathers' cognomen, sometimes also his nomen where desired; in the case of multiple daughters, they might receive an additional personal name to distinguish between the different women, but these names are not always preserved.

Chapter 1

1. Livy, *The History of Rome* 1.8 (hereafter Livy).
2. Livy 1.36.
3. Velleius 2.117.2.
4. Murdoch 2008: 51.
5. Syme 1986: 313.
6. On ancestor worship in ancient Rome see MacMullen 2014.
7. Syme 1986: 313–328.
8. Livy 30.18. It is not clear exactly where the battle took place – Livy only notes that it took place in the territory of the Insubrian Gauls in northern Italy, in the area of modern Lombardy.
9. A proconsul was a former consul awarded (or prorogued) the powers of a consul outside Rome, without having been elected to the position of consul again. A proconsul was also granted so that he could command military forces in the field – it basically served as an extension of the military authority previously held by the individual as consul, without any of the powers of the public office in Rome.
10. Syme 1986: 313.
11. Syme 1986: 313.
12. Velleius 2.119.3. Although he does not give the cause of the grandfather's suicide, from the context it seems likely to be the result of a public disgrace, such as in the aftermath of a military defeat.
13. On the potential identity of Varus' mother as the daughter of Gaius Claudius Marcellus Minor see Settipani 2000.
14. The alliance was informal and based on mutual advantage – 'Thus these three most powerful men co-operated together for their mutual advantage' (Appian, *Civil*

Wars 2.8–9). See also Plutarch (*Life of Caesar* 13.3): 'This policy was to reconcile Pompey and Crassus, the most influential men in the city. These men Caesar brought together in friendship after their quarrel, and by concentrating their united strength upon himself, succeeded, before men were aware of it, and by an act which could be called one of kindness, in changing the form of government.' Suetonius (*Life of Julius Caesar* 19.2) added: '[Caesar] made a compact with both of them that no step should be taken in public affairs which did not suit any one of the three'. See also Cassius Dio 37.54.

15. Suetonius (*Life of Caesar* 30.3–4) suggested that Caesar expected to face trial on his return to Rome for irregularities in his conduct in Gaul; however, more recent studies have suggested that the risk of prosecution was minimal, and was not a concern for Caesar when considering his return to Rome (see especially Ehrhardt 1995 & Morstein-Marx 2007).

16. The events of the civil war are far too extensive to be summarized here. Ancient accounts survive written by Caesar (*The Civil War*) and Appian (*The Civil War*). See also Fields 2008 or Westall 2018 for summaries of the conflict and the rivalry between Caesar and Pompey.

17. Velleius 2.16.4.

18. Caesar *Civil War* 1.23; *cf.* Dio 43.13.3. See also Morstein-Marx 2021: 433, who discusses the mercy shown by Caesar towards Sextus Quinctilius Varus, suggesting that it may have been the result of personal intercession between Caesar and a third-party who pleaded on Sextus' behalf.

19. Morstein-Marx 2021: 445–446.

20. Caesar, *Civil War* 2.28.

21. Caesar, *Civil War* 2.35.

22. Unlike Publius Attius Varus, who died later in the conflict, in battle against Caesar in Spain (Vell. Pat. 2.55.4).

23. On the potential assassins, see Strauss 2015, & Stothard 2020.

24. Murdoch 2008.

25. On the Second Triumvirate see Eck 2003: 15–21.

26. Velleius 2.71.2. Velleius also notes (2.119.3) that Varus' father committed suicide just as Varus' grandfather had, in the context of Varus' own suicide in the Teutoburg in AD 9. In mentioning all the deaths together, he may have been making a direct connection between the three deaths, two of which took place during or after a humiliating military defeat; the third, that of Varus' grandfather, may well have happened under similar circumstances.

Chapter 2

1. On the *cursus honorum* in Rome see Duncan-Jones 2016: 22–35.

2. Based on the dates of their marriages.

3. Morstein-Marx (2021: 478–487) notes that more than seventy prominent individuals were pardoned by Caesar during and after the after the civil war, and allowed to return to Rome with no obvious censure.

4. Morstein-Marx 2021. Cicero (*Philippics* 2.5) took a more negative view of Caesar's clemency in the aftermath of the civil war, suggesting that Caesar's decision to grant his enemies their lives was no more generous than a highwayman not killing his victims – 'such a kindness as is done by banditti, who are contented with being able to boast that they have granted their lives to all those men whose lives they have not taken?'

5. Bonner 1977: 14.
6. Murdoch 2006: 52.
7. Horace, *Ars Poeticai* 438–444; *Odes* 1.24.
8. Coarelli 2014: 692.
9. https://www.tate.org.uk/art/artworks/turner-view-of-tivoli-from-the-ruins-of-the-villa-of-quintilius-varus-d15483
10. E.g. Barolini 1969.
11. Education for the elites in Rome aimed to prepare males for a career in public life, focusing on writing, memorization, and speaking, themed particularly around great works of ancient literature. Many would also have been taught Greek in addition to Latin. For more on Roman education see Bonner 1977.
12. Octavian because he had been named heir in Caesar's will, as his closest living male relative; Mark Antony because he was older, more experienced, and had been Caesar's loyal second-in-command for many years prior.
13. Lepidus was a capable military commander who had been awarded a triumph for quelling a rebellion in Spain. He was also a staunch ally of Julius Caesar, who had been named as Caesar's Master of Horse (*magister equitum*) shortly before his death.
14. Dio 48.49; making Agrippa the first Roman commander since Caesar to lead troops across the river.
15. Octavian campaigned in Illyria, Antony in the East, particularly in Parthia.
16. His full name translates as 'Ptolemy Caesar, beloved of his father, beloved of his mother'. Caesarion was never formally acknowledged by Caesar as his child, although he did bring both of them to Rome, where they were living in one of his houses at the time of the assassination.
17. Plutarch, *Life of Antony* 57.4–5; Dio 50.3.2.
18. Both would have expected some form of humiliating public scene which they were evidently keen to avoid. It is likely that both would have been displayed as captives in a triumphal parade in Rome, a common treatment for enemy commanders captured in warfare (see Beard 2007: 108–142, especially 114–118 for Cleopatra's attitude towards the prospect of public display, and similar incidents with other defeated enemies of Rome). Cleopatra might have faced execution, a punishment given to some captured enemy leaders, although in reality relatively few were actually killed this way (Beard 2014: 128–132). It was more likely that she, and probably Antony, would have been imprisoned instead.
19. It is not impossible that he took some part in the final stages of the conflict, although this is not documented by any surviving sources; however, given Varus' later disgrace, it would not necessarily be surprising to see his connections to Octavian/Augustus and the Imperial regime be minimized in the historical record.
20. Suetonius, *Augustus* 35.1.
21. Tacitus, *Annals* 11.25; Julius Caesar had enacted a similar policy, of which Octavian's family had been beneficiaries, with Octavian's father the first to sit in the senate (Suetonius, *Augustus* 2.3).
22. Pliny, *Natural History* 7.45.
23. Suetonius *Augustus* 38.2.

Chapter 3
1. It is not certain what point Pliny's narrative continued to, however, and it remains uncertain whether it would have included the events in the Teutoburg which might

have led to a biographical digression about Varus. It is likely that the narrative extended at least to the start of Tiberius' reign, however, as Tacitus (*Annals* 1.69) reports an incident on the Rhine in AD 14 based on the narrative of Pliny the Elder, suggesting that his history of the German Wars may well have encompassed this earlier period.

2. The ancient sources do not provide a comprehensive narrative of the Cantabrian Wars; there may have been a fuller account in Augustus' own autobiography, which has not survived (Goldsworthy 2014: 253–257); it was also likely narrated by Livy, but the relevant books have been lost. Dio discusses it only briefly (53.25), and Florus (*Epitome* 2.33) also gives a cursory account, focusing mainly on a near-disaster for the Romans, the mass suicide of some Cantabrians, and the personal actions of Augustus.

3. Suetonius, *Tiberius* 9.1; Dio 53.26.1. At the time, both were considered likely future heirs of Augustus, although neither had been named as such by this point.

4. See Peralta Labrador *et al* 2019 for the conditions of the conflict, particularly the difficult, mountainous terrain which the Romans had to cope with.

5. Santos Yanguas 2007.

6. For a narrative of Augustus' Cantabrian War see Powell 2018: 36–68.

7. Dio 53.12.4–13.1.

8. *Res Gestae* 26.3; Suetonius, *Life of Augustus* 21.

9. Bleicken 2015: 296–298.

10. Strabo, *Geography* 3.4.18. He also added that they carried with them a poison which would provide them with a swift and painless death in case of capture or other misfortune – but, if so, evidently not everyone got the chance to take it in time.

11. According to Dio (53.25.7) as a result of exhaustion and stress, the latter particularly because he was repeatedly unable to draw the enemy into a pitched battle.

12. Suetonius, *Augustus* 20.1; Dio 53.25.5–7; Florus 2.33.

13. Dio, 53.26.5; Florus, *Epitome* 2.33.53; *Res Gestae* 4.

14. Polito 2012.

15. Strabo, *Geography* 3.4.18.

16. Dio 53.25.6–7. The historian also notes that Augustus himself got caught up in some of these ambushes, and struggled to deal with the situation – this was not the kind of warfare his earlier experiences had prepared him for.

17. For detailed discussion of the archaeological evidence for the Roman conquest of Spain see Morillo *et al.* 2020.

18. Excavations and analysis have been particularly prominent at the site of Monte Bernorio, where the Roman use of the landscape to attack the town have been well-illustrated through the archaeology; see Brown *et al.* 2017.

19. Fonte *et al.* 2021.

20. Unzueta and Ocharán 1999, 2006. The finds include lead sling-bullets, iron arrowheads, catapult bolts, military kit fragments, and coins, as well as more than 600 iron hobnails from military sandals. A partially-constructed Roman field fortification was found in the midst of the assemblage, which was overrun by the ambushing force before the defences could be finished. It is possible that this was an overnight camp which was in the process of being dismantled when the ambush came, but it is more likely that the fortification was thrown up in a desperate Roman attempt to build a secure defensive compound; this was the typical Roman response to an attack in the open.

21. There are various discussions about the average age at which a Roman man first married (particularly those of the elite), ranging from low estimates of around 19 or 20 years for men and 14 or 15 for women, to around 30 for men and 18 to 20 for women; although the evidence is still far from conclusive, estimates towards the higher age ranges are most convincing. For a summary of the evidence, and scholarship see Scheidel 2007.

22. With most Roman elite males marrying in their later twenties/early thirties. Crosby (2016: 124) suggests that Varus may have entered into an early marriage in an attempt to endear himself to Augustus, who by as early as 28 BC was encouraging the Roman elite to marry and have children. Syme (1986: 314–315) agrees that the Imperial favour shown to Varus in the late 20s BC suggests that he was suitably married by this point.

23. Josephus, *AJ* 17.288; *cf.* Crosby 2016.

24. Josephus, *BJ* 2.68; on an earlier marriage and older son of Varus see also Reinhold 1972, Crosby 2016. An early marriage and son has been completely rejected by some (particularly John 1958), although his piece pre-dated the discovery of several pieces of evidence which showed Varus' personal life to be more complicated than his reading had allowed.

25. Levick (2003: 36) suggests that this earlier child of Varus may have been adopted by one of Varus' sisters and her husband Lucius Nonius Asprenas, and renamed Sextus Nonius Quinctilianus. There is little to this suggestion beyond a similar cognomen and the broad coincidence of their birth, with no further indication that Quinctilianus was not the natural son of Quinctilia and her husband.

26. Velleius Paterculus 2.89.3.

27. Crosby (2016: 124) suggests that Varus may have married early to improve his chances of being made a quaestor.

28. Murdoch 2006: 53.

29. Dio 54.7.1–6.

30. Dio 54.7.2–3.

31. Dio 54.7.6; he had done the same to the city of Cyzicus in the province of Asia. On Augustus and the imposition of slavery-like conditions on provincial civilians, see Lavan 2013.

32. Plutarch, *Life of Crassus* 21.1–5.

33. On the battle see Plutarch, *Life of Crassus* 23–31; Dio 40.16–30.

34. Plutarch, *Life of Crassus* 31.7; on the unreliability of Roman casualty figures see Brunt 1971: 694–697.

35. Plutarch, *Life of Crassus* 31.5–6; Dio 40.27.2–3. Dio also mentions the infamous story that Crassus had molten gold poured down his throat, in mockery of his powerlessness [greed surely?], although this is not mentioned in any other source; Plutarch, by contrast, suggests that Crassus' head was used as a prop in a performance of Euripides' *Bacchae* before the Parthian king, Orodes II (*Life of Crassus* 33.2–4).

36. Plutarch, *Life of Antony* 37.3, 40.4; Dio 49.24.5. On Antony's attempt to recover the standards from Parthia, and their importance as a propaganda tool, see Patterson 2015: 81–82.

37. Dio 54.8.1.

38. Dio 54.8.2.

39. *Res Gestae Divi Augusti* 29.

40. On the iconography of the Augustus of Prima Porta's breastplate, see Squire 2013: 249–253.

41. Dio 54.7.5.
42. Tenos inscription - IG XII 5, 940 = ILS 8812; Pergamon inscription IGR IV 418 f.; Athens inscription IG II/III2 4124.
43. Braund 1985, n. 368.
44. A German travelogue from 1934 suggests that the stone was given to the museum at Haltern as a gift, and was on display when the writer visited in 1933; further research discovered it was donated by the Imperial Osmanic Museum in Istanbul to the Römisch-Germanisches Museum in Haltern, facilitated by Alexander Conze, a German archaeologist who headed excavations at Pergamon from 1879 to 1894. The inscription was still in the museum when it was destroyed in March 1945 by a bomb-hit (it was not part of the collection which was evacuated during the war) and was likely either completely destroyed, or lies in fragments among the bomb debris which now lies buried below more modern development at the site (details from a press release by the LWL in 2009). For an image, see https://www.livius.org/pictures/turkey/bergama-pergamon/pergamon-museum-pieces/pergamon-squeeze-of-an-honorific-inscription-for-quintilius-varus/
45. Eck 2010: 18.
46. Dio 55.24.9.
47. Syme 1986: 313–328.
48. Tansey 2000: 270. It had previously been thought that Quinctilia married a different Publius Cornelius Dolabella, who had served as consul in 44 BC, and had initially fought for Pompey during the civil war before defecting to Caesar, and who had been married to Cicero's daughter Tullia 50–46 BC (Syme 1986: 316/361). He was later declared a public enemy and died by suicide in 43 BC. Given that Quinctilia would only have been a few years old at most by this time, a marriage between her and this Publius Cornelius Dolabella is most unlikely. Although this Dolabella and the one who did marry Quinctilia were part of the same wider family, they were probably not father and son (Tansey 2000).
49. *AE* 1966, 422; Syme 1986: 316.
50. Appuleia Varilla is mentioned by Tacitus (*Annals* 2.50.1) as the niece of Augustus' sister, although her wider familial connections are not mentioned in the passage.
51. Pliny, *Natural History* 35.46; Suetonius, *Life of Augustus* 56.3–4.
52. Levick 2003: 36.
53. Sextus Nonius Quinctilianus was consul in AD 8, suggesting he was born around 22 BC (or between then and 17 BC if he was given a waiver on the age requirement to serve), when Varus would likely have been married to his first wife; it seems unlikely that he would have given away a son at this early stage in his life.
54. 'Pri(vat) tus caloni(bus) ser(vus) P(ublii) Q(uinctilii) Vari leg(ati) L(egionis) XIX c(o)h(ortis) I'; on the interpretation of the disc, see Nuber 2008.
55. There have been some concerns raised over Varus' presence with the Nineteenth Legion in 15 BC, namely that he was not old enough to hold the command (he was probably aged 30/31 years at the time), as the minimum age to hold the necessary *Imperium* required to command troops abroad was 39, with the position of praetor (Abdale 2016: 44–45). However, the lower age limits for positions on the *cursus honorum* were reduced under Augustus, with around 30 years of age being the new requirement for the office of praetor. In addition, all age limits were fairly elastic in the early Imperial period, with the emperor able to create a special dispensation to allow individuals to serve at much younger ages.

56. Dio 55.22.1–5.
57. Duncan-Jones 2016: 36–37.
58. See Rageth & Zanier 2010/2013 on the conflict landscape around Oberhalbstein (Switzerland), particularly at the Crap Ses gorge and the Septimer Pass. Finds include Roman iron projectiles and projectile points, caligae nails, entrenchment tools, tent pegs, and Republican coins. Lead sling-bullets, some bearing stamps identifying the Third, Tenth and Twelfth legions have also been recovered.
59. See Zanier 1997.
60. Kinnee 2018: 105–129.
61. Pliny, *Natural History* 3.24.
62. *Res Gestae Divi Augusti* 26.
63. Velleius Paterculus 2.104.4: 'Indeed, words cannot express the feelings of the soldiers at their meeting, and perhaps my account will scarcely be believed – the tears which sprang to their eyes in their joy at the sight of him, their eagerness, their strange transports in saluting him, their longing to touch his hand, and their inability to restrain such cries as "Is it really you that we see, commander?" "Have we received you safely back among us?" "I served with you, general, in Armenia!" "And I in Raetia!" "I received my decoration from you in Vindelicia!" "And I mine in Pannonia!" "And I in Germany!"'
64. E.g. Tacitus, *Annals* 1.25.
65. As per traditional naming conventions for girls, with the first name a feminized version of her father's *nomen* – in this case, Vipsania for Vipsanius – and a second name as needed to distinguish between different daughters who would share the first name, often drawn from the mother's familial connections – consequently Marcella, from her mother Claudia Marcella, part of the Marcellus clan.
66. Kölner Pap. I.10; *cf.* Koenen 1970; Reinhold 1972.
67. Her name and identity is mysterious, not least as it was long thought that Agrippa and Claudia Marcella Major only had one daughter, while three now seem to be referred to in various inscriptions and other sources (Powell 2015). There is some suggestion that Vipansia Marcella might have been Varus' wife as early as the 20s BC, accounting for why he appears to have an otherwise unknown early marriage, but again, there is little beyond speculation to endorse this reading of the limited evidence.
68. As discussed previously, Varus may already have had a son from an earlier marriage in the 20s BC, who appears alongside his father in Syria in 4 BC. Even if Varus and Vipsania had children, a son of theirs would not be old enough to be the individual cited by Josephus. Some have suggested that Varus and Vipsania Marcella did have a son who was adopted by one of Varus' sisters and her husband, Lucius Nonius Asprenas, based in part on the name of the boy, Sextus Nonius Quinctilianus. However, examination of the timescale makes this hypothesis unlikely. Sextus Nonius Quinctilianus was consul in AD 8, putting his birth at some point between 22 BC and 17 BC (and the latter date only if the minimum age was waived for him, a privilege that he does not seem important enough to have been given). Given that Vipsania Marcella was born at some point between 28 and 24 BC, she would not have been old enough to have been married to Varus early enough to be the mother of Sextus Nonius Quinctilianus. If he was the biological son of Varus, Sextus Nonius Quinctilianus could only have been born to Varus' first marriage, but there is no clear reason why he would have been adopted by Quinctilia and Asprenas, not least as they already had a son. On the available evidence, Sextus Nonius Quinctilianus was probably not the son of Varus, but indeed of his sister and her husband; his name

may have been intended to emphasize the connection of himself and his family to Varus, who was already by that time showing himself to be a man to watch under the Imperial regime.

69. See Powell 2015: 155–179.
70. Plutarch, *Life of Antony* 87.1; Dio, *Roman History* 53.1.2, 54.6.4.
71. Dio 53.1.6, 53.27.5
72. Hurlet 2011: 322. Augustus served as consul himself every year from 29–23 BC, choosing members of his inner circle to serve alongside him, even if, like Agrippa, they did not come from senatorial backgrounds.
73. Dio 54.12.4.
74. See Stevenson 2013.
75. On Agrippa's building works in Rome see Richardson 2012: 93.
76. Dio 53.27.
77. Dio 53.30.
78. *Cf.* Valerius Maximus, *Memorable Deeds and Sayings* 7.8.5
79. Dio 53.26.1.
80. Dio 53.28.3.
81. See Stevenson 2013: 124– ; *cf.* Eck 2007 157: 'When it came to the descent of his line of blood the behaviour of Augustus could almost be described as obsessive'.
82. Suetonius, *Augustus* 66; Dio 53.32.1.
83. Stevenson 2012: 125.
84. Dio 53.30.4. No accusations were made of Agrippa having been responsible for Marcellus' death, convenient as it was for him – although they were levelled against Augustus' wife Livia, with suggestions that she killed Marcellus due to her husband's preference for him over her sons (his step-sons) Tiberius and Drusus (Dio 53.33.4). However, this kind of accusation was made against Livia all the time, with no real proof in most cases. Given that illness was reported to be widespread in Rome at the time – and had, of course, also afflicted the emperor – Marcellus' death was probably just an unfortunate accident of fate.
85. Plutarch, *Life of Antony* 87.2; according to Plutarch, Claudia Marcella's own mother, Octavia (Minor) – Augustus' sister – urged Agrippa to divorce her daughter in favour of Julia, apparently to ensure that the emperor would have a son-in-law that he could fully trust. Marcella went on to marry Iullus Antonius, a son of Mark Antony by his wife Fulvia (Mark Antony having been Marcella's step-father at one point); Iullus Antonius would later be found guilty of adultery with (of all people) Augustus' daughter Julia the Elder, and committed suicide.
86. Dio 54.6.5.
87. Dio 54.6.5.
88. Suetonius, *Augustus* 64; Dio 54.18.1. Dio says that he hoped to discourage plotting against him by showing that the succession was already decided.
89. Vipsania Agrippa was Agrippa's daughter by his first wife, Pomponia Caecilia Attica. The marriage took place around 42–37 BC, and was apparently arranged by Mark Antony (Nepos, *Titus Pompomius Atticus* 12).
90. Dio 54.25.1; *Res Gestae Divi Augusti* 12.
91. For a full discussion of the role of consuls in Republican Rome see Pina Polo 2011.
92. If a consul was to die while in office, a replacement would be elected to serve the rest of his term, known as a suffect consul; he would ostensibly have the same range of powers as a fully elected consul, although in reality would often be considered less senior than consuls serving a full term.

93. Gaius Marius was appointed as consul seven times (107, 104, 103, 102, 101, 100, 86 BC), although he died very early on in his seventh and final time; Julius Caesar was appointed as consul five times (59, 48, 46, 45, and 44 BC).

94. In 44 BC, Caesar was consul for the fifth time, alongside his long-time companion Mark Antony.

95. Not particularly because Augustus enacted any legislation which removed powers from the consuls, but because their pre-eminence could not survive in a system where the emperor ultimately held supreme power at all times – see Hurlet 2011 for discussion of the consulship under Augustus. Indeed, a perception that Augustus held less power in Rome than the consuls held in 19/18 BC led to the emperor effectively being given consular powers for life even without holding the office itself, as it was considered intolerable to let the current situation continue (Stevenson 2013: 127).

96. Augustus (Octavian) had been appointed consul in 43, 33, 31, 30, and 29–23 BC, and would serve twice more before his death (5 BC and 2 BC); Agrippa held the consulship in in 37, 28, and 27 BC, the latter alongside Augustus.

97. Although he had frequently returned to the city during this period.

98. See Goldsworthy 2014: 353–354.

99. Dio 54.20.4–6.

100. Dio 54.23.7.

101. *Res Gestae Divi Augusti* 12. This was not the first altar dedicated to celebrate Augustus' safe return from provincial travels – the *Res Gestae* (11) also details an altar constructed following the emperor's return from Syria in 19 BC (the tour Varus had accompanied him on), on this occasion dedicated to Fortuna Redux (the aspect of Fortuna who oversaw safe returns from long journeys), on which annual sacrifices were also to be made by the pontiffs and Vestal Virgins on 12 October. Following Augustus' death, this sacrificial day became the Augustalia festival, becoming an important element in the development of the Imperial cult.

102. On the identification of these figures as Varus and Tiberius see Toynbee 1953: 82, with fuller discussion in Pollini 1986.

103. Pollini 1986: 460.

104. Dio 54.25.1–2.

105. Dio 54.28.3–5; despite the fact that Agrippa had prepared his own tomb in the Campus Martius. See also Powell 2015: 180–187 for the aftermath of Agrippa's death.

106. Seneca, *De Beneficiis* 6.32.

107. Kölner Pap. I.10; *cf.* Koenen 1970; Reinhold 1972.

108. Suetonius, *Life of Augustus* 63.

109. Suetonius, *Life of Tiberius* 7.2–3; Tacitus, *Annals* 1.53. Suetonius recounts how Tiberius once caught sight of Vipsania Agrippina by chance, and followed her with such longing that pains were taken to ensure that he never saw her again. Suetonius suggests that the marriage was harmonious in its early stages, but that this state soon faded, with the couple living apart. The marriage would not produce any children.

110. Stevenson 2013: 131–133.

Chapter 4

1. Duncan-Jones 2016: 32–33.

2. Dio 53.31.2–4, 54.34.1–4. The senate voted to give Tiberius a triumph for his success in the field, which was blocked by Augustus – although he did grant Tiberius triumphal privileges.

3. Dio 53.32.1–55.33.5. Drusus was also denied a triumph by Augustus.
4. Duncan-Jones 2016: 36–37, 159.
5. Dio 53.13.1–8; Strabo *Geography* 17.3.25; see Millar 1966.
6. Duncan-Jones 2016: 37–38.
7. Dio 53.14.2 – although Syme (1986: 318) notes that this period was flexible in practice, and ex-consuls move to senatorial provinces after a much shorter period should the emperor wish them to.
8. Duncan-Jones 2016: 59–60.
9. Millar 1966: 159–160; although it is unlikely that the emperor would have hesitated to interfere with senatorial provinces if he thought it necessary. See also Millar 1982.
10. See Eck 2012: 187–195 for the administration of the provinces more widely.
11. Millar 1966: 158.
12. Raven 1993: 57.
13. Raven 1993: 56–58. The legion was based in Africa until at least the late fourth century AD, although it was stationed at several different bases during this time; at times, detachments from the legion were sent to fight elsewhere, and soldiers from Third Augusta could be transferred to other legions that were depleted in manpower. It is unknown what happened to the legion after the fourth century AD.
14. Raven 1993: 59–61. Four different governors in Africa would face off against Tacfarinas, mostly ineffectively due to the rebels' use of guerrilla tactics, including ambushes of Roman troops on the march. It was only the fourth governor, Publius Cornelius Dolabella, who was able to finally end the rebellion. He is likely to have been Varus' nephew, and perhaps had learned from the example of his uncle about how not to handle provincial uprisings.
15. Dio 53.14.2.
16. Raven 1993: 79–99. By the mid-first century AD, Africa produced two-thirds of the grain consumed by the city of Rome.
17. Some historians suggested that Varus was not appointed governor of Africa until 7 BC, based particularly on coin issues from the province featuring Gaius and Lucius, which were said only to have been minted in 7/6 BC (e.g. Syme 1986: 319, although he does not rule out the earlier year). Although possible, this re-dating would have unaddressed implications for Varus' appointment to Syria, which is also dated to 7 BC.
18. In the Republic, he would still not yet have been age-eligible for many of the more senior positions he had already held, including the consulship.
19. Duncan-Jones 2016: 38.
20. The portrait may have served to emphasize his individual authority as he took on a long-term Dictatorship, particularly by February 44 BC when he had been named Dictator for Life. The coins were not without controversy at the time, seeming to suggest to some in Rome that Caesar intended to make himself king, a fear of which apparently underlay his assassination. The reverse designs of the portrait coins were often used to highlight personal achievements of Caesar (particularly his victories in the Gallic War) or emphasize his ancestral right to power (with allusions to Venus, whom Caesar claimed as an ancestor).
21. RPC I 798; https://rpc.ashmus.ox.ac.uk/coins/1/798.
22. Burnett *et al* 1992: 39–40.
23. On coinage and Imperial authority in the Augustan period see Wallace-Hadrill 1986.
24. RPC I 775; https://rpc.ashmus.ox.ac.uk/coins/1/775.

25. RPC I 776; https://rpc.ashmus.ox.ac.uk/coins/1/776.
26. Some suggest that Varus' governorship in Syria began in 6 BC not 7 BC, particularly for those who think he was appointed to Africa in 7/6 BC rather than 8/7 BC.
27. Like Varus, Saturninus was favoured by Augustus, who had previously served as governor in Africa (probably in 14/13 BC), and had earlier been appointed consul in 19 BC, evidently performing exceedingly well during his year in office, which took place while Augustus was largely still away from Rome touring the eastern provinces (Velleius Paterculus 2.92). In many ways, Varus' career followed that of Saturninus, although the latter had evidently never been brought into the Imperial family by marriage (the identity of his wife is unknown). That said, an inscription from Rome (ILS 8892) reveals that Saturninus was the cousin of Scribonia, Augustus' first wife and the mother of Julia, his only biological child, making him part of the wider circle of the Imperial family.
28. Butcher 2003: 19–23.
29. Syme 1986: 321.
30. Butcher 2003: 87–98.
31. On client kingship in the Roman world see Braund 1984.
32. Duncan-Jones 2016: 49, 52–55.
33. Butcher 2003: 82.
34. Several governors of Syria were accused of plotting against the emperor over the first two centuries of Imperial rule, including Gnaeus Calpurnius Piso, who was accused of plotting civil war after being appointed governor of the province early in the reign of Tiberius. He was put on trial by the Senate but committed suicide before sentencing (Tacitus, *Annals* 3.15). Others accused during governorships of Syria included Avidius Cassius and Pescennius Niger, who nearly seized the Empire during the civil wars which followed Commodus' death in AD 192 – see Butcher 2003: 82–83.
35. Following Marcus Terentius Varro, Marcus Agrippa, Marcus Titius, and Gaius Sentius Saturninus.
36. The provinces of Britannia and Dacia would later require similar levels of seniority from their governors, but neither had yet been conquered (Britain in AD 43 onward; Dacia in AD 101 onward).
37. Butcher 2003: 81.
38. On political structures in Syria and the wider region see Butcher 2003: 79–121.
39. Dio 48.24.1–48.26.5. Quintus Labienus was the son of Titus Labienus, one of Julius Caesar's officers in the Gallic Wars, who defected to Pompey after Caesar took troops over the Rubicon River into Italy in 49 BC. He was killed at the Battle of Munda in 45 BC.
40. See Josephus, *AJ* 14.13.1–10 on the events of the invasion.
41. These would be among the eagles returned by the Parthians to Augustus in 19 BC to such public acclaim.
42. Dio 49.19.1–49.20.5.
43. Velleius Paterculus 2.78.1.
44. Howgego 1982: 7.
45. RPC 1: 4242, 4245, 4252.
46. Butcher & Ponting 2015: 554
47. Howgego 1982: 7–8.
48. On the messages and significance of the SC issues in Augustan coinage see Russell 2020.

49. Velleius Paterculus 2.117.2
50. Suetonius, *Life of Augustus* 41. Augustus was said to have made up the difference for favoured individuals who had previously satisfied the wealth criteria but found themselves short under the increased levels.
51. For details on charges brought for provincial corruption see Brunt 1961.
52. For general background on the life and times of Herod the Great see Richardson & Fisher 2008.
53. Josephus, *AJ* 14.1.3.
54. Josephus, *AJ* 14.8.5.
55. Josephus, *AJ* 14.9.2.
56. Josephus, *BJ* 1.10.8. On Herod's rise to power in more detail, see Smallwood 1976: 44–59.
57. Including Julius Caesar, Cassius Longinus (Brutus' co-conspirator against Caesar), Mark Antony, and finally Octavian, as well later as the various Roman governors of Syria, particularly Marcus Agrippa.
58. Josephus, *AJ* 14.13.10.
59. Josephus, *AJ* 14.14.1–3.
60. Josephus, *AJ* 14.14.4–5.
61. Josephus, *BJ* 1.14.4.
62. Josephus, *AJ* 14.16.1–3.
63. Josephus, *AJ* 14.16.3.
64. Josephus (*AJ* 15.1.2) and Plutarch (*Life of Antony* 36) say that Antigonus was beheaded. Dio (49.22.6) says that he was crucified.
65. Josephus, *AJ* 15.3.8.
66. Josephus, *AJ* 15.6.6.
67. Plutarch, *Life of Antony* 71.
68. Richardson & Fisher 2018: 136–138.
69. Josephus, *BJ* 1.20.1–2.
70. Josephus, *BJ* 1.20.3–4. Although one historian points out that in reality there was little risk for Octavian in this decision; if Herod proved disloyal, or a disappointment, he could be easily replaced (Hohlfelder 2000: 242).
71. On the building works at Caesarea Maritima see Bergin 2018. On the suggestion that Caesarea Maritima was built and named to ingratiate Herod with Augustus and the Imperial regime see Hohlfelder 2020.
72. Berlin 2014.
73. Josephus, *AJ* 15.3.5.
74. For Josephus on Herod see Rajak 2007. Josephus' main source for Herod's reign was probably the work of Nicolaus of Damascus, Herod's court historian, which may have come with inherent interpretational biases (Paltiel 1981: 109–111). Josephus used the reign of Herod as background to contextualise the conflict between the Jews and Rome in his own times, which had culminated in the First Roman-Jewish War (AD 66–73), which Josephus himself had fought in.
75. Josephus, *AJ* 16.5.4.
76. On the reception of Herod by historians see McCane 2008.
77. Magness 2021: 126.
78. On Herod's reign more widely see Smallwood 1976: 60–104; Richardson & Fisher 2018: 140–196.
79. See Richardson & Fisher 2018: 119–139 for a detailed narrative of events during the first decade of Herod's reign.

80. Mariame was the granddaughter of Hyrcanus II, the High Priest and king who had been deposed by the Parthians in favour of Aristobulus II.

81. Josephus, *AJ* 15.2.5–7, 15.7.4–6. Aristobulus' claim to the throne had been championed by his mother Alexandra, who had unsuccessfully petitioned Antony and Cleopatra to intervene to replace Herod with her son, hoping that Cleopatra could use her influence on Mark Antony to effect the regime change – apparently forgetting that Antony had been one of Herod's strongest advocates in Rome, and was indeed the main reason that he had been made king of Judaea in the first place. Mariamne was executed because she had apparently planned to poison Herod, in part after discovering that he had left instructions that she should be killed.

82. Josephus, *AJ* 15.6.2.

83. Josephus, *AJ* 16.2.2. Later members of the Herodian dynasty would be named for Agrippa, including Herod's grandson, Marcus Julius Agrippa (born in 11 BC), and his son, Herod Agrippa II (born AD 27/28), who was the last king to rule Judaea, until his death some time in the last decade of the first century AD.

84. Richardson & Fisher 2018: 190.

85. Josephus, *AJ* 16.4.1. Josephus suggests in the wider narrative that it was the rivalry between Herod's eldest son Antipater, and the younger Alexander and Aristobulus that led to the deaths of the latter, as Antipater wanted to remove these preferred heirs.

86. Josephus, *AJ* 16.8.4.

87. Josephus, *AJ* 16.11.1.

88. Josephus, *AJ* 16.11.3.

89. Josephus, *AJ* 16.11.7.

90. Josephus, *AJ* 17.5.2

91. Richardson & Fisher 2018: 187–188.

92. Josephus, *AJ* 17.1.1.

93. See Richardson & Fisher 2018: 187–192 for details of the plots against Herod in this period.

94. Josephus, *AJ* 17.5.2–7.

95. Josephus, *BJ* 1.33.5; Herod also apparently wrote to Augustus about Antipater. Elsewhere (*AJ* 17.5.7) Josephus does not mention Varus writing to Augustus, only Herod, but given the importance of the matter an Imperial governor would be expected to consult the emperor about what to do, suggesting the account in the *Jewish War* is the more accurate of the two.

96. Yoder 2014: 154–155.

97. Josephus, *AJ* 17.8.1; *BJ* 1.33.7. Antipater mistook the commotion caused by an attempt by Herod to commit suicide (due to the pain of his illness) for the reaction to his father having been found dead, and immediately tried to bribe his jailer to let him go. This was the final straw for Herod regarding his eldest son (Richardson & Fisher 2018: 42).

98. Josephus, *AJ* 17.5.7.

99. Josephus, *AJ* 17.6.5, *BJ* 1.33.5. For further details and discussion of possible diagnoses (including arterio-sclerosis, cancer, and cirrhosis of the liver) see Smallwood 1976: 103–104. However, one modern historian (Ladouceur 1981: 27–28) points out that in the case of a controversial figure like Herod, historical descriptions of their symptoms were subject to the influence of literary *topoi* which defined how illness would be described – and gruesome symptoms used as a physical illustration of the underlying immorality of the victim. As such, he advises not to read too much into

potential diagnoses of Herod's illness, while acknowledging that knowing what it was would be a useful tool for historians attempting to understand Herod's mindset and actions in his later years.

100. Bowersock 1965: 22.
101. For discontent in the later years of Herod's reign see Smallwood 1976: 96–100; Richardson & Fisher 2018: 182–196.
102. This is likely why there is little record of Varus' activities in Africa – he did not oversee any major provincial problems, therefore nothing was written about him.
103. Josephus, *AJ* 17.8.1.
104. Richardson & Fisher 2018: 39–41; actions included the tearing down of a golden eagle statue from the wall over a gate of the Temple, which was said to be offensive to Jewish law.
105. See e.g. Smallwood 1976; Steinmann 2009. One modern historian rightly notes that 'The question has been debated more than it deserves' (Paltiel 1981: 107, n. 1).
106. Herod was clearly long dead by the time Quirinius was appointed governor of Syria (whatever date is decided for his death, it was inarguably before AD 1). Academic consensus now suggests that the Gospel of Luke mistakenly dated the census of Quirinius to the reign of Herod (e.g. Brown 1993: 17), although some attempt to reconcile the timeline by suggesting that Quirinius may have earlier served in Syria as a more minor Roman functionary, possibly under Varus, during which time he may have conducted a census. However, although it was normal for a census to be conducted in a Roman province, it would have been a very different prospect to carry one out in a client kingdom, making this reconstruction less than likely.
107. A census of a kind was carried out in Judaea after Herod's death, under the governorship of Varus, to establish the extent of Herod's estate, which could have been mistaken for a larger-scale event conducted across the kingdom's population. Even a factual or transcriptional error between 'Quirinius' and 'Quinctilius' may have played a role in the confusion.
108. Josephus, *AJ* 17.6.4. Another eclipse took place in 5 BC, another possible date for Herod's death, although this is likely too early a date; nevertheless, it technically remains a viable hypothesis.
109. 4 BC – Bernegger 1983; Richardson & Fisher 2018;
110. Josephus, *AJ* 17.8.1.
111. One modern historian suggests that Herod also left Augustus himself a substantial bequest in his will (Miller 1993: 41), perhaps to make it more likely that the emperor would approve the document.
112. Yoder 2014: 154.
113. Josephus, *AJ* 17.9.3. Aside from this appearance in Josephus, Sabinus is otherwise undocumented in the historical record – even his full name is unknown.
114. Antipas had been named as Herod's primary heir in an earlier version of his will.
115. Josephus, *AJ* 17.9.5–7.
116. Yoder 2014: 154, n. 102.
117. Josephus, *AJ* 17.9.1–2.
118. Josephus, *AJ* 17.9.3.
119. Josephus, *AJ* 17.9.3.
120. Josephus, *AJ* 17.9.3.
121. Josephus, *AJ* 17.9.4–5.
122. Josephus, *BJ* 2.3.1, *AJ* 17.10.1. It is not clear whether Varus personally visited Jerusalem on his way back to Antioch. Josephus indicates in the *Jewish War* that he

did, but makes no mention of this in the *Jewish Antiquities*. While in Jerusalem Varus may have witnessed a smaller-scale uprising, which may have been the reason that he left the legion behind (Yoder 2014: 156, n. 107). However, Smallwood (1976: 110–111) suggests that the act of garrisoning Jerusalem may have provoked resentment from the local population, adding to that already stirred by Sabinus and Archelaus.

123. Josephus, *AJ* 17.10.1.
124. Josephus, *AJ* 17.10.2. Yoder (2014: 156–157) notes that this action exposes as false the concern Sabinus expressed for the fate of the legion, as he showed no hesitation about sending them out into a potential massacre.
125. Josephus, *AJ* 17.10.2. Some of the Jewish fighters were said by Josephus to be so despairing of the misery around them that they committed suicide, by throwing themselves onto their own swords, or into the fire.
126. Josephus, *AJ* 17.10.3.
127. See Smallwood 1976: 110–113.
128. Josephus, *AJ* 17.10.8.
129. Josephus, *AJ* 17.10.4–7.
130. Athronges was said to have drawn support for no better reason than his height and physical strength (Josephus, *AJ* 17.10.7).
131. Josephus, *AJ* 17.10.6.
132. Josephus, *AJ* 17.10.7; the leaders of Athronges' force were later either killed in battle or taken captive by the Judaean regime (Athronges' fate was one of these, but it is uncertain which), although Josephus notes that this was some time after the period immediately following Herod's death.
133. Josephus, *AJ* 17.10.9.
134. Formerly the Greek city of Ake; later the Crusader city of Acre.
135. Josephus, *AJ* 17.10.9; *BJ.* 2.5.1; see also Crosby 2016. If this was a son of Varus, it cannot be the only son documented historically (Publius Quinctilius Varus the Younger), as he had probably not even been born yet. It would be most likely therefore that this was a much older son, probably from Varus' first marriage to an unknown woman in the later 20s BC, who would be in his late teens/early twenties by this point, and therefore exactly the right age to serve as a tribune under his father in Syria. Some argue that Josephus' reference to a son in the *Antiquities* is simply incorrect, and that there was no son of Varus involved in the Judaean campaign. However, these arguments were largely made before it was known that Varus was married at least once earlier in his life, and their hesitation over ascribing to him an adult son is therefore more understandable.
136. Yoder 2014: 158–159. Yoder notes that Varus likely had the opportunity to end the 'fire and slaughter' of the allied troops but chose not to, probably because he needed the manpower. They would then provide a useful scapegoat for the bad behaviours of Varus' army later.
137. Josephus, *AJ* 17.10.10.
138. Likely to deter future would-be rebels.
139. Josephus, *BJ* 2. 77–788; *AJ* 17. 297.
140. Miller 1966: 159.
141. Josephus does not mention exactly what happened to them; presumably they were executed.
142. Josephus, *AJ* 17.11.1; *BJ* 2.6.1.
143. Josephus, *AJ.* 17.9.4.
144. Josephus, *AJ* 17.11.1

145. Josephus, *AJ* 17.11.1–4.
146. Josephus, *AJ* 17.13.1–5. In the earlier years after annexation, some parts of the former kingdom of Judaea maintained a level of autonomy, while the Roman portion was administered as a satellite territory of Syria, and governed by an equestrian prefect. Under Claudius, the kingdom was even partially restored, with Herod Agrippa (Herod's grandson) named 'King of the Jews', although direct Roman control of the territory appears to have been maintained. Herod Agrippa died in AD 44, and his son, Herod Agrippa II, inherited his position, albeit not until AD 48. Judaea remained in this mixed situation of province-client kingship until the death of Agrippa II in the last decade of the first century AD, despite major uprisings in the region (including the seven-year First Roman-Jewish War), governed by a legate and garrisoned by Tenth Fretensis. Rule by legate continued until the AD 130s, when in the aftermath of the devastating Second Roman-Jewish War (also known as the Bar Kokhba Revolt) Hadrian renamed the province Syria-Palaestina, and ended any special privileges.
147. Murdoch 2008: 63.
148. See Smallwood 1976: 113.
149. RPC 1: 4535; https://rpc.ashmus.ox.ac.uk/coins/1/4535.
150. See Yoder 2014: 156–158.
151. Yoder 2014: 157; *cf.* Mason 2008: 32, n. 278: 'It is telling that he [Sabinus] must dramatize the legion's possible fate in order to get Varus' attention; there seems to be no love lost between Varus and Sabinus'.
152. Josephus wrote in the later first century AD, and would likely have been well aware of the ultimate fate of Varus in Germany, although he makes no reference to this in his work, as it happened well outside his remit. Josephus' description of Varus' actions in Judaea nevertheless go some way to rehabilitating his reputation as a military commander, even if this was not the original intention.
153. Yodel 2014: 158, n. 113 suggests that the actions of Varus in the aftermath of the Judaean uprising were described in such a way that they would act as a sharp contrast to the Roman response after the First Roman-Jewish War decades later, in which a Roman official had also been partly to blame for the stirring up of discontent, but in which case the governor of Syria did not recognize the innocence of most of the Jewish inhabitants of Jerusalem, nor was he able to successfully calm the situation down without a fight; both Rome and Judaea would suffer.
154. Yoder 2014: 158–159.
155. Yoder 2014: 158.
156. Smallwood 1976: 113.
157. Yoder 2014: 154.
158. John 1963: 960.
159. Murdoch 2008: 62.
160. Paltiel 1981: 114.
161. Josephus *AJ* 17.10.6.
162. E.g. Murdoch 2008: 65.
163. See Steinmann 2009: 17–18 for further discussion.
164. It would also, of course, have a potential impact on the possible date-range for the birth of a historical Christ, whose birth could then be put anywhere in the period leading up to 1 BC.
165. CIL XIV 3613 = *ILS* 918. A translation from Kokkinos (1995: 22) reads: '[k]ing, which (aforementioned tribe?) having been brought into the pow[er of Imperator Caesar] Augustus and the Roman People, the Senat[e decreed to the immortal gods]

two thanksgivings for success[ful achievements, and] triumph[al] ornaments to himself; as proconsul he he[ld] the province of Asia; [as legatus propraetore]; of the Divine Augustus for another time [he held] Syria and Phoenicia]…'. Kokkinos notes that sections are missing from both the top and bottom of the inscription.

166. Suggestions have been made that this does not necessarily mean that the subject of the inscription outlived Augustus on the basis that the fragment could be from a later honorific (re)dedication (e.g. Taylor 1936: 167–168), although others point out that this leap is usually made to support an identification of the subject as someone who predeceased Augustus, rather than on any inherent attribute of the artefact itself (e.g. Atkinson 1958: 316 n.73; Kokkinos 1995: 22).

167. On the Roman governors of Syria see Atkinson 1958.

168. Atkinson 1958: 314–319; see Kokkinos 1995: 23 n.6 for a full discussion of the Quirinius advocates.

169. Saturninus – Kokkinos 1995; Piso – Syme 1986: 338–340; Titius – Taylor 1936.

170. The identification of Varus with the inscription first emerged in Martin 1980, seen as 'the only attempt at reinterpretation after Syme' (Kokkinos 1995: 23 n.7).

171. On Quirinius in Asia in AD 1–2 see Atkinson 1958: 164–169.

172. Duncan-Jones 2016: 38–41.

173. There are a few years in this period in which the identity of the governor of Asia is less than clear, including 1 BC–AD 1, AD 1–2, and AD 2–3/3–4 (a senator named Gaius Antistius Vetus held the position in one of these last two periods, but which one is uncertain); but Varus has never been considered likely to have been a governor of Asia in this period (see Atkinson 1958).

174. As yet, no archaeological evidence has been recovered that associates Varus with a place or position during this period.

175. Cassius Dio 55.6.5.

176. Suetonius, *Life of Tiberius* 10.

177. It seems to have been an unfortunate problem for the emperors that if they spent too much time in Rome they became unpopular, making it necessary to spend time away from the city – but this in turn could lead to political issues going under their radar, as well as accusations that they were no longer in touch with the mood of the city.

178. Cassius Dio 55.9.4–8. Dio suggests that Gaius and Lucius were at the time failing to live up to the high behavioural standards Augustus expected of them, and that Augustus became concerned when Gaius received the popular vote for a consulship before he was even old enough to serve as a tribune (around 20 years old). The emperor apparently attempted to shock them into better behaviour by giving Tiberius tribunician powers and the governorship of Armenia, and denying Gaius the consulship. This apparently backfired, leading to the tension described by Dio. However, the historian also cites the poor relationship between Tiberius and Julia as another possible cause. He also mentions that there were rumours that Tiberius had been exiled from Rome after Augustus discovered he had been plotting against Gaius and Lucius, but there is little credibility to the claims in the form made.

179. Cassius Dio 55.10.12–14.

180. Suetonius, *Life of Tiberius* 11.4.

181. Suetonius, *Life of Tiberius* 11.5. By then, both Gaius and Lucius had held commands of cavalry units (Cassius Dio 55.9.9–10), and Gaius had been given a legionary command as well, although acknowledged to be relatively inexperienced (Cassius Dio 10.10.17).

182. Suetonius, *Life of Tiberius* 12. Tiberius evidently became concerned over time that his absence from Rome would be used to cover his assassination, far from the public eye, which Suetonius suggests made him increasingly keen to return to Rome.
183. Cassius Dio 55.10.9–10.
184. Cassius Dio 55.10.10; Suetonius, *Life of Tiberius* 13.
185. Cassius Dio 55.10.7–9.
186. This led to widespread suggestions that Tiberius' mother Livia was responsible for the deaths of Gaius and Lucius (Cassius Dio 55.10.10), to return her son to prominence and the Imperial succession, although there seems to be very little direct evidence, only the inevitable supposition which seemed to follow ambitious women around under the early Empire.
187. Cassius Dio 55.13.1. Tiberius was also compelled to adopt his nephew Germanicus, the son of his younger brother Drusus, as his own heir – apparently worrying that Tiberius would behave unpredictably again, as he had done in exiling himself to Rhodes, or that he would somehow spark a rebellion somewhere.
188. Cassius Dio 55.13.1; Suetonius, *Life of Tiberius* 16.1.
189. Cassius Dio 55.32.1–2. Dio suggests that Agrippa Postumus was disrespectful to his adopted Imperial parents, insulting Livia, and berating Augustus for holding on to the inheritance which should have come to him from his father's estate.
190. Murdoch 2008: 65.
191. Murdoch 2008: 65.
192. Claudia Pulchra's mother Claudia Marcella Minor and Vipsania Marcella's mother Claudia Marcella Major were full sisters, born to Octavia the Younger through her first marriage, to Gaius Claudius Marcellus. Through her maternal line, she was also a cousin of varying degrees to several other prominent figures in the later Imperial regime.
193. Claudia Pulchra's parents did not marry until 14 BC, making this the earliest possible date for her birth (even allowing for a pre-marriage conception).

Chapter 5
1. For Roman perspectives on Germany, see Caesar, *Gallic Wars* 4.1–3.
2. On the German tribes, see Tacitus, *Germania* 1–2; *cf.* Strabo, *Geography* 7.1.3–5.
3. Strabo, *Geography* 7.1.2.
4. Strabo, *Geography* 7.1.3;
5. Strabo, *Geography* 7.2.3. Human sacrifice had been banned by Rome in 97 BC, having been used on extreme occasions during the earlier Republic. Although claims about human sacrifice on the part of the Germanic peoples was clearly meant to shock Roman readers, anthropological and archaeological studies suggest that most of the claims are not entirely fictitious, even if they were exaggerated for effect. On this argument, and human sacrifice in later prehistoric western Europe more widely, see Green 1998.
6. For more on Late Pre-Roman Iron Age Germany see Sievers 2020.
7. Caesar, *Gallic Wars* 4.5–6.
8. Caesar, *Gallic Wars* 4.17–19.
9. Caesar, *Gallic Wars* 6.1–10, 28–44.
10. During the 55 BC campaign; see Roymans 2017.
11. Plutarch, *Caesar* 58.7.
12. Florus, *Epitome* 2.30.22.

13. On political hostage-taking in the Roman world see Allen 2006.
14. See Gruen 1996 for a detailed discussion.
15. Virgil, *Aeneid* 1.278–9.
16. Livy 21.30.10.
17. Dio 54.11.2; on the protection of Gaul from Germany, see Wells 2003: 76–78.
18. See Wells 1972 and Gruen 1996: 178–188.
19. Powell 2011: 57–59.
20. Strabo, *Geography* 7.1.4.
21. Dio 55.10a.3.
22. Strabo, *Geography* 4.1.1. The divisions were said to have been drawn broadly along pre-existing cultural and ethnic lines, as perceived by the Romans at least.
23. Wolters 2020: 29.
24. For these early campaigns see Powell 2011: 18–48.
25. Dio 54.20.4–6; Florus, *Epitome* 2.30.24.
26. Dio 54.20.4–6.
27. Like Varus, Lollius had been a prominent figure in the early Imperial regime, likely also hand-picked by Augustus to serve in the provinces because of his administrative and military abilities. Lollius appears to have come from a non-Patrician family, making him a *homo novus*, 'new man', and the first of his family to enter the Senate. The most likely source of this upward mobility was a personal relationship with the emperor and the patronage which followed, possibly fostered while Augustus was still Octavian and in conflict with Mark Antony. There is some suggestion that Lollius was mentioned in Appian's account of the civil war which followed Caesar's assassination, as 'Marcus', originally an ally of Brutus captured after the Battle of Philippi, who pretended to be a slave to avoid the proscription which awaited him back in Rome (Appian, *The Civil War* 4.49). His 'master', referred to in Appian's text as Barbula, suspected that his slave was in fact a proscribed Roman, and brought him to Rome in search of the truth, where Marcus was recognized by one of Barbula's friends. Through the intercession of Marcus Agrippa, this Marcus was granted an amnesty from proscription by Octavian, was freed from slavery, and became a friend of Octavian, fighting in his army at the Battle of Actium. Barbula had fought for Antony at the battle, and afterwards was seemingly bought by Marcus so that he could be brought before Octavian and ask to be pardoned, which was evidently granted.
28. It was originally intended that Lollius serve as consul alongside Augustus himself, although this plan had been abandoned when Augustus decided not to hold the consulship again after 23 BC, and left Rome to tour the eastern provinces soon afterwards (the tour that Varus accompanied him on as *quaestor*). After civic disturbances during the selection of a new co-consul, Quintus Aemilius Lepidus was appointed – who was, according to Appian, the Barbula who had saved Marcus at Philippi, and had been saved by him in turn at Actium (Tansey 2008). Augustus was absent from Rome during Lollius' term in office (Dio, *Roman History* 54.7.2), which suggests that the emperor had a degree of faith that he left Rome in capable hands, and indeed, little of significance appears to have happened that year, beyond improvements to the Bridge of Fabricius across the Tiber following damage sustained in a floor several years earlier (Syme 1986: 41–42; the improvements are recorded on an inscription still extant on the bridge). In 19/18 BC, Lollius was appointed governor of Macedonia, where he enjoyed military success against an invading Thracian Bersi tribe. This experience likely led to his appointment as the governor of Gaul, at that

time the northernmost province, during which the disaster against the German tribes would take place.

29. Velleius 2.97.1 – an accusation which will sound similar to that which Velleius directed towards Varus as well.

30. Velleius 2.97.1; Tacitus, *Annals* 1.10; Dio 54.20.4–6. The exact year/date of the battle is a matter of debate.

31. Velleius 2.97.1 reveals that the Fifth Alaudae Legion lost their legionary eagle in the engagement.

32. Powell 2011: 19.

33. This is perhaps surprising, as many Roman military commanders committed suicide during or soon after a substantial military defeat, either to avoid falling into enemy captivity or to avoid shame in the aftermath (on Roman military suicide, see van Hooff 1990: 87–110). Contrary to this, Rauh 2015 suggests that 'shame' has been overexaggerated as a cause for Roman military suicide, and that it was primarily fear of capture that prompted this action. As such, soldiers and commanders at no risk of capture might be considered less likely to commit suicide than previously imagined.

34. Dio, *Roman History*, 54.19.1, 54.20.4; Velleius Paterculus 2.97.1. Dio suggests that Augustus was glad to have an excuse to leave Rome, as his long-standing presence in the city had seemingly led to discontent – or because he wanted to escape salacious gossip about his relationship with another woman.

35. Dio, *Roman History* 54.20.6.

36. Horace, *Odes* 4.9; although see Ambrose 1965 for a suggestion that the ode was actually 'censure ironically disguised as praise' (p 2).

37. Suetonius, *Life of Augustus* 23.1. However, others argue that the Lollian Disaster was highly significant in Rome until it was overshadowed by events under Varus, and that the collective trauma of the event can be seen in several pieces of cultural work from the time, including poetry (Kerremans 2018).

38. Relations between Lollius and Gaius Caesar seemingly became strained during the expedition. During a visit to Tiberius, during his self-imposed exile on Rhodes, one historian claims that it emerged that Lollius had been slandering Tiberius to Gaius, leading to tensions between them (Suetonius, *Life of Tiberius* 12.2). However, Velleius Paterculus, makes no mention in his brief account of the meeting between Tiberius and Gaius, claiming that Gaius treated Tiberius 'with all honour as his superior' (Velleius Paterculus 2.101.1). Given the fact that Velleius was actually on the expedition as an officer, his account probably has more credibility. Later in the excursion, Lollius was accused by Gaius of taking bribes and exhorting tribute from local leaders for his own personal gain, with the result that Gaius denounced Lollius to Augustus. Tiberius also appears to have been involved in Lollius' downfall, seemingly corresponding for months with an officer who was part of Gaius Caesar's party, probably Publius Sulpicius Quirinius, who was praised in the Senate after his death by Tiberius, noting the services he had performed in helping to bring down Lollius (Pettinger 2012: 53–58). This led to Lollius' downfall and death – according to Pliny the Elder, a suicide in disgrace (Pliny the Elder, *Natural History* 9.58). Velleius Paterculus also suggests that Lollius' death may have been suicide, and claimed that the news was greeted with widespread joy (Velleius Paterculus 2.102.1). Pliny also claimed that some of the treasures acquired by Lollius in the East were passed down as family treasures, eventually ending up in the hands of his granddaughter Lollia Paulina, who was briefly the third wife of the emperor Caligula. The worth of these treasures was said to be more than 400,000 sestertii. Tiberius later condemned

Lollius' actions in the Senate, and blamed him for corrupting the mind of Gaius Caesar (Tacitus, *Annals* 3.48).

39. Although flawed and flexible in reality, there was a semi-formal requirement in Rome for conflicts to be 'just wars', launched not to fuel Roman imperialist expansionism, but to 'defend' their territories, although the justifications could be fairly flimsy in some cases.

40. This is the provincial tour that Augustus returned to Rome from in 13 BC, during Varus' consulship, as commemorated by the Ara Pacis. Concerns about the emperor's safety might have been raised by several bad omens which had occurred around the same time (see Powell 2011: 21).

41. On the Alpine War, see Powell 2011: 33–48. A short account of the conflict was written by Dio (54.20–23), and is very briefly referred to by Florus (2.22).

42. Dio 54.22.1.

43. Suetonius, *Life of Tiberius* 9.

44. Dio 54.25.1.

45. Powell 2011: 61–63; Wolters 2020: 29–30.

46. Powell 2011: 61–62.

47. On Drusus' expedition north see Powell 2011: 75–80.

48. Dio 54.32.1. On the campaign of 11 BC more widely, see Dio 54.32.1–33.5; *cf.* Powell 2011: 83–84.

49. Dio 54.33.2–3. Dio also suggests that a swarm of bees seen in Drusus' marching camp was interpreted as an omen of coming disaster, and another reason to head to safety on the Rhine.

50. Dio 54.33.3–4.

51. For a conditional reconstruction of the ambush see Powell 2011: 88–89.

52. Pliny, *Natural History* 11.18. Pliny therefore suggested that this battle demonstrated that a swarm of bees in the camp, as Drusus had, could also be seen as a good omen.

53. Pliny, *Natural History* 11.18. Dio (54.3.3) mentions only that it took place in a 'narrow pass', which is of limited use in determining the location.

54. Dio 54.33.5.

55. Powell 2011: 89–91. Aliso is usually identified as the fort at Haltern, 54km beyond the Rhine, although a case has also been made for Bergkammen-Oberaden. Both sites have remains from roughly the correct date.

56. See Rasbach 2020 on the Augustan-period military infrastructure east of the Rhine.

57. Powell 2011: 102–103.

58. Dio 55.1.2. Velleius (2.97.3) is at pains to point out that the majority of the blood shed in the campaign was German, not Roman.

59. Suetonius, *Claudius* 1.4. See also Rich 1999.

60. Dio (55.1.3) and Suetonius (*Claudius* 1.4) both recount this episode – that Drusus saw a vision of a woman of 'superhuman size', who foretold his death should he attempt to advance any further. The episode clearly became a popularized story in the aftermath of his death. Powell (2011: 104–105) suggests the event may have been an episode of sleep paralysis, noting that Drusus clearly took the warnings seriously. Dio 55.1.4; Suetonius, *Claudius* 1.5

61. Strabo, *Geography* 7.1.3; Velleius 2.97.3.

62. Rasbach 2020: 27.

63. Powell 2011: 103. On the practice generally see Allen 2006.

64. Dio 55.1.4; Velleius 2.97.3.

65. Suetonius, *Claudius* 1.5. On Drusus' death more widely, see Powell (2011: 105–108).

66. Livy, *Periochae* 142.2.
67. Dio 55.2.1; Valerius Maximus 5.5.3.
68. Dio 55.2.4.
69. Velleius 2.97.4.
70. Tacitus, *Annals* 4.44. Ahenobarbus is better known as the grandfather of the emperor Nero.
71. Velleius 2.104.2. It was to this Marcus Vinicius that Velleius dedicated his work, the full title of which was *Roman History Dedicated to Marcus Vinicius*.
72. Velleius Paterculus, *Roman History* 2.105.1–2.106.3.
73. Velleius Paterculus, *Roman History* 2.108.1.
74. Strabo, *Geography* 7.1.3.
75. Velleius Paterculus, *Roman History* 2.109–110.
76. Tacitus, *Annals* 2.46.
77. For the fortress at Marktbreit see Pietsch 2003.
78. Dio, *Roman History* 55.28.5–7.
79. Or 'The War of the Batos'. The conflict gained its name as the two major Illyrian rebel leaders were both named Bato, one the chieftain of the Daesitiates, the other of the Breuci.
80. On the Illyrian Revolt generally see Abdale 2019.
81. After the revolt, the province of Illyricum was dissolved, and the regions of Dalmatia and Pannonia became their own provinces – the conflict perhaps having demonstrated the dangers inherent in administrating the region as a single province.
82. Velleius 2.110.6.
83. Suetonius, *Tiberius* 16.1.
84. Suetonius, *Tiberius* 16.1.
85. Velleius 2.111.1.
86. Velleius 2.111.4–116.5.
87. See Rasbach 2020.
88. Murdoch 2008: 65.
89. Tacitus, *Annals* 4.44.
90. Suetonius, *Augustus* 71.2. In a letter sent by Augustus to Tiberius he mentions Vinicius coming to a dinner party at which the guests gambled during the meal.
91. Velleius Paterculus 2.105.1
92. Velleius Paterculus 2.105.2. This character portrait could hardly be in greater contrast to that Paterculus gave of Varus soon after (2.117.2).
93. Wells 1972: 156.
94. Eck 2010: 13–14.
95. Rasbach 2020: 27, 31.
96. Timpe 1970: 86; see also Syme 1986: 325–326.
97. Velleius 2.118.1.
98. Dio 56.18.1–3.
99. Dio, *Roman History* 56.18.1.
100. See Millar 1982 for a detailed discussion of the involvement of the emperor in decision-making in the provinces.
101. Velleius 2.117.4.
102. Keppie 1997.
103. Velleius 2.120.3.
104. Syme 1986: 314.
105. Rasbach 2020.

106. See Eck 2009.
107. Dio 56.18.1–3.
108. The idea that newly-conquered populations underwent a process of deliberate top-down 'romanization' – with the imposition of Roman law, customs, and institutions on the new population – has by now largely been rejected as a nineteenth- century idea which reflects British Imperialism rather than Roman reality – for a full discussion see e.g. Freeman 2006. The literature on 'romanization' is extensive; work over the last three decades has made it fairly clear that Roman culture was not imposed top-down on unwilling provincial populations, but rather made available without any particular onus on the majority of the people to adopt it – although, likely for reasons of availability and affordability, many likely did over time.
109. On the archaeology of Waldgirmes see von Schnurbein 2003, Curry 2017, and Rasbach 2020: 27–36.
110. Rasbach 2020: 30.
111. Rasbach 2020: 35.
112. Most of the statue pieces were recovered during excavations in the 1990s, although the discovery of the horse's head was not announced until 2009.
113. Eck 2009.
114. Tacitus, *Germania* 5.
115. Wells 1972: 156.
116. Dio 56.18.2.
117. Velleius 2.117.3–4; Dio 56.18.2–4.
118. Dio 56.18.2.
119. Velleius 2.117.3.
120. Dio 56.18.3.
121. Velleius 2.117.4.
122. Velleius 2.118.1.
123. Dio 56.18.3.
124. It may well have been the start of taxation in Germany. There were ever-increasing financial demands on the Empire, for the ongoing building projects, grain supply, and to pay the mounting costs of the Illyrian Revolt, which as an internal conflict brought in much less in terms of booty than a normal campaign of conquest. Augustus may have been aiming to maximize all his possible revenue sources, including sourcing more payments from the provinces (Levick 2010: 98–99)
125. Dio 56.18.4.
126. Florus, *Epitome* 2.30.30–33.
127. E.g. Creasy (1851).
128. Florus, *Epitome* 2.30.32.
129. Dio 56.19.1.
130. Abdale 2016: 123.
131. Velleius 2.120.5.
132. As suggested by Gruen 1996: 184–185, who further suggests that the Romans recognised the German distaste for their way of life, even if they could not understand it.
133. Timpe 1970: 49.
134. Velleius 2.118.2.
135. The Netflix show *Barbaren* speculated that Arminius was raised within Varus' own household, but there is absolutely no evidence for this.
136. Tacitus, *Annals* 2.10.

137. Tacitus, *Annals* 2.10. See also Timpe 1970 on the recruitment of Cheruscan auxiliaries between 12 BC and AD 9.
138. Murdoch 2008: 84.
139. Flavus certainly served under Tiberius at least once, either during one of these conflicts or in the Roman campaigns which followed the Teutoburg. Tacitus (*Annals* 2.9) notes that he lost an eye while under Tiberius' command.
140. Velleius 2.118.2.
141. Velleius 2.118.1.
142. Tacfarinas, another ex-auxiliary rebel, used similar intelligence to great effect in a seven-year uprising against Rome in North Africa, employing guerrilla-type tactics which the Roman army struggled to resist. He was only defeated when the Romans responded by adapting their own tactics to neutralize his (on Tacfarinas, see Tacitus *Annals* 2.52, 3.73–74, 4.23–25).
143. Tacitus, *Annals* 2.9–10. In Tacitus' account, even at this late stage Flavus attempted to convince Arminius to surrender to Rome, while his brother in turn urged him to defect back to the Germans. However, given that Tacitus reports this as a private conversation between the brothers the exchange sadly has little historical authenticity, although it provides a fitting pretext for Tacitus to lay out the Roman and German perspectives on Imperial rule and the value of service to Rome.
144. Tacitus, *Annals* 2.88.2. Tacitus notes that Arminius was 37 years old when he died in AD 21, putting his birth-date in 18/17 BC.
145. Winkler 2015: 2; *cf.* Timpe 1970.
146. Dio 56.19.2.
147. Dyson 1971: 255.
148. Velleius 2.118.2.
149. Velleius 2.119.2.
150. Dio 56.18.2.
151. See Sheldon 2001 for a discussion of Roman intelligence in Germany during Varus' time on the Rhine.
152. Velleius 2.118.2.
153. Suetonius, *Life of Tiberius* 17.1.
154. Velleius 2.117.1, Dio 56.18.1.
155. Dio 56.18.4.
156. Dio 56.19.1.
157. Velleius 2.118.4; Tacitus *Annals* 1.55; Florus *Epitome* 2.30.31.
158. Tacitus, *Annals* 1.58.
159. Tacitus, *Annals* 1.58.
160. Tacitus, *Annals* 1.55.
161. Velleius, 2.118.4.

Chapter 6
1. Velleius Paterculus 2.117.1–2.119.5; Florus 2.30; Cassius Dio 56.18–24; Tacitus 1.60–1.61.
2. Strabo, *Geography* 7.1.4; Manlius, *Astronomica* 898–901; Frontinus, *Stratagems* 3.15.4, 4.7.8; Seneca, *Controversiae* 1.3.10; Pliny, *Natural History* 7.46. It has also been suggested that Ovid's poem *Tristia 2* was inspired by the events in the Teutoburg, particularly in references to Germany and Tiberius waging war there (2.165–178 and 2.225–231), but it is not certain that the poem was composed after the battle had taken place (see Thakur 2014 for discussion of the date of *Tristia 2*).

3. Velleius 2.119.1.
4. On the treatment of Tiberius in Velleius' work see Balmaceda 2014.
5. Lucian, *How to Write History* 49.
6. Lucian (*How to Write History* 11–13) also cautioned that some military historians deliberately distorted or falsified their accounts, to gain praise and flatter contemporaries that they thought they might profit from.
7. Thucydides, *History of the Peloponnesian War* 7.44.1, 1.22.3.
8. Aristotle, *Parva Naturalia* 1.450b.15–25.
9. Caesar, *Gallic Wars* 1.22.
10. Pliny, *Natural History* 7.24.
11. Two particularly relevant studies are Baddeley 1972 and Fruzetti *et al* 1992, which both specifically address memory and performance during dangerous situations, particularly battle.
12. Velleius 2.117.1. On the histories of the Seventeenth, Eighteenth and Nineteenth legions see Keppie 1997.
13. The Marcus Caelius tombstone, found in Xanten, now in Bonn; CIL XIII 8648; the Nineteenth legion is mentioned in the context of the eagle being recovered during a subsequent campaign in the region under Germanicus during the early reign of Tiberius, AD 15–17 (see Tacitus, *Annals* 1.60). Keppie notes that even the existence of the Seventeenth is speculative, as there is no historical or epigraphic evidence of a legion of this number existing in the Augustan army. He suggests that the absence of a legion with this number in the later historical/epigraphic record, combined with the numbers of the other German legions in the Teutoburg, makes it probable that that the third, unspecified legion was the Seventeenth.
14. On the disbandment of legions after defeats see Ward 2020.
15. No inscriptions have been found from any legions, not just the Seventeenth, Eighteenth, and Nineteenth. Several artefacts bear the name of cohorts within the legion, alongside the owner of the artefact in some cases, but as the numbered cohorts are found associated with every legion, they are not particularly helpful in confirming the identity of the units involved. The artefacts comprise a scabbard fragment from the Oberesch, reconstructed as 'T. Vibi(i) (centuria) Tadi(i) l(egionis) P(rimae) A(ugustae) X LX'; an armour fitting inscribed 'M. Aii (cohort) I (centuria) Fab(ricii); and a plumbob inscribed 'CHOI' (= c(o)ho(rtis) I) - see Harnecker & Franzius (2008, find numbers 26, 114, & 315) for more details.
16. This hypothesis was first developed by Peter Norris while a student at the University of Liverpool; I advance it here with his permission. On the *evocati* see also Dio 45.12.3.
17. Velleius 2.111.1.
18. Velleius 2.111.2. The praise is qualified by the excellence of the army being used as yet another way to attack Varus, although this does not mean that the comments were untrue.
19. The stone was dedicated by his brother, and reads 'To Marcus Caelius, son of Titus, of the Lemonian district, from Bologna, first centurion of the Eighteenth legion. 53½ years old. He fell in the Varian War. His freedman's bones may be interred here. Publius Caelius, son of Titus, of the Lemonian district, his brother, erected (this monument)'. CIL 13.8648.
20. No other reference to the 'Varian War' is made in either archaeological or historical sources. It is possible that the inscription refers to the later campaigns of Germanicus,

which were conducted in revenge for the Teutoburg, although it is difficult to imagine that these would have been named after Varus.

21. On Roman military decorations more widely see Maxfield 1981: 85–99.
22. Velleius 2.117.1.
23. Dio 56.19.1.
24. 10,000 – Abdale 2016: 110–117; 10–15,000 – Rost & Wilbers-Rost 2010: 119; up to 14,000 – Murdoch 2006: 105; nearly 20,000 – Sheldon 2020: 1014.
25. Dio 56.20.2. At this time soldiers below the rank of centurion were not legally allowed to marry, although it is certain that they did so anyway, albeit that these unions would have no legal status in Roman law; for Roman military marriage, see Phang 2001.
26. Painter 2001: 15.
27. Although it has been suggested that the silverware in the Hildesheim Treasure was distributed by Varus as diplomatic gifts, rather than being looted from the baggage-train following the battle.
28. On Roman strategies for avoiding and coping with ambush see Onasander, *The General* 6.7; Vegetius, *Epitome of Military Science* 3.6, 3.9, 3.13.
29. Vegetius, *Epitome of Military Science* 3.6. For tribal use of irregular tactics around this period see Caesar, *Gallic Wars* 5.26–38; Tacitus, *Annals* 1.10, 1.65, 14.32; Dio 56.18–22. See also Bellino 2011 for a comparison with the military tactics which the Romans faced in Wales just a few decades later.
30. Sheldon 2020: 1030.
31. According to Tacitus (*Annals* 2.14), Germanicus would later try and assure his soldiers that Roman weaponry and training was equally well, if not better, suited to fighting in forests and marshes than that of the Germans, although his assertions were not necessarily borne out – his army was only victorious in Germany after managing to meet the enemy in pitched battle.
32. Dio 56.19.5–20.1.
33. Velleius 2.105.3. But Velleius was often overly praising of Tiberius' actions.
34. Dio 56.18.2.
35. Dio 56.19.3.
36. Murdoch 2006: 103; Abdale 2016: 108–109. Abdale consequently rejects the hypothesis that Varus' summer camp was based at Porta Westfalica/Minden as this would broadly fall into the territory of the Angrivarii, making it unlikely that Varus could be lured into an ambush approaching a territory he was already present in; he suggests a summer base at Aliso. However, siting the 'rebellion' in another part of the same tribal territory is not an impossibility, and would also explain why Varus felt comfortable trying to deal with a rebellion in the short period before winter set in. The name of the tribe Angrivarii literally translates as 'angry with the Varians', and although the name is documented in a source long pre-dating AD 9 (Ptolemy's, *Geography*, 2.10), the tribe may have become linked with the Battle of the Teutoburg for no other reason than their name fitting in nicely with an attack on Varus and his army. None of the Roman sources link the tribe with the rebellion, even when they crop up in later narratives – such as their complete surrender to Germanicus in his later wars in Germany (Tacitus, *Annals* 2.22).
37. Abdale 2016: 110–111. It is interesting that Varus is generally accused in the ancient sources of not being 'military enough', but is criticized by some subsequent sources as reacting too strongly to an uprising, despite that being one of his purposes on the Rhine.

38. The idea of the expedition as an opportunity for diplomacy and an enjoyable experience for the soldiers originated with Phil Freeman of the University of Liverpool (but any errors associated with it are mine).

39. Based on the finds recovered from the Kalkriese area. Some of the more luxurious finds may be associated with Varus' personal baggage, as commanders in the Roman army could bring large quantities of their personal belongings on campaign, which would usually be kept separate from the rest of the train (see Josephus, *Jewish War* 5.49 (5.2.1). For more on Roman military baggage trains, see Roth 1999: 79–90. Roth notes that it is unclear exactly how many pack animals were used by a Roman army on the march, but suggests estimates of around 1,000–1,500 animals per legion are not unrealistic; even if his units were under strength, Varus' train may have comprised some 2,000–3,000 animals, not an inconsiderable number.

40. Dio 56.20.2.

41. Vegetius, *Epitome of Military Science* 3.6.

42. Dio 56.20.5.

43. Dio 56.20.2.

44. Tacitus, *Annals* 2.46.

45. Dio 56.19.4.

46. Vegetius, *Epitome of Military Science* 3.6.

47. Dio 56.19.4.

48. Dio 56.19.5.

49. Dio 56.19.5–20.1. This kind of engineering and building activity seems to have been an accepted part of campaigning in areas lacking these facilities. Similar scenes of forest clearance and construction are seen on Trajan's Column in Rome during the Dacian Wars almost a century later.

50. Dio 56.20.3.

51. Dio 56.20.4.

52. Dio 56.20.4–5.

53. Tacitus, *Germania* 6.

54. For more on the German fighting style at the time of the Teutoburg see Abdale 2016.

55. Very little German weaponry or other military equipment is found from the battlefield at Kalkriese, and this may partially explain why – because many of the German soldiers were actually using Roman kit.

56. Sheldon 2020: 1030.

57. Dio 56.20.2; Florus, *Epitome* 2.30.34.

58. Vegetius, *Epitome of Military Science* 3.6.

59. Vegetius, *Epitome of Military Science* 3.6.

60. Austin & Rankov 1995: 42–54; see also Polybius. 9.13.6, 9.14.2–3; Onasander, *The General* 6.7; Vegetius, *Epitome of Military Science* 3.6, 3.9, 3.13, 3.22.

61. Sheldon 2020: 1015.

62. On cultivation around Kalkriese see Tolksdorf-Lienemann 2004; for native settlements in the region, see Rost & Wilbers-Rost 2019.

63. Wilbers-Rost 2009: 125.

64. See Riggsby 2006.

65. Östenberg 2018: 243.

66. See Anders 2015: 284–286.

67. On combat disintegration see Wesbrook 1980.

68. Tacitus, *Annals* 1.65.

69. On the ambush at Trasimene see Polybius 3.82.9–84.15; Livy, *History of Rome* 22.4–7.
70. Polybius 3.84.5.
71. Dio 56.21.3.
72. Dio 56.21.1; Tacitus, *Annals* 1.61.
73. Tacitus, *Annals* 2.21.
74. Unzueta & Ocharán 2006.
75. Rasbach 2020.
76. On the ambush see Caesar, *Gallic Wars* 5.26–37.
77. Tacitus (*Annals* 4.73) describes a similar situation during the Frisian Revolt, in which a detachment of 400 Roman soldiers trapped in a villa complex committed suicide by falling on each other's swords, fearing betrayal and capture.
78. Morgan 2019: 93, 99–100.
79. Dio 56.21.1.
80. See Morgan 2019: 99–100.
81. Caesar, *Gallic Wars* 3.3, 5.33; Plutarch, *Life of Crassus* 28.1.
82. See Wilbers-Rost & Rost 2009, and Rost 2017.
83. Rost 2017: 561.
84. Morgan 2019: 100.
85. Dio 56.20.5; the soldiers were mixed in with the wagons from the march, and could not get around them to try and adopt a battle array.
86. Dio 56.20.5 suggests the Romans sustained heavy casualties as they were unable to defend themselves effectively, although he does not indicate whether these soldiers were wounded or killed.
87. Rost 2012/13: 106.
88. Tacitus, *Annals* 1.64.
89. Dio 56.21.1.
90. Dio 56.21.2.
91. Dio 56.21.4.
92. Dio 56.21.4.
93. Dio 56.21.3.
94. E.g. Sabin 2000. This approach is broadly based on the 'Face of Battle' studies developed by John Keegan (see Keegan 1976).
95. Anders 2015; see also Coulston 2013 and Whateley 2021.
96. Coulston 2013: 27–28.
97. Whateley 2021: xv-xx.
98. Tacitus, *Annals* 1.65.
99. Tacitus has Arminius declare 'Varus and the legions… enchained once more in the old doom!', a statement with a lot of power, but one which Tacitus cannot possibly have heard him state. According to Tacitus, Arminius intended to let Caecina's men start out towards the Rhine and to then fall on them in ambush again – the same tactic used against Varus – but Caecina anticipated the attack and took the Germans by surprise with a strong counter-attack, which forced them to retreat. Caecina may well have learned from Varus' example, that attempting to escape to the Rhine was an ineffective way to deal with an Arminian ambush, despite it being the tactic of choice to deal with an ambush until the Teutoburg had demonstrated its weaknesses.
100. Coulston 2013: 30.
101. Rost 2009.

102. On the rampart at the Oberesch see Wilbers-Rost 2003.
103. Rost & Wilbers-Rost 2010: 119–120.
104. For discussion of tactical implications of the rampart in the pass see Sheldon 2001.
105. See Müller-Scheeßel 2012 for a summary of the arguments. The current director of excavations at Kalkriese, Salvatore Ortisi, believes that the rampart is Roman work, while other specialists on the site, particularly Achim Rost and Susanne Wilbers-Rost, maintain that it was a German-built rampart.
106. Murdoch 2008: 111–112.
107. Wilbers-Rost 2017: 573–574; observed also by Morgan 2019: 95, n. 62.
108. By contrast, in the Roman camp overrun by the enemy at Andagoste, there was substantial deposition in the interior, evidence of the fierce fighting which took place there (see Unzueta & Ocharán 2006).
109. See Rost 2009, 2012/13 and Wilbers-Rost 2009.
110. The same phenomenon was seen in the 1876 Battle of the Little Bighorn. Archaeological exploration demonstrated that, in the final stages of that battle, the last surviving US cavalrymen abandoned their training, bunching together and no longer defending themselves – many of the bodies from Last Stand Hill show evidence of being killed at close quarters, including with edged weapons, without attempting to defend themselves (see Fox 1993: 48–49). This discovery helped to reconcile Native American accounts of the battle, which had stated that the US cavalrymen committed suicide at this stage – something unacceptable to the American public. To the Native Americans, the cavalrymen's lack of defensive action was tantamount to suicide, but would not be recognized as such by the defeated side.
111. Tacitus, *Annals* 1.61.
112. Velleius 2.119.3; Dio 56.21.5; Tacitus *Annals* 1.61; Florus, *Epitome* 2.30.35.
113. Tacitus, *Annals* 1.61.
114. Velleius 2.119.3.
115. Cicero (*De Officiis* 3.114) notes that the Roman state did not ransom captured prisoners 'in order that our soldiers might have the lesson planted in their hearts that they must either conquer or die'. See Ulpian (*Digest* 49.15.19.2) for the rights Romans lost in captivity, including their citizenship (should they hold it) and the validity of their wills and other legal documents. If Roman PoWs escaped captivity they could become citizens again, but had to go through a purification ceremony first; at this point, their legal status would also be restored.
116. See van Hooff 1990: 87–89, 109–110 and Hill 2004: 198–201. See also Ball (*forthcoming*).
117. Polybius 3.84.10.
118. Caesar, *Gallic Wars* 5.37.6.
119. Coulston 2013: 27–28.
120. In recent decades, several prominent Roman commanders had killed themselves in the wake of defeat, mostly in the immediate aftermath of battle but sometimes later on – including Cassius and Brutus in the wake of the loss at Philippi (Dio 47.46.3–5, 47.49.1–3; most of the other commanders still alive also killed themselves, including Varus' father), and Mark Antony, when Octavian captured the city of Alexandria and Antony risked falling into his hands (Dio 51.10.7–9; Plutarch, *Life of Antony* 76.4).
121. One suggestion is that the shame and humiliation that would result from capture made it almost inevitable that commanders and rulers would commit suicide rather than fall into enemy hands. In most cases, the Romans were the victors and therefore

the ones doing the capturing, but the same clearly worked in the opposite direction (see Hill 2004: 201–202).

122. Tacitus, *Annals* 1.71.

123. Velleius 2.119.5.

124. Perhaps as a tribute, or as a veiled insult, given that Maroboduus had declined to join Arminius in his rebellion against Rome.

125. Velleius 2.119.5.

126. Florus, *Epitome* 2.30.38.

127. Or perhaps they were worried about being haunted by his ghost should they fail to, although with the unburied casualties already sustained one more unrested spirit should not have been a huge problem; Varus' ghost was said by Tacitus (*Annals* 1.65) to have appeared to Aulus Caecina in a dream some years later, where the dead commander arose from a marsh and called to Caecina, reaching out his hand to the living.

128. Pliny, *Natural History* 7.54.

129. Noy 2000: 188–191. The practicalities of cremating even a single member of the battle-dead would often have been prohibitively difficult – see Rees 2018 for a discussion in the context of ancient Greek warfare.

130. See Carroll 2009.

131. Dio 56.22.1.

132. In ancient warfare the psychological shock of a commander's death could lead to tactical disintegration, frequently resulting in a rout – see Sabin 2007: 431–432.

133. Velleius 2.119.4.

134. Tacitus, *Annals* 1.61.

135. Florus, *Epitome* 2.30.37.

136. Florus, *Epitome* 2.30.36.

137. Velleius 2.120.6.

138. Dio 56.120.4.

139. Dio does not give an explanation for this prohibition, nor does he make it clear when it happened – it could have been during the last years of Augustus' reign, or under that of Tiberius, as there is no indication of how long the Romans concerned were captive before being liberated. It was an unusual decision to make, with no comparable parallels, and the legality of such an order would be questionable. On the legal implications see Lica 2001. Perhaps Augustus hoped by the order to avoid potentially traumatized survivors coming into contact with the general population of Italy and Rome, for fear that they might spread alarm and despondency, or provide an inconvenient correction to the accepted historical record of the battle.

140. Tacitus, *Annals* 12.27.

141. The find has not yet been fully published, but see a summary online at https://the-past.com/news/uncovering-kalkriese/. A press release (in German) is also available: https://www.kalkriese-varusschlacht.de/fileadmin/user_upload/varusschlacht/0_aktuelles/museumsblog/Archiv_Museumsblog_2016_-_2021/61_Der__Block-Blog_-_Teil_1_Achtung_Schienenpanzer__-_14.11.2020.pdf

142. Tacitus, *Annals* 1.60–61; see also Dio 56.24.1.

143. Tacitus, *Annals* 2.15.

144. Rost 2017; see also Morgan 2019: 96.

145. At Carrhae, a small group of Roman survivors at the end of the battle, who stood with their weapons still ready to fight, inspired fear among the victorious Parthians, who hesitated to engage this group of desperate men (Dio 40.24.3).

146. Rost & Wilbers-Rost 2019.
147. Rost & Wilbers-Rost 2009: 76–77, 2010: 133; *cf.* Moosbauer 2020: 156–157.
148. Particularly in the landscape around Abritus, the site of a comprehensive Roman defeat in AD 251. In particular, high-denomination coins were buried, including within the area of the Roman camp before it was abandoned (see Radoslavova *et al* 2011).
149. But even if casualty figures were mentioned, they would not necessarily be reliable – Roman losses in battle tended to be inflated or deflated according to the needs of the author in question (on this issue more generally see Brunt 1971: 694–697 and Campbell 2002: 68–70). Although it has been argued that specified Roman casualty numbers are generally accurate, particularly in the Republican period (Rosenstein 2004: 113–117).
150. On average casualties in Roman warfare see Rosenstein 2004: 109–25; Gabriel & Boose 1994: 29–34; Sabin 2000: 5–6.
151. On the general identification of the Roman battle-dead see Peretz 2005: 131–137.
152. Velleius 2.119.4.
153. Velleius 2.119.4.
154. For more on Caelius see Schalles & Willer 2009.
155. Florus, *Epitome* 2.30.38.
156. Tacitus, *Annals* 1.61.
157. Estimate of eight days travel time, using rapid horse relay covering 250km per day, over the 1,505km from Cologne, calculated via ORBIS (the Stanford Geospatial Network Model of the Roman World; https://orbis.stanford.edu/) which suggests 7.9 days would be needed to complete this journey at maximum speed.
158. Dio 56.23.1.
159. Velleius 2.120.3.
160. On German looting processes at Kalkriese see Rost 2009, 2012/13 and Rost & Wilbers-Rost 2010. For post-battle looting more widely, see Ball 2015.
161. Rost & Wilbers-Rost 2016: 27.
162. Tacitus, *Annals* 2.45.
163. Rost & Wilbers-Rost 2012. There appears to have been a second phase of looting some weeks later, during which time more of the assemblage was recovered. In this intervening period, parts of the rampart at the Oberesch had collapsed, preserving a snapshot of the partially-looted battlefield, which contains a significantly higher density of artefacts than the rest of the Oberesch.
164. Wilbers-Rost 2009: 129. The Germans lacked the technology to re-smelt the iron artefacts, although they might have sold some of the surplus as a raw material to those who could.
165. Tacitus, *Annals* 1.57.
166. Storgaard 2003.
167. Dio 56.22.2.
168. Velleius 2.117.1; Dio 56.18.1.; *cf.* Suetonius, *Life of Tiberius* 17.1.
169. Velleius 2.120.4; Frontinus, *Stratagems* 4.7.8. Frontinus is particularly praising of Caedicius, noting a stratagem that he employed at Aliso: 'Caedicius, a centurion of the first rank, who acted as leader in Germany, when, after the Varian disaster, our men were beleaguered, was afraid that the barbarians would bring up to the fortifications the wood which they had gathered, and would set fire to his camp. He therefore pretended to be in need of fuel, and sent out men in every direction to steal it. In this way he caused the Germans to remove the whole supply of felled trees.'

170. Frontinus (*Stratagems* 3.15.4) mentions survivors of the Teutoburg taking refuge at Aliso.
171. Dio 56.22.2.
172. Dio 56.22.2. Arminius likely did not have much experience of sieges from his time in the Roman army.
173. Frontinus (*Stratagems* 3.15.4); it was included in the section 'How to Produce the Impression of Abundance of what is Lacking'.
174. The local archaeological authorities are firmly behind the identification, as demonstrated in a press release about the site: https://www.lwl.org/pressemitteilungen/mitteilung.php?urlID=22740
175. Dio 56.23.2–3.
176. Velleius 2.120.1.
177. Velleius 2.120.2.
178. Dio 56.22.2–3.
179. Velleius 2.120.4.
180. Velleius 1.122.1.
181. Suetonius, *Life of Augustus* 23.2.
182. Dio 56.23.1; Suetonius, *Life of Augustus* 23.2.
183. Levick 2010: 99–100. At this point, the majority of legionary soldiers were from Italy, as citizenship had not yet spread far enough in the provinces to alter the traditional recruitment patterns (this would only change over the following century). Marcus Caelius, for example (the soldier whose tombstone was found in the fort at Xanten) was originally from Bononia (modern Bologna, in northern Italy).
184. Suetonius, *Augustus* 23.2; Suetonius is unclear on whether the entire period was taken as one of mourning, or just one of the associated days.
185. Dio 56.24.1.
186. Suetonius, *Life of Augustus* 22.1.
187. Dio 56.24.2; Suetonius, *Life of Augustus* 23.
188. Dio 56.23.4.
189. There appear to have been a number of protocols followed in Rome when a Roman army was annihilated and a direct threat to the city was anticipated,. They included the suspension of normal business, and the rapid recruitment of men of military age into the armed forces. Livy (10.3.7–10.4.2) describes a similar situation in the Third Samnite War, when a Roman foraging party was attacked by Etruscan raiders and suffered heavy casualties; Rome was put on immediate guard for the enemy, the men were forced into armed service, and legal activities were cancelled.
190. Turner 2018: 264.
191. Dio 56.24.1.
192. Dio 56.24.2–3.
193. Dio 56.24.3.
194. Tacitus, *Annals* 1.10; Suetonius, *Augustus* 23.1; *cf.* Levick 2010: 96–100.
195. Suetonius, *Life of Augustus* 66.
196. Velleius 2.119.5.
197. Suetonius, *Life of Augustus* 25.4.
198. Dio 53.25.6–7.
199. Tacitus, *Annals* 1.11. Tiberius largely adhered to this policy, although not every future emperor did.
200. Murdoch 2008: 37–40. The slightly mysterious death of Drusus the Elder in Germany had been one catalyst for such sentiment.

201. On Imperial expansion under Augustus see Gruen 1996.
202. Rasbach 2020: 29.
203. On Germanicus in Germany more widely see Powell 2013:85–118.
204. Tacitus, *Annals* 1.3.
205. Tacitus, *Annals* 1.61–62. On Germanicus seeing to the burial of the Teutoburg dead also see Dio 57.18.1.
206. For discussion of literary convention in Tactitus' description of the Teutoburg see Pagán 1999 and Siedman 2014.
207. Tacitus, *Annals* 2.7.
208. Tacitus, *Annals* 1.62.
209. In the Roman world it was largely believed that the unburied dead could become restless and haunt the living, and pains were taken to ensure the bodies received some level of mortuary processing. However, this was not always possible during war, and it was probably accepted that the battle-dead might on some occasions lie unburied; Cicero (*Philippics* 14.34) suggests that when a citizen laid down his life for Rome he did not need a burial to avoid becoming a member of the restless dead. See also Hope 2003, 2015, 2018 on Roman military burial practices.
210. Likely nothing should be read into the fact that the bones were buried rather than cremated, despite the latter being the predominant form of battlefield disposal at the time. The practicalities of cremating skeletal material would hardly have been worth the effort, especially given that the purpose of the disposal method was to prevent the despoilment of the dead, which had already taken place years earlier (see also Wilbers-Rost 2012/13).
211. See Großkopf 2012/13 and Uerpmann & Uerpmann 2007 for the contents and laying-out of the bone pits.
212. See Großkopf 2007: 167 and Rost 2012/13: 106 for discussion of armour/bandaging. The partially-articulated remains include a skull and upper vertebrae, a right arm (radius, ulna, carpal and metacarpal bones) and a right hand (carpal and metacarpal bones). A number of bones from the hands and feet survived in the pits, particularly Bone-pit 1, in far higher numbers than most post-exposure burials. Unusually, the hand bones survive in greater quantity than those of the feet, despite the greater size and integrity of the latter.
213. Burmeister 2015: 22.
214. Wilbers-Rost 2012/13.
215. Plutarch, *Life of Marius* 21.3.
216. Tacitus, *Annals* 1.63.
217. Tacitus, *Annals* 1.63–68.
218. Tacitus, *Annals* 2.9–10.
219. Lucius Stertilius, who had been the one to recover the eagle of the Nineteenth legion.
220. Tacitus, *Annals* 2.16.
221. Tacitus, *Annals* 2.18.
222. Tacitus, *Annals*, 2.20–21.
223. Tacitus, *Annals*, 2.23–34.
224. Tacitus, *Annals* 2.26, 2.41; 'There was a procession of spoils and captives, of mimic mountains, rivers, and battles; and the war, since he had been forbidden to complete it, was assumed to be complete'.
225. On the revolt of the Rhine legions see Tacitus, *Annals* 1.31–46.
226. Tacitus, *Annals* 1.34.
227. Tacitus, *Annals* 1.44.

228. Murdoch 2006: 136.
229. Tacitus, *Annals* 1.60, 2.25.
230. Tacitus, *Annals* 2.41.
231. Dio 60.8.7.
232. Tacitus, *Annals* 1.58.
233. The name of Arminius' son is preserved by Strabo (*Geography* 7.1.4).
234. Tacitus, *Annals* 1.59.
235. Tacitus (*Annals* 1.16) alludes to a 'humiliation' which he later suffered, saying that he would recount the details later, in a section of the *Annals* which has not survived. Thumelicus appears to have been dead by the later 40s. Thumelicus was almost certainly dead by AD 48, when the Cherusci applied to Emperor Claudius to appoint a chieftain as internal conflict had wiped out their ruling elite, but it is unclear how long ago he might have died. Claudius ended up appointing Arminius' nephew Italicus, the son of his brother Flavus and a Germanic chieftain's daughter, who had apparently been trained in both Roman and German ways of war and custom, although this led to some questioning his fitness to rule, referencing how unhappy the Germans would have been if Arminius' son had returned from being raised in Rome to rule them. Italicus was later exiled by the Cherusci, although he did return to rule them once more. Italicus in turn was succeeded as chieftain by Chariomerus, probably his son, who was driven out of Germany due to his loyalty to Rome (Dio 67.5.1).
236. Strabo, *Geography* 7.1.4.
237. Tacitus, *Annals* 2.88.

Chapter 7
1. On other Roman military disasters and the responses to them, see Chrystal 2015.
2. Rasbach 2020: 29.
3. Claudius sent campaigns over the Rhine in AD 41, 47, and 50. In 82/83, Domitian sent an army to fight against the Chatti. The most extended campaigns were the Marcomannic Wars (AD 166–180) during the reign of Marcus Aurelius.
4. On the archaeology of the battle see Berger *et al.* 2010/13.
5. *Historia Augusta, The Two Maximini* 12.4. It does not help that the *Historia Augusta* is a notoriously unreliable source.
6. Wolters 2008: 125–149.
7. Timpe 1970: 49.
8. On Tiberius' reign see Levick 2003.
9. Eck 2009.
10. See Rich 2012 and Östenberg 2018 for how commanders were blamed for military defeats. Although Rosenstein 1990 notes that in the Republican period at least, this did not necessarily end a commander's career, if exculpating factors for the reverse could also be found.
11. Although it was more customary for the name of the war to refer to the enemy, rather than the Roman commander.
12. Use of *clades*: Velleius Paterculus 2.117.1, Tacitus, *Annals* 1.10.4. It was also used by Pliny the Elder (*Natural History* 7.46).
13. Generally they were referred to by the place-name they happened closest to, within a war that was usually named after the enemy they were fighting.
14. See Wardle 2011.
15. Velleius 2.117.2.

16. Velleius 2.105.1–2.
17. E.g. As a youth 'Tiberius gave early promise of becoming the great man he now is' (Velleius 2.94.3), and Velleius' statement (2.104.3) that while in military service under Tiberius 'I was a spectator of his superhuman achievements'; see also 2.106.1–3, 2.12.1–2.
18. Velleius 2.117.4; Dio 56.18.3.
19. Velleius 2.117.3.
20. Dio 56.18.3.
21. Velleius 2.118.2.
22. Velleius 2.117.3–4, 2.118.1.
23. Dio 56.16.3.
24. Dyson 1971: 251.
25. Velleius 2.118.4.
26. Suetonius, *Life of Tiberius* 18.2.
27. Velleius 2.119.2.
28. Velleius 2.20.4–5.
29. Dio 56.22.1.
30. See Östenberg 2018 for a discussion of how terrain was blamed for Roman military defeats.
31. Östenberg 2018.
32. See chapter 6 for a fuller discussion of the landscape of Kalkriese at the time of the battle.
33. Östenberg 2018: 242.
34. Tacitus, *Annals* 1.61–62; *cf.* Östenberg 2018: 242–243.
35. Livy 9.5.6–8: 'the men could hardly keep from laying violent hands on those through whose rashness they had been led into that place, and through whose cowardice they were now to depart more shamefully than they had come. they bethought them how they had been unprovided either with guides or with patrols, but had been driven blindly, like wild beasts, into a trap'.
36. Dio 56.20.3. For a discussion of the impact of the weather on the outcome of the battle see Durschmied (2012) and Östenberg 2018.
37. Dio 56.21.3.
38. Östenberg 2018: 249–251. Weather is particularly cited in defeats when the effects were seen to have a much greater impact on the Romans than their opponents.
39. Velleius 2.119.1.
40. Velleius 2.120.5.
41. Velleius 2.120.4–5.
42. Rosenstein 1990 noted that through to the Late Republican period Roman soldiers were frequently blamed for battlefield defeats, alongside the gods.
43. Velleius 2.119.2.
44. Östenberg 2018: 252. Although they both had knowledge that Varus did not – namely, the Teutoburg battle itself, which would have provided a rich example of i) how the Germans fought under these circumstances and ii) what actions were likely to prove effective and ineffective against them.
45. Millar 1982.
46. On Roman citizenship more generally see Sherwin-White 1979.
47. Velleius 2.118.1.
48. Dio 55.29.1.
49. Dio 56.18.3.

50. Levick 2010: 98–99.
51. Rasbach 2020: 32.
52. Dio 56.20.1.
53. Dio 56.18.3.
54. Dio 56.18.3.
55. Velleius 2.118.4.
56. On the psychological impact of the commander's death in battle see Sabin 2007.
57. Morgan 2019: 99–100.
58. Morgan 2019: 100.
59. Sheldon 2001: 29–30.
60. Morgan 2019: 101. It is worth noting that Arminius' brother Flavus was a scout for the Roman army (Tacitus *Annals* 11.16).
61. Morgan 2019: 100–101.
62. Morgan 2019: 101, 102; Dio (54.33.3–4) noted that when Drusus the Elder had been trapped in an ambush by the Germans, their attention had been distracted, allowing the Romans to escape the attack.
63. Sheldon 2001: 30.
64. On Roman military vulnerabilities in passes and defines see Östenberg 2018: 244–247.
65. Schlüter 1999: 131–133.
66. Sheldon 2020: 1013.
67. Sheldon 2020: 1030.
68. See Morgan 2019 for an extensive discussion of Varus' generalship in the Teutoburg.
69. On the involvement of the emperor in deciding policy at all levels in the provinces, particularly the Imperial ones, see Millar 1996.
70. Velleius 2.117.3; Dio 56.18.3.
71. Morgan 2019.
72. See Levick 2010: 115–154.
73. On this type of evasion see particularly Cheung 1998, Wardle 2011, and Turner 2018.
74. Cheung 1998: 109–110.
75. Turner 2018: 265 notes the contradictory reports about Augustus' response to the Teutoburg: 'we can identify two competing, although not necessarily mutually exclusive, portrayals of Augustus' reaction and response. One, emotional, even hesitant, appears to challenge his grip on authority, if not reality. The other, practical, authoritative, and even traditional, illustrates the emperor's care and control of the state'.
76. For problems in the later years of Augustus' reign see Levick 2010: 96–100.
77. By contrast, Dio's account, while still largely placing the blame with Varus, is more circumspect, as though the temporal distance from the event allowed a slightly higher degree of neutrality, in a way that was not possible at the time Velleius was writing.
78. Dio 56.22.4.
79. Levick 2010: 238.
80. Wardle 2011.
81. Tacitus, *Annals* 2.10.
82. Tacitus, *Annals* 2.9–10.
83. Tacitus, *Annals* 2.9.
84. Tacitus, *Annals* 2.10. Flavus was married to the daughter of Actumerus, chief of the Chatti tribe (Tacitus, *Annals* 11.16).

85. Tacitus, *Germania* 33; *cf* Sheldon 2020: 1025–1026.
86. Dio 56.18.3.
87. Dio 55.21.1.
88. On the development and use of the Roman *auxilia* see Haynes 2013.
89. Tacitus, *Annals* 2.16–18, 2.20–21.
90. See also Dyson 1971 for in-depth discussion of native revolts against Rome, particularly in the first century AD.
91. On Tacfarinas – see Tacitus, *Annals* 2.52, 3.73–74, 4.23–24.
92. Tacitus, *Annals* 2.52.
93. Tacitus, *Histories* 4.13.
94. Tacitus, *Histories* 4.1–37, 4.54–79, 5.14–26.
95. Dio (55.29.2–3) suggests that Bato, one of the leaders of the Great Illyrian Revolt (AD 6–9), may also have been a former auxiliary soldier in a unit of Dalmatians who had been recruited to fight in Tiberius' German campaign. See also Dyson 1971: 251–252.
96. Keppie 1997; Ward 2018.
97. Tacitus, *Annals* 4.5.
98. Keppie 1998, Appendix 4. Keppie suggests that the historical sources were likely hesitant of mentioning large-scale losses and legionary disbandment, suggesting that it may have been more common than the written sources suggest. Legions known to be disbanded, in addition to the Teutoburg legions, were: First Germanica, Fifteenth Primigenia (c. AD 70), Fifth Alaudae (c. AD 85–86), Twenty-first Rapax (c. AD 92), and Twenty-second Deiotariana (c. AD 132–135). The Ninth Hispana, once thought lost in Scotland, may also have been lost in the Bar Kokhba Revolt in Judaea (AD 132–135), or disbanded either during the reign of Hadrian or Marcus Aurelius (see Elliot 2021). Ward 2018: 293 notes that Augustus' action in effectively disbanding the Teutoburg legions may have set a precedent followed by subsequent emperors, that if a legion lost almost all its manpower in battle it was not to be reconstructed.
99. For a general discussion of legionary disbandment in the Imperial period see Ward (2018).
100. Velleius 1.97.1.
101. Seneca the Younger, *De Beneficiis* 6.32.
102. Keppie 1997.
103. Dio 54.11.5; it was probably a First Legion, as a legion of this title without an honorific is referred to in an inscription from Spain, suggesting the title was not replaced for some time (see Ward 2018: 291).
104. Ward 2018: 284.
105. Suetonius, *Life of Augustus* 92.1.
106. Ward 2018: 292.
107. Tacitus, *Annals* 1.71.
108. In the process of *damnatio memoriae* ('condemnation of memory'), a severe, usually post-mortem, public punishment of an individual thought to have unforgivably transgressed against the state. Individuals condemned would literally be removed from public record – their name was erased from official inscriptions, statues of them reworked or destroyed, and where relevant and possible, their coinage melted down (although this could take several years). For *damnatio memoriae* more widely, see Calomino 2020, who provides an overview of the circumstances under which individuals were condemned, and why.
109. Calomino 2020: 25–27.

110. *Res Gestae Divi Augusti* 12: 'When I returned from Spain and Gaul, in the consulship of Tiberius Nero and Publius Quintilius, after successful operations in those provinces, the Senate voted in honour of my return the consecration of an altar to Pax Augusta in the Campus Martius, and on this altar it ordered the magistrates and priests and Vestal Virgins to make annual sacrifice'.
111. Tacitus, *Annals* 4.55.
112. She was the daughter of Marcus Agrippa and Augustus' daughter Julia.
113. Barrett 1996: 42. Others had been punished for the same 'crime', including a woman named Sosia Galla and her husband Gaius Silius, who had been friends with Agrippina and her former husband Germanicus; Sosia ended up in exile, while Silius committed suicide (Tacitus, *Annals* 4.19–20).
114. Bauman 1992: 147–149.
115. Details on the persecution of Agrippina and her allies was preserved in a memoir written by her daughter, Agrippina Minor (Tacitus, *Annals* 4.53), which probably dealt with the prosecution of Claudia Pulchra in greater detail.
116. Tacitus, *Annals* 4.66.
117. It is not certain which Publius Cornelius Dolabella was the father of this one, as there are several possible candidates (see Syme 1986: 316; Tansey 2000: 267–270). But Tacitus is certain of there being a familial connection between Dolabella and Varus the Younger, which firmly suggests that he was the one who married Quinctilia.
118. Barrett 1996: 42.
119. Seneca, *Controversiae* 1.3.10; Seneca notes that the taunt was met with disapproval by those who heard it.
120. Tansey 2000: 267–270.
121. Tacitus, *Annals* 4.23–24.
122. Through the marriage of her father, Lucius Marcius Philippus, to Augustus' mother Atia, in 56 BC.
123. CIL XI, 1362 = ILS 935. 'To Sextus Appuleius, son of Sextus, grandson of Sextus, great-grandson of Sextus, of the tribe Galeria, born of Fabia Numantina, the last in his family'.
124. Tacitus, *Annals* 2.50.
125. Syme 1986: 314–315.
126. Syme 1986: 431.
127. Tacitus, *Annals* 1.53.
128. On the death of Gracchus see Rogers 1967.
129. Tacitus, *Annals* 3.18.

Chapter 8

1. Strabo, *Geography* 7.1.4. The date range is based on the fact that Strabo refers to Arminius continuing the war, and that he was murdered in AD 21. A date in the first few years of Tiberius' reign is most likely, probably in or around AD 17; Strabo died around AD 24, giving a latest possible date for the composition.
2. Dyson 1971.
3. Eck 2009: 13.
4. See Balmaceda 2014 on Velleius and Tiberius.
5. Seneca the Elder (*Controversiae* 1.3.10).
6. Manlius, *Astronomica* 1.896–901.
7. Pliny, *Natural History* 7.46.

8. Suetonius, *Life of Gaius* 31.1: 'He [Gaius] even used openly to deplore the state of his times, because they had been marked by no public disasters, saying that the rule of Augustus had been made famous by the Varus massacre... while his own was threatened with oblivion because of its prosperity; and every now and then he wished for the destruction of his armies, for famine, pestilence, fires, or a great earthquake.'

9. Such as the Battle of Adrianople (AD 378), fought against the Goths, in which the eastern Roman Emperor Valens was killed, alongside two-thirds of his army (around 20,000 men).

10. Including the *Chronica sive Historia* (1143–1146) by Otto von Freising, and chronicles by Sigismund Meisterlin (1522), Adilbert (1516) and Konrad Peutinger (1520) – see Derks 2017: 158–160.

11. Schlüter 1991: 14.

12. Derks 2017: 158, note 36. See also Murdoch 2006: 156–159.

13. Dio 56.22.1.

14. Derks 2017: 161.

15. Derks 2017: 160–161.

16. Benario 2004: 87–88.

17. Creasy 1851: 132

18. For a comprehensive study of how Arminius has been used in later history and culture see Winkler 2015; Wolters 2008: 174–201 also discusses the legacy of Arminius, with a particular focus on the sixteenth to nineteenth centuries. Murdoch 2006: 155–280 also provides an excellent summary of the use of Arminius in German nationalism.

19. Murdoch 2006: 156.

20. Barbon & Plachta 1994.

21. Derks 2017.

22. The statue was the lifelong dream of German architect and artist Joseph Ernst von Bandel, who was responsible for the monument's design. It was originally commissioned in the 1830s as a symbol of German unity and money was raised by subscription for the project, but as the prospect of a unified German state began to fade (particularly following a failed revolution in 1848) the work largely ceased. Interest was revived in the 1860s following German victory in the Franco-Prussian War, and from 1871 von Bandel was once again working at the site. The monument was eventually inaugurated on 16 August 1875, in the presence of Emperor William I of Prussia, his son Frederick William (the Crown Prince), and a crowd of some 20–30,000 spectators.

23. Emperor Napoleon III commissioned a corresponding statue of the Gallic resistance leader Vercingetorix on Mont Auxois, near Alise-Sainte-Reine in eastern France, thought (almost certainly correctly) to be the site of the Battle of Alésia against Julius Caesar in 52 BC. The Vercingetorix statue was dedicated in 1865, after several years of excavations at the site from 1861 onwards, which had uncovered significant evidence of the battle. It also aimed to promote national unity, despite the fact that Vercingetorix had ultimately been defeated by Rome and Gaul conquered. The eventual benefits of the Roman conquest for the ancient and nineteenth-century population of France were emphasized around its dedication – although the statue also became a symbol of anti-German sentiment in France (see Dietler 1998).

24. Although as the events took place between 13–24 August there is no real likelihood that they matched the days that the battle was actually fought; these dates were likely picked just as a convenient time to hold the event.

25. Murdoch 2006: 174–178, Derks 2017: 171.
26. Holland 2016: 393–394.
27. Murdoch 2006: 1677–178.
28. Derks 2017: 171. It has already been noted that Creasy 1851 (among others) also claimed Arminius as an English folk hero, due to the movement of Saxon peoples to England in the early medieval period. A nationalist symbol who could also be claimed by the enemy as their own was of little use.
29. Derks 2017: 171.
30. Derks 2017: 187.
31. Todd 2004: 48.
32. E.g. Eck 2009.
33. Sheldon 2005, 2020.
34. Durschmied 2012; Östenberg 2018.
35. Inscription: 'Publius Quinctilius Varus erlitt als Oberbefehlshaber der römischen Truppen in der Schlacht des Jahres 9 n. Chr. eine schmachvolle Niederlage. Sieger ware der Cheruskerfürst Arminius. Als Anführer germanischer Hilfstruppen und Angehöriger des römischen Adels besaß er das besondere Vertrauen des Varus. Deshalb kommt seine Verschwörung gegen Rom einem Verrat gleich. Nicht nur die militärische Katastrophe, sondern auch der verachtenswerte Grund des Scheiterns an seiner historischen Aufgabe veranlassten Varus, sich selbst zu töten. Durch den Untergang der römischen Vormachtstellung östlich des Rheins blieben die Germanen für Jahrhunderte von der hoch entwickelten rümischen Kultur ausgeschlossen'.
36. Akin to the ongoing interest in the 'disappearance' of the Ninth Hispana Legion, which has attracted a disproportionate amount of discussion – see Elliott 2021 for more details.
37. See Roymans & Fernandez-Götz 2017.
38. The landscape was opened up in 2000 as the *Varusschlacht Museum Park* ('Varus Battle Museum Park'), supplemented by a small museum exhibition from 2001, and the full museum in 2002. On the development of the museum and park see Murdoch 2006: 189–194.
39. Derks 2017: 178.
40. Derks 2017: 180.
41. Derks 2017: 176.

Bibliography

Abdale, J.R. (2016). *Four Days in September: The Battle of Teutoburg.* 2nd Edition. Barnsley (Pen & Sword Military).

Abdale, J.R. (2019). *The Great Illyrian Revolt.* Barnsley (Pen and Sword Military).

Allen, J. (2006). *Hostages and Hostage-taking in the Roman Empire.* Cambridge (Cambridge University Press).

Ambrose, J.W. (1965). 'The Ironic Meaning of the Lollius Ode'. *TAPA* 96: 1–10.

Anders, A.O. (2015). 'The Face of Roman Skirmishing'. *Historia* 64 (3): 263–300.

Atkinson, K.M.T. (1958). 'The Governors of the Province Asia in the Reign of Augustus'. *Historia* 7 (3): 300–330.

Austin, N.J.E., & Rankov, N.B. (1995). *Exploratio: Military and Political Intelligence in the Roman World from the Second Punic War to the Battle of Adrianople.* London (Routledge).

Baddeley, A.D. (1972). 'Selective Attention and Performance in Dangerous Environments'. *British Journal of Psychology* 63 (4): 537–546.

Ball, J. (2015). 'To the Victor the Spoils? Post-Battle Looting in the Roman World'. In Lee, G., Whittaker, H., & Wrightson, G. (eds.) *Ancient Warfare: Introducing Current Research.* Cambridge (Cambridge Scholars Press): 309–330.

Ball, J.E. (forthcoming). 'Terrible but Unavoidable? Combat trauma and a Change to Legal Proscriptions on Roman Military Suicide under Hadrian'. In Crowley, J., Hurlock, K., & Rees, O. (eds.) *Combat Stress in Pre-modern Europe.* London (Palgrave Macmillan).

Balmaceda, C. (2014). 'The Virtues of Tiberius in Velleius "Histories"'. *Historia* 63 (3): 340–363.

Barbon, P., & Plachta, B. (1994). '"Chi la dura la vince" – "Wer ausharrt, siegt". Arminius auf der Opernbühne des 18. Jhds". In Wiegels, R., & Woesler, W. (eds.) *Arminius und die Varusschlacht: Geschichte - Mythos - Literatur.* Paderborn (Schöningh): 265–290.

Barolini, H. (1969). 'Excursion'. *The Kenyon Review* 31 (1): 8+10+12+14–15.

Barrett, A.A. (1996). *Agrippina: Mother of Nero.* London (B.T. Batsford).

Bauman, R.A. (1992). *Women and Politics in Ancient Rome.* London (Routledge).

Beard, M. (2007). *The Roman Triumph.* Cambridge, MA (The Belknap Press of Harvard University Press).

Bellino, V. (2011). 'Romans, Silures and Ordovices: the experience of low intensity warfare in Wales'. *Archaeologia Cambrensis* 160: 13–38.

Benario, H.W. (2004). 'Arminius into Hermann: History into Legend'. *Greece & Rome* 51 (1): 83–94.

Berger, F. (1996). *Kalkriese 1. Die römischen Fundmünzen.* Mainz (Philipp von Zabern).

Berger, F., Bittman, F., Geschwind, M., Lönne, P., Meyer, M., & Moosbauer, G. (2010/13). 'Die römisch-germanische Auseinandersetzung am Harzhorn, Lkr. Northeim, Niedersachsen'. *Germania* 88: 313–402.

Bergin, B.M.D. (2018). 'The Innovative Genius of Herod at Caesarea Maritima'. *Cultural and Religious Studies* 6 (7): 377–390.

Berlin, A.M. (2014). 'Herod the Tastemaker'. In *Near Eastern Archaeology* 77 (2): 108–119.

Bernegger, P.M. (1983). 'Affirmation of Herod's Death in 4 B.C.'. *The Journal of Theological Studies* 34 (2): 526–531.

Bleicken, J. (2015). *Augustus: The Biography.* London (Allen Lane).

Bonner, S.F. (1977). *Education in Ancient Rome: From the Elder Cato to the Younger Pliny.* London (Methuen).

Bowersock, G.W. (1965). *Augustus and the Greek World.* Oxford (Clarendon).

Braund, D. (1984). *Rome and the Friendly King: The Nature of Client Kingship.* London (Croom Helm).

Braund, D.C. (1985). *Augustus to Nero: A Sourcebook on Roman History 31 BC–AD 68.* Totowa, NJ (Barnes & Noble Books).

Brown, C.J., Torres-Martínez, J.F., Fernández-Götz, M., & Martínez-Velasco, A. (2017). 'Fought under the walls of Bergida: KOCOA analysis of the Roman attack on the Cantabrian oppidum of Monte Bernorio (Spain)'. *Journal of Conflict Archaeology* 12 (2): 115–138.

Brown, R.E. (1993). *The Birth of the Messiah: A Commentary on the Infancy Narratives in the Gospels of Matthew and Luke.* 2nd Edition. New York (Doubleday).

Brunt, P.A. (1961). 'Charges of Provincial Maladministration under the Early Principate'. *Historia* 10 (2): 189–227.

Brunt, P.A. (1971). *Italian Manpower, 225 B.C.–A.D. 14.* London (Oxford University Press).

Brunt, P.A. (1984). 'The Role of the Senate in the Augustan Regime'. *The Classical Quarterly* 34 (2): 423–444.

Burmeister, S. (2015). 'Die Örtlichkeit der Varusschlacht: Eine anhaltende Kontroverse'. *Archäologie in Deutschland Special Issue – Ich Germanicus: Feldherr Priester Superstar*: 17–23.

Burnett, A., Amandry, M., & Ripollès, P.P. (1992). *Roman Provincial Coinage. Volume I: From the Death of Caesar to the Death of Vitellius (44 BC–AD 69)* . Cambridge (Cambridge University Press).

Butcher, K. (2003). *Roman Syria and the Near East.* London (The British Museum Press).

Butcher, K., & Ponting, M. (2015). *The Metallurgy of Roman Silver Coinage: From the Reform of Nero to the Reform of Trajan.* Cambridge (Cambridge University Press).

Calomino, D. (2020). 'The Other Side of *damnatio memoriae*: Erasing Memory to Assert Loyalty and Identity in the Roman Empire'. In Fuglerud, Ø., Larsen, K., & Prusac-Lindhagen, M. (eds.) *Negotiating Memory from the Romans to the Twenty-First Century: Damnatio Memoriae.* New York (Routledge): 23–43.

Campbell, B. (2002) *War and Society in Imperial Rome, 31 BC–AD 284.* New York (Routledge).

Carroll, M. (2009). 'Dead Soldiers on the Move: Transporting bodies and commemorating men at home and abroad'. In Morillo, Á., Hanel, N., & Martín, E. (eds.) *Limes XX.* Madrid (Polifemo): 823–832.

Chantraine, H. 2002. "Varus oder Germanicus? Zu den Fundmünzen von Kalkriese." *Thetis* 9: 81–93.

Cheung, A. (1998). 'The Political Implications of Imperial Military Defeat'. *Scholia* 7 (1): 109–117.

Chrystal, P. (2015). *Roman Military Disasters: Dark Days and Lost Legions.* Barnsley (Pen & Sword Military).

Clunn, T. (2005). *The Quest for the Lost Roman Legions.* Spellmount (Savas Beatie).

Coarelli, F. (2014). *Rome and Environs: An Archaeological Guide.* Updated Edition. Oakland, CA (University of California Press).

Coulston, J. (2013). 'Courage and Cowardice in the Roman Imperial Army'. *War in History* 20 (1): 7–31.

Creasy, E. (1851). *The Fifteen Decisive Battles of the World: From Marathon to Waterloo.* New York (Harper & Brothers).

Crosby, D.J. (2016). 'The Case for Another Son of P. Quinctilius Varus: a re-examination of the textual and scholarly traditions around Joseph. *BJ* 2.68 and *AJ* 17.288'. *Journal of Ancient History* 4 (1): 113–129.

Curry, A. (2017). 'The Road Almost Taken'. *Archaeology* 70 (2): 32–37.

Derks, H. (2017). 'The Varus Battle in the Year 9 CE – or How to Escape the "Memory" Trap'. In Bernbeck, R., Hifmann, K.P., & Sommer, U. (eds.) *Between Memory Sites and Memory Networks: New Archaeological and Historical Perspectives.* Berlin (Edition Topoi): 151–197.

Dietler, M. (1998). 'A Tale of Three Sites: The Monumentalization of Celtic Oppida and the Politics of Collective Memory and Identity'. *World Archaeology* 30 (1): 72–89.

Duncan-Jones, R. (2016). *Power and Privilege in Roman Society.* Cambridge (Cambridge University Press).

Durschmied, E. (2012). *The Weather Factor: How Nature Has Changed History.* 2nd Edition. New York (Arcade Publishing).

Dyson, S.L. (1971). 'Native Revolts in the Roman Empire'. *Historia* 20 (2/3): 239–274.

Eck, W. (2003). *The Age of Augustus.* Oxford (Blackwell Publishing).

Eck, W. (2009). 'Triumph und Katastrophe: Die römische Provinz Germanien und Varus' Scheitern'. *Antike Welt* 40 (3): 8–13.

Eck, W. (2010). 'P. Quinctilius Varus, seine senatorische Laufbahn und sein Handeln in Germanien: Normalität oder aristokratische Unfähigkeit?'. In Capelle, T. (ed.) *IMPERIUM: Varus und seine Zeit. Beiträge zum internationalen Kolloquium des LWL-Römermuseums am 28. und 29. April 2008 in Münster.* Munich (Aschendorff): 13–28.

Eck, W. (2012). 'Administration and Jurisdiction in Rome and in the Provinces'. In van Ackeren, M. (ed.) *A Companion to Marcus Aurelius.* Malden & Oxford (Blackwell Publishing Ltd): 185–199.

Ehrhardt, C.T.H.R. (1995). 'Crossing the Rubicon'. *Antichthon* 29: 30–41.

Elliot, S. (2021). *Roman Britain's Missing Legion: What Really Happened to IX Hispana?* Barnsley (Pen & Sword Military).

Fields, N. (2008). *Warlords of Republican Rome: Caesar Versus Pompey.* Barnsley (Pen & Sword Military).

Fonte, J., Costa-García, J.M., & Gago, M. (2021). 'O Penedo dos Lobos: Roman military activity in the uplands of the Galician Massif (Northwest Iberia)'. *Journal of Conflict Archaeology* online, DOI: 10.1080/15740773.2021.1980757.

Fox, R.A. (1993). *Archaeology, history, and Custer's last battle: the Little Big Horn reexamined.* Norman, OK: University of Oklahoma Press.

Freeman, P. (1996). 'British Imperialism and the Roman Empire'. In Webster, J., & Cooper, N. (eds) *Roman Imperialism: Post-Colonial Perspectives.* Leicester (School of Archaeological Studies, University of Leicester): 19–34.

Fruzzetti, A.E., Toland, K., Teller, S.A., & Loftus, E.F. (1992), 'Memory and Eyewitness Testimony'. In Gruneberg, M., & Morris, P. (eds.) *Aspects of Memory. Volume 1: The Practical Aspects.* 2nd Edition. London (Routledge): 18–50.

Gabriel, R.A., & Boose, D.W. (1994). *The Great Battles of Antiquity: A Strategic and Tactical Guide to Great Battles That Shaped the Development of War.* Westport, CT (Greenwood).

Goldsworthy, A. (2014). *Augustus: From Revolutionary to Emperor.* London (Weidenfeld & Nicholson).

Green, M. (1998). 'Humans as Ritual Victims in the Later Prehistory of Western Europe'. *Oxford Journal of Archaeology* 17 (2): 169–189.

Großkopf, B. (2012/13). 'The Human Remains from the Oberesch Site'. In Harbeck, M., von Hayking, K., & Schwarzberg, H. (eds.), *Sickness, Hunger, War and Religion: Multidisciplinary perspectives*. Munich (Rachel Carson Centre): 97–101.

Gruen, E.S. (1996). 'The Expansion of the Empire Under Augustus'. In Bowman, A.K., Champlin, E., & Lintoot, A. (eds.) *The Cambridge Ancient History. Volume 10: The Augustan Empire, 43 BC–AD 69*. 2nd Edition. Cambridge (Cambridge University Press): 147–197.

Harnecker, J., & Franzius, G. (2008). *Kalkriese 4. Katalogue Der Römischen Funde Vom Oberesch. Die Schnitte 1 Bis 22*. Mainz (Philipp von Zabern).

Harnecker, J., & Mylo, D. (2011). *Kalkriese 5. Katalogue Der Römischen Funde Vom Oberesch. Die Schnitte 23 Bis 39*. Mainz (Philipp von Zabern).

Haynes, I. (2013). *Blood of the Provinces: The roman Auxilia and the Making of Provincial Society from Augustus to the Severans*. Oxford (Oxford University Press).

Hill, T. (2004). *Ambitiosa Mors: Suicide and the Self in Roman Thought and Literature*. London (Routledge).

Hohlfelder, R.L. (2000). 'Beyond Coincidence? Marcus Agrippa and King Herod's Harbor'. *Journal of Near Eastern Studies* 59 (4): 241–253.

Holland, J. (2016). *The Rise of Germany, 1939–1941: The War in the West Volume One*. London (Corgi).

Van Hooff, A.J.L. (1990). *From Autothanasia to Suicide: Self-Killing in Classical Antiquity*. London (Routledge).

Hope, V. (2003). 'Trophies and Tombstones: commemorating the Roman soldier'. *World Archaeology* 35 (1): 79–97.

Hope, V. (2015). 'Bodies on the Battlefield: The Spectacle of Rome's Fallen Soldiers'. In Hope, V. & Bakogiannia, A. (eds) *War as Spectacle. Ancient and Modern Perspectives on the Display of Armed Conflict*. London (Bloomsbury): 157–178.

Hope, V. (2018). '"Dulce et Decorum Est Pro Patria Mori": The Practical and Symbolic Treatment of the Roman War Dead'. *Mortality: Promoting the interdisciplinary study of death and dying* 23 (1): 35–49.

Howgego, C.J. (1982). 'Coinage and Military Finance: the Imperial Bronze Coinage of the Augustan East'. *The Numismatic Chronicle* 142: 1–20.

Hurlet, F. (2011). 'Consulship and consuls under Augustus'. In Beck, H., Duplá, A., Jehne, M., & Pina Polo, F. (eds.) *Consuls and Res Publica: Holding High Office in the Roman Republic*. Cambridge (Cambridge University Press): 319–335.

John, W. (1958). 'Zu den Familienhältnissen des P. Quinctilius Varus.' *Hermes* 86 (2): 251–255.

John, W. (1963). '20) P. Quinctilius Varus'. In Ziegler, K. (ed.) *Paulys Real-Encyclopädie der classischen Alterumswissenschaft*, Volume 24. Stuttgart (Alfred Druckenmüller): 907–984.

Keegan, J. (1976). *The Face of Battle*. London (Cape).

Kehne, P. (2000). 'Zur Datierung von Fundmünzen aus Kalkriese und zur Verlegung des Enddatums des Halterner Hauptlagers in die Zeit der Germanienkriege unter Tiberius und Germanicus (10–16 n.Chr.)'. In Wiegels, R. (ed.) *Die Fundmünzen von Kalkriese und die frühkaiserzeitliche Münzprägung*. Möhnesee (Bibliopolis): 47–79.

Keppers, F., & Myrberg, N. (2001). 'Rethinking Numismatics: The Archaeology of Coins'. *Archaeological Dialogues* 18 (1): 87–108.

Keppie, L. (1997). 'Legiones XVII, XVIII XIX: Exercitus Omnium Fortissimus'. In Groenman-van Waateringe, W. (ed.) Roman Frontier Studies 1995: Proceedings of the XVIth International Congress of Roman Frontier Studies. Oxford (Oxbow): 393–398.

Keppie, L. (1998). *The Making of the Roman Army*. 2nd Edition. London (Routledge).

Kerremans, B. (2018). 'A Real Roman Defeat: Memory, Collective Trauma and the *Clades Lolliana*'. *Acta Classica* 61: 69–98.

Kinnee, L. (2018). *The Greek and Roman Trophy: From Battlefield Marker to Icon of Power*. London (Routledge).

Koenen, L. (1970). 'Die "Laudatio funebris" des Augustus für Agrippa auf einem neuen Papyrus'. *Zeitschrift für Papyrologie und Epigraphik* 5: 217–284.

Kokkinos, N. (1995). 'The Honorand of the Titulus Tiburtinus: C. Sentius Saturninus?'. *Zeitschrift für Papyrologie und Epigraphik* 105: 21–36.

Ladouceur, D.J. (1981). 'The Death of Herod the Great'. *Classical Philology* 76 (1): 25–34.

Lavan, M. (2013). 'Florus and Dio on the Enslavement of the Provinces'. *The Cambridge Classical Journal* 59: 125–151.

Levick, B. (2003). *Tiberius the Politician*. 2nd Edition. London (Routledge).

Levick, B. (2010). *Augustus: Image and Substance*. Harlow (Longman).

Lica, V. (2001). '"Clades Variana" and "Postliminium"'. *Historia* 50 (4): 496–501.

MacMullen, R. (2014). 'The End of Ancestor Worship: Affect and Class'. In *Historia: Zeitschrift für Alte Geschichte* 63 (4): 487–513.

Magness, J. (2021). *Masada: From Jewish Revolt to Modern Myth*. Princeton (Princeton University Press).

Martin, E.L. (1980). *The Birth of Christ Recalculated*. (Foundation for Biblical Research).

Mason, S. (2008). *Flavius Josephus: Translation and Commentary. Volume 1b – Judean War 2*. Leiden (Brill).

Maxfield, V.A. (1981). *The Military Decorations of the Roman Army*. London (Batsford).

McCane, B.R. (2008). 'Simply Irresistible: Augustus, Herod, and the Empire'. *Journal of Biblical Literature* 127 (4): 725–735.

Mellor, R. (1993). *Tacitus*. New York (Routledge).

Millar, F. (1966). 'The Emperor, the Senate and the provinces'. *Journal of Roman Studies* 56 (1/2): 156–166.

Millar, F. (1982). 'Emperors, Frontiers and Foreign Relations, 31 B. C. to A. D. 378'. *Britannia* 13: 1–23.

Millar, F. (1993). *The Roman Near East: 31 BC–AD 337*. Cambridge, MA & London: Harvard University Press.

Mommsen, T. (1885). *Die Ortlichkeit Der Varusschlacht*. Berlin (Weidmann).

Moosbauer, G. (2020). 'Roman Battlefields in Germany: Kalkriese and Harzhorn'. In James, S., & Krmnicek, S. (eds.) *The Oxford Handbook of the Archaeology of Roman Germany*. Oxford (Oxford University Press): 149–165.

Morgan, D. (2019). 'The Generalship of P. Quinctilius Varus in the Clades Variana'. *Antichthon* 53: 87–107.

Morillo, Á, Adroher, A.M., Dobson, M., & Martín Hernández, E. (2020). 'Constructing the archaeology of the Roman conquest of Hispania: new evidence, perspectives and challenges'. *Journal of Roman Archaeology* 33: 36–52.

Morstein-Marx, R. (2007). 'Caesar's Alleged Fear of Prosecution and His "Ratio Absentis" in the Approach to the Civil War'. *Historia* 56 (2): 159–178.

Morstein-Marx, R. (2021). *Julius Caesar and the Roman People*. Cambridge (Cambridge University Press).

Müller-Scheeßel, N. (2012). 'Die Fundverteilungen von Kalkriese "Oberesch" im Rahmen einer "Schlachtfeldarchäologie": Neue Aspekte zur Interpretation des Fundplatzes'. *EAZ* 53 (1/2): 108–121.

Murdoch, A. (2006). *Rome's Greatest Defeat: Massacre in the Teutoburg Forest*. Sutton (Stroud).

Noy, D. (2000). 'Half-Burnt on an Emergency Pyre': Roman Cremations Which Went Wrong'. *Greece & Rome* 47 (2): 186–196.

Nuber, H.U. (2008). 'P. Quinctilius Varus, Legatus legionis XIX. Zur Interpretation der Bleischeibe aus Dangstetten, Lkr. Waldshut'. *Archäologisches Korrespondenzblatt* 38 (2): 223–232.

Östenberg, I. (2018). 'Defeated by the Forest, the Pass, the Wind: Nature as an Enemy of Rome'. In Clark, J.H., & Turner, B. (eds.) *Brill's Companion to Military Defeat in Ancient Mediterranean Society*. Leiden (Brill): 240–261.

Pagán, V. (1999). 'Beyond Teutoburg: Transgression and Transformation in Tacitus *Annales* 1.61–62'. *Classical Philology* 94 (3): 302–320.

Painter, K. (2001). *The Insula of the Menander at Pompeii. Volume 4: The Silver Treasure*. Oxford (Clarendon Press).

Paltiel, E. (1981). 'War in Judaea – After Herod's Death'. *Revue belge de philologie et d'histoire* 59 (1): 107–136.

Patterson, L.E. (2015). 'Antony and Armenia'. *TAPA* 145 (1): 77–105.

Peralta Labrador, E.J., Camino Mayor, J., & Torres-Martínez, J.F. (2019). 'Recent Research on the Cantabrian Wars: The Archaeological Reconstruction of a Mountain War'. *Journal of Roman Archaeology* 32: 421–438.

Peretz, D. (2005). 'Military Burial and the Identification of the Roman Fallen Soldiers'. *Klio* 87 (1): 123–138.

Pettinger, A. (2012). *The Republic in Danger: Drusus Libo and the Succession of Tiberius*. Oxford (Oxford University Press).

Phang, S.E. (2001). *The Marriage of Roman Soldiers (13 B.C. - A.D. 235)*. Leiden (Brill).

Pietsch, M. (2003). 'Die augusteische Legionslager Marktbreit'. In Wiegels, R., & Woesler, W. (eds.) *Arminius und die Varusschlacht: Geschichte, Mythos, Literatur*. Paderborn (Schöningh): 41–66.

Pina Polo, F. (2011) *The Consul at Rome: The Civil Functions of the Consuls in the Roman Republic*. Cambridge (Cambridge University Press).

Polito, E. (2012). 'Augustan Triumphal Iconography and the Cantabrian Wars: Some Remarks on Round Shields and Spearheads Depicted on Monuments from the Iberian Peninsula and Italy'. *Archivo Español de Arqueología* 85: 141–148.

Pollini, J. (1986). 'Ahenobarbi, Appuleii and Some Others on the Ara Pacis'. *American Journal of Archaeology* 90 (4): 453–460.

Powell, L. (2011). *Eager for Glory: The Untold Story of Drusus the Elder, Conqueror of Germania*. Barnsley (Pen & Sword Military).

Powell, L. (2013). *Germanicus: The Magnificent Life and Mysterious Death of Rome's Most Popular General*. Barnsley (Pen & Sword Military).

Powell, L. (2015). *Marcus Agrippa: Right-Hand Man of Caesar Augustus*. Barnsley (Pen & Sword).

Powell, L. (2018). *Augustus at War: The Struggle for the Pax Augusta*. Barnsley (Pen & Sword Military).

Radoslavova, G., Dzanev, G., & Nikolov, N. (2011). 'The Battle at Abritus in AD 251: Written Sources, Archaeological and Numismatic Data'. *Archaeologia Bulgarica* 15 (3): 23–49.

Rageth, J., & Zanier, W. (2010/2013). 'Crap Ses und Septimer: Archäologische Zeugnisse der römischen Alpeneroberung 16 / 15 v. Chr. aus Graubünden'. *Germania* 88: 241–283.

Rajak, T. (2007). 'The Herodian Narratives of Josephus'. In Kokkinos, N. (ed.) *World of the Herods: Volume 1 of the International Conference, The World of the Herods and the Nabataeans, held at the British Museum, 17–19 April 2001.* Stuttgart (Steiner): 23–34.

Rasbach, G. (2020). 'Germany East of the Rhine, 12 BC–AD 16: The First Step to Becoming a Roman Province'. In Curcă, R.-G., Rubel, A., Symonds, R.P., & Voß, H.-U. (eds.) *Rome and Barbaricum: Contributions to the Archaeology and History of Interaction in European Protohistory.* Oxford (Archaeopress): 22–38.

Rauh, S.H. (2015). 'The Tradition of Suicide in Rome's Foreign Wars'. *TAPA* 145 (2): 383–410.

Raven, S. (1993). *Rome in Africa.* 3rd Edition. London (Routledge).

Reece, R. (1981). 'Roman Monetary Impact on the Celtic World – Thoughts and Problems'. In Cunliffe, B. (ed.) *Coinage and Society in Britain and Gaul: Some Current Problems.* CBA Research Report 38. London (Council for British Archaeology): 24–28.

Rees, O. (2018). 'Picking over the bones: the practicalities of processing the Athenian war dead'. *Journal of Ancient History* 6 (2): 167–184.

Reinhold, M. (1972) 'Marcus Agrippa's Son-in-Law P. Quinctilius Varus'. *Classical Philology* 67 (2): 119–121.

Rich, J.W. (1999). 'Drusus and the *Spolia Opima*'. *The Classical Quarterly* 49 (2): 544–555.

Rich, J.W. (2012). 'Roman Attitudes to Defeat in Battle under the Republic'. In Marco Simón, F., Pina Polo, F., & Remesal Rodríguez, J. (eds.) *Vae Victis! Perdedores en el Mundo Antiguo.* Barcelona (Universitat de Barcelona): 83–111.

Richardson, J. (2012). *Augustan Rome 44 BC to AD 14: The Restoration of the Republic and the Establishment of the Empire.* Edinburgh.

Richardson, P., & Fisher, A.M. (2018). *Herod: King of the Jews and Friend of the Romans.* 2nd Edition. London (Routledge).

Riggsby, A.M. (2006). *Caesar in Gaul and Rome. War in Words.* Austin, TX (University of Texas Press).

Rogers, R.S. (1967). 'The Deaths of Julia and Gracchus, A.D. 14'. *Transactions and Proceedings of the American Philological Association* 98, 383–390.

Rosenstein, N. (1990) *Imperatores Victi: Military Defeat and Aristocratic Competition in the Middle and Late Republic.* Berkeley (University of California Press).

Rosenstein, N.S. (2004). *Rome at War: Farms, Families and Death in the Middle Republic.* Chapel Hill, NC (University of North Carolina Press).

Rost, A. (2009). 'The Battle between Romans and Germans in Kalkriese: Interpreting the Archaeological Remains from an Ancient Battlefield'. In Morillo, Á., Hanel, N., & Martín, E. (eds.) *Limes XX.* Madrid (Polifemo): 1339–1345.

Rost, A. (2012/13). 'Methods in Battlefield Archaeology: A Critical Analysis of the Distributional Pattern'. In Harbeck, M., von Heyking, K., & Schwarzberg, H. (eds.) *Sickness, Hunger, War and Religion: Multidisciplinary Perspectives.* Munich (Rachel Carson Centre): 92–111.

Rost, A. (2014). 'Schlachtfeld und Massengrab'. In Eickhoff, S., & Schopper, F. (eds.) *Schlachtfeld und Massengrab.* Wünsdorf (Brandenburgisches Landesamt für Denkmalpflege): 9–15.

Rost, A. (2017). 'Remains of the Roman Baggage Train at the Battlefield of Kalkriese'. In Hodgson, N., Bidwell, P., & Schachtmann, J. (eds.) *Roman Frontier Studies 2009: Proceedings of the XXI International Congress of Roman Frontier Studies (Limes Congress) held at Newcastle upon Tyne in August 2009.* Oxford (Archaeopress): 559–564.

Rost, A., & Wilbers-Rost, S. (2009). 'Kalkriese: Die Archäologische Erforschung einer Antiken Feldschlacht'. In Meller, H. (ed.) *Schlachtfeldarchäologie/Battlefield Archaeology.* Halle/Saale (Landesmuseum für Vorgeschichte): 67–79.

Rost, A., & Wilbers-Rost, S. (2010). 'Weapons at the Battlefield of Kalkriese'. *Gladius* 30: 117–136.

Rost, A., & Wilbers-Rost, S. (2012). *Kalkriese 6. Verteilung der Kleinfunde auf dem Oberesch in Kalkriese, Kartierung und Interpretation der römischen Militaria unter Einbeziehung der Befunde.* Mainz (Philipp von Zabern).

Rost, A., & Wilburs-Rost, S. (2016). 'The Extensive Battlefield of Kalkriese (Varus Battle 9 AD): A Challenge for Archeological Research and Monument Presentation'. In Smith, S. (ed.) *Preserving Fields of Conflict: Papers from the 2014 Fields of Conflict Conference and Preservation Workshop.* Columbia, SC (South Carolina Institute of Archaeology and Anthropology): 25–30.

Rost, A., & Wilbers-Rost, S. (2019). 'The Ancient Conflict Landscape of Kalkriese (Varian Disaster 9 CE): New Insights into the Course of the Battle and the Post-Battle Processes'. In Moreira, N., Derderian, M., & Bissonnette, A. (eds.) *Fields of Conflict 2018 Pequot Museum: Conference Proceedings. Volume 4.* Mashantucket, CN (Mashantucket Pequot Museum): 40–49.

Roth, J.P. (1999). *The Logistics of the Roman Army at War (264 B.C. – A.D. 235).* Leiden (Brill).

Roymans, N. (2017). 'A Roman massacre in the far north Caesar's annihilation of the Tencteri and Usipetes in the Dutch river area'. In Fernández-Götz, M., & Roymans, N. (eds.) *Conflict Archaeology: Materialities of Collective Violence from Prehistory to Late Antiquity.* London (Routledge): 167–181.

Roymans, N., & Fernandez-Götz, M. (2018). *Conflict Archaeology: Materialities of Collective Violence from Prehistory to Late Antiquity.* London & New York (Routledge).

Russell, A. (2020). 'The SC coinage and the role of the Senate under Augustus'. In Powell, A., & Burnett, A. (eds.) *Coins of the Roman Revolution (49 BC–AD 14): Evidence Without Hindsight.* Swansea (The Classical Press of Wales): 157–173.

Sabin, P. (2000). 'The Roman Face of Battle'. *Journal of Roman Studies* 90: 1–17.

Sabin, P. (2007). 'Battle'. In Sabin, P., Van Wees, H., & Whitby, M. (eds.) *The Cambridge History of Greek and Roman Warfare. Vol I: Greece, the Hellenistic World and the Rise of Rome.* Cambridge (Cambridge University Press): 399–433.

Sallmann, K. (1984). 'Der Traum des Historikers: Zu den 'Bella Germaniae' des Plinius und zur julisch-claudischen Geschichtsschreibung'. *Aufstieg und Niedergang der römischen Welt* 2.32.1: 578–601.

Santos Yanguas, N. (2007). 'El ejército romano de conquista en el norte de la Península Ibérica'. *Hispania Antiqua* 31: 51–86.

Schalles, H.-J., & Willer, S. (2009). *Marcus Caelius: Tod in der Varusschlacht.* Darmstadt (Primus-Verlag).

Scheidel, W. (2007). 'Roman Funerary Commemoration and the Age at First Marriage'. *Classical Philology* 102 (4): 389–402.

Schlüter, W. (1991). *Römer im Osnabrücker Land. Die archäologischen Untersuchungen in der Kalkrieser-Niewedder Senke.* Bramsche (Rasch).

Schlüter, W. (1992). 'Archäologische Zeugnisse zur Varusschlacht? Die Untersuchungen in der Kalkrieser-Niewedder Senke bei Osnabrück'. *Germania* 70 (2): 307–402.

Schlüter, W. (1999). 'The Battle of the Teutoburg Forest: Archaeological Research at Kalkriese near Osnabrück'. In Creighton, D., & Wilson, R.J.A. (eds.) *Roman Germany: Studies in Cultural Interaction.* Portsmouth, RI (*Journal of Roman Archaeology*): 125–159.

Von Schnurbein, S. (2003). 'Augustus in Germania and his new 'town' at Waldgirmes east of the Rhine'. *Journal of Roman Archaeology* 16: 93–107.

Scott, D.D., Fox, R.A., & Connor, M.A. (1989). *Archaeological Perspectives on the Battle of the Little Bighorn*. Norman, OK (University of Oklahoma Press).

Scott, D.D., & McFeaters, A.P. (2011). 'The Archaeology of Historic Battlefields: A History and Theoretical Development in Conflict Archaeology'. *The Journal of Archaeological Research* 19 (1): 103–132.

Seidman, J. (2014). 'Remembering the Teutoburg Forest: *Monumenta* in *Annals* 1.61'. *Ramus* 43 (1): 94–114.

Settipani, C. (2000). *Continuité gentilice et continuité familiale dans les familles sénatoriales romaines a l'époque impériale: mythe et réalité*. Oxford (Unit for Prosopographical Research, Linacre College).

Sheldon, R.M. (2001). 'Slaughter in the Forest: Roman Intelligence Mistakes in Germany'. *Small Wars & Insurgencies* 12 (3): 1–38.

Sheldon, R.M. (2005). *Trust in the Gods, but Verify: Intelligence Activities in Ancient Rome*. London (Routledge).

Sheldon, R.M. (2020). 'Insurgency in Germany: The Slaughter of Varus in the Teutoburger Wald. *Small Wars & Insurgencies* 31 (5): 1010–1043.

Sherwin-White, A.N. (1979). *The Roman Citizenship*. 2nd Edition. Oxford (Clarendon Press).

Sievers, S. (2020). 'The Lands of Germania in the Later Pre-Roman Iron Age'. In James, S., & Krmnicek, S. (eds.) *The Oxford Handbook of the Archaeology of Roman Germany*. Oxford (Oxford University Press): 5–27.

Smallwood, E.M. (1976). *The Jews under Roman Rule: From Pompey to Diocletian*. Leiden (Brill).

Squire, M. (2013). 'Embodied Ambiguities on the Prima Porta Augustus'. *Art History* 36 (2): 242–279.

Steinmann, A.E. (2009). 'When Did Herod the Great Reign?'. In *Novum Testamentum* 51 (1): 1–29.

Stevenson, T. (2013). 'The Succession Planning of Augustus'. *Antichthon* 47: 118–139.

Storgaard, B. (2003). 'Cosmopolitan aristocrats'. In Jørgensen, J., Storgaard, B., & Thomsen, L.G. (eds.) *The Spoils of Victory. The North in the Shadow of the Roman Empire*. Copenhagen (National Museum): 106–125.

Syme, R. (1986). *The Augustan Artistocracy*. Oxford (Clarendon Press).

Tansey, P. (2000). 'The Perils of Prosopography: The Case of the Cornelii Dolabellae'. *Zeitschrift für Papyrologie und Epigraphik* 130: 265–271.

Tansey, P. (2008). 'Q. Aemilius Lepidus (Barbula?) Cos. 21 B.C.'. *Historia: Zeitschrift für Alte Geschichte* 57 (2): 174–207.

Thakur, S. (2014). 'Tiberius, the Varian disaster, and the dating of Tristia 2'. *Materiali e discussioni per l'analisi dei testi classici* 73: 69–97.

Timpe, D. (1970). *Arminius-Studien*. Heidelberg (Bibliothek der klassischen Altertumswissenschaften).

Todd, M. (2004). *The Early Germans*. 2nd Edition. Hoboken (Wiley-Blackwell).

Tolksdorf, J.F., Elburg, R., & Reuter, T. (2017). 'Can 3D scanning of countermarks on Roman coins help to reconstruct the movement of Varus and his legions'. *Journal of Archaeological Science* 11: 400–410.

Tolksdorf-Lienemann, E. (2004). 'Naturräumliche Situation und Böden ausgewählter Fundstellen in den Landschaftseinheiten'. In Harnecker, J., & Tolksdorf-Lienemann,

E. (eds.) *Kalkriese 2: Sondierungen in der Kalkrieser-Niewedder Senke: Archäologie und Bodenkunde.* Mainz (Philipp von Zabern): 108–119.

Toynbee, J.M.C. (1953). *The Ara Pacis Reconsidered and Historical Art in Roman Italy.* London (Oxford University Press).

Turner, B. (2018). 'Imperial Reactions to Military Failures in the Julio-Claudian Era'. In Clark, J.H., & Turner, B. (eds.) *Brill's Companion to Military Defeat in Ancient Mediterranean Society.* Leiden (Brill): 262–283.

Uerpmann, H.-P., & Uerpmann, M. (2007). 'Tierknochfunde aus den Grabungen auf dem Oberesch'. In Wilbers-Rost, S. (ed.) *Kalkriese 3. Interdisziplinäre Untersuchungen auf dem Oberesch in Kalkriese.* Mainz (Philipp von Zabern): 126–144.

Unzueta Portilla, M., & Ocharán, J.A. (1999) 'Aproximación a la conquista romana del cantábrico oriental: El campamento y/o campo de batalla de Andagoste (Cuartango, Álava)'. In Iglesias, J.M., & Muñiz, J.A. (eds.) *Regio Cantabrorum.* Santander (Caja Cantabria): 125–142.

Unzueta Portilla, M., & Ocharán Larrondo, J.A. (2006). 'El campo de batalla de Andagoste (Álava)'. In García-Bellido, M.P. (ed.) *Los campamentos romanos en Hispania (27 a.C.-192 d.C.). El abastecimiento de moneda, II.* Madrid (CSIC – Polifemo): 473–492.

Wallace-Hadrill, A. (1986). 'Image and Authority in the Coinage of Augustus'. *Journal of Roman Studies* 76: 66–87.

Ward, G.A. (2018). '"By Any Other Name": Disgrace, Defeat, and the Loss of Legionary History'. In Clark, J.H., & Turner, B. (eds.) *Brill's Companion to Military Defeat in Ancient Mediterranean Society.* Leiden (Brill): 284–308.

Wardle, D. (2011). 'The Blame Game: An Aspect of Handling Military Defeat in the Early Principate'. *Hermes* 139 (1): 42–50.

Wells, C.M. (1972). *The German Policy of Augustus: An Examination of the Archaeological Evidence.* Oxford (Clarendon).

Wells, P.S. (2003). *The Battle that Stopped Rome: Emperor Augustus, Arminius, and the Slaughter of the Legions in the Teutoburg Forest.* New York (W. W. Norton & Company).

Wesbrook, S.D. (1980). 'The Potential for Military Disintegration. In Sarkesian, S.C. (ed.) *Combat Effectiveness: Cohesion, Stress, and the Volunteer Military.* Beverly Hills (Sage Publications): 244–278.

Westall, R.W. (2018). *Caesar's Civil War: Historical Reality and Fabrication.* Leiden (Brill).

Whateley, C. (2021). *A Sensory History of Ancient Warfare: Reconstructing the Physical Experience of War in the Classical World.* Barnsley (Pen & Sword Military).

Wigg-Wolf, D. (2007). 'Dating Kalkriese: the numismatic evidence. In Lehmann, G.D., & Wiegels, R. (eds.) *Römische Präsenz und Herrschaft im Germaniem der augusteischen Zeit: Die Fundplatz von Kalkriese im Kontext neuerer Forschungen und Ausgrabungsbefunde.* Göttingen (Vandenhoeck and Ruprecht): 119–134.

Wilbers-Rost, S. (2003). 'Der Hinterhalt gegen Varus. Zu Konstruktion und Funktion der Germanischen Wallanlage auf dem ‚Oberesch' in Kalkriese'. *Die Kunde, N.F.* 54: 123–142.

Wilbers-Rost, S. (2009). 'Total Roman Defeat at the Battle of Varus (9 AD)'. In Scott, D., Babits, L., & Haecker, C. (eds.) *Fields of Conflict: Battlefield Archaeology from the Roman Empire to the Korean War.* Washington D.C. (Potomac Books): 121–132.

Wilbers-Rost, S. (2012/13). 'Results of Excavations on the Oberesch Site'. In Harbeck, M., von Hayking, K., & Schwarzberg, H. (eds.), *Sickness, Hunger, War and Religion: Multidisciplinary perspectives.* Munich (Rachel Carson Centre): 93–97.

Wilbers-Rost, S. (2017). 'The Battlefield of Kalkriese: The Rampart at the Site "Oberesch" During and After the Battle'. In Hodgson, N., Bidwell, P., & Schachtmann, J. (eds.)

Roman Frontier Studies 2009: Proceedings of the XXI International Congress of Roman Frontier Studies (Limes Congress) held at Newcastle upon Tyne in August 2009. Oxford (Archaeopress): 571–576.

Wilbers-Rost, S., & Rost, A. (2009). 'Bones and Equipment of Horses and Mules on the Ancient Battlefield of Kalkriese, Northern Germany'. *Baltica* 11: 220–228.

Winkler, M.M. (2015). *Arminius the Liberator: Myth and Ideology.* New York & Oxford (Oxford University Press).

Wolters, R. (2008). *Die Schlacht im Teutoburger Wald: Arminius, Varus und das roemische Germanien.* Munich (Verlag C.H. Beck).

Wolters, R. (2020). 'Emergence of the Provinces'. In James, S., & Krmnicek, S. (eds.) *The Oxford Handbook of the Archaeology of Roman Germany.* Oxford (Oxford University Press): 28–50.

Yoder, J. (2014). *Representatives of Roman Rule: Roman Provincial Governors in Luke-Acts.* Berlin (Walter de Gruyter GmbH).

Zanier, W. 1997. 'Ein einheimischer Opferplatz mit romischen Waffen der fruhesten Okkupation (15–10 v. Chr.) bei Oberammergau'. In Groenman-Van Waateringe, W., van Beek, B.L., Willems, W.J.H., & Wynia, S.L. (eds.) *Roman Frontier Studies 1995: proceedings of the XVIth International Congress of Roman Frontier Studies.* Oxford (Oxbow Books: 47–52.

Index